*To my wife, Marlis, born and raised a European,
without whose assistance, advice, love, and companionship
this book could scarcely have been created.*

The European Culture Area

A SYSTEMATIC GEOGRAPHY

Third Edition

TERRY G. JORDAN

Walter Prescott Webb Professor
University of Texas

HarperCollins*College*Publishers

COVER ILLUSTRATION: "Europe, a Portrait from Space," natural color, taken in 1992 from a height of 850 km (528 mi.) above the earth's surface by a camera in an orbital weather satellite. Compiled by the Natural Oceanic and Atmospheric Administration (USA) and by the National Remote Sensing Centre, Ltd., Farnborough, Hants (GB). Published by WorldSat Productions, Inc., Mississauga, Ontario, CDN. Used with permission.

Acquisitions Editor: Alan McClare
Project Coordination and Text Design: Electronic Publishing Services Inc
Cover Designer: Mary McDonnell
Electronic Production Manager: Mike Kemper
Manufacturing Manager: Helene G. Landers
Electronic Page Makeup: R.R. Donnelley Barbados
Printer and Binder: R.R. Donnelley & Sons Company
Cover Printer: The Lehigh Press, Inc.

The European Culture Area: A Systematic Geography, Third Edition

Copyright © 1996 by HarperCollins College Publishers

HarperCollins ® and ▆ ® are registered trademarks of HarperCollins Publishers Inc.

Library of Congress Cataloging-in-Publication Data

Jordan, Terry G.
  The European culture area : a systematic geography/ Terry G. Jordan.—3rd ed.
      p. cm.
  Includes bibliographical references and index.
  ISBN 0–06–500729–8
  1. Europe—Geography. 2. Europe—Description and travel.
  I. Title.
  D907.J67   1995
  940—dc20   95-17408
                                                              CIP

96 97 98 9 8 7 6 5 4 3 2 1

Contents

CHAPTER SIX

DEMOGRAPHY   157

CHAPTER SEVEN

GEOPOLITICS   195

CHAPTER ELEVEN

PRIMARY AND SECONDARY INDUSTRIES   353

CHAPTER TWELVE

SERVICE INDUSTRIES   381

CHAPTER THIRTEEN

REGIONS   411

Preface

The third edition of the *European Culture Area* reflects one geographer's interpretation of a fascinating, influential, and ever-changing part of the world. Firmly based in my experiences gained during seventeen seasons of travel and field research in Europe, it reflects journeys from Gibraltar to North Cape, from the westernmost promontories of Ireland to the Russian steppes and taiga, from Cyprus to Iceland the Faeroes.

Fundamentally revised from its 1988 predecessor, the present edition reflects the far-reaching changes that have reshaped Europe in the 1990s. The book derives from the rich humanistic tradition of geography and represents an attempt to interpret Europe as a cultural entity. It treats Europe both as one and many, as a people adhering to an overarching culture while at the same time exhibiting a bewildering internal regional variety.

Throughout the book, preference will be given to the indigenous form of place names, as for example *Napoli* instead of *Naples* and *Bayern* instead of *Bavaria*. I felt that the English forms of these toponyms serve no useful purpose and often lead to confusion. One American tourist bound for the wonders of Florence reportedly refused to get off the train at the station bearing the placard "Firenze," convinced that the conductor intended to cheat him! Why bother to learn names that the local citizenry do not use? A few exceptions have been made. The names of independent countries appear in English form, even though this leads us to the absurdity of calling Hrvatska "Croatia" and Deutschland "Germany." Also, if a river, city, mountain range, or other geographic feature extends across linguistic borders and is as a result known by more than one native name, then the English version receives preference. Thus I use Danube instead of Donau/Duna/Dunarea. The English version of names occasionally appear in parentheses following the native form, and the *Index* also directs the reader from English to native forms.

Similarly, preference is given to the metric system, which enjoys almost universal usage in Europe. English measure equivalents follow in parentheses, and a conversion table is included here (see Metric Conversion and Abbreviation Table, page xv). Also, since metric measures often appear in abbreviated form, such as *km* instead of *kilometer*, a key to these is contained in the same table.

Use will also be made of the internationally approved postal code abbreviations for European and neighboring countries. These abbreviations appear in bibliographies, on many maps, and in some captions. In Europe they are used in postal zip codes and often are affixed to the rear of automobiles. For example, the letter code for Germany is D (see Table of Official Letter Codes for Countries, page xvi). Also in that same table are listed the native forms of the names for countries.

Statistical subdivisions of most countries appear on maps throughout the text, in order to present a more detailed geographical pattern of data. While based upon administrative and censal units, these subdivisions almost always represent some lumping of units, in order that the maps not become overly complicated.

Numerous persons have contributed to the writing of the third edition by providing ideas, suggestions, data, assistance, and criticism. My research assistants, Alyson Greiner and Jane Manaster, deserve special thanks, as do the professors who read the first draft and offered numerous suggestions for improvement, including Dr. Mary Lee Nolan of Oregon State, Dr. Ary J. Lamme III of the University of Florida, Dr. Brad Baltensperger of Michigan Tech, and Dr. John U. Marshall of York University. Other valuable contributions came from professors Guy Manaster, Andreas Grotewold, Bruce S. Young, Kirk H. Stone, Kazimierz J. Zaniewski, John Sallnow, Wilbur Zelinsky, Michael Kukral, Robert A. Sirk, Dale J. Stevens, Robin Elisabeth Datel, Ramesh Dhussa, H. Gardiner Barnum, and Joseph Brownell.

Dr. John Cotter of Austin created nearly all of the attractive, functional cartographic work for this book. His maps reveal the human touch that can only be achieved the old-fashioned way, by rejecting computer graphics and employing instead a skilled hand and sensitive eye. I am fortunate to have had his services. Long may his eyes remain keen and his hand steady.

The modest success of *The European Culture Area* reflects in part the resurgence of interest in regional geography and in the humanistic method of study. Renewed and growing attention to the geography of Europe was also revealed in the 1992 establishment and subsequent growth of a "European Specialty Group" within the Association of American Geographers. Earlier editions of *The European Culture Area* have been translated into Italian and Japanese, suggesting an international appeal, and the book has often been cited in European scholarly journals, both within and outside the discipline of geography. The third edition now renews the availability of *The European Culture Area* to the English-speaking countries, presenting the geography of a dynamic and influential region on the eve of a new century.

Terry G. Jordan

METRIC CONVERSION AND ABBREVIATION TABLE

METRIC SYSTEM	AMERICAN MEASURES
Length	
1 meter (m) = 3.281 sq. ft.	1 ft. = 0.348 m
1 kilometer (km) = 0.621 mi.	1 mi. = 1.609 km
1 centimeter (cm) = 0.3937 in.	1 in. = 2.54 cm
Area	
1 sq. m = 10.764 sq. ft.	1 sq. ft. = 0.092 sq. m
1 sq. km = 0.386 sq. mi.	1 sq. mi. = 2.59 sq. km
1 hectare (ha) = 2.471 acres	1 acre = 0.405 ha
100 ha = 1 sq. km	
Volume/Capacity	
1 cu. m = 35.3 cu. ft.	1 cu. ft. = 0.028 cu. m
1 cu. cm = 0.061 cu. in.	1 cu. in. = 16.39 cu. cm.
1 liter (l) = 0.264 gal.	1 gal. = 3.785 l
1 hectoliter (hl) = 2.84 bu.	1 bushel = 0.35 hl
Weight	
1 kilogram (kg) = 2.2 lbs.	1 lb. = 0.45 kg
1,000 kg (1 metric ton) = 2,205 lbs.	1 ton = 0.91 metric ton
100 kg = 1 centner (ct) = 220.5 lbs.	

TABLE OF OFFICIAL LETTER CODES FOR COUNTRIES

EUROPE

A	Austria (Österreich)
AL	Albania (Shqiperi)
AM	Armenia (Hayastan)
AND	Andorra
B	Belgium (Belgie/Belgique)
BA	Bosnia-Herzegovina (Bosna-Hercegovina)
BG	Bulgaria (Balgarija)
BY	Belarus
CH	Switzerland (Helvetia)
CY	Cyprus (South) (Kipros)
CZ	Czech Republic (Čechy)
D	Germany (Deutschland)
DK	Denmark (Danmark)
E	Spain (España)
EW	Estonia (Eesti)
F	France
FL	Liechtenstein
FR*	Faeroe Islands (Føroyar)
GB	United Kingdom
GBZ*	Gibraltar
GE	Georgia (Sakartvelo)
GR	Greece (Hellas)
H	Hungary (Magyarorszag)
HR	Croatia (Hrvatska)
I	Italy (Italia)
IRL	Ireland
IS	Iceland (Island)
L	Luxembourg
LR	Latvia (Latvija)
LT	Lithuania (Lietuva)
M	Malta
MC	Monaco
MD	Moldova
MK	Macedonia (Makedonija)

N	Norway (Norge)
NL	Netherlands (Nederland)
P	Portugal
PL	Poland (Polska)
RO	Romania
RSM	San Marino
S	Sweden (Sverige)
SF	Finland (Suomi)
SK	Slovakia (Slovensko)
SLO	Slovenia (Slovenija)
SU	Russia (Rossiya)
UKR	Ukraine (Ukraina)
V	Vatican City (Citta del Vaticano)
YU	Yugoslavia (Jugoslavija)

BORDERING COUNTRIES

AZ	Azerbaijan
DZ	Algeria
ET	Egypt
HKJ	Jordan
IL	Israel
IR	Iran
IRQ	Iraq
KWT	Kuwait
KZ	Kazakhstan
LAR	Libya
MA	Morocco
RL	Lebanon
SYR	Syria
TCY	Turkish Cyprus
TM	Turkmenistan
TN	Tunisia
TR	Turkey

* = dependent territory

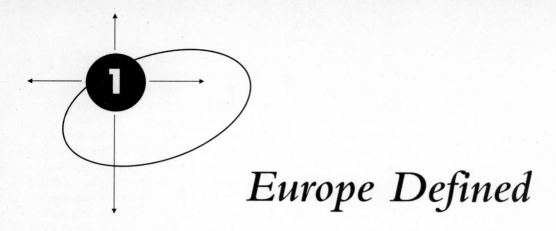

Europe Defined

Europe as a Continent

What is Europe? The answer is by no means as simple as might be imagined, for Europe represents, in the words of Norwegian geographer Leif Ahnström, "an elusive notion." Even so, most people would probably define Europe as a *continent*. You may recall from elementary school days being asked to recite the names of the family of continents, in which Europe held a place of full membership. Support for the continental status of Europe appears in various dictionaries and in the writings of numerous geographers. For example, *Webster's New World Dictionary* defines Europe as a "continent between Asia and the Atlantic Ocean," while the British geographer Lionel Lyde entitled his textbook *The Continent of Europe*. In this view, then, we are led to believe that Europe constitutes a distinct *physical* entity because a continent is a sizable landmass standing more or less separate from other landmasses. North and South America, connected by the narrow Isthmus of Panama, form continents, as do Africa, linked to Asia only by the severed land bridge at Suez, and Australia, fully separated from other landmasses by surrounding seas.

Europe, however, cannot meet the definition of a continent since it does not form a separate landmass. To be sure, the Mediterranean Sea provides a clear separation from Africa in the south, while the Atlantic and Arctic oceans well define Europe's western and northern limits, but in the east, the notion of continentality founders. Only the beginning of a water separation appears in the southeastern fringe, where an arm of the sea reaches northward from the Mediterranean, through the Aegean, Dardanelles, and Bosporos to the Black Sea, and still beyond to the Sea of Azov. There the division ends, and to the north of Azov stretches the vast East European Plain. Instead of a narrow isthmus similar to Panama or Suez, the map reveals a wedge of land broadening steadily to the east, welding Europe and Asia into one large continent called Eurasia. Europe lacks a clear-cut oceanic border and as a result is not a continent. In fact, a glance at a map of the Eastern Hemisphere reveals Europe as simply one rather small appendage of the continent Eurasia, merely a westward-reaching peninsula. At most, Europe forms only about one-fifth of the area of Eurasia.

The erroneous belief that Europe possesses the characteristics of a continent came down to the modern day from the civilizations of the ancient Mediterranean, in particular from the Greeks and Romans (Figure 1.1). The Greco-Roman world view in turn owed much to other, older cultures. One theory concerning the origin of the words *Europe* and *Asia* relates them to the Semitic Assyrian-Phoenician *ereb* ("sunset") and *acu* ("sunrise"). The "land of the sunset," Europe, may have first appeared as an entity among the peoples of the Fertile Crescent, meaning simply "the western land." Too, an ancient, mythological ruler of Sidon in Phoenicia reputedly had daughters named *Europa* and *Asia*. The legendary Europa married the Greek king of gods, Zeus, and accompanied him back to the Aegean, while her sister remained in the east.

From their vantage point on the Aegean, the ancient Greeks perceived a world divided into three parts—Europe, Africa (then called Libya), and Asia—and the Romans accepted the Greek outlook. Greece was always a nation of seafarers, and its sailors from the time of Ulysses and earlier had charted the marine separation of Europe and Africa. In addition, the classical Greeks knew of the division of Africa and Asia, for the Phoenicians before them had apparently circumnavigated the African continent. The Argonauts and other Greek explorers had probed into the Black Sea, founding trading colonies as far away as present-

FIGURE 1.1 World map drawn by the ancient Greek geographer Hecataeus about 500 B.C. Note that he erroneously linked the Caspian Sea to the open ocean so that Europe and Asia joined only at the Caucasus isthmus. (Source: Adapted from Parker, 1960.)

day Ukraine. Intrepid Greek merchants probed beyond the Black Sea to the shores of the landlocked, saltwater Caspian Sea. Certain Greek scholars evaluating the information brought back by traders assumed that the saline Caspian was part of the ocean. To them, the Caucasian isthmus between the Black and Caspian seas was the only land bridge connecting Europe and Asia (Figure 1.1). Little did they know that the Caspian was an inland sea, with no opening to the ocean, and that north of the Caspian stretched a huge expanse of land. Certain other classical scholars, including Strabo, Pomponius Mela, and Ptolemy, mistakenly believed that only a narrow isthmus lay north of the Black Sea and the Sea of Azov, separating them from the Arctic Ocean, and they placed the Europe-Asia border along the course of the Don (ancient Tanais) River (Figure 1.2). Their lack of accurate information led them to whittle down the expansive Russian plains to a narrow land bridge. The classical Greeks and Romans, then, believed in a threefold division of the landmasses, and Europe was to them a separate physical entity, a mere geographic term.

From the Greeks and Romans, the concept of the three continents passed intact to monastic scholars of the medieval period. Perpetuation of the classical view became guaranteed when a Christian religious significance was attached to it in the Roman church. The result of churchly interpretation of cartography was the famous "T in O" map. The map of the known world was deliberately simplified in such a way that the pattern of land and seas formed the letters T, for *terrarum* ("earth") and O, for *orbis* ("circle"), suggesting that God had shaped the world in a sort of Latin shorthand. The Mediterranean Sea represented the lower

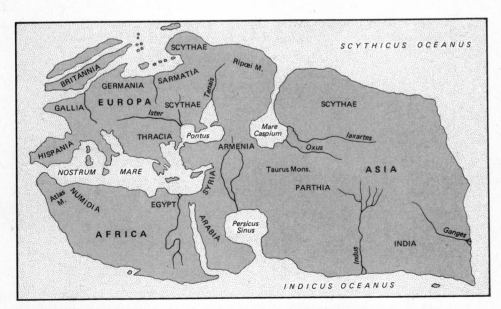

FIGURE 1.2 World map of the Roman geographer Pomponius Mela, drawn in A.D. 43. The Caspian Sea is still depicted as an arm of the ocean, but Russia has also been narrowed to form an isthmus. (Source: Adapted from Parker, 1960.)

bar of the T, and the top of the map was east rather than north. The Nile River (or Red Sea)–Aegean Sea–Black Sea–Don River line formed the horizontal bar of the T. Some medieval Christian scholars created water separations of Europe, Asia, and Africa by severing Suez and widening the Don to marine proportions. The letter O lay between the outer perimeter of the three continents and the presumed edge of the world (Figure 1.3). On many such ethnocentric Christian maps, the hub, or center, of the world was the holy city of Jerusalem, while the lost Garden of Eden lay far out in the inaccessible reaches of hinter Asia. We should not judge "T in O" maps by modern standards because their purpose, as interpretative art, was to depict religious mysteries and offer a stylized stage for the Christian drama, rather than to picture the world accurately. It is sufficient to know that medieval scholars perpetuated the pre-Christian notion of Europe as a continent.

Even after the Age of Discovery added new continents to the world map, some erroneous views persisted. As late as 1532, cartographers such as Grynaeus continued to show Russia as a narrow isthmus (Figure 1.4). Later in that century, a fairly accurate world map first appeared. It revealed that no isthmus existed north of the Black Sea and that the Don was a rather insignificant river whose headwaters did not even approach the great frozen ocean to the north. Instead of a relatively narrow land bridge, the mapmakers of Europe encountered a 2000-kilometer-wide wedge of land (about 1200 miles) between the White Sea in the north of Russia and the Sea of Azov in the south.

Europe was not, after all, a continent, but a 2,000-year-old belief is not easily discarded. Even to the present day, as we have seen, some continue to speak of the "continent of Europe." In the absence of an isthmus, geographers began looking for other environmental features to use as Europe's eastern border. Even if it

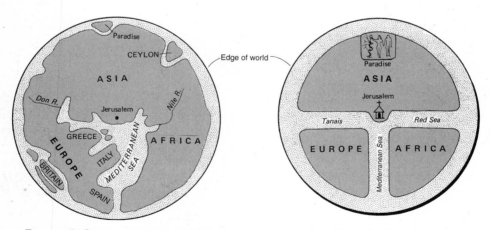

FIGURE 1.3 Two versions of the medieval European "T in O" map. Europe remained, as in classical times, a separate continent. (Source: Adapted from David Woodward, "Reality, Symbolism, Time, and Space in Medieval World Maps," *Annals of the Association of American Geographers,* 75, 1985, 510–521.)

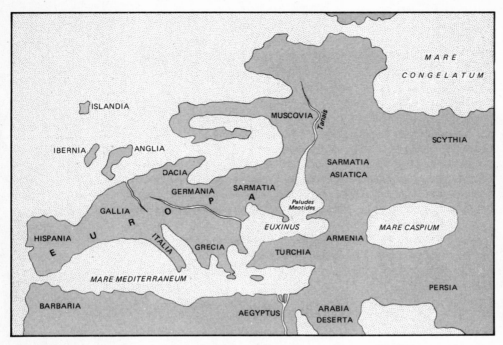

FIGURE 1.4 A portion of the world map by Grynaeus, 1532. Russia remains an isthmus and the headwaters of the Tanais (Don) River incorrectly lie near the Arctic shore. Europe is still a continent. (Source: Adapted from Parker, 1960.)

was not a continent, perhaps it could still be bounded physically. Maybe Europe was a **subcontinent** like India, walled off from the rest of Eurasia by the Great Himalaya Mountains. The Swedish geographer Strahlenberg first proposed, in 1730, that the Ural Mountains, a low range running in a due north-south direction across the heart of Eurasia, should be used as the border, and many have adopted his view. The Uralian border today enjoys greater acceptance than any other, even though it severs Russia in half (Figure 1.5). Another range, the impressive snow-capped Caucasus Mountains, provided another link in the border of Europe, stretching between the Black and Caspian seas. Certain other geographers, more sensitive to the nuances of terrain, suggested that Europe did not extend beyond those regions where the land lay partitioned into small, discrete landform units, banishing to the Asian world the great expanses of unbroken plains that dominate the Eurasian interior, including most of Russia (see Chapter 2) (Figure 1.5).

Some other geographers, continuing the ancient classical tradition, award certain rivers the status of European border. The Don formed one part of Strahlenberg's proposed border, and the Dnipro (Dnieper) and Ural rivers have found similar honor among certain scholars. The suggestion has also been made that Europe should exclude all areas of interior, Arctic and Indian Ocean drainage,

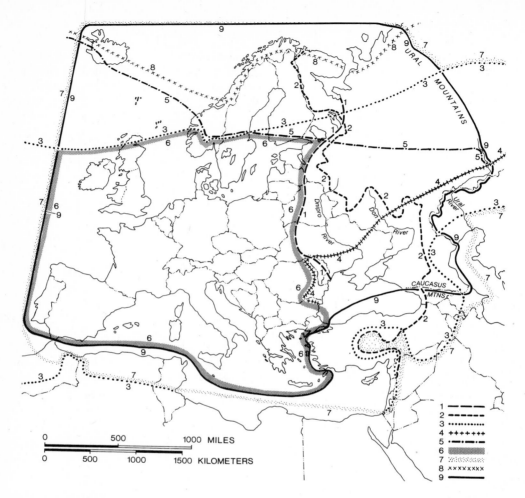

FIGURE 1.5 The European ecumene: diverse proposals for defining Europe physically. Mountain ranges, rivers, drainage basins, terrain patterning, and climatic traits have all been suggested. Borders: **1** = eastern border of small discrete terrain regions, beyond which lie boundless plains; **2** = western border of interior-Arctic-Indian Ocean drainage; **3** = Louis' borders, based on warmth and rainfall; **4** = northern limit of the steppe grasslands; **5** = northern limit of temperate climates; **6** = the European ecumene narrowly defined, including lands accepted by all who seek to bound Europe on a physical environmental basis; **7** = the European ecumene most broadly defined, including lands accepted by at least one scholar seeking a physical boundary; **8** = southern border of Arctic tundra; **9** = most widely accepted border of Europe today. Europe, environmentally, thus becomes a temperate, well-watered land of variegated terrain. Louis extended it far into southern Siberia, off our map. (Sources: Hahn 1881, plate 3; Louis 1954, map following 80; Eric R. Wolf, *Europe and the People without History*, Berkeley, USA: University of California Press, 1982, 31; Parker 1953; Parker 1960.)

content to include only those lands whose rivers drain to the Atlantic Ocean, Baltic, Mediterranean, and Black Sea (Figure 1.5).

Still others prefer to seek a climatic border, defining Europe as a temperate, well-watered land flanked by deserts, steppes, and frigid subarctic wastes. To the south lies the great arid belt consisting of the Sahara, Arabian, Central Asian, Takla Makan, and Gobi deserts (look ahead to Figure 1.7). The geographer Herbert Louis adopted this southern border, placing it at the limits of unirrigated farming. He further proposed that Europe reached only as far north and east as those lands having at least two months averaging +15°C. (54°F.) or warmer and a total of four months above +10°C (50°F), a limit judged critical for grain cultivation (Figure 1.5). Some scholars would also exclude from Europe the steppe grasslands that intrude from Asia north of the Black Sea, regarding them as alien in appearance and utilization. The northern tundras, beyond the treeline in an Arctic environment, merit similar disapproval from a few. From all these attempts at bounding the European ecumene comes an image of a temperate, humid land of highly variegated terrain.

But of what value are these diverse suggestions for an ecologically determined Europe? Why, in fact, does the concept of "Europe" survive so long after continentality has been disproven? Why do we teach courses in the geography of Europe, instead of Eurasia? Why is there a "European Specialty Group" within the Association of American Geographers? Indeed, why do the Europeans themselves continue to believe that a separate and distinct Europe exists? Why do they speak of their "common European home"? Clearly, the answers do not lie in the contrived and discordant physical boundaries discussed above. Instead, we must agree with the Russian geographer, E. M. Murzayev, who concluded that "any attempt to divide Europe from Asia on a systematic physical-geographical basis is doomed to fail."

Europe as a Human Entity

Let us instead seek a definition of Europe based in human, rather than environmental, characteristics. Europe is a *culture* that occupies a *culture area.* A culture may be defined as a community of people who hold numerous features of belief, behavior, and overall way of life in common, including ideology, technology, social institutions, and material possessions. A culture area is any large area inhabited by people of a particular culture, a land upon which the visible imprint of that culture has been placed. Geographer W. H. Parker perhaps put it best when he said that Europe represented "a cultural concept" and that "its eastern limits have been cultural and never long stable." Europeans belong to a cultural community rooted in a Judeo/Christian/Hellenic heritage.

During the long period of belief in continental status, Europe evolved and expanded as a culture area. Only gradually, and amid confusion that lingers still today, did Europe make the transition from physical to human entity. As late as the 1200s, *Europe* continued to mean simply a continent, though by then some had adopted the view that Europeans were distinctive as the descendants of Japheth, one of the sons of the biblical Noah. Slowly, in the period 1300 to 1600, *Europe* came to mean "Christendom," says historian Denys Hay, "and the emotional content of the word Europe significantly increased." A European self-consciousness, centered in the church, emerged. By 1571 the Pope revealingly referred to "Europeans, or those who are called Christians." *Europe* had acquired a positive, cultural meaning, and Europeans a distinctive world view based in a vivid and flattering self-image. Four centuries later, in 1991, another Roman Pope exhorted Europe to return "to its Christian roots." In that same year, the president of Turkey, frustrated at the failure of his dominantly Muslim country to be accepted as a member of the European Union, lamented that "some people maintain that the E.U. should be a Christian club." A British periodical recently described "a Muslim crescent curling threateningly around the southern and eastern edges of Europe."

Christianity, for at least the last eight centuries, has allowed Europeans to remain a self-conscious, distinct culture. The church helped create a we/they mentality that separated Christian-European from barbarian/heathen/infidel/fiend. All along the outer margins of Europe, religion still today engenders a virulent sense of separation and demonization, causing Spaniards to despise Arabs, Greeks-Bulgars-Armenians to hate Turks, Russians to revile Mongols, Serbs to murder Bosnians, and Georgians to battle Ossetians and Abkhazis (look ahead to Figure 3.18). Even in the very heart of Europe and in the present century, the religious issue has remained sufficiently potent to deny European residence, and even life itself, to Jews.

The second basic cultural trait that helps define Europe is *language*. The great majority of Europeans speak one or another of the **Indo-European** tongues, an extended family of related languages that all derive from a common ancestral speech. Flanking the Indo-Europeans on all sides are speakers of unrelated language families, such as Uralic, Altaic, and Caucasic (Figure 1.6). The language pattern will be considered in greater detail in Chapter 4.

Race provides the third basic human trait that helps distinguish Europeans from their neighbors. Europe is the homeland of the **Caucasian,** or white, race. Beyond the Sahara Desert to the south, in Africa, live the **Negroid** peoples, while most Asians belong to the **Mongoloid** race. In other words, Europeans differ in physical appearance from neighboring peoples, and these differences have become enmeshed in their self-identity. Racism remains common among Europeans, as in virtually all cultures. The question of race will be addressed in Chapter 5.

In a narrow sense, then, Europe can be defined as those parts of the Eastern Hemisphere where the people are Christians, speak an Indo-European language, and exhibit Caucasian physical traits (Figure 1.7). For the sake of simplicity, we might sever the awkward "tail" of European culture extending eastward along the line of the Trans-Siberian Railroad, perhaps cutting it off at the point where Altaic and Uralic speakers cause a constriction and forking, very near the widely accepted Uralian border (Figures 1.6, 1.7).

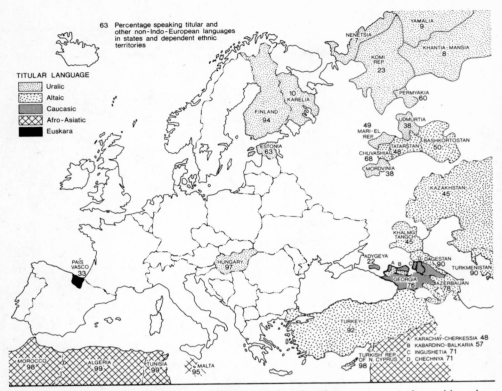

FIGURE 1.6 The non–Indo-European borderlands of Europe, as indicated by ethnically based independent states and dependent territories of five different language families. While these nominal, non–Indo-European groups do not always form a majority in these territories, their ethnicity remains strong enough to dilute the Europeanness of the areas. Only the Hungarians do not occupy a peripheral position. Can we bound Europe accordingly?

By the sixteenth century, when continentality was proven invalid, the human Europe was already well developed. This evolution of a culture area explains not only the numerous efforts to find a satisfactory eastern boundary for Europe since the 1500s, but also the remarkable survival of the myth of continentality in the face of contradictory evidence. Cartographers, aware that Europe was different from Asia, were simply trying to express this idea on their maps. Continentality had become merely a surrogate for culture.

Still, if Europe is to be defined in terms of human characteristics, then the three basic criteria of religion, language, and race hardly suffice, for European culture is complex and has changed remarkably through time. In order to define *modern* Europe, we must add many more defining traits to the basic ones. Any such list can only be subjective and the resultant definition can only be a personal one, but that should not deter the search. The following are suggested as additional ways in which Europeans differ from their neighbors:

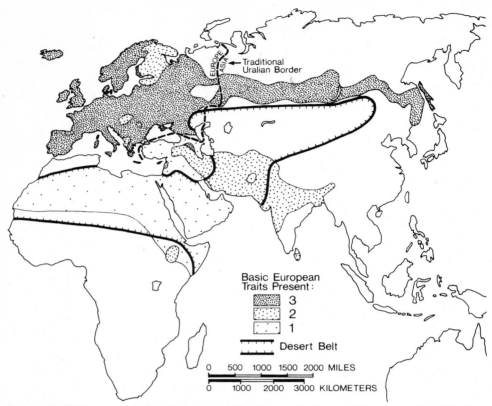

FIGURE 1.7 Europe defined geographically on the basis of Christian religion, Indo-European language, and Caucasian race. Note how Europe, so defined, nestles against but does not intrude into the great desert belt to the south.

1. **A well-educated population.** The European culture, more than most others, places a high value on the written word as opposed to oral tradition. As a result, more than 90 percent of all Europeans in most countries are literate, and in some nations it is illegal not to be. In Germany, for example, 99 percent of the population can read and write, and in Spain the proportion is 97 percent. By contrast, as near as the southern shore of the Mediterranean, in Morocco, only about half of the people are literate as is also true in India to the east.

2. **A healthy population.** Europeans enjoy a far-above-average life expectancy—well in excess of 70 years in some countries. Perhaps an even better measure of health is provided by the infant mortality rate—the number of children per thousand who do not survive to the age of 1 year. For much of Europe the rate stands below 10, while across the Mediterranean and Aegean one encounters rates such as Turkey's 59. Most Europeans benefit from splendid medical facilities and an abundant, nutritious diet.

3. **Stabilized population size.** The European population is scarcely growing at present; "zero population growth" has essentially been achieved. In fact, some European countries, such as Germany, have declining populations. In startling contrast, all countries in neighboring North Africa and Asia Minor, as well as in Africa and Asia at large, experience more than 2 percent natural increase in the population annually and suffer an ongoing "population explosion."

4. **A wealthy population.** The typical European receives enough not only for the necessities of life but also for many luxuries. The net result is a very high standard of living, as judged by the precepts of Western civilization. In areas adjacent to Europe, the large majority of Africans and Asians, often less materialistic in their outlook, achieve a bare subsistence and live in what Europeans call poverty. Per capita incomes drop drastically as one crosses into Africa or Asia.

5. **An urbanized population.** The great majority of Europeans live in cities and towns of 10,000 or more population, and in some countries the proportion exceeds 80 percent. By way of comparison, only 26 percent of the people in India and China are urbanites, 44 percent in Egypt, and 21 percent in Sudan.

6. **An industrialized economy.** All sectors of industry, especially the services, are well developed in Europe and collectively employ the far greater part of the labor force. Some even speak of Europe as an "industrial civilization." By contrast, agriculture remains the dominant form of economy in most of Africa and Asia.

7. **A dense transport network.** Europe is crisscrossed by an unparalleled system of highways, railroads, canals, pipelines, and airline routes. Few areas can be called remote, and the "friction of distance" has been minimized. By contrast, in much of Asia and Africa a network scarcely exists, few people own automobiles, and movement of people over any considerable distance remains rare.

8. **Freely elected governments.** Europeans invented democracy and took the first major steps toward limiting the power of leaders, producing political freedom and pluralism. Competing ideologies are tolerated, and *individualism*, the cardinal European virtue, flourishes in such political conditions. In most of Africa and Asia, by contrast, authoritarianism and collectivism remain the rule.

By this necessarily personal definition, then, Europe includes that part of the Eastern Hemisphere where people are not merely Christian, Caucasian, and Indo-European, but also educated, free, healthy, individualistic, wealthy, materialistic, mobile, urbanized, employed preponderantly in industry, and demographically stable. As a result of sharing these and other diverse, important traits, Europeans are, in the barely exaggerated words of the Italian Luigi Barzini, "all basically the same kind of people, comfortable in each other's countries and in each other's homes." They have developed a *geo-ideology*, which links perception of a common cultural heritage—**Western civilization**—to a particular piece of the earth's surface.

European Great Ideas

If a single word can epitomize the human Europe, it is *dynamism.* Europe provid-ed nearly all **great ideas**—those that have, for better or worse, substantially changed human existence and destiny—in the past millennium. To see the dis-tinctiveness of Europe, to appreciate the degree to which this culture area has been a center of innovation, one need but plot on a map the place of origin of the great ideas that have revolutionized life since about A.D. 1000 (Figure 1.8).

Among the great ideas of Europeans is *democracy,* the child of classical Greece, which reappeared in medieval Iceland and in the city-states of the Middle Ages and burst forth over much of Europe in the late 1700s and 1800s. Nowhere in Asia or Africa did this noble idea arise of its own accord, for tyranny and servitude have been the rule there. The *Age of Discovery,* primarily the accomplishment of Italian and Iberian Europeans, allowed Europe to discover the remainder of the world, rather than the converse. The peoples of the great Asian civilizations did not choose to follow the stepping-stone islands to discov-er and colonize America or Australia. It was not the Chinese who sent traders and explorers to Europe but rather the Italian Marco Polo who journeyed to China. In the process, as they encountered strange and to them barbarous foreign cultures, Europeans developed a heightened self-awareness that helped shape their geo-ideology.

The *printing press,* a gift from the artisans of the German Rhine Valley, has had a tremendous impact in most parts of the world, revolutionizing people's means of communication. The concept of *the earth's sphericity,* developed by the classical Greeks, was revived by Italians and Iberians in the Age of Discovery, and the Polish astronomer Copernicus was the first to proclaim the heliocentric notion that the *earth revolves about the sun.* If Copernicus dealt a first great blow to human ego by removing the earth from the center of the universe, his fellow European Charles Darwin struck another in his *theory of evolution* by proposing that humans were animals of humble biological ancestry rather than divine crea-tures made in the image of God. A Czech, Gregor Mendel, provided the basis for *genetic science,* and Sigmund Freud, born a short distance from Mendel in Morava (Moravia), founded modern psychology, the scientific study of the mind. The Englishman Sir Isaac Newton, in his *laws of motion and gravity,* established mod-ern physics, while the German-born Albert Einstein, through his *theory of relativi-ty,* ushered in the nuclear age. Discovery of bacterial and viral *causes of disease,* the beginning of modern medicine, was the work of the German country doctor Robert Koch and the Frenchman Louis Pasteur. Dutch and Italian inventors developed the first *microscope* and *telescope,* allowing humans for the first time to inspect objects too small or too distant to be studied with the naked eye.

The most far-reaching impact has resulted from the *Industrial Revolution* (see Chapter 11), the invention of diverse machines and harnessing of inanimate power that began in Great Britain in the 1700s. Its technology became a hallmark of European civilization and involved countless crucially important inventions, including the steam engine, railroad, internal-combustion engine, automobile, expressway, radio, orbital satellites, manned space flight, and digital computer,

Figure 1.8 Sources of selected European great ideas. These help define geographically the European culture area. Key: **1** = democracy (ancient Greece, French Revolution, Magna Carta); **2** = Age of Discovery (Genova, Venèzia, Cádiz, Lisboa); **3** = printing press (Gutenberg, at Mainz); **4** = concept of the spherical earth (classical Greeks at Miletus, now in Turkey); **5** = concept of the heliocentric solar system (Copernicus in Frombark); **6** = the Industrial Revolution (English Midlands); **7** = the steam engine (Watt in Glasgow); **8** = the railroad (northeast England); **9** = the internal-combustion engine (Lenoir in Paris, Otto and Daimler in Germany); **10** = the automobile (Daimler and Benz in Germany); **11** = the laws of motion and gravity, providing the basis of modern physics (Newton in England); **12** = science of modern genetics (Mendel in Morava); **13** = the theory of evolution (Darwin in England); **14** = the theory of relativity (Einstein in Bern); **15** = discovery of bacterial and viral causes of diseases (Koch in Ostpreussen and Pasteur in Paris); **16** = the radio (Marconi in Bologna); **17** = the modern study of the mind (Freud in Wien); **18** = socialism (Marx in Trier and London); **19** = productive capitalism (Holland and Vlaanderen); **20** = nationalism (Switzerland and France); **21** = the nation-state (Greece); **22** = expressways (Germany; **23** = orbital satellites and manned space flight (Russia); **24** = microscope and telescope (Lippershey and Janssen in Holland; Galileo in Padova; and **25** = digital computer (Babbage in England.)

to mention but a few. All of these came from Europe (Figure 1.8). Prometheus was unbound, and it was Europeans who loosened his bonds. *Modernity* and the concept of *progress,* quintessentially European, sprang into being.

Other cornerstones of modernity were also laid in Europe, including capitalism, socialism, nationalism, and the nation-state. *Productive capitalism,* distinguished by the application of capital to innovation in order to elevate levels of production, spread from an early nucleus in the Low Countries, and soon "overtly commercial values" permeated European civilization, leading to an economic miracle that spread prosperity through a larger segment of the population than ever before in world history. When linked to the Industrial Revolution, productive capitalism reshaped the world. *Socialism* arose in Europe as a movement to spread prosperity still more widely and to prevent the migration of great wealth back into the hands of the few. Practiced in moderation, Socialism led to the enviable quality of life achieved in the Scandinavian welfare states, but applied in Asiatic extremes, it led to the economic and political catastrophe of Communism.

Nationalism, in which citizens transferred allegiance from monarch to state, with potentially dangerous results, began perhaps in Switzerland and later appeared more forcefully in revolutionary France. Still later came, as another gift from Europe, the most virulent form of nationalism, the *nation-state,* in which nationality became linked to a common language and/or religion. The nation-state concept, perhaps born in the Greek struggle for independence from the Turks, subsequently infected most of Europe and much of the world at large.

Collectively, the impact of these diverse European great ideas has been prodigious. Try to imagine a world never touched by them. The Eurocentric notion that European culture is, as a result, a *superior* one follows easily. Certainly most Europeans believe this to be true. Listen, for example, to the words of the great German writer Thomas Mann. In his novel *The Magic Mountain,* Mann described two opposed principles in conflict for possession of the world—"force and justice, tyranny and freedom, superstition and knowledge, permanence and change. One may call the first Asiatic, the second European because Europe was a center of rebellion, the domain of intellectual . . . activity leading to change, while the Orient was characterized by quiescence and lack of change." Similar, even stronger views found expression in the works of the famous Greek author Nikos Kazantzakis, who grew to manhood on the very outermost periphery of Europe, confronting a hostile, alien culture. Kazantzakis, in his book *Report to Greco,* compared his own culture to that of Asia Minor. Greece, he wrote, "is the filter which . . . refines brute into man, eastern servitude into liberty, barbaric intoxication into sober rationality." Cultural impulses received from the east, from Asia, were refined and transubstantiated by the Greeks into more civilized forms. Greece's "fated location" on the borders of Asia produced, said Kazantzakis, "a mystic sense of mission and responsibility," a buffer against the "barbaric" and "bestial" east.

When confronted by Eurocentrism and cultural arrogance, we should remind the Europeans that many of their gifts to the world proved malevolent and destructive, in some cases threatening the very existence of the human race. Europe gave us ethnic cleansing, genocide, imperialism, colonialism, mechanized total warfare, and ecocide. In the words of geographer Yi-fu Tuan, the Europeans, by discarding "the ageless fear of the greater power and potency of nature," assumed "an arrogance based on the presumed availability of almost unlimited power." Europe means progress, but where that progression ultimately will lead, to good or evil, remains unclear. Europeans developed a high culture, but it could not, in the final analysis, prevent them from committing unspeakable atrocities, even in the German heart of Europe, nor does it allow them to control the powerful technology they unleashed. No, European culture is not superior. The world might be a better place had they never existed. Rather, let us regard Europe merely as a *distinctive* culture, one devoted to individualism, innovation, and change. The definition of Europe lies in that unique culture rather than in the physical earth.

Boundaries

Earlier, we rejected the diverse attempts to find physical borders for Europe (Figure 1.5), while at the same time presenting a map based on the three basic European traits (Figure 1.7). Now we must seek more refined, culturally based limits.

Perhaps the best place to begin our search is with the subjective perceptions of Europeans themselves. Listen when they speak, and you will hear revealing if often bigoted remarks, such as:

"Africa begins at the Pyrenees." (A. Dumas, Frenchman)

"We were, and will be, Europeans." (Latvia's prime minister, 1991)

"The principles of Europe can't exactly be implanted in Bulgaria." (Vladimir Andreev, Bulgarian filmmaker, 1995)

"Scratch a Russian and you will wound a Tatar." (Napoleon)

"Russians: a European people or some mongrel Asian one?" (Steven Erlanger, 1995)

"Can we become a part of Europe?" (anonymous Albanian, 1992)

"My country has joined Europe again." (Czech official, 1991)

"When the rest of [medieval] Iberia was under Arab domination, Catalonia was part of Europe, an important difference." (Catalunya's director of linguistic policy, 1991)

"Napoli must stop being a Middle Eastern city." (Sergio Baronci, bureaucrat in Roma)

"Ukrainians have a decided Oriental kink in their brains." (British Foreign Office internal memo, 1939)

Implicit in many such inflammatory remarks is the notion that Russia, or even Russian-dominated buffer states, do not belong in Europe; many scholars would place the European border at the western limits of that country. Yet the Russian Mikhail Gorbachev coined the term "our common European home," and, as Milan Hauner notes, many Russians today ask "what is Asia to us?" Most geographers seek to compromise, drawing the border of Europe *through* Russia, thereby claiming a part of it—*Eurorussia*—for the European culture area (Figure 1.9). We will do precisely that in this text, whenever a statistical boundary of Europe

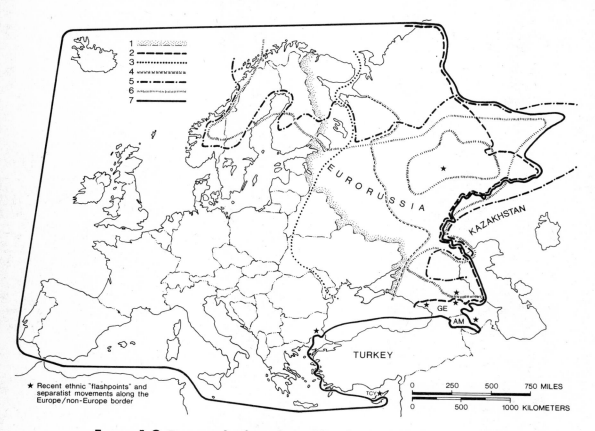

FIGURE 1.9 Proposed culture-based borders of Europe. 1 = western border of Russia; **2** = eastern border of Europe proposed by the Russian geographer Murzayev, based upon internal administrative units; **3** = border proposed by the German geographer Banse, 1912; **4** = border proposed by the French geographer Thevet, 1575; **5** = border of the "European space economy," according to geographer Andrew Dawson, 1993; and **6** = borders of "sedentary agricultural Europe," proposed by the Frenchman Delaisi, 1929. The border shown as **7** is the one used when defining Europe for statistical purposes throughout this book. (Sources: After Parker 1960; Delaisi 1929, 24–25; Hahn 1881 plate 3; Murzayev 1964; Andrew H. Dawson *A Geography of European Integration*, London, GB: Belhaven, 1993.)

In some places, a sharp cultural border for Europe seems simple to draw, as is true at Gibraltar and in the Aegean, where different shores belong to sharply contrasted cultures. It is also true along the partition line in Cyprus, where, in the words of one United Nations official, crossing from the Greek to the Turkish sector "is like suddenly stepping into Asia." Greek Nicosia's "skyline is an enormous wall of high-rises," while Turkish Lefkosa's consists of "low, red-tiled roofs, homes to craftsmen and shopkeepers." We deal in these places with Christian/Islamic confrontation and dichotomy.

In recent times, some segments along this well-defined border of Europe have become flashpoints of conflict, separatism, and ethnic cleansing, as happened in Cyprus in 1974; in Bulgaria, where expulsions of ethnic Turks flared anew in the late 1980s; in Azerbaijan, where the Armenian Christian minority in Nagorno-Karabakh province rebelled; in Georgia, where Abkhazi Muslims seceded amid civil war in 1993; in the Russian Caucasus, where Muslim Chechenya declared an abortive independence in 1991; and even along that most Russian of rivers, the Volga, where Muslim Tatarstan attempted to break away in 1992 (Figures 1.6, 1.9, 1.10). In some of these conflicts, Asian-ness was flaunted, as in Cyprus, where Turkey code-named its 1974 invasion "Attila," after the infamous Hunnic warrior from Asia who attacked Europe long ago. In the aftermath, Turkish Cypriots quickly expunged Greek place names from the map in their new republic. The border of Europe tends to grow sharper as a result of such conflicts.

Still, seeking a sharp cultural border for Europe proves futile in some places, especially in the east. There, the attempt to draw a precise line separating Europe from Asia becomes a fool's errand, with no two geographers agreeing (Figure 1.9). There, at least, Europe has no sharp borders. As long ago as the 1920s, geographers had "largely emancipated themselves from the hypnotic effect of terms like Europe and Asia," wrote the geographer Marion Newbigin, stressing instead the gradual transition from European to non-European. The Russian geographer Murzayev agreed, concluding that "there is no clear boundary," though he believed that Europe obviously ended "at some sensitive point" in Russia and that a purely utilitarian border based on political-administrative subdivisions could be useful (Figure 1.9).

The absence of a sharp border for Europe becomes even more evident when the various defining criteria are mapped. Even if the definition includes only the three basic traits—religion, language, and race—transitional zones appear in both south and east (Figure 1.7). The Caucasus region reveals a chaotic cartography when we limit consideration to just two traits, religion and language (Figure 1.10).

If instead, we map all eleven of the earlier-mentioned human defining characteristics of Europe, a broad transitional zone replaces any notion of sharp borders. From a core in central and northwestern Europe, where all the defining traits appear, "European-ness" declines gradually to the east and south. Europe, culturally, yields slowly to Asia and Africa (Figure 1.11).

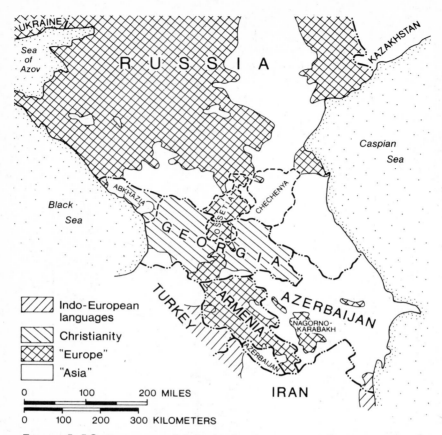

FIGURE 1.10 Europe and Asia in the Caucasus, based on the distribution of Christianity and the Indo-European languages. Notice how complicated the border of Europe becomes even when only these two criteria are employed.

Core and Periphery

Implicit in the transition-zone concept of the European boundary is a contrast between *core* and *periphery*. The core of Europe includes those inner provinces in which all of the defining traits are present, while the periphery consists of countries and districts in which only some of the European characteristics appear. Peripheries tend to be dependent upon or dominated by the core, controlling at best only their own resources. They occupy the outskirts of a system, in this case the European culture area.

Europeans regularly acknowledge the core/periphery configuration; for centuries residents of Europe's core have looked down upon the various peoples of the periphery, disparaging their quasi-European character. The snobbery of the core and inferiority complex of the periphery find expression in some of the quotations presented earlier, particularly those directed against Russians and Iberians. Figure 1.12 contains a variety of others. In countries whose boundaries

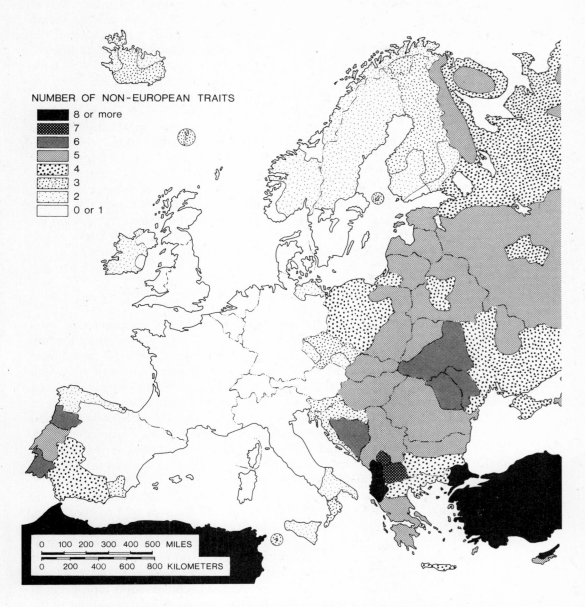

NUMBER OF NON-EUROPEAN TRAITS

- ■ 8 or more
- ▦ 7
- ▨ 6
- ▦ 5
- ⣿ 4
- ⣀ 3
- ⢀ 2
- □ 0 or 1

| 0 | 100 | 200 | 300 | 400 | 500 MILES |
| 0 | 200 | 400 | 600 | 800 KILOMETERS |

FIGURE 1.11 A measure of "European-ness," by province, based upon 11 European traits. **1** = over 80% Christian; **2** = over 80% Indo-European; **3** = over 90% Caucasian; **4** = infant mortality rate below 10; **5** = per capita gross domestic product of U.S. $10,000 or more; **6** = over 90% of people literate; **7** = 400 or more km of highway per 100 sq km of territory; **8** = less than 15% of workforce employed in agriculture; **9** = over 50% of people live in towns and cities; **10** = less than 1% annual natural population increase; and **11** = no totalitarian governments or military coups since 1980.

overlap core and periphery, separatist movements often exist, as in Italy, where the *Liga Nord* seeks autonomy for the northern part of the country. In an Italian movie comedy of the 1950s, a policeman from the north of Italy, part of the European core, is stationed in Sicilia (Sicily). Frustrated by the local lawless ways, alien to his orderly world, he, in one wordless but revealing scene, approached a large wall map of Italy and, at arm's length, conceals Sicilia with one hand to see how his country would look without that troublesome island.

So profound is the core/periphery configuration that Francis Delaisi gave the title *Two Europes* to a book on the subject. Another revealing example of the core/periphery mindset can be found in the pattern of "sister-cities," a system in which urban areas in different countries are "twinned" for the purposes of increasing international contacts and understanding. These ties are generally sought within the core region, rather than between core and periphery. In France, for example, 1,500 cities were twinned with Germany and 664 with the United Kingdom, but only 134 French sister-cities lie across the Pyrenees in Spain, in the "Africanized" part of Europe. In other words, the French turn their backs on fellow Romance speakers and forge ties to Germanic Europe.

Advance and Retreat

Once we adopt the notion that Europe should be defined in human terms, then we must also realize that its geographic extent can change. People and ideas are mobile, and so is Europe. To bound Europe today means drawing different lines than would have been used 1000 or 2000 years ago (Figure 1.13). Both expansion and retreat have marked Europe's past. One thousand years before Christ, a small European nucleus had formed around the shores of the eastern Mediterranean, a Greek embryo of Western civilization. The Greeks had to fight off the Asiatic Persians among others, to preserve their infant European culture. By the beginning of the Christian era, Europe coincided with the territorial extent of the Roman Empire, a considerable expansion from the nucleus of 1000 B.C., though the core still lay in the Mediterranean basin.

The passage of still another millennium, to about A.D. 1000, brought dramatic areal changes. The Arabs, driven by the evangelical spirit of a new religion, Islam, wrested away all of North Africa, most of Iberia, and the larger islands in the Mediterranean Sea. The deepest intrusion of the Arabs reached into central western France, where they were finally turned back on the battlefield of Tours. Asiatic horsemen from the East, the Magyars, penetrated as far as southern Germany, where a major battle was fought on the Lechfeld. After long years of raiding, these mounted warriors eventually abandoned all but a foothold in the grassland of Hungary, where their linguistic descendants still remain today. The first thousand years after Christ were not, however, entirely years of retreat. The loss of North Africa was paralleled by an expansion into heathen Germanic and Slavic realms, which Christian missionaries brought into the European community.

The territorial ebb and flow of Europe continued into the present millennium. Spaniards and Portuguese, gripped by a religious fervor reminiscent of the

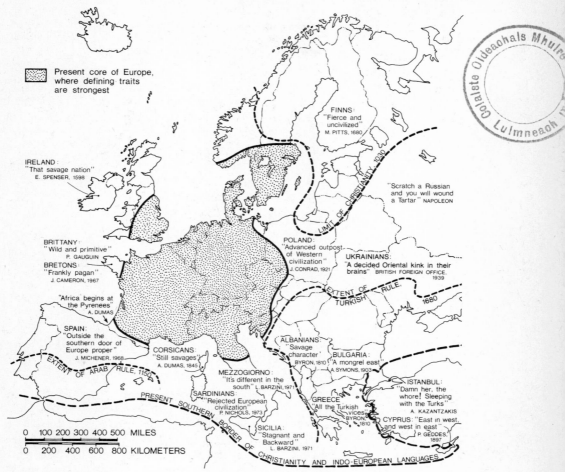

FIGURE 1.12 Core and periphery in Europe, a subjective delimitation. Cultural residues of African and Asian rule persist, as, perhaps, does the later Christianization of the north. Europeans themselves perceive these gradations, as suggested by the quotations and sayings, though they often reflect the biases and prejudices of the core inhabitants. (Sources: Edmund Spenser, *A View of the Present State of Ireland,* Oxford, GB: Clarendon Press, 1970, 1; Nikos Kazantzakis, *Report to Greco,* trans. P.A. Bien, New York, USA: Bantam Books, 1966, 410; Karl Peltzer, *Das treffende Zitat,* Thun, CH and München, D: Ott Verlag, 1957, 11; Alexandre Dumas, *The Corsican Brothers,* trans. Metcalfe Wood, London, GB: Readers Library Publishing Co., 1928, 34; Philippe Huisman, *René Jacques Brittany,* trans. Gladys Wheelhouse, Garden City, USA.: Doubleday, 1965, 5; Sylvie Nickels et al., *Finland: An Introduction,* New York, USA Praeger, 1973, 302; Luigi G. Barzini, *From Caesar to the Mafia: Sketches of Italian Life,* New York, USA: Library Press, 1971, 68, 259; Bergen Evans (ed.), *Dictionary of Quotations,* New York, USA: Delacorte Press, 1968, 602; Peter Yapp (ed.), *The Travellers' Dictionary of Quotation,* Boston, USA: Routledge & Kegan Paul, 1983, 6, 54, 158, 185, 428, 693; Gary Dunbar, "The Forests of Cyprus Under British Stewardship," *Scottish Geographical Magazine,* 99: 7 (1983), 111; James A. Michener, *Iberia,* New York, USA: Random House, 1968.)

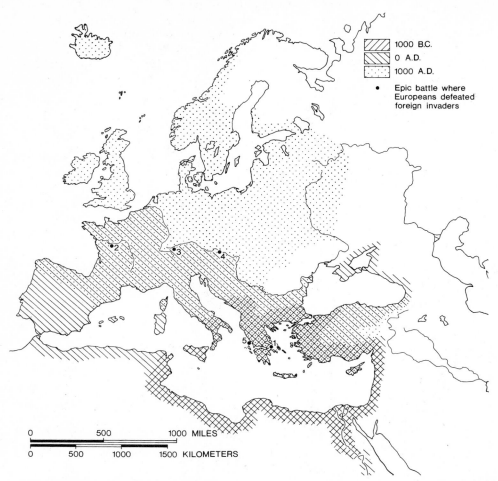

FIGURE 1.13 Territorial extent of Europe, 1000 B.C. to A.D. 1000 Europe shifted north and west. The battles include: **1** = Marathon and Salamis (Greeks defeated Persians, 490 and 480 B.C.); **2** = Tours (Franks turn back Arabs, A.D. 732); **3** = Lechfeld (Germans rout the Asiatic nomads at the deepest penetration into Europe in A.D. 955); **4** = Wien (European alliance three times repelled the Turks in 1529, 1532, and 1683) and **5** = Lepanto (Spaniards and Venetians crush Turks, 1571). (Source: Based in part upon Derwent Whittlesey, *Environmental Foundations of European History*, New York, USA: Appleton, 1949.)

earlier Muslim expansion, drove the Arabic Moors from Iberia, a reconquest that was completed in 1492. In the East, however, two serious setbacks occurred. The Tatars, or Golden Horde, followed the path of their earlier Asiatic kinsmen, sweeping across southern Russia to fall on Europe in the 1200s. Scarcely had they fallen back when a new peril appeared in Asia Minor, where the Muslim Turks overwhelmed the Greeks in Asia Minor and pressed on beyond the Dardanelles-Bosporos to seize permanently the center of Orthodox Eastern Christianity, Constantinople. From there the Turks spread northward to occupy most of the

Balkan Peninsula. Repeatedly, Europe's warriors gathered to turn the Turks back from the gates of Wien (Vienna) and at the naval battle of Lepanto, preserving European culture. The Turkish tide gradually receded, leaving only Muslim relics in the Balkans and a small Turkish bridgehead on the north shore of the Dardanelles and Bosporos around Istanbul. Even the most persistent efforts by Europeans failed to destroy this bridgehead, and it, along with Asia Minor, remains lost to Europe.

Another area of contest within the last thousand years has been Palestine. The Europeans seized a temporary foothold in the Holy Land during the Crusades, only to suffer eventual defeat. Renewed efforts to claim the area began with the Zionist movement, the British takeover after World War I, the flood of Jewish migration after the Nazi disaster, and the creation of Israel. To be sure, the Israelis are not Christian, and they abandoned the Indo-European Yiddish language in favor of Semitic Hebrew, but in standard of living and economic development, their nation represents a transplanting of Europe to the eastern Mediterranean shores.

The truly spectacular European expansion, however, has been accomplished over the past 400 to 500 years by Germanic peoples, Slavs, and Iberian Latins. The French scholar Pierre Chaunu views this global expansion as primarily the work of "Latin Christendom," including the adherents to both its Roman Catholic and Protestant components. Germanic-speaking peoples, in particular the English, created overseas Europes in Anglo-America, Australia, New Zealand, and South Africa, while Spaniards and Portuguese transplanted much that is European in large parts of Latin America. The overseas activities of the Iberians and Germans coincided with a major Slavic expansion overland, accomplished by the European Russians, who busily pushed Europe deep into the previously alien heartland of Eurasia and on beyond to the Pacific shore.

In addition to the middle- and upper-latitude areas to which large European populations were transplanted bodily, destroying or subjugating the native peoples, great tropical colonial empires were established by the Spaniards, Portuguese, British, French, Dutch, Belgians, and Germans. In the entire world, only China, Japan, Thailand, Iran, Arabia, and Turkey failed to fall under European rule at some time between 1500 and 1950. Colonialism brought the imprint of Europe. Consequently, India has a railroad system founded by the British, the Haitian speaks a form of French, and the Filipino adheres to the Roman Catholic faith. Europeans carried their mode of life throughout the world, transplanting it to thinly occupied lands or grafting it onto societies too firmly rooted to be dislodged (Figure 1.14). The world has been Europeanized in numerous, fundamental ways. Even those few areas never ruled from Europe have felt its cultural impress. Japan accepted the Industrial Revolution, China adopted Marxist socialism, and Turkey replaced Arabic script with the Latin alphabet.

At the same time, other parts of the world also helped shape Europe. Influence flowed both ways, and the European way of life has been profoundly altered in the process. Indeed, prior to about A.D. 1500, Europe could best be regarded as peripheral to the great culture centers of the Old World, receiving far more than it gave. Even Christianity, the traditional basis for much of Europe's distinctiveness, originated in the Middle East and attained its first major foothold

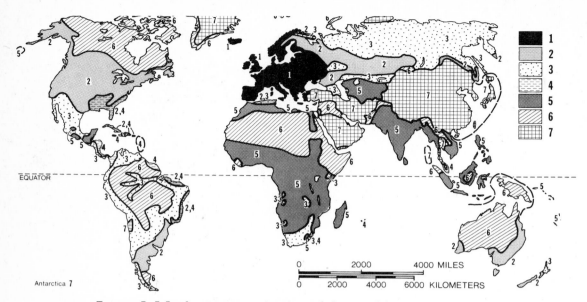

FIGURE 1.14 The Europeanization of the world. Key: **1** = European hearth area, A.D. 1500; **2** = neo-European areas; population and culture almost wholly of European derivation; **3** = mixed European and aboriginal areas, but culture strongly influenced or dominated by European practices; **4** = plantation culture; small European-derived minority traditionally dominated a large non-European labor force; **5** = exploitive or custodial occupation by Europeans in colonial era; minute numbers of Europeans implanted some durable customs and artifacts; **6** = loose, ineffective, or brief European control and impact; **7** = areas never directly occupied or controlled by Europeans, but indirect penetration of European influence often significant. (Source: Modified from Wilbur Zelinsky, *A Prologue to Population Geography*, Englewood Cliffs, USA: Prentice Hall, 1966, 74–75.)

in Asia Minor. African Arabs taught Iberians some of the navigational secrets that permitted the Age of Discovery, and Muslims preserved much ancient Greco-Roman knowledge during Europe's lengthy Dark Age. Asiatic philosophical influences reached some European intellectuals, such as the twentieth-century German writer Hermann Hesse. Agriculture originally reached Europe from a western Asian hearth, and the later introduction of American Indian crops, such as the potato, tomato, tobacco, and maize, greatly altered the European agrarian system.

Nor has European influence always found acceptance overseas. Recent events suggest a substantial, rising resistance to Europeanization, as is seen in the demise of colonialism and the Islamic cultural revival. In Africa, Islam rather than Christianity is the fastest-growing religious faith, and generations of Christian missionaries failed to make significant inroads in India, China, or Japan. Finally, demographic stagnation means that Europeans form an ever-smaller part of the world population, a trend that will presumably further undermine their influence.

Still, the importance of Europe remains profound. Let us turn our attention now to a geographical analysis of this small but remarkable corner of the world.

Sources and Suggested Readings

Leif Ahnström. "Europe: Culture Area, Geo-ideological Construct, or Illusion?" *Norsk Geografisk Tiddskrift*. 47:2 (1993), 57–67.

Luigi Barzini. *The Europeans*. New York, USA: Simon & Schuster, 1983.

Brian W. Beeley. "The Greek-Turkish Boundary: Conflict at the Interface." *Transactions of the Institute of British Geographers*. 3 (1978), 351–366.

Hans Bobek. "The Main Stages in Socio-Economic Evolution from a Geographical Point of View." In Philip L. Wagner and Marvin W. Mikesell (eds.). *Readings in Cultural Geography*. Chicago, USA: University of Chicago Press, 1962, 218–247.

Pierre Chaunu. *European Expansion in the Later Middle Ages*. Trans. Katharine Bertram. Amsterdam, NL: North-Holland Publishing Co., 1979.

Francis Delaisi. *Les deux Europes*. Paris, F: Payot, 1929.

Robert A. Dodgshon. "The Role of Europe in the Early Modern World-System: Parasitic or Generative?" *Political Geography*. 11 (1992), 396–400.

John Fells and Józef Niznik. "What Is Europe?" *International Journal of Sociology*. 22 (1992), 201–207.

Eric Fischer. *The Passing of the European Age: A Study of the Transfer of Western Civilization and Its Renewal in Other Continents*. Cambridge, USA: Harvard University Press, 1943.

F. G. Hahn. "Zur Geschichte der Grenze zwischen Europa und Asien." *Mitteilungen des Vereins für Erdkunde zu Leipzig*. 1881,83–104.

Milan Hauner. *What Is Asia to Us? Russia's Asian Heartland Yesterday and Today*. Boston, USA: Unwin Hyman, 1990.

Denys Hay. *Europe: The Emergence of an Idea*. Edinburgh, GB: University Press, 1957.

Michael J. Hebbert and Jens C. Hansen (eds.). *Unfamiliar Territory: The Reshaping of European Geography*. Aldershot, GB: Avebury, 1990.

Günter Heinritz. "Der griechisch-türkische Konflikt in Zypern." *Geographische Rundschau*. 27 (1975), 93–99.

Brian W. Ilbery. "Core-Periphery Contrasts in European Social Well-Being." *Geography*. 69 (1984), 289–302.

Sarah Ladbury and Russel King. "Settlement Renaming in Turkish Cyprus." *Geography*. 73 (1988), 363–367.

Herbert Louis. "Über den geographischen Europabegriff." *Mitteilungen der Geographischen Gesellschaft in München*. 39 (1954), 73–93.

Lionel Lyde. *The Continent of Europe*. London, GB: Macmillan, 1926.

E. M. Murzayev. "Where Should One Draw the Geographical Boundary Between Europe and Asia?" *Soviet Geography: Review and Translation*. 5 (1964), 15–25.

Marion I. Newbigin. *The Mediterranean Lands*. London, GB: Christophers, 1924.

W. H. Parker. "Europe: How Far?" *Geographical Journal*. 126 (1960), 278–297.

W. H. Parker. "Europe and the New Civilization." *Canadian Geographer*. 3 (1953), 53–60.

Alan Pred. *Recognising European Modernities*. London, GB: Routledge, 1995.

Marina Tolmacheva. "Cultural Perceptions of the Islamic Frontier in Arabic Geographical Literature." In *Contacts Between Cultures: West Asia and North Africa,* ed. A. Harrak. Lewiston/Queenston,/Lampeter, CDN: Edwin Mellen 1992, v. 1, 361–368.

Yi-fu Tuan. "Cultural Pluralism and Technology." *Geographical Review*. 79 (1989), 269–279.

Wilbur Zelinsky. "The Twinning of the World: Sister Cities in Geographic and Historical Perspective." *Annals of the Association of American Geographers*. 81 (1991), 1–31.

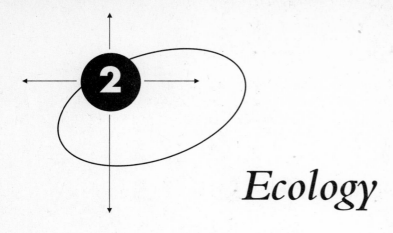

Ecology

While Europe constitutes a human and largely cultural entity, its natural setting should not be slighted in a geographical analysis. The story of the human Europe has been acted out on a segment of the physical earth—a peninsula composed of many constituent peninsulas attached to the western extremity of Eurasia. In this chapter we will consider Europe's terrain, climate, natural vegetation, soils, and hydrogeography.

The physical environment of Europe has influenced the inhabitants' way of life in diverse ways, and we cannot understand Europe thoroughly without knowing the nature of its physical framework. At the same time, Europeans have massively altered their environment, for both better and worse, to the extent that a "natural" environment no longer exists: the geographer, environment, people, and place remain abstractions unless considered together. This intertwining of culture and milieu, this cultural ecology, provides another focus of the present chapter.

The European Mountains

The physical geography of Europe displays considerable internal variety. Nowhere is that areal variation more visible than in terrain, or landforms. The European land ranges from high, rugged mountains to featureless flat plains. We will employ a threefold classification of terrain types: mountains, hills, and plains (Figure 2.1).

Mountains are confined largely to the southern half of Europe, except for one major chain in Scandinavia, and in marked contrast to the ranges of the Americas, most European mountains are oriented in an east-west direction. The southern concentration of mountain ranges is largely a result of *plate tectonics*, as the African and Eurasian plates slowly collide, a process begun some 50 million years ago—recent by geologic standards. The collision has caused folding, fracturing, and uplifting of the earth's surface, building the mountains.

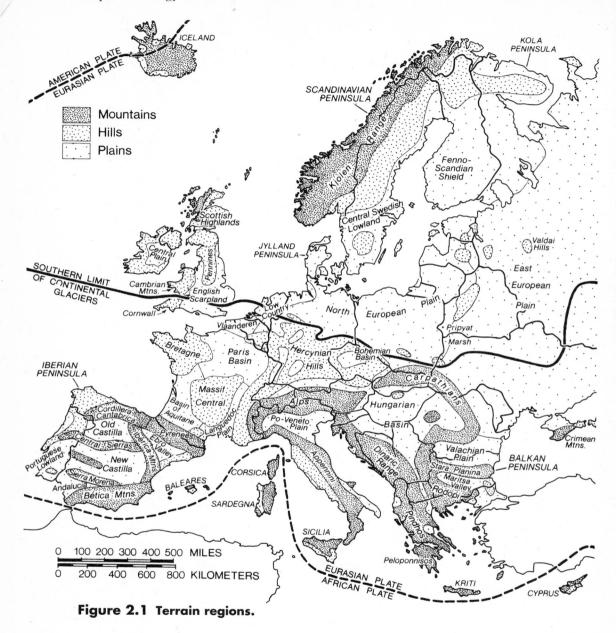

Figure 2.1 Terrain regions.

Beginning in the southwest, in Iberia, we find the *Bética* (Baetic) Mountains, paralleling the south coast of Spain. They consist of several ridges—including the *Sierra Nevada*—and several longitudinal valleys, stretching from the Rock of Gibraltar to the vicinity of Valencia. There the mountains disappear beneath the sea only to emerge again to the east as the Baleares (Balearic) Islands. The Bética area, which includes peaks of more than 3350 m (11,000 ft.), was the final strong-hold of the Moors, or Arabs, in Europe, and their influence is seen in the architecture of the city of Granada, which lies in one of the longitudinal valleys at the foot of the Sierra Nevada. Arabic place names also survive as a Moorish relic, including Gibraltar, which is derived from *gebel-al-Tariq,* or the "rock of Tariq," who was a Moorish ruler. The last Arab Muslim revolt against Spanish rule, in the late 1500s, occurred in the Bética range, and villages founded by the Berbers—an African tribal group that accompanied the Moorish invasion—still today retain a special cultural character. Truly, Europe meets Africa in these mountains. The southernmost ridge of the Bética Range fronts on the Mediterranean Sea, creating a rocky and picturesque coast, but in a number of places the ranges draw back from the shore, allowing small pockets of coastal plain, called *huertas,* literally "gardens." These permit intensive irrigation agriculture, as in the Huerta of Valencia, famous for its orange groves. The *Ibérica (Iberian) Mountains,* a fragmented arc trending inland north and northwest from the general area of Valencia, might best be regarded as a lower continuation of the Bética Range. They do not exceed elevations of 2300 m (7500 ft.) and in general are not a major hindrance to transportation.

The Pyrenees, much more impressive, form a true barrier range along the border of Spain and France. Rivers that cut back into the main, northern ridge of the Pyrenees from the Spanish and French sides are not longitudinally aligned, and as a consequence no low passes have been carved out by adjacent headwaters. The resultant isolation aided the survival of Andorra, a mountain nation whose people long relied on smuggling as a livelihood. The lesser, southern ridges of the Pyrenees are also difficult to pass since the rivers that sever them have cut deep gorges. The barrier effect of the Pyrenees was reduced by tunnel construction when the Val d'Aran, a small part of Spain lying north of the main Pyrenean ridge and traditionally reached only through French territory, was connected to Spain. A lower, westward mountain projection from the Pyrenees is the *Cordillera Cantabrica* (Cantabrians), reaching 2600 to 2750 m (8500 to 9000 ft.) at the highest and paralleling the north coast of Spain. The steepest face of this range faces north, to the Atlantic, producing a rocky coast with numerous small protected bays called *rías,* long used as fishing harbors.

Farther south in Iberia lie the *Central Sierras,* an east-west-tending mountain complex about the same height as the Cantabrica and bearing several local names, in particular the sierras of *Gredos, Guadarrama,* and *Gata* in Spain and the *Serra de Estrêla* in Portugal. Still farther south one finds other parallel, lower mountain areas, most notably the *Sierra Morena.* Collectively, the Iberian ranges partition the peninsula, fostering cultural variation and even political separatism.

The *Alps,* the highest and most famous European mountains, stretch from the French Riviera in an arc eastward through Switzerland to the Wienerwald (Vienna Woods) on the bank of the Austrian Danube (Figure 2.2). The inhabitants use almost countless local names to designate different parts of the range, such as the *Cottienne, Maritime, Berner* (Bernese), *Dolomitic,* and *Julian* Alps. For purposes of description, the range is best divided into three parts—the southern, western, and eastern Alps. Bordering the Mediterranean, the southern Alps form the narrowest segment of the range and consist of one main ridge along the French-Italian border. About the latitude of Grenoble and Torino (Turin), the southern section gives way to the western Alps, in the process acquiring a second main

FIGURE 2.2 Spur ridges of the eastern Alps, bearing a winter's snow cover. While the Alps appear formidable, low passes and water gaps make them relatively easy to traverse. (Photo by the author, 1974.)

ridge to parallel the first and changing direction to arc eastward. Extending as far east as a line from Lake Como to the Bodensee (Lake Constance), the western Alps form the highest and most spectacular part of the range, with deeply incised valleys and impressive remnant glaciers. Mont Blanc, towering 4813 m (15,781 ft.) above sea level, is the highest in Europe. Deep, sheer-sided, U-shaped valleys, hollowed out by glaciers during the Ice Age, sometimes have floors 2750 m (9000 ft.) lower than the adjacent peaks.

While impressive in appearance, the southern and western Alps never served as a true barrier. So many low passes exist through which invaders can move that the Italians, who live south of the mountains and look to them as a "natural" border, refer to the range as the "magnificent traitor." The Carthaginian general Hannibal successfully moved a cavalry of elephants and 30,000 men through the southern Alps to attack Italy. Centuries later came various German tribes from the north, who slipped through to deal a deathblow to the Roman Empire. The ease of access through the western Alps is attributable to streams. The valley lying between the two ridges is drained by a succession of rivers, including the Isère, Arc, Rhône, Reuss, and Rhine. All of these sever the northern-western ridge, providing access into the heart of the range as they flow into the plains and hills beyond the Alps. Headwater tributaries of these rivers have cut into the southern-eastern ridge directly opposite streams leading to the

Po River of Italy, producing a series of remarkably low passes. The most famous of these are the Mont Cenis (2083 m, 6834 ft.), Great Saint Bernard (2470 m, 8100 ft.), and Simplon (2010 m, 6600 ft.) passes, lying on ancient routes from Italy to France, as well as the Saint Gotthard and Splügen passes (both 2100 m, 6900 ft.), linking the German-speaking lands with Italy. This combination of river gaps and low passes produce the "magnificent traitor."

The eastern Alps, much broader than the other two sections, reach a width of 240 km (150 mi.) along a line from Verona to München (Munich). Instead of one longitudinal valley, two, three, or even four exist, guiding the courses of rivers such as the Inn, Adige, Mur, and Drau. The peaks of the eastern Alps rarely exceed 3000 m (10,000 ft.). In spite of their greater width, the eastern Alps are also relatively easy to cross. The great north-south route is the Brenner Pass (1375 m, 4500 ft.), carved by tributaries of the Inn and Adige rivers through the middle of three ridges that are found in this part of the Alps. Water gaps created by these same rivers and others sever the northern and southern ridges.

The *Appennini (Apennine) Mountains,* which form the backbone of the Italian Peninsula, branch out from the southern Alps in the Riviera district, parallel the coast of the Gulf of Genova (Genoa), and then arc gently to the southeast to approach Italy's Adriatic shore and south and west to return to the western coast and form the toe of the Italian boot. Structurally, they reappear bearing different names in the island of Sicilia. The Appennini, both narrow and low, offer many easy passes and have never presented much of a barrier.

The *Dinaric Range* begins at the Alps near the point where Italy, Slovenia, and Austria meet and stretches southeastward along the Adriatic coast through the western Balkan peninsula, continuing as the *Pindhos (Pindus) Mountains* and others through to the tip of the Pelopónnisos. While not unusually high, the Dinaric Range is in many sections rugged and difficult to traverse, especially in areas of *karst* topography, where water filtering down from the surface dissolved permeable limestone, forming numerous large sinks or troughs called *dolines* and *polje* that are used for farming activity. One of the few easy passages through the Dinaric Range occurs in the extreme north, at the juncture with the Alps, where Pear Tree Pass allows access from the plains of Hungary into the Po-Veneto Plain of Italy, another "betrayal" by the magnificent, traitorous mountains that rim the northern edge of the Italian Peninsula. While Pear Tree Pass enjoys less significance today, both Hunnish and Gothic warriors poured through it to attack the Roman Empire. Today, the Zagreb-to-Rijeka route possesses greater importance. To the south, about midway through Albania, the Dinaric Range becomes more open and accessible, a condition that persists through Greece.

Just east of Wien (Vienna), across the Danube River in Slovakia, the *Carpathian Mountains* begin, almost as a continuation of the Alps. Their directional course inscribes a huge mirror-image C through southern Poland, a corner of Ukraine, and Romania, ending as they began on the shores of the Danube at the Iron Gate. The southern part of the Carpathians in Romania bears the name Transylvanian Alps. High elevations rarely occur in the Carpathians,—few peaks are over 2500 m (8000 ft.)— and they form a narrow range with numerous low passes. South of the Iron Gate on the Danube, the same mountain structure turns back eastward in two prongs as the *Stara Planina (Balkan Mountains)* and *Rodopi*

(Rhodope) Mountains, mainly in Bulgaria. To the east, the *Crimean Mountains* occupy the southern side of a large peninsula jutting into the Black Sea in Ukraine and shelter the famous resort of Yalta from the brutal East European winter. Still farther east and in the popular mind serving as boundaries for Europe lie the *Caucasus Mountains,* a towering, rugged range that has provided refuge for numerous small ethnic groups between the Black and Caspian seas, and the *Urals,* a low, easily penetrated mountain ridge reaching from the Arctic Ocean shore southward into central Eurasia (see Figure 1.5).

The final major mountain area of Europe is the *Kjölen Range,* which forms the spine of the Scandinavian Peninsula in Norway and Sweden. It was heavily glaciated in the Ice Age, and remnant glaciers are still present. As a result, the soil cover is extremely thin or absent altogether, and the coastline is deeply indented by ice-carved fjords, U-shaped glacial valleys later flooded by the ocean. One of the most spectacular is the long, narrow Hardangerfjord (Hairstring Fjord). The Kjölen Range contains very few inhabitants, but at the upper end of most Kjölen fjords, a small patch of flat, unflooded land known as a *vik* occurs, backed by a steep head wall and flanked by nearly perpendicular valley sides (Figure 2.3). Long ago the inhabitants derived their very name, Vikings ("people of the inlet"), from these small plains. Virtually forced by the local

Figure 2.3 A branch of the Sognefjord and an inhabited *vik* at its head. In the Norwegian Kjölen Range, only small agricultural areas occur. The fjords provide an excellent transportation facility. (Photo by the author, 1981.)

Kjölen terrain to look outward, down the fjord to the sea, the Vikings became famous as traders and sea raiders.

Earthquakes and Vulcanism

Closely linked to the mountain ranges of Europe, particularly in the southeast and on the island of Iceland, are the related phenomena of *earthquakes, vulcanism,* and *tidal waves* (Figure 2.4). The mountain areas most repeatedly and catastrophically affected include the Appennini, Caucasus, Rodopi, and Dinaric/Pindhos, as well as many islands of the eastern Mediterranean and Iceland. Huge losses of life sometimes accompany European earthquakes, as was the case when 60,000 Sicilians died in an early twentieth-century disaster and 25,000 Armenians in 1988. The fatalities are often caused by the collapse of stone houses and tiled roofs, both common in southern Europe.

Volcanoes can also bring grief. The eruption of Vesùvio (Vesuvius) near Napoli (Naples) in A.D. 79 destroyed the Roman city of Pompeii, while on Sicilia over 500 recorded eruptions of Etna, the largest continental volcano in the world, claimed an estimated 1 million lives over the past 2500 years. The perpetually active volcano called Stromboli lies in the Aeolian Isles, north of Sicilia.

The most violent and powerful volcanic eruption ever known in Europe occurred on the small Greek Aegean island of Thíra, which today consists of a shattered volcanic crater. Thíra erupted and collapsed with incredible force about 1600 B.C. The noise was likely heard as far away as Scandinavia and central Africa; a huge tsunami, perhaps 200 m (650 ft.) tall, crashed against the shore of nearby islands; and the sky was soon blackened with falling volcanic debris. Parts of Kriti (Crete) may have become temporarily uninhabitable as volcanic ash killed vegetation. Altogether, some 54 km³ (13 mi.³) of material was removed in the explosion of Thíra, in the process perhaps giving rise to the legend of the lost continent of Atlantis. Archaeologists found the remains of dwellings beneath 30 m (100 ft.) of ash cover on the remnant of Thíra.

On the mountainous island of Iceland, astride a tectonic plate divide at the opposite territorial extremity of Europe from Thíra, vulcanism and earthquake activity occur frequently. Iceland, with 30 volcanic systems, has experienced over 250 eruptions in the past 1100 years. Just within the past four decades, a new island—Surtsey—appeared as a volcanic peak off Iceland's southern shore, and a massive eruption occurred on a nearby, older island, creating a natural harbor. Small wonder that this northern island is called "the land of fire and ice."

The Plains of Europe

At the opposite extreme of terrain types are the **plains** areas of Europe. To a much greater extent than the mountains, the plains have been the scene of human activity, and for this reason they are of greater importance to the European culture area. The plains are concentrated in the north and east, in contrast to the southern dominance of mountains (Figure 2.1).

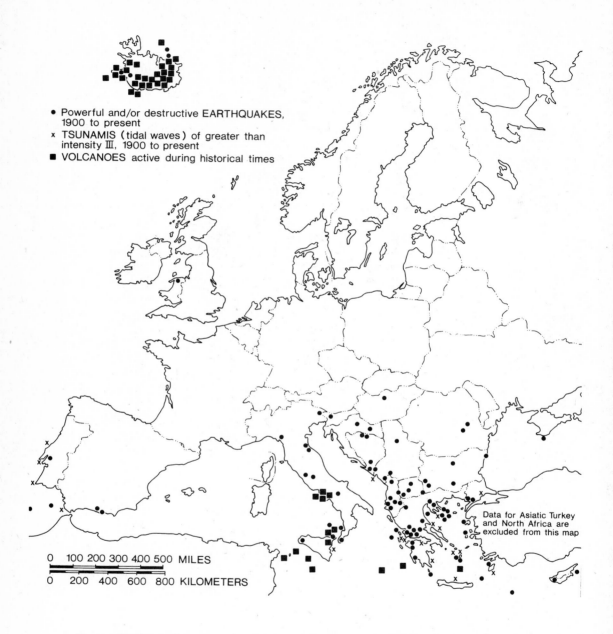

- Powerful and/or destructive EARTHQUAKES, 1900 to present
x TSUNAMIS (tidal waves) of greater than intensity III, 1900 to present
■ VOLCANOES active during historical times

Data for Asiatic Turkey and North Africa are excluded from this map

0   100 200 300 400 500 MILES

0   200   400   600   800 KILOMETERS

FIGURE 2.4 Earthquakes, vulcanism, and tsunamis in Europe. (Sources: Vít Kárník, *Seismicity of the European Area,* Dordrecht, NL: D. Reidel, Vol. II, 1971, p. 203; Tom Simkin et al., "This Dynamic Planet: World Map of Volcanoes, Earthquakes, and Plate Tectonics," Washington, USA: Smithsonian Institution and U.S. Geological Survey, 1989; data gathered by C. F. Richter, B. Gutenberg, and N. N. Ambraseys; Glen Reagor, U.S. Geological Survey, National Earthquake Information Center.)

A large, compartmentalized lowland, collectively called the *Great European Plain,* extends from the foot of the Pyrenees in southwestern France, arcing northward and eastward along the coast through Germany and Poland as far as the Baltic states. Many different sections of the Great European Plain can be distinguished, each bearing its own name and special character. European landscapes tend to be small, by American standards, and to know Europe well, we must think in terms of diminutive regions, each with its own identity, both physically and culturally. All facets of European culture, from languages to the pattern of independent states, reflect this physical and perceptual compartmentalization.

Europeans, then, do not think geographically at the scale of the Great European Plain but instead prefer to distinguish its constituent parts. Beginning in the southwest the first segment encountered is the *Basin of Aquitaine,* largely fertile and producing France's famous Bordeaux wines. Only the sandy section bordering the coast, the *Landes,* is infertile. The basin is connected to neighboring lowlands by two famous and important natural corridors: the Gap of Carcassonne, leading eastward to the Mediterranean Sea and guarded by the walled town of the same name, and the Gate of Poitou, a plains pathway some 65 km (40 mi.) wide, leading into the north of France toward Paris. The Moorish invaders entered the Basin of Aquitaine by way of Carcassonne and turned northward to the Gate of Poitou, where they were met and defeated by Frankish forces near Tours. Later, the basin provided a natural core area for the development of the medieval feudal states of Aquitaine and Gascogne. The orientation of the basin, facing outward toward the Atlantic, contributed to its long dominance by English rulers.

Beyond the Gate of Poitou lies a second major part of the North European Plain, the *Paris Basin,* occupying the larger part of northern France. In surface configuration this basin resembles a series of concentric, progressively larger saucers, with the city of Paris and the surrounding district, known as the Île de France, occupying the smallest, central saucer. In every direction from Paris, the land rises gently until a sharp drop-off is reached, formed by outward-facing *cuestas,* or escarpments. From the foot of the cuesta, the countryside again gradually increases in elevation until another cuesta is reached. To the east, seven such cuestas are present in at least fragmentary form (Figure 2.5). These escarpments proved valuable as natural defense walls for the French nation in wars with Germany. Invaders had to fight their way up the steep cuesta slopes in the face of French fortifications in order to reach Paris. The city of Verdun, which lies at the foot of one of the east-facing cuestas, was the scene of bitter fighting in World War I, and 600,000 Germans and French died fighting for command of the slope during a six-month period in 1916. This series of natural defense lines made the Île de France an ideal birthplace for the French state (see Chapter 7).

Across the English Channel in the southeastern part of the island of Great Britain lies a third segment of the Great European Plain, the *English Scarplands.* It is in many respects simply a continuation of the Paris Basin, including a series of west-facing cuestas. The Cotswolds and Chilterns are eroded hilly areas along the cuesta lines, with considerable land still forested, a rarity in Britain. At the eastern foot of the hilly escarpments are long valleys, oriented roughly southwest to northeast, including the Vale of Oxford and the once-marshy Fens. Just as the

FIGURE 2.5 An outward-facing cuesta just west of the Paris Basin city of Troyes, looking toward the city of Paris. Such cuestas protect the capital of France. As recently as World War I, they played a strategic role. The fertility of the Paris Basin is suggested by the expanse of grainfields. (Photo by the author, 1978.)

Paris Basin was the nucleus of the French state, so the scarpland was the scene of initial nation building by the Saxon invaders of Britain.

North from the Paris Basin, the European Plain again narrows to form a gateway, Vlaanderen (Flanders Plain) centered in western Belgium. As was true of Carcassonne and Poitou, Vlaanderen has strategic value. In World War I "Flanders Fields" connoted bitter fighting and high casualties, and its name lives on in the English poetry and literature of that era. Beyond Vlaanderen, the plain once again broadens to the north and east to form the *Low Country*, distinguished by almost total flatness. It consists of the communal delta of the Rhine, Maas, Schelde (Scheldt), Ems, and several lesser rivers. The greater part of the Low Country lies in the Netherlands, whose very name describes the terrain. Some of the area lies below the level of the sea. Much of the land that the Dutch struggle to keep is quite fertile, but the Low Country also contains sizable sandy districts, including the Kempenland (Campine) on the Belgium-Netherlands border, as well as areas of peat bog.

On the east, the Low Country borders the much larger *North European Plain*, which broadens as it extends through Germany, Denmark, southernmost Sweden, and Poland, increasing from 160 km (100 mi.) in width at the German-

Dutch border to nearly 500 km (300 mi.) in the Polish Lowlands to the east. The North European Plain, the western half of which has traditionally been called the North German Plain, differs markedly from the Low Country. It displays considerably more surface irregularity, a great part of which can be attributed to the effects of the Ice Age, in particular the last southward advance of the glaciers from their Scandinavian source. Parallel chains of *moraine* hills, glacial deposits formed wherever the ice mass paused in its retreat to leave behind a greater thickness of debris, extend east-west across the North European Plain, from the Jylland (Jutland) Peninsula of Denmark on into northern Poland, parallel to the Baltic shore. Between the hill chains are extensive zones covered with a layer of *ground moraine*, or *till*, where the continental glaciers deposited less material. The till surface is quite irregular or hummocky with many enclosed depressions of widely varied sizes that contain lakes or bogs. These are so numerous that the coastal part of the North European Plain is called the Baltic Lake Plain. The glaciers did not entirely cover the plain, but even the areas south of the ice mass were altered by its proximity. Beyond the terminal moraine, the southernmost line of glacially deposited hills, meltwater streams from the ice mass washed down finer sand and gravel, forming what are known as *outwash plains*. These remain today as infertile heath areas. The Lüneburger Heath south of Hamburg provides a fine example.

If the Ice Age produced much inferior land, it also helped form some of the most fertile districts of the plain. Winds sweeping down from the ice mass picked up fine particles of earth and carried them to the southern edge of the plain, where the lowlands give way to a zone of hilly terrain. The forced ascent blunted the velocity of the winds, causing them to drop at the foot of the hills much of their load of dust. These wind-deposited, fine-textured parent materials, known as *loess*, weathered into fertile and easy-to-work soils. The greatest depths of loess accumulated in numerous "embayments" of the North European Plain, called *Börde*, which reach south into the hills. Since the dawn of agriculture the loessial belt has been the most thickly populated part of the North European Plain, while the outwash areas supported only scattered inhabitants engaged mainly in herding.

To the east, beyond a parted veil of hill areas, large lakes, and the inhospitable Pripyat Marsh, lies the greatest of all the lowlands, the expansive *East European Plain* (Figure 2.1), spanning the entire breadth of the European peninsula from the Arctic Ocean in the north to the Black Sea in the south. Quite simply, this plain is not drawn on the "European" scale. Its vastness and lack of compartmentalization lend an alien aspect, and invading European armies, such as those led by Napoleon and Hitler, felt overwhelmed here. A huge independent state, Russia, arose to match this great plain, and its size, too, is atypical for Europe. Small wonder that most Europeans look upon Russia, seated in this massive lowland, as marginally European at best.

That is not to say that internal variety is lacking in the East European Plain. In the southern, unglaciated part, three major east-facing cuestas parallel the Dnipro, Don, and Volga rivers, vaguely reminiscent of the Paris Basin but on a far grander scale. The northern half of the plain abounds in the same glacial features that dominate the North European Plain.

To the north lies another fairly extensive plains region, the *Fenno-Scandian Shield*. Massively glaciated and underlain by ancient rocks, some of which lie exposed at the surface, the shield is centered in Finland and Russian Karelia. Two great moraine walls, called the Salpausselkä, parallel the south coast of Finland and serve to dam up much of the interior, producing an intricate system of connecting lakes. The Finns and Karelians long used these waterways as their dominant mode of transportation, but in the age of highways, roads follow sinuous *eskers*—high ground laid down as the beds of ancient rivers flowing in hollows beneath the glaciers. The eskers run at right angles to the Salpausselkä and provide some of the main north-south highway links. Parts of Sweden also belong to the Fenno-Scandian Shield, including the lake-rich *Central Swedish Lowland*.

All of the other plains areas lie in the south, wreathed by the mountain ranges that dominate that part of Europe. Most are small with the bordering ridges always visible. An exception is the large *Hungarian Basin*, also known as the Pannonian Plain, surrounded by the Alps, Carpathians, and Dinaric Range and including the nation of Hungary, as well as parts of every neighboring country. The fringing mountains provide no isolation for the Hungarian Basin. The Italian lands are easily reached through the Pear Tree Pass, while the Black Sea lies beyond the Iron Gate on the Danube, where the river severs the Carpathians from the Stara Planina. In the northwestern corner of the basin, the Moravian Gate provides egress north to the North European Plain, and the valley of the upper Danube leads on beyond Wien into southern Germany. Greece and the Aegean are accessible southward through the long, narrow Morava-Vardar Depression, a rift valley wedged between the Dinaric and Stara Planina ranges. Furthermore, there are numerous low passes in the Carpathian Mountains that lead into Russia. Through one or another of these numerous leaks and seams in the mountain wall, representatives of just about every major linguistic group in Europe and adjacent parts of Asia have passed as conquerors or refugees, and the recorded history of the basin is one of continued turbulence. It has been a zone of conflict between Roman and barbarian, Turk and Christian, Hun and German, Magyar and Slav. Warpaths have also been trade routes from the time of the amber trade through the Moravian Gate several thousand years ago and earlier. The diverse ethnic makeup of the basin today, including German, Hungarian, Slav, and Romanian, is the heritage of a long history of warfare, trade, and migration.

The *Valachian* (Wallachian) *Plain* and *Maritsa Valley* form two small, fingerlike lowlands reaching eastward into the Balkan peninsula from the Black Sea, flanking the Stara Planina on both sides. The Valachian Plain measures only about 300 by 125 km (200 by 70 mi.) in size, a typical European dimension. Valachia has witnessed the comings and goings of a great variety of invaders and migrating peoples, including the Huns, Slavs, Magyars, and Mongols. Today, the Valachian Plain is the heartland of the Romanians, who have somehow managed to preserve a language derived from the legions of the Caesars, perpetuating an isolated eastern bastion of Romance speech.

The *Po-Veneto Plain* of northern Italy, rimmed by the Alps and Appennini, is the only sizable plains area in that country. It represents a continuation of the structural depression containing the Adriatic Sea, filled to above the level of the sea with materials brought down from the surrounding mountains by streams and ice. Glaciers moving down into the fringe of the Po-Veneto Plain from the north deposited moraines, which dammed up the mouths of tributary Alpine valleys, creating a chain of beautiful natural lakes, including Como, Maggiore, Lugano, Iseo, and Garda. South of the moraine dams is an infertile outwash plain similar to that found in northern Germany. Beyond the outwash plain lies the greater part of the Po-Veneto Plain, an area of fertile, river-deposited soils. At the juncture of alluvium and outwash, the groundwater table reaches the surface, resulting in an east-west line of springs called *fontanili.* From ancient times the fontanili attracted human settlement, and today a row of cities, including Torino (Turin) and Milano (Milan), traces the course of the spring sites. Still another line of cities, including Parma, Modena, and Bologna, lies along the southern edge of the plain, at the foot of the Appennini. The western, uppermost part of the plain served as the political nucleus of Italian unification in the nineteenth century, and today the same area contains the industrial heart of the nation. France's gateway to the Mediterranean is the *Languedoc Plain,* a narrow coastal lowland reaching from the Pyrenees to the Riviera. Two strategic routes connect the plain to the heart of France: To the west one finds access through the previously mentioned Gap of Carcassonne to the Basin of Aquitaine, and the Rhône-Saône Corridor leads north into the Paris Basin.

The mountain ranges of Iberia divide that peninsula into a series of separate plains, each of which is home to people of a distinct subculture. The *Lowland of Andalucía (Andalusia),* wedged in between the Bética Mountains and the Sierra Morena in far southern Spain, is a land of olive groves dotted with place names that recall the Moorish occupation. The main river draining the lowland is the Rio Guadalquivir, a name derived from *Wadi-al-Kabir,* Arabic for "the great river." The narrow *Portuguese Lowland,* which fronts the Atlantic coast of Iberia, and the *Ebro Valley* in northeastern Spain are the other major peripheral Iberian regions of level terrain. The interior plains of Iberia, collectively known as the *Meseta,* differ from all the others in Europe previously discussed because they are plateaus rather than lowlands, elevated about 800 m (2500 ft.) above sea level. The Central Sierras divide the plateau into two parts, *Old* and *New Castilla* (Castile), the homeland of the people who have traditionally dominated and ruled Spain. The New Castilla Meseta contains the capital city of Madrid and also includes both Extremadura in the southwest and the plains of La Mancha near the center.

The European Hills

The third, and final, terrain category includes the major **hilly** areas of Europe. Hills dominate the European midsection, just as mountains occur mainly in the south and plains in the north (Figure 2.1). From the coast of France, a broad, compartmentalized belt of hills extends eastward through France and central Germany.

Among the more important constituent hilly districts are *Bretagne* (also known as the *Armorican Massif*) in western France, the *Massif Central* to the southeast, and the *Hercynian Hills,* which reach across Germany and into the Czech Republic. The Hercynian region is itself subdivided into a myriad of small, separate hill complexes, such as the Ardennes of Belgium and Luxembourg, Vosges of eastern France, Schwarzwald (Black Forest), Jura, Harz, Bohemian Forest, and Sudety. Scattered among these hill units are equally numerous small lowlands, such as the Upper Rhine Plain, Bohemian Basin, and Alpine Foreland, the latter a plateau situated just north of the Alps. These many small plains have long served as clusters of dense population, and the weblike gateways linking them have been routes of trade and invasion. The intervening hill areas, more sparsely settled, retain remnant forests and sometimes provided refuge for retreating ethnic minorities, such as the Celts of Bretagne and the Protestants of the Massif Central.

Some major hill lands lie outside the main belt in Central Europe, including the highlands of the British Isles. In Great Britain, hills dominate the west and north, confining the English Scarplands to the southeastern part of the island. *Cornwall* is the hilly peninsula reaching southwest to Land's End, and the *Cambrian Mountains* occupy the larger part of the province of Wales. The *Pennine Chain* and hilly *Lake District* of northern England blend into the *Scottish Highlands.* On the island of Ireland, a hill rim parallels the coast except in the east, including among others the mountains of Mourne, Antrim, Wicklow, and Knockmealdown. In northern Ireland, where the effects of glaciation appear abundantly, numerous elongated, streamlined hills called *drumlins* occur. Glaciers planed off the drumlins, and the long axis of such hills parallels the direction of ice flow. The hills of the British Isles have been the primary refuges of the Celtic people, where they were, for a time at least, able to resist the Anglo-Saxon invaders and preserve their customs and language. Gaelic, Erse, and Welsh are still spoken today as mother tongues in parts of the hills. In contrast, the lowlands and plains were invariably the scene of early Celtic defeat and assimilation. In Roman times the pattern was identical, for while the legions of Rome were able to secure the English Scarplands, they rarely ventured out against fierce hill tribes such as the Picts. Hadrian's Wall, built across the waist of Great Britain to restrain the Picts, still stands as a monument to Roman failure in the hilly north. The lesson of British terrain is that a hill area can be held by its inhabitants against repeated thrusts of a militarily and numerically superior enemy based in adjacent plains. Part of the reason for the success of hill refuges is that such regions are less valuable than fertile lowlands, not worth the effort of conquest.

If a recurrent trait can be detected in the terrain makeup of Europe, it is *compartmentalization.* The segmentation into numerous peninsulas and islands helps create this image, but it is heightened by the fact that individual terrain units are small and possess individuality. The Basin of Aquitaine differs from its neighbor, the Paris Basin, and the western Alps differ from the eastern Alps. Rarely does homogeneity of terrain dominate a sizable area, and each small landform district possesses its own special character. Where nature is drawn on a grand regional scale, the European is not at home.

Human Modification of Terrain

If terrain influences Europeans in certain ways, then they have most assuredly responded in kind. It is true that the "everlasting hills" have not been as drastically altered as some other facets of the European physical environment, but the work of the ever-active human hand is definitely visible. One example, confined to limited areas, is *terracing*. This ancient technology, probably derived from the mountain fringe of the Fertile Crescent in the Middle East, has enabled people to "level" mountains for agricultural use. A river journey on the Rhine from Bonn to Mainz reveals one of the most thorough jobs of terracing in all of Europe— huge, vine-covered stairsteps rising from the riverbank to the adjacent heights. In the Mediterranean lands, where level land is in short supply, terraced hillsides are also common, especially in Greece.

People have even gone so far as to build hills. Huge slag piles rise from the green valleys of Wales, and on the North European Plain near Berlin stands the Teufelsberg, or "Devil's Mountain." Building material for the Teufelsberg was obtained from the rubble of the war-destroyed German capital, and the peak reaches sufficient height to allow use as a ski slope in winter. In eastern Ireland there are numerous small hills called *motes,* erected as fortifications by invading Normans in the Middle Ages. Similar artificial hills or mounds dot the delta plains on the approach to the ruins of Pella, the capital of the Macedonian Empire in northern Greece at the time of Alexander the Great (Figure 2.6). If people build, they also excavate, forming open-pit mines that scar the landscape in many regions.

Tunneling represents another device by which Europeans have modified terrain, in this case to reduce the barrier effect of mountain ridges. Norway has begun to impose an effective highway network upon the Kjölen Range in this way, and the Pyrenees have lost much of their barrier effect. Even the gentle Appennini are now pierced. Nowhere has tunneling been so frequently employed as in the western Alps because that range lies in the core of Europe, where the need for effective, rapid ground transportation is greatest. Italy is now linked to both France and Germany by tunneled routes.

Major Climate Types

Tucked safely north and west of the Eastern Hemisphere's great desert belt, Europe enjoys climates that are generally humid and exceptionally mild, considering the rather high latitudes involved. These temperate, moist conditions favored Europe and helped it become one of the major homelands of humanity.

We can recognize three major climate types (Figure 2.7). One of these is the **marine west coast,** bearing a name that describes both its location and predominant *air mass.* To simplify, we can say that an air mass is just that—a large mass of air relatively uniform in temperature and moisture content. Marine air masses, which in the case of Europe originate over the Atlantic Ocean, are moisture-laden, cool in summer, and mild in winter. Coming ashore from the west, since

FIGURE 2.6 A huge artificial mound at the ancient Danish capital of Jelling, on the Jylland Peninsula. Europe abounds in such anthropogeomorphic features, helping produce the image of a thoroughly humanized landscape of great antiquity. (Photo by the author, 1981.)

Europe lies in the wind belt of the *westerlies,* this marine air meets little topographic resistance due to the east-west alignment of most mountain ranges. As a result, it regularly penetrates fairly deeply into Europe, producing the marine west-coast climate zone. This includes the British Isles, northern Iberia, most of France, western Germany, the Low Country, and part of the fjord coast of Norway (Figure 2.7). Temperatures remain mild all year, with cool summers and relatively pleasant winters (Table 2.1). The coldest month averages above freezing and generally below 7°C (45°F). Temperatures do not differ greatly between winter and summer. Dublin, Ireland, averages only 10°C (18°F) warmer in July than in January, and the difference at Tórshavn in the Færoe Islands is only 7°C (13°F). The majority of January nights in London do not have frost. Even in the Shetland Islands, far to the north, snow is relatively rare, occurring only three days in the winter of 1991–92, and temperatures rarely fall below –10°C (+14°F).

Occasional bitter cold waves do occur in the marine west coast climate, but many winters pass without one. London has recorded –16°C (4°F), and in one severe cold spell in February 1929, the temperature remained constantly below

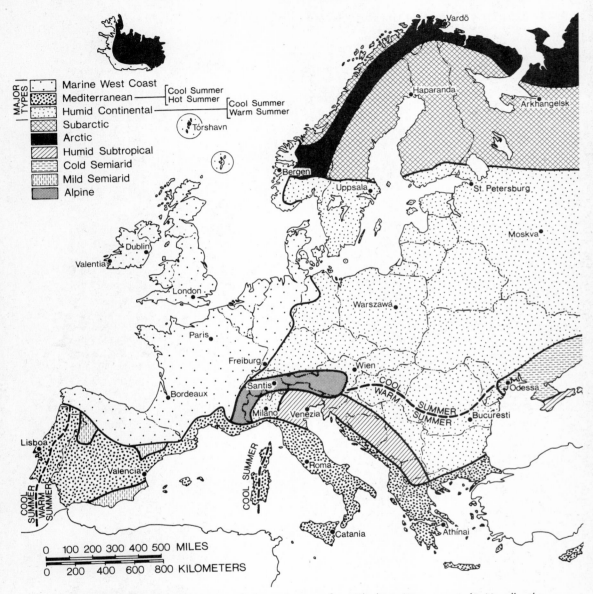

FIGURE 2.7 Climate types. (Source: In part after Wladimir Köppen, et al., *Handbuch der Klimatologie*, Berlin, D: Borntraeger, 3 vols., 1930–36, with substantial modifications.)

freezing for 226 hours in the British capital. The surprising appearance of a few palm trees at places on the southwest Irish coast, however, suggests the overall mildness of the winters. It was not always so. During the colder climatic phase known as the Little Ice Age, from about A.D. 1200 to 1800, the marine west coast winters were more severe. The canals of Holland often froze over, permitting the

TABLE 2.1 Climatic Data for Selected European Stations

	Station	July average temperature	January average temperature	Average annual precipitation
		Marine west coast		
	Valenta, IRL	15°C (59°F)	7°C (44°F)	142 cm (56 in.)
	Freiburg-im-Breisgau, D	19°C (66°F)	1°C (34°F)	86 cm (34 in.)
	Paris, F	19°C (66°F)	3°C (37°F)	58 cm (23 in.)
	Tórshavn, FR	11°C (51°F)	3°C (37°F)	145 cm (57 in.)
	Bergen, N	14°C (58°F)	1°C (34°F)	213 cm (84 in.)
	Bordeaux, F	20°C (68°F)	5°C (41°F)	84 cm (33 in.)
		Mediterranean		
warm summer subtype	Roma, I	24°C (76°F)	7°C (45°F)	84 cm (33 in.)
warm summer subtype	Athínai, GR	27°C (80°F)	9°C (48°F)	41 cm (16 in.)
cool summer subtype	Lisboa, P	21°C (70°F)	11°C (51°F)	74 cm (29 in.)
		Humid continental		
cool summer subtype	Moskva, SU	18°C (64°F)	−10°C (14°F)	53 cm (21 in.)
cool summer subtype	St. Petersburg, SU	17°C (63°F)	−8°C (18°F)	48 cm (19 in.)
cool summer subtype	Uppsala, S	17°C (63°F)	−4°C (24°F)	53 cm (21 in.)
cool summer subtype	Warszawa, PL	19°C (66°F)	−3°C (26°F)	56 cm (22 in.)
cool summer subtype	Wien, A	20°C (68°F)	−2°C (29°F)	64 cm (25 in.)
cool summer subtype	Milano, I	24°C (75°F)	−1°C (31°F)	102 cm (40 in.)
cool summer subtype	Bucureşti, RO	23°C (73°F)	−3°C (27°F)	58 cm (23 in.)
		Subarctic		
	Arkhangelsk, SU	15°C (59°F)	−13°C (8°F)	54 cm (21 in.)
	Haparanda, S	16°C (60°F)	−10°C (14°F)	53 cm (21 in.)
		Arctic		
	Vardö, N	9°C (48°F)	−6°C (22°F)	66 cm (26 in.)
		Humid subtropical		
	Venèzia, I	24°C (75°F)	3°C (37°F)	86 cm (34 in.)
		Cold semiarid		
	Odesa, UKR	22°C (72°F)	−4°C (25°F)	41 cm (16 in.)
		Alpine		
	Säntis, CH	5°C (41°F)	−9°C (16°F)	244 cm (96 in.)

ice skating shown in the paintings of some of the Dutch masters. Marine west coast summers are cool, with July averages generally below 21°C (70°F), and sweaters or coats feel comfortable on many days. Heat waves, with temperatures above 32°C (90°F), do occur rarely in parts of the marine west coast area. The record high temperature at Paris is 38°C (100°F).

Because the marine air masses contain great amounts of moisture, the west coast climate is quite humid, with adequate precipitation all year round. Normally between 50 and 100 cm (20 to 40 in.) fall each year, though some stations record more. In plains areas, the amounts are rather modest, as for example Paris, which receives only 58 cm (23 in.) annually, and London 62 cm (25 in.). However, the cool temperatures retard evaporation, as does prevalent cloudiness, and precipitation is adequate to produce humid conditions. Stations situated in or at the western edge of hills and mountains receive considerably more precipitation. Freiburg-im-Breisgau, western Germany, at the foot of the Schwarzwald (Black Forest), averages 86 cm (34 in.) annually, and the slopes above Bergen, Norway, on the west flank of the Kjölen Range, receive 213 cm (84 in.) in an average year. This increased amount is the product of the so-called *orographic* factor. Humid air masses moving from the west into Europe are forced to rise over hill and mountain barriers, which block the path. In the process of rising, the air mass cools, thereby lowering its ability to hold moisture in an evaporated state, and the excess is precipitated on west-facing slopes.

Very little precipitation typically falls on any given day in the marine west coast areas. Gentle showers or drizzles are the rule. Paris, for example, has its modest annual precipitation spread over 188 days, or about 0.30 cm (0.12 in.) per rainy day, involving over half of all days in the year. A pervasive wetness, then, results from persistent light rain and feeble evaporation, rather than from large amounts of rainfall. On one occasion London had 72 consecutive days in which precipitation fell. Clouds obscure the sun most of the time, and the marine west coast climate seems unpleasant to most people. Seventy percent or even more of the daylight hours each year are marred by cloudiness, and the British Isles average less than 1500 hours of sunshine annually, about 4 hours per day or less. Fog and mist also commonly occur, and one town in Denmark reports an average of 54 foggy days each year. This cheerless climate drives numerous inhabitants to seek vacations in the sunny southern part of Europe. Jean Rouaud summed it up nicely when he wrote that "in the lower Loire," in the west of France, "rain is a life companion."

The precipitation and cloudiness reach the marine west-coast climate region borne by an endless succession of *cyclonic storms*, centers of low pressure embedded in the wind belt of the westerlies. In most cases these storms are gentle, as the modest precipitation amounts suggest, but on occasion they reach violent proportions. For example, a cyclonic storm that struck England and northwestern France on October 15–16, 1987, the most severe recorded in 250 years, in many places produced sustained winds of 70 to 115 km per hour (45 to 70 mph.) and gusts of up to 175 km/hr. (110 mph.). Millions of trees were felled, 13 people died, and extensive property damage occurred.

Generally, storm-induced winds are gentler, and often they come so regularly and predictably as to have names. One of the best known is the *Föhn* of southern Germany, a warm, dry wind from the south that results when a cyclonic storm moves just north of the Alps. The low pressure serves to draw winds over the mountains from the Mediterranean lands, dropping orographic precipitation and growing cooler in ascent, and then descending into Germany, warming as they progress downslope. A föhn blowing in midwinter can produce a sudden false springtime, with fair skies and pleasant temperatures, a delightful though short-lived respite from the dreary, damp winter conditions.

Southern Europe, in particular the three southward-reaching peninsulas of Iberia, Italy, and Greece, is dominated by the **Mediterranean** type of climate. Also included are the various European islands of the Mediterranean, southern coastal France, and the Adriatic coast of Croatia (Figure 2.7). Certainly the most distinguishing trait of the Mediterranean climate is the concentration of precipitation in the winter season, with exceptionally dry summers. Generally, less than one-tenth of the annual precipitation falls in the quarter-year comprising the summer months of June, July, and August, and the month of July is almost totally rainless. Lisboa (Lisbon), Portugal, averages only 0.5 cm (0.2 in.) in July; Roma, Italy, but 1.8 cm (0.7 in.); and Athínai (Athens), Greece, only 0.8 cm (0.3 in.). This seasonality of precipitation reflects the transitional position of the Mediterranean basin between the humid marine west coast to the north and the parched Sahara in the south. In winter the Mediterranean lands lie in the belt of the westerlies and receive the impact of precipitation-producing marine air masses and migrating storm centers, while in summer the region comes more under the influence of a great subtropical high-pressure center, which causes fair weather in North Africa and the Mediterranean peninsulas alike. Winter precipitation usually occurs as rainfall in the small lowland plains, but snow is common in the numerous mountain ranges concentrated in the Mediterranean climate region. Accumulated snow in the highlands is of crucial importance to the farmers of the region because the meltwater runoff in spring and summer provides a source of irrigation water for the drought season.

Temperatures in the Mediterranean climate are warmer than those of the marine west coast area because of a more southerly location and a lower incidence of cloudiness. Summers are hot in the greater part of the Mediterranean climate zone, with July averages usually in the 24° to 28°C (75° to 82°F) range. The record high temperature at Athínai is 40.5°C (105°F), at Valencia in Spain 42.8°C (109°F), and at Catania in Sicilia 40°C (104°F), the highest ever recorded in Italy. However, the relative humidity in summer tends to be low, and fairly rapid nighttime cooling occurs. A cool-summer subtype of the Mediterranean climate also appears in places, confined to the Atlantic littoral of Portugal and certain other windward coastlines (Figure 2.7). Lisboa provides an example (Table 2.1). In the cool-summer subtype, warmest-month averages do not exceed 22°C (72°F). Throughout the Mediterranean climate area, except in the mountain ranges, winters remain mild and extended periods of frost are unknown. Groves of citrus fruit dot the lowlands of the Mediterranean, a good indicator of the absence of severe cold. The record low of –7°C (20°F) for Athínai is typical of the region. Cloudiness is at a minimum, particularly in the summer, a striking contrast to the marine west coast. Parts of Italy receive more than 2500 hours of sunshine per year, almost twice as much as the British Isles.

The local winds of the Mediterranean reflect its location between the marine west coast and the desert. Winter storm centers moving through the basin draw cold, damp winds down from the north, including the *mistral* and the *bora*. The mistral blows with some fury down the Rhône-Saône Corridor into the Mediterranean coastal fringe of France and on beyond to the islands of Corsica and Sardegna (Sardinia), while the bora strikes the eastern coast of Italy from across the Adriatic Sea. From the opposite direction, dry, hot *sirocco* winds are drawn up from the Saharan region by cyclonic storms to afflict southern Italy and Greece. A similar wind, the *leveche,* brings hot, dusty conditions on occasion into the south of France, while in Andalucía the same phenomenon is called the *solano.* All serve to introduce a parched, warm continental tropical air mass from the Sahara Desert to the south. In Italy, the sirocco blows from 30 to 50 times annually, lasting 80 to 120 days per year and occurring most often from March through May and again in November. The Saharan winds are least common in summer, but when they do happen in that season, the searingly hot effects are most unpleasant and potentially damaging to crops and orchards.

The third of the major climate types found in Europe, the **humid continental,** dominates the eastern part of the culture area, from southern Scandinavia to the eastern Balkans and deep into Russia (Figure 2.7). Here, as the climate's name implies, *continental* air masses, born over the vast Eurasian interior and frozen Arctic Ocean, prevail over those of marine origin. These air masses display a great annual range of temperature, becoming very cold in the winters and surprisingly warm in the summers, producing a climate given to seasonal extremes (Table 2.1). In particular, the winters are colder and become progressively more bitter toward the east. The disasters that befell the armies of Hitler and Napoleon in Russia were in no small part the work of numbing cold. January averages in the humid continental area range from about –12°C to 0°C (10°F up to freezing), and low readings below –18°C (0° F) are common. In the bitter winter of 1986–87, Moskva (Moscow) recorded –26°C (–32°F) and St. Petersburg –29°C (–34°F). The difference between January and July averages runs double or more the annual range of many marine west coast stations. Winter temperatures are low enough to cause a durable snow cover to develop, with usually at least one month in which the ground remains blanketed. In more eastern areas, the continuous snow cover can last for three or four months. Rivers, lakes, and shallow ocean inlets freeze over, including the Baltic Sea. Occasionally during winter in the East European Plain, the heart of the humid continental climate zone, cloudy and mild spells of weather occur. Russians, who prefer clear, cold conditions, contemptuously refer to these marine-influenced spells as "European" weather.

Summer temperatures are remarkably similar to those in the marine west coast area. The July average at Moskva, and Warszawá (Warsaw) is identical to that at Paris, and most stations fall in the 16°C to 21°C (60°F to 70°F) range for the warmest month average. Only in the southern extremity of the humid continental area, in the Balkans and in an outlier in the upper Po-Veneto Plain does a warm-summer subtype of the humid continental climate occur (Figure 2.7). Milano and Bucureşti (Bucharest) are representative. In this zone, July averages exceed 22°C (72°F), and some summer days are unpleasantly hot. Throughout the humid continental climate region, precipitation is adequate if not abundant at all seasons, owing in part to the low evaporation rate associated with cool and cold weather. Between 48 and 65 cm (19 to 26 in.) of precipitation can be expected each year at typical humid continental stations, only slightly less than is the rule in marine west coast areas.

Minor Climate Types

The greater part of Sweden and Finland lie in the zone of the **subarctic** climate, more severe than the humid continental (Figure 2.7). Only one to three months average over 10°C (50°F), and the proximity to the pole in a continental location means bitter, dark winters. Summers are very cool and short, and winter is clearly the dominant season (Table 2.1). In January, 1987, a temperature of –45°C (–53°F) was recorded at an arctic climate station in Norway's Kjölen Range. The precipitation total is modest and comes mainly as snow, but the resultant climate is humid, due to very low evaporation. Few Europeans choose to live in this cold zone, and most of those who do have come as a result of a severe shortage of good land, as in Finland, or to exploit the fisheries or mineral wealth such as northern Sweden's iron ore.

Still more severe is the **arctic** climate, a region largely devoid of trees (Figure 2.7). It lacks a summer altogether, and the warmest month averages below 10°C (50°F, Table 2.1). Surprisingly, the adjacent Barents Sea, part of the Arctic Ocean, does not freeze in winter, and the entire Norwegian coast and the Russian Arctic port of Murmansk remain open to shipping, thanks to the influence of the easternmost branch of a warm ocean current known as the North Atlantic Drift.

The Dinaric Range and coastal portion of the Po-Veneto Plain are characterized by the **humid subtropical** climate, similar to the Mediterranean area in temperature but lacking the pronounced summer drought. Here the summers are hot with high humidity, and the July visitor to Venèzia may well be reminded of New Orleans or Brisbane.

Nearly all of Europe receives adequate precipitation, even if it is seasonal as in the Mediterranean. The only exceptions are some peripheral semiarid regions, where moisture deficiency prevails because evaporation from the land exceeds available precipitation. In these places, the great desert belts of Africa and Eurasia gently touch Europe. Two minor types result: (1) the **cold semiarid** climate, typical of the lands north of the Black and Caspian seas that share the bitter continental winter, made all the more fierce here by the absence of trees to block the wind; and (2) the **mild semiarid** climate, sharing the temperatures of the Mediterranean winter but lacking its precipitation (Figure 2.7) (Table 2.1). The mild semiarid districts lie in Iberian *rainshadow* areas east of the Bética, Ibérica, and Cantabrica ranges, where the moisture-bearing westerlies are orographically drained of their moisture. Included are the Ebro Valley, the coastal huertas flanking the Bética Range, and the western reaches of the Meseta in Old Castilla.

The final type, the **Alpine** climate, occurs to some extent in all the mountain ranges of Europe, though shown in Figure 2.7 only in the Alps. The key causal factor is elevation above sea level. Mountain heights cause the climate to be colder, so that Säntis in Switzerland, for example, actually has an arcticlike climate, differing only in the enormous amount of orographic precipitation, a total of almost 250 cm annually (Table 2.1). The Alpine climate varies greatly from valley to valley and slope to slope, creating a pattern too chaotic to map on a small scale.

All of the minor climate types occur in peripheral parts of Europe and are, as a consequence, only marginally "European." Recognizing their alien character, relatively few Europeans choose to live in such regions. We can regard the marine west coast, Mediterranean, and humid continental climates as "core" European, while the minor types represent a transition toward non-European conditions.

Human Influence on Climate

Europeans, usually unintentionally, alter the climates of their culture area. This happens both on a local scale and much more broadly. They live preponderantly in cities, each of which, in some measure, suffers from air pollution and experiences temperature alteration. London's *anthropoclimate* has been studied for centuries, and we know a lot about the human-induced changes there. As early as 1661, John Evelyn wrote in reference to London that "the weary traveler, at many miles distance, sooner smells, than sees the city." When the coal smoke poured through a myriad of chimneys, "London resembles the face rather of Mount Etna, the Court of Vulcan, Stromboli, or the suburbs of hell than an assembly of rational creatures." In more recent times geographers came to speak of London's "heat island," a reference to the fact that temperatures are consistently higher over the built-up portion of the city than over the surrounding rural greenbelt (Figure 2.8). Minimum nighttime temperatures are at times 7°C (12°F) higher over the central portion of London than in the greenbelt, and daytime maxima are also higher. This results from the inability of heat radiation from surfaces to penetrate the pollution haze that hangs over the city; the retention of heat by paved streets and buildings; and the heat produced locally by fuel combustion in vehicles, factories, and homes. At times, isotherms, lines connecting points with the same temperature, take on the same shape as the London urban area. Human activity also influences rainfall and humidity characteristics of the London area. More thunderstorms occur over the city, more precipitation, and a distinctly higher absolute humidity than in adjacent rural areas. The cause apparently lies both in the greater amount of thermal convection resulting from more surface heating and in the superabundance of microscopic particulate matter associated with air pollution. Drops of condensation are built around such nuclei. A decrease in coal burning has lessened the degree of air pollution in London since about 1960, but one can still observe the pronounced effect of humans on the local climate.

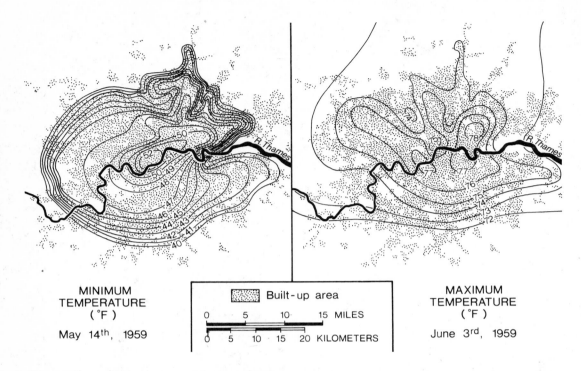

MINIMUM
TEMPERATURE
(°F)

May 14th, 1959

Built-up area

0   5   10·   15 MILES

0   5   10   15   20 KILOMETERS

MAXIMUM
TEMPERATURE
(°F)

June 3rd, 1959

Figure 2.8 Temperature modification in the greater London area. The presence of a large urban conglomeration stimulates daytime heating and retards night cooling. (Source: After T. J. Chandler, "The Changing Form of London's Heat Island," *Geography*, 46 (1961), 300, 303.)

This same effect can be detected in many other areas of Europe. In fact, every city has a heat island, and severe air pollution remains a problem in many countries.

The corridor of worst air pollution lies in the humid continental climate, along the southern margins of the North European Plain and in the Bohemian Basin, from eastern Germany and the Czech Republic into Poland. This corridor, not coincidentally, also appears as the worst concentration of *acid rain* (Figure 2. 9). Various chemicals released into the air as a consequence of burning fossil fuels are cleansed from the atmosphere by precipitation. The resultant rainfall has a much higher than normal acidity, diminishing soil fertility, poisoning fish, and damaging vegetation. Air pollution extends to the outermost peripheries of Europe, as in the far north, where the phenomenon called "Arctic haze" has recently appeared.

Also found on a wide scale and likely the result of human industrial activity is a pan-European warming of climate. In effect, the entire core of the culture

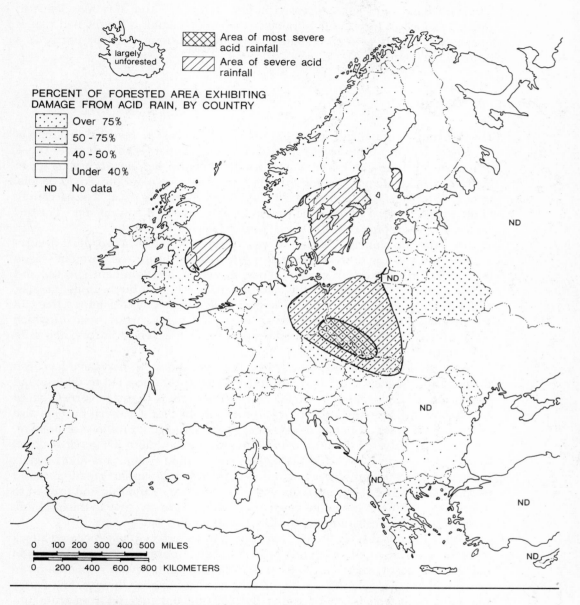

FIGURE 2.9 Acid rain problem. (Sources: *National Geographic Magazine,* June 1991, 45; *The Economist Atlas of the New Europe,* New York, USA: Henry Holt, 1992, 211.)

area seems to have become a heat island. Recent decades have been unusually warm, Atlantic cyclones have taken more northerly tracks, and sirocco-type winds off the Sahara have increased in both frequency and duration. Semiarid climate regions in Iberia and Ukraine perhaps now stand at heightened risk of *desertification,* or degeneration into fully arid conditions, perhaps partly as a result of the warming.

Vegetation Regions

The distribution of natural vegetation in Europe can best be revealed in a map of *biotic* (or *floristic*) *provinces* (Figure 2.10). To a considerable degree, these provinces coincide with the climate types discussed earlier, not surprising given the fact that climate has a major shaping influence upon plant life. So do people. In fact, Europeans have so massively altered the vegetative cover that we cannot know precisely what these biotic provinces were like in a natural state. For this reason, biogeographers often speak of *potential* vegetation.

The **Atlantic** biotic province was once largely covered by a broadleaf decidu- ous forest, consisting of trees which drop their leaves during the dormant season in winter. *Oaks*, including various types, served as the dominant species, and other common trees included the ash, linden, beech, and birch. Elms, maples, willows, and hornbeams were also well represented among the canopy trees. In the vegetative understory grew yews, hollys, and hazel shrubs, beneath which lay a groundcover of ivy, heather, anemone, ferns, bracken, primrose, and wild strawberry.

No fully intact Atlantic biotic system survives today, so pervasive has been the human influence. Clearing the forest for agricultural use led to widespread destruction of the deciduous broadleaf forest, a process begun in earnest about A.D. 500 by the Germanic peoples invading from the east. Charcoal burners also exacted a toll on the Atlantic woodlands, as in the Belgian province of Brabant, where in the place of the once great Forest of Carbonnière (charcoal makers) today stretches an unwooded plain. This devastation by farmers and burners continued unabated into the 1300s, when pestilence and warfare greatly reduced the population. The Hundred Years' War between France and England proved so destructive of human life in the Basin of Aquitaine as to give rise to the local folk saying that "the forests returned to France with the English."

Following this respite, the Atlantic forests were subjected to a renewed attack by ax wielders. Population decline proved to be temporary, and a final phase in the clearing occurred in the 1500s and 1600s. To the renewed demands of an expanding farm population were added the needs of English, French, and Dutch shipbuilders, as well as other artisans. By 1550 England suffered from acute tim- ber shortages, and France reached the same predicament a century later. Both came to rely on their American colonies to supply much-needed lumber. Considerable forests remained in Ireland during the late 1500s, for contemporary documents mention the difficulty of conducting military campaigns against Irish rebels in their woodland refuges. It seems likely that the English felled many Irish woods for military reasons, to destroy these refuges. Profit-hungry land-

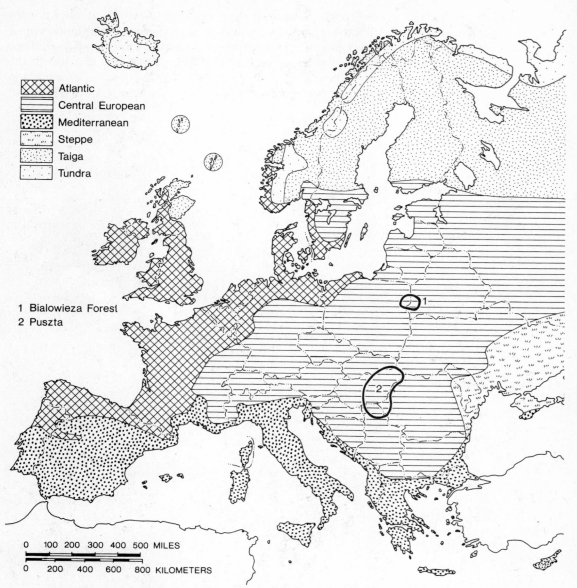

Atlantic
Central European
Mediterranean
Steppe
Taiga
Tundra

1 Bialowieza Forest
2 Puszta

| 0 | 100 | 200 | 300 | 400 | 500 | MILES |

| 0 | 200 | 400 | 600 | 800 | KILOMETERS |

FIGURE 2.10 Biotic provinces. (Sources: Jalas and Suominen; Polunin and Walters.)

lords completed the process of deforestation in Ireland in the 1600s, selling the timber abroad. By the year 1700, woodlands had vanished from the Irish scene, and oak virtually disappeared from the pollen record after that time. In England, similarly deforested, the word *wold* (as in Cotswold), which originally meant "forest," came to mean instead "an upland area of open country."

So catastrophic was the assault on the woodland that in several countries lying within the Atlantic biotic province, less than 10 percent of the land bears a forest cover today, and much of this meager woodland results from twentieth-century *afforestation*, the replanting of forests (Figure 2.11). Hill districts of the British Isles have been the scene of some of the most impressive afforestation projects, especially the Scottish Highlands and islands. However, trees planted in

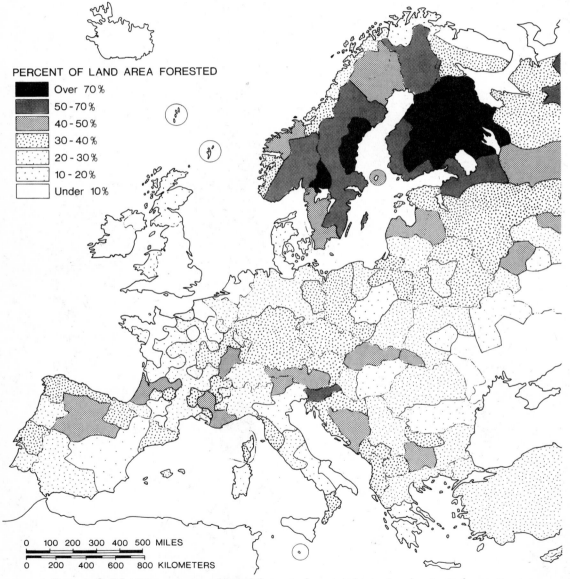

PERCENT OF LAND AREA FORESTED

- Over 70 %
- 50 - 70 %
- 40 - 50 %
- 30 - 40 %
- 20 - 30 %
- 10 - 20 %
- Under 10 %

0   100 200 300 400 500 MILES

0   200   400   600   800 KILOMETERS

FIGURE 2.11 Percentage of land forested, mainly by national units. Deforestation is greatest in the west and south.

these projects tend to be commercially valuable exotics such as Douglas fir and Sitka spruce. The soil must be regularly limed, often by helicopter drop, to counteract natural acidity so that the desired exotic trees will survive.

Only scattered patches of forest containing native Atlantic trees remain. Some owe their existence to royal protection, as for example England's Sherwood Forest. In places, rough terrain, unattractive to farmers, sheltered a remnant of woods (Figure 2.12). The tiny vestiges of Atlantic woodland are today carefully tended, with heavy penalties for unauthorized cutting. Often these tidy groves resemble parks more than natural woodlands, particularly to the American eye. Western Europeans value remnant forests as recreational areas and have laid out a splendid network of hiking trails, and it is rare to find a forest area that is not open to the public.

Representative of the destruction of the Atlantic forests of Europe are wide expanses of treeless *moor* and *heath*, especially in the British Isles and Denmark. As a general rule, "heath" is the term used for hilly areas or undulating plains, while "moor" describes level surfaces. Both are covered with a variety of low

Figure 2.12 "The forest's in trouble on Wenlock Edge," according to an old English saying. Reference is to a ridge in the Scarplands of western England near the border of Wales. Only the steep slopes of Wenlock Edge, unattractive to farmers, retain a forest cover. In contrast, the fertile vales below were stripped of trees and are well cultivated. The remnant forests resemble dark caps on the steep leading edges of a succession of great earthen "waves." (Copyright Aerofilms Limited, London.)

shrubs, including heather, juniper, and gorse (reedlike, with abundant yellow flowers). Peat bogs abound. Experts now believe that nearly all such areas are human induced, except in small exposed heights and coastal locations. Fire, used to create pastureland, was apparently the most important device employed to establish these open landscapes.

Ironically, these heaths and moors are themselves now under human attack and rapidly declining in area. Afforestation projects are partly responsible, and one can still see the rock fences that once enclosed Scottish sheep pastures zigzagging through new forests of spruce and fir. In other cases, especially in Denmark, heath has been converted to agricultural use, especially improved pastures for dairy cattle (Figure 2.13). In other words, people first removed the forests in ancient times to produce rough pasture of heath, and then much later they destroyed the heath to obtain a better grassland. Clearly, the concept of *natural* vegetation is largely alien to Europe.

The **Central European** biotic province lies east of the Atlantic woodlands, covering the core of the culture area. Here the *beech* dominates the natural climax forest, with many oak, larch, and hornbeam. Unlike the Atlantic forest, the Central European province has abundant coniferous needleleaf evergreen trees such as fir, spruce, and the Scottish pine, especially in hilly, mountainous, and sandy regions. The understories are similar to those in the Atlantic forest, and orchids and sedges also abound.

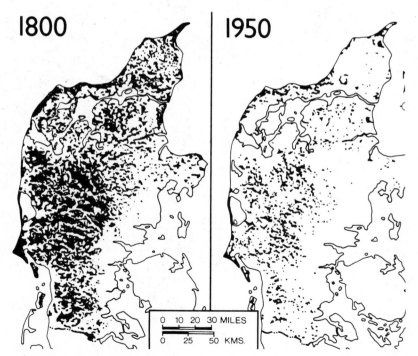

FIGURE 2.13 Reduction of heath in the Jylland Peninsula of Denmark, 1800–1950. The land was reclaimed for agricultural use. (Source: After Thorpe, 88.)

While less catastrophically influenced by human activity, the mixed decidu-ous/coniferous forest of Central Europe has also been greatly altered. As in areas farther west, Germanic farmers engaged in a great era of forest clearance during the Middle Ages to create new farming colonies (Figure 2.14). Often, evidence of the initial clearing survives in the present-day village and town names. In Germany, the common suffixes *-rod, -rot, -reuth,* and the like, as in Wernigerode, Heiligenroth, and Bayreuth, are all related to the modern German verb *roden,* which means "to root out," or "to clear." The German suffix or prefix *brand* and the like, exemplified by Branderoda and Oberbränd, indicate that the original clearing was accomplished by burning, for it derives from a Germanic root word meaning "fire."

Germanic forest removal typically began with small, roughly round clear-ings. As population grew, the settlers worked communally to push the perimeter of farmland outward at the expense of the forest, until finally the clearings of adjacent villages joined, sometimes leaving small isolated groves of trees at points farthest from the settlements (Figure 2.15). Less-common and confined mainly to valleys in the hill lands of central and eastern Germany, a second linear pattern of clearing began with a long, narrow cut along the valley to serve as a road. The colonists each received a ribbon-shaped farm stretching in a narrow strip back away from the road. Each colonist family cleared their own property. In the absence of communalism, the more ambitious settlers rapidly cleared the forest toward the hinter portions of their land, while their neighbors lagged behind, producing an uneven linear swath of farmland advancing from the val-ley toward the adjacent ridgecrest.

From the Germans, extensive clearance of the Central European forests spread east to the Slavs, who had already made modest inroads before A.D. 500. Slavic forest removal is indicated by place names containing the word elements *kop, lazy,* and *paseky,* all of which specifically indicate "clearing."

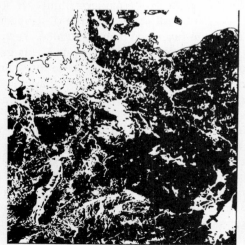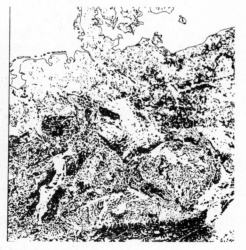

FIGURE 2.14 The retreat of woodland in central Europe, A.D. 900–1900. (Source: After Otto Schlüter, as reproduced in Darby, "Clearing of Woodland," 1956.)

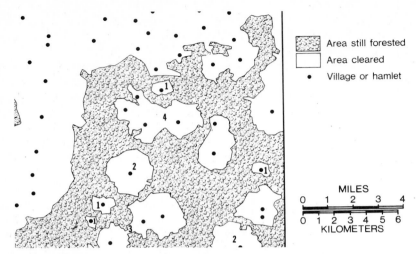

FIGURE 2.15 Stages of forest clearance in the southeastern outskirts of München, Germany. The map reveals typical Germanic clearance at almost every stage, curiously preserved to the modern day. The smaller clearings (#1) are suggestive of the early stage, while those marked #2, almost perfectly circular, reflect a somewhat later stage. Symbol #3 indicates the earliest phase of coalescence of adjacent clearings, while #4 illustrates more mature coalescence. To the north and west, more complete clearing occurred. (Source: After Jean Brunhes.)

A conservation movement arose in time to rescue substantial wooded areas in the Central European biotic province. As in the west, the nobility, anxious to preserve recreational hunting grounds, took the lead. An example, rare because it stands in the middle of a great city, is Berlin's *Tiergarten,* literally "animal garden," long the royal hunting preserve of the Hohenzollern family. It survived until the winter of 1945–46, when desperate inhabitants of the destroyed capital cut the trees for firewood. The Tiergarten has since been replanted. Terrain also protected some of the forest, for woodland cover on steep slopes was generally spared by the farmers. So close became the identification between forest and hilly or mountainous areas in Germany that the word *Wald,* "forest," appears as the name for areas of rough terrain, as in Schwarzwald (Black Forest) or Thüringerwald (Thuringian Forest).

The most impressive remnant of the Central European woodland is the Bialowieza Forest on the eastern margin of the North European Plain, straddling the border between Poland and Belarus (Figure 2.10). It encompasses some 127,000 ha (313,000 acres), and about 4 percent is preserved as a national park in Poland. Earlier, it enjoyed royal protection. The Bialowieza Forest houses at least 4000 plant species, including immense specimens of hornbeam, spruce, and oak. Here, and only here, one can glimpse the great forest of the European heartland in its very nearly pristine condition, but access is strictly regulated.

No native open grasslands existed within the original Central European woodland, and the prairies of the central Hungarian Basin, called the *Puszta* or *Alföld* (Figure 2.10), are apparently human induced, maintained by fire and grazing. A fair amount of woodland survives in the Puszta, causing it to be described as a "wooded steppe." Traditionally, the Hungarians raised large herds of open-range cattle here.

To the south, generally corresponding to the climate region of the same name, we find the **Mediterranean** biotic province. The natural vegetation consisted of relatively open forests of broadleaf evergreen live oaks and olives, as well as Aleppo and stone pines, chestnuts, myrtles, walnuts, cypresses, and, in the mountains, fir trees. The dominant tree was the holm oak. Beneath and between the trees grew an evergreen shrub layer of juniper, honeysuckle, heather, and spiny broom. The groundcover included various grasses, especially esparto, as well as spurge and spleenwort.

This vegetative cover must withstand the pronounced summer drought of the Mediterranean region. Most trees and shrubs exhibit *sclerophyllous* features—an exceptional development of protective external tissue, as in the thickening of leaves and bark, in order to retard evaporation. This is well illustrated by the thick, deeply fissured bark of the cork oak and the stiff, leathery leaf of the olive. Also, leaves are small, and the upper side is shiny, further retarding evaporation.

The destruction of the Mediterranean evergreen forest has been virtually complete. Alteration began in prehistoric times, and the initial effect was probably to produce a parkland in which live oaks were scattered in a grassland. Stretches of this sort of vegetation can still be seen in Extremadura, on the Meseta of southwestern Spain. In most cases, though, a far more complete alteration was achieved.

The process was well under way by Homer's time, some 3000 years ago. He wrote of ongoing forest removal, both accidental and purposeful. In the rainless summers, "fierce fire rages through the glens on some parched mountainside, and the deep forest burns. The wind driving it whirls the flames in every direction." Shipbuilding also took a heavy toll, including the "thousand" ships launched for the sake of fair Helen of Troy. Homer, in describing the incredible carnage on the battlefield in front of Troy, compared the deaths of warriors to the felling of trees, and a soldier speared in the throat "fell as an oak, or a poplar, or tall pine tree which craftsmen have felled in the hills with freshly whetted axes to be a ship's timber," while another warrior, speared just below the ear, "fell as an ash, on the crest of a distant hill, which is smitten by the bronze axe and falls to the ground." Timber also provided charcoal for smelting, particularly after the use of iron replaced bronze. The construction of buildings, including temples and palaces, demanded still more lumber, until finally a shortage of wood forced acceptance of stone as the primary Mediterranean building material. Considerable damage had already occurred by the 400s B.C., prompting Plato to compare deforested, eroded Attiki (Attica) to "the skeleton of a sick man, all the fat and soft earth have been wasted away, leaving only the bare framework of the land" (Figure 2.16).

People, then, using both fire and ax, assaulted the Mediterranean woodlands in preclassical times and continued the destruction for many centuries. Unfortunately, the forest proved unable to reestablish itself after having been cleared. Removal of trees tended to be permanent for two major reasons. First, most of the Mediterranean open forest occupied steep slopes, for mountainous

FIGURE 2.16 Deforested, rocky landscape on the Aegean island of Patmos.
Thousands of years of grazing, accidental fires, and the need for lumber have left this
Greek hillside denuded of forest, with much exposed rock. Tall stone fences have been built
to separate adjacent herds of goats and sheep. Most of the Greek islands were once much
more forested than they are today. (Photo by the author, 1971.)

terrain dominates Southern Europe. When the trees were removed from the
slopes, the soil soon washed away with the winter rains, stripping the mountains
to bare rocky skeletons unfit for reforestation. The second retarding factor in
woodland regeneration was the lowly goat, a domestic animal of great importance to most Mediterranean rural people. The goat, quite at home in the rugged
terrain, devours the tender young shoots of trees newly broken through the soil.
This single animal contributes greatly to the permanence of deforestation in
many Mediterranean lands. Still, much timber survived in the classical period, as
is indicated by the writings of numerous scholars of the time. Destruction continued in postclassical times. Venetian and Genovese merchant fleets and
Byzantine, Spanish, and Portuguese imperial navies made the same demands on
the forests as had their Greek and Roman predecessors. The craftsmen of Firenze
(Florence), Toledo, and Byzantium (modern Istanbul) needed charcoal as had
their classical forerunners, and the ever-present herdsmen and farmers continued to regard the woodland as an enemy to be conquered.

Expanses of bare rock devoid of vegetation today represent the most extreme
result of human activity in the Mediterranean (Figure 2.17). More common, however, are regions covered with thickets of evergreen shrub growth a meter (3 ft.)
or more in height, known in French as *maquis,* in Italian as *macchia* or *maki,* and in

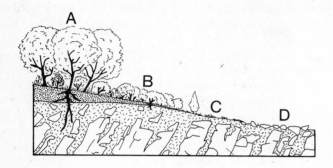

A   LIVE OAK FOREST: rendzina soil over terra rosa

B   LIVE OAK GARRIGUE: some rendzina soil left

C   TURF: terra rosa only

D   LITTLE VEGETATION LEFT: nearly all soil gone

FIGURE 2.17 Diagram of Mediterranean floral and edaphic destruction. The alterations involve forest removal and subsequent erosion and overgrazing. Large areas of southern Europe have been degraded in this way. (Source: After C. Delano Smith, *Western Mediterranean Europe,* London, GB: Academic Press, 1979, 283; and J. Braun-Blanquet, "La forêt d'yeuse Languedocienne," *Mémoires de la Société des Sciences Naturelles de Nîmes,* 5 (1936).)

Spanish as *matorral*. Such thickets served as hiding places by the French underground in World War II, with the result that the resistance movement became known as the Maquis. Areas of *garrigue* vegetation, a thin cover of scattered dwarf evergreen scrub less than a meter high and rooted in very shallow soil or in fissures in bare rock, also abound. In either case, *maquis* or *garrigue*, people produced a badly damaged environment of little further use. Some limited afforestation has been accomplished in the Mediterranean biotic province in recent times, often with exotics such as eucalypts, now widespread in Portugal. Most of the region, however, remains deforested.

The **steppe** biotic province, dominated by tallgrass prairies, lies in far southeastern Europe, in Ukraine and parts of Russia. It represents an extension of the expansive grasslands that dominate the heart of Asia, reaching to Mongolia and beyond. As such, the steppes appear alien to the European eye and are, at best, only peripherally a part of Europe. Pointed like an extended finger toward Europe, this *steppe corridor* served repeatedly as a natural route of invasion by mounted Asiatic nomad-warriors, who found the treeless country well suited to their mode of warfare and the abundant grasses excellent for their flocks and herds. For a thousand years and more, wave after wave of Asian intruders passed this way—Hun, Bulgar, Magyar, Avar, Tartar. Most remained to become more or less Europeanized, and some pressed on into the heart of Europe, where, with few exceptions, they failed militarily. The great prairie that led the Asian nomadic tribes into Europe has largely vanished. The steppe proved too fertile to escape the plow, and today domesticated grasses, mainly wheat, grow in place of the natural grassland.

The **taiga** biotic province, sometimes called *boreal*, is also peripheral to Europe. These are the great coniferous evergreen forests of the north, and they, too, represent a projection westward from an Asian core. Dominant species include the Norway spruce and Scottish pine. The downy birch, a broadleaf deciduous tree, also abounds, as does the gray alder. In poorly drained places, abundant due to the heavy hand of glaciation, peat bogs and mires support a growth of mosses, grasses, and shrubs, while some hilly areas have heaths. Europeans have also found the taiga province inhospitable. It remains thinly populated and a refuge for non–Indo-European Finnic peoples. Most of the land retains a forest cover, as in Finland, 76 percent wooded (Figure 2.11). The taiga represents the last substantial forest in Europe and is the focus of a large lumbering and paper-pulp industry (Figure 2.18). As a result, most of the taiga is no longer a natural forest but instead is planted and regularly harvested. Nor does this represent a new industry. For centuries the northern lands have supplied lumber for the European core countries, and the coat-of-arms of Taivalkoski County in Finland's Kainuu region shows forest trees and a two-man saw.

The final biotic province, the **tundra**, occurs north of the tree line along the Arctic coast of Scandinavia and Russia, on the island of Iceland, in the higher ele-

FIGURE 2.18 Logs floating to Joensuu, Finland, in the taiga region of the Fenno-Scandian shield. The great needleleaf evergreen forests of the European north provide the basis for a large-scale wood-processing industry, dealing in lumber and pulp. Such activity is evident in this view. (Source: Photo by author, 1985.)

vations of the Kjölen Range (where it bears the name *fjell*), and above the limit of forest growth in certain mountain ranges such as the Alps. Tundra vegetation consists largely of lichens, mosses, sedges, rushes, dwarf beech and birch, stunted or creeping evergreen shrublets, and some grasses. Rarely do these plants exceed 30 cm (1 ft.) in height, though in the transition zone between the tundra and taiga, scrub birch forests grow somewhat taller. The brief Arctic summer brings an outburst of flowery plants of unique coloring and beauty. *Permafrost,* or permanently frozen subsoil, occurs in many places, causing waterlogging of the upper layers and a variety of surface soil hummocks. As a result, walking across the tundra in summer can be very difficult. Few Europeans live here, leaving it as a refuge for the Sami (Lapps) and other Finnic minorities. The tundra, too, serves more to bound Europe than as a part of it.

Forest Death

Of crucial significance to the fate of the remnant woodlands of Europe, whether Atlantic, Central European, Mediterranean, or taiga, is the recently detected phenomenon of *Waldsterben,* or "forest death." About 1975 forestry experts began to notice tree damage, especially in needle-leaf species. Then, as if some critical threshold had been crossed, the percentage of trees exhibiting damage increased very rapidly. In western Germany, only 8 percent of the forest showed visible damage in 1982, in the form of leaf or needle loss or discoloration. A year later the proportion had increased dramatically to 34 percent, and by 1984 to 50 percent. Switzerland's forest damage rose from 17 percent in 1984 to 40 percent by 1988. In the Czech Republic, well over two-thirds of the woodland exhibited damage by 1988, and forest death was widespread in the hill lands along the border with eastern Germany. The Schwarzwald (Black Forest) of southwestern Germany became another center of the phenomenon. Even peripheral lands such as Greece, Norway, the Kola Peninsula of Russia, and Estonia had damage in over half of their forests by the late 1980s, and annual reports by the European Union reveal that in the 1990s "there is an overall tendency toward a worsening of the forest condition in Europe." Every fifth tree throughout Europe showed damage by 1991.

We must conclude that the remaining forests of Europe are in danger of dying. The culprit, almost certainly, is acid rain (Figure 2.9), produced by burning fossil fuels. Unless drastic corrective action is taken, byproducts of the industrial age will complete the deforestation of Europe begun millennia ago by axwielding agriculturists.

Soil Regions

Climate, vegetation, and parent materials combine to yield a variety of soil types in Europe, varying greatly in texture, depth, and fertility. Eleven types appear on the accompanying map (Figure 2.19). Of these, the most widespread are the

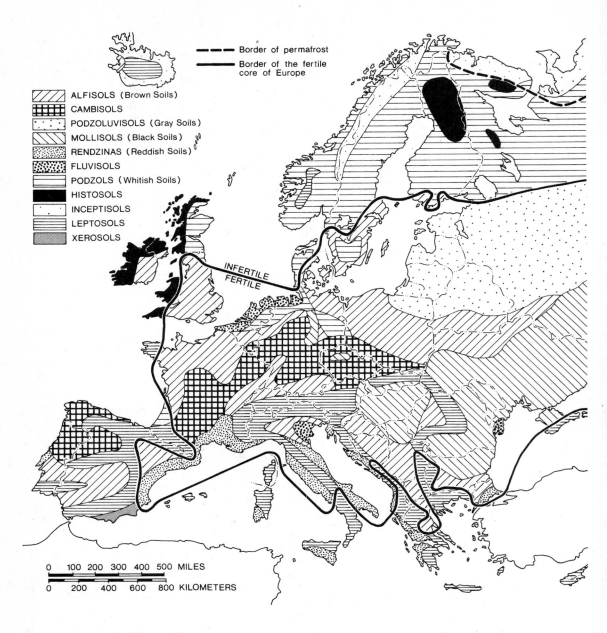

FIGURE 2.19 Soil Regions. This classification, better called a scientific grouping, draws upon both the American and European classification systems. Soils vary in an incredibly complex pattern, and any attempt to map large areas, such as Europe, necessarily requires an excessive amount of generalization. You should be aware that far greater complexity exists than is depicted here. (Sources: F.A.O. UNESCO, *Soil Map of the World,* Vol. 5 (Europe), Paris, F: United Nations, 1981; F.A.O. UNESCO, *Soil Map of the World: Revised Legend,* Roma, I: United Nations, 1988.)

alfisols, found particularly on the Great European Plain. They generally exhibit a brown or gray-brown surface color with a loamy texture, possess good fertility for farming, and overlay thick clay accumulations. Sufficiently attractive to motivate the difficult work of forest removal, the alfisols still today support a large farm population. Surprisingly little erosion has occurred, due to the gentleness of rainfall, the level terrain, and conservational farming methods. **Cambisols**, especially common in the hilly lands of Central Europe, are lighter in color, thin, often stony, deficient in humus, and only moderately productive agriculturally. The **mollisols**, by contrast, are dark, rich in humus, extremely fertile, and derived from a parent material of thick loess deposits. Included are *chernozems*, the famous "black earths" of the Ukrainian and Russian steppes. The dark color of mollisols comes from the humus created by decaying prairie grasses. Some mollisols have a chestnut color. Wheat, in particular, thrives on the mollisols and has always been the major bread grain in those regions. **Rendzinas**, represented in Europe by the *terra rossa*, or "red earth" soils found in some Mediterranean lands, derive from limestone parent material and are usually fertile, but most are thin, lacking distinct *horizons* (or layers) and occurring as a mantle over bedrock. Of all the soil types in Europe, the rendzinas have suffered the greatest abuse by humans (Figure 2.17). In Spain, about half of the agricultural area in many provinces is seriously or severely eroded, prompting land abandonment in a few cases. Some orchards, vineyards, and fields there lost a meter (3 ft.) of soil, causing irrigation reservoirs to silt up and streams to clog. Terra rossa, in fact, is actually a subsoil from which the upper horizons have been eroded. **Fluvisols**, most evident in delta areas, dominate the Low Country and a few other small regions. Deposited by rivers, this alluvium has undergone little alteration and is very fertile. Countless small pockets of fluvisols dot the Mediterranean area, including the previously mentioned *huertas* of Iberia.

Podsols occur mainly in northern Europe, with notable outliers in the North European Plain and Scottish Highlands. Their name means "white earth" or "ash-colored soil." They are humus deficient, due to *leaching*, the downward movement of plant nutrients to lower soil layers beyond the reach of crop roots. Podsols are highly acidic and sterile. Before they can yield satisfactory harvests, the farmer must add lime to counteract the acidity and compost to correct the lack of humus. In fact, most podsol areas do not support crop agriculture and remain largely covered by coniferous forests. In the North European Plain, podsols are most closely associated with sandy outwash plains and terminal moraines, while in the north they correspond to the taiga belt. **Podzoluvisols** appear in a broad belt across the East European Plain, mainly in Russia, and derive from glacial deposits. They possess greater natural fertility than podsols, with less profound acidity and leaching, and a gray color often results. Clays dominate the horizon just below the topsoil. We might best regard podzoluvisols as a transitional type between podsols and alfisols. They support a crop-based agriculture but require fertilization.

Some soil types occur in such small, scattered patches as to be invisible on a map such as Figure 2.19. Yet some of these are important locally. An example, the **andosols**—dark, extremely fertile soils derived from volcanic ash—attract dense populations to the environs of volcanoes in Italy and Greece.

At the opposite extreme in terms of fertility, the sterile **inceptisols** occur in the Arctic north, where cold temperatures retard both chemical weathering of bedrock and biological decay of the plant life, the two main processes by which soils are created. Highly acidic bogs occur widely, particularly in permafrost areas, and agriculture is absent. Similar to the inceptisols but not quite so sterile are the **histosols** of highland areas in the British Isles and also parts of northern Scandinavia. While rich in organic matter, the histosols suffer from moisture saturation and acidity, often forming peat bogs. **Leptosols**, meaning "thin soils," are typical of most mountain belts. Some scholars refer to these instead as *lithosols*, or "rocky soils." Because of the steep slopes, erosion has been profound, especially in Southern Europe. Little crop farming occurs in leptosol regions. **Xerosols**, found in the semiarid rainshadow districts of Iberia, are humus deficient, light colored, and often plagued by salinity.

Agriculturists have greatly modified nearly all of these soil types, creating in the process **anthrosols**, or human-induced soils. The topsoil is often artificial, produced by composting. Celtic farmers on the coasts of Scotland and Ireland formerly overcame the problems associated with histosols and expanses of bare rock by creating soil from composted seaweed. Deep plowing sometimes mixes soil horizons, and irrigation can cause sediments to build.

To generalize concerning Europe's soil geography, we can identify a core/periphery pattern (Figure 2.19). The fertile core, dominated by alfisols, mollisols, podzoluvisols, and cambisols, is surrounded by an infertile periphery of podsols, histosols, inceptisols, and leptosols.

Hydrogeography

The waters of Europe, including flanking seas, connecting straits, rivers, and marshes, intertwine intimately with human occupation. Europe's highly indented coastline causes most parts of the culture area to be no more than 650 km (400 mi.) from the sea. Only eight sizable independent countries in Europe lack a coastline, as contrasted to 29 major states that enjoy access to the sea. Winter ice troubles only the Baltic and White seas.

These *flanking seas*, named on the accompanying map (Figure 2.20), are in turn linked by numerous strategic **straits**, facilitating a movement of people and goods around the perimeter of Europe. Control over the connecting straits has long been the goal of many competing European powers, and many of these waterways have often been militarily contested. The *Bosporos* and the *Dardanelles*, two narrows that join the Black and Aegean seas, have alternately been controlled by the seagoing Greeks, most notably in the period of the Byzantine Empire, and by the land-based Turks. The Russians, who attach great importance to these straits, also once sought to exert influence there, though Turkey presently rules the area. Similarly, Arabs and Spaniards contested *Gibraltar* before it fell to the British, who hold it as a vestige of a sea-based empire. Wider, but still of great strategic importance, the so-called "waist" of the Mediterranean divides the sea into two halves. Control of the axis from Sicilia to Tunisia, spanning the waist

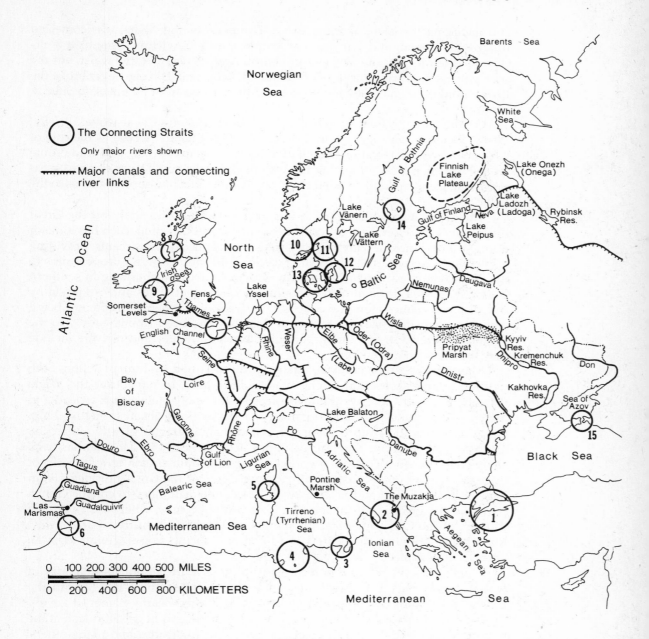

FIGURE 2.20 Hydrogeographic features. Europe is characterized by a highly indented coastline of surrounding seas and connecting straits. Key to connecting straits: **1** = Bosporos-Dardanelles, **2** = Otranto, **3** = Messina, **4** = "waist" of the Mediterranean, **5** = Bonifacio, **6** = Gibraltar, **7** = Dover, **8** = North Channel, **9** = Saint George's Channel, **10** = Skagerrak, **11** = Kattegat, **12** = Øresund, **13** = the Belts, **14** = Åland, **15** = Kerch.

and including the islands of Pantelleria, Lampedusa, and Malta, was contested first by the Roman and Carthaginian empires, and the victors assembled a circum-Mediterranean state of great durability. Arabs later ruled the waist, but the Axis powers in World War II, who controlled Sicilia and Tunisia, never broke the British hold on Malta, allowing west-east Allied access from Gibraltar to Suez to continue.

On the Atlantic front of Europe, the most crucial strait is at Dover. Briefly, this white-cliffed passage and the adjacent English Channel served as the core of a Norman French state, but ultimately it became a natural moat and trade route for the British. Instead of joining the mainland and Britain, Dover came to separate them. Denmark and Sweden have long commanded the several entries to the Baltic Sea.

The great, navigable **rivers** of Europe lie disproportionately on the Great European Plain. Flowing in a southeast-to-northwest direction, each has a major port city at its juncture with the sea. Canals interconnect these streams, providing a splendid waterway system. Most of eastern and southeastern Europe drains to the Black Sea, in particular through the great Danube, which, rising in southern Germany, passes through or borders nine independent states and is known by five different names along its course. The rivers of southern Europe, not being navigable, generally lack port cities at their mouth. Iberia drains largely to the Atlantic in the west, and the important European Mediterranean rivers include only the Ebro, Rhône, and Po.

Many European rivers have been greatly modified by human action, both deliberate and accidental. Some seas and streams, in particular the Wisla (Vistula) River, are severely polluted—laced with heavy metals such as lead and mercury, coal-mine salts, and organic carcinogens (look ahead to Figure 11.5). Others, such as the Dnipro River, have had their character greatly altered by reservoir construction. The Drin, a minor river of northern Albania, has been completely transformed from a gorge-cutting mountain stream to a stairstep of three lakes, now open to boat traffic. Many rivers of the Great European Plain have been *channelized* and *canalized* with locks and small dams to enhance transport, and the great rapids at the Iron Gate of the Danube, where the river cuts through at the Carpathian-Stara Planina juncture, have been dynamited away. River banks are often manicured and lined with facing stones, giving them an artificial appearance.

Marshes were once common in many parts of Europe, but the majority of wetlands have been drained and converted to agriculture. The *Fens* in the English Scarplands disappeared in this way, as did the nearby Somerset Levels, the Pontine Marshes near Rome, much of Las Marismas, a huge salt marsh at the mouth of the Guadalquivir in Spain, the Muzakja in Albania, and many others. Some marshes were, instead, created by human action, as in the Val di Chiana in Toscana (Tuscany), Italy. There, Etruscan forest removal in ancient times began siltation, which in time clogged the valley's drainage system, forming a large malarial marsh and allowing the Tevere (Tiber) River eventually to capture the area from the Arno. Later, farmers drained the Val di Chiana marshes and made them productive. The greatest surviving European wetland, the Pripyat (Pripet) Marsh, lies along the border of Belarus and Ukraine.

Dutch Coastline Alteration

The coastlines of Europe have also been altered by human action. Nowhere is this change more evident than in the Low Country. The Dutch live on the wrong end of a huge geomorphological seesaw. Their deltaic homeland in the Low Country is gradually sinking, at the rate of about 20 cm (8 in.) per century, coincident with an increase in elevation along the Swedish shore of the Baltic Sea. Since the end of the period of Pleistocene glaciation about 10,000 years before the Christian Era, the coastal fringe of the Netherlands has sunk some 20 m (65 ft.). Silt brought in and deposited by the Rhine, Maas, and Schelde rivers has partially offset the sinking of the land, but without active human efforts, the coastline would have drastically deteriorated.

Before the encroachment by the sea began, the ancient Dutch coast was apparently quite straight and paralleled by a protective wall of sand dunes. The only breaks in the dunes occurred where the many distributaries of the Rhine, Maas, and Schelde cut through to reach the North Sea. As thousands of years passed and the level of some lands on the inland side of the dunes fell below sea level, parts of the Low Country flooded. Driven by storms, the North Sea broke through the sand-dune barrier in the northern and southwestern Netherlands and permanently inundated large areas. This damage can still be seen today, especially in the north. The Friesche (Frisian) Islands, which lie in an east-west string along the northern coast, represent all that remains of the sand-dune wall in that sector, and the shallow saltwater Waddenzee, which separates the islands from the coast, was once dry land. Besides the Waddenzee, the other major marine incursion helped create a huge flooded river mouth, or estuary, where the Rhine, Maas, and Schelde rivers came to the sea on the southwestern coast.

Still, deterioration continued. Parts of the coastal margin of the Low Country fragmented into marshy tidal islands, and numerous lakes formed in depressions. From time to time storm tides broke through to join some of these lakes to the sea. When the Romans came to the Low Country, they found a large freshwater lake just south of the Waddenzee, fed and drained by a distributary of the Rhine, and called it the Flevo Lacus. The Roman lake became a saltwater embayment of the North Sea, when a series of storms about A.D. 1200 cut through the ribbon of dry land separating it from the Waddenzee. This created the shallow, saline Zuider Zee, or "southern sea," to replace Flevo Lacus. Other freshwater lakes in the coastal fringe awaited their turn to be joined to the sea.

Another type of deterioration involved the slow eastward migration of what remained of the sand-dune barrier. The prevailing westerly winds gradually moved the dunes inland, and the sea followed close behind. A fortress built during the Roman occupation on the landward side of the dunes was covered by drifting sands, disappeared and was soon forgotten after the legions left, only to reappear during the Christmas season in the year 1520 on the *seaward* side of the dune wall. Soon thereafter the ruins were flooded by the advancing North Sea. This involved an eastward migration of about 3 km (2 mi.) in 1500 years, and it is estimated that in the vicinity of the city of 's Gravenhage (The Hague) the dunes have moved at least 5 to 8 km (3 to 5 mi.).

Human action to resist the environmental deterioration gained momentum over the last 1500 to 2000 years. At first the early Dutch inhabitants did nothing more than to pile up mounds of earth upon which to build their homes. These mounds, variously called *terp* (Dutch), *warft* (Frisian), and *wurt* (low German) can be seen today in parts of the Low Country and are generally still inhabited (Figure 2.21). During periods of high water, the *terpen* temporarily became little islands protecting the people in clustered dwellings on top. These mounds were 3.7 to 12 m (12 to 40 ft.) high and varied in area from 1.5 to 16 ha (4 to 40 acres). The *terpen* were built mainly from the third to the tenth centuries A.D., and some 1500 of them still survive at least in rudiment. Somewhat later, in the A.D. 900s, the Dutch began placing obstructions along the coast to catch and hold accretions of sand and silt and built walls to trap silt being washed down the rivers. In these ways they induced island building in the delta (Figure 2.22).

FIGURE 2.21 An ancient *terp* in the Dutch coastal province of Friesland. This artificial mound dates from the earliest period of the Dutch battle against the sea and today contains the church and cemetery of the village of Jelsum. Before the era of dike building, the country-side all around the *terp* was subject to periodic inundation by the waters of the sea. (Copyright Marianne Dommisse, from Netherlands Information Service, used with permission.)

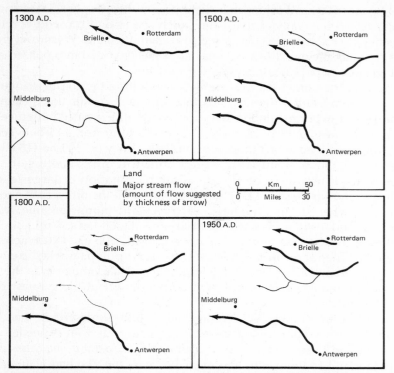

FIGURE 2.22 Humans at work modifying the Dutch coastline, 1200–1950.
Both the advance of the North Sea and the subsequent work of humans to push back the
waters are evident in these maps of the Rhine-Maas-Schelde Estuary in the Zeeland province
of the Netherlands. The Delta Project is not shown. (Source: After *Westermanns Atlas zur
Weltgeschichte,* Part 2, Braunschweig, D: Georg Westermann, 1963, 97.)

    Dike building began about A.D. 900 in the extensive tidal marsh areas of
Vlaanderen and Zeeland, provinces of what are today the southern Netherlands
and adjacent Belgium. The dikes protected lands above the low-tide level that
were subject to periodic flooding, and sluice gates were opened at low tide to
allow gravity discharge of the water that had accumulated through seepage.
Such protected areas became known as *polders,* a term first used in 1138 in
Flanders Plain. Dike building and poldering spread northward into the province
of Holland, where Count William the Diker directed poldering in an area of peat
bogs, lakes, and marshes south of Amsterdam in the early 1200s. A peak of dike
construction occurred in the 1300s to protect cropland from the unpredictable
seas, lakes, and rivers. Human reaction remained largely defensive.

    The development of polders in areas too low to be drained by gravity at low
tide awaited the invention of a mechanical water lifter. The windmill, known in
the Low Country at least since the late 1100s, initially served the Dutch only as a
grinder of grain, but in the year 1408 the windmill was first employed as a water

lifter and by the 1600s had achieved general use for this purpose. The same westerlies that pushed the waters against the Dutch shores and caused the retreat of the protective sand dunes was harnessed to reclaim the land. Within several centuries nearly all of the marshes and bogs had been converted into polders, with a resultant increase in population and food production.

Drainage of the numerous freshwater lakes dotting the coastal fringe of the Low Country represented the next advance in Dutch reclamation technology. Two centuries of experimentation with the windmill convinced engineers that sizable water bodies could be converted to agricultural use, and between 1609 and 1612 the combined work of 49 windmills laid dry a 7300-ha (18,000-acre) freshwater lake. Other small lakes were drained in quick succession. More-powerful water lifters were needed to allow reclamation of large lakes and oceanic inlets, and for these the Dutch had to wait until the nineteenth and twentieth centuries, when steam- and, later, electric-engine pumps became available. Between 1840 and 1846, a dike was built around the 60-km (37-mi.) circumference of the freshwater Haarlemmer Lake, covering 17,800 ha (44,000 acres) west of Amsterdam. Then three British-built steam-engine pumps worked continually for five years, from 1847 to 1852, to drain the lake. Haarlemmer was the largest water body yet to surrender to the Dutch at that time, but the greatest projects still lay in the future.

The treacherous Zuider Zee, whose origin has been described, had been a menace to the Low Country ever since its formation. Its waters needed only a strong north wind to send them raging against the vulnerable sea dikes protecting the polderland to the south, and over the years the Zee had claimed many victims. One particularly severe flood in 1916 finally prompted the Netherlands government to take action. The Zuider Zee Project gained approval in 1918, and actual work began seven years later. The key to the project, a huge sea dike called the Afsluitdijk was completed in 1932 and cut off the narrow mouth of the Zuider Zee from the ocean (Figure 2.23). The streams that flooded into the Zee soon flushed it clean of salt water, creating the freshwater Lake Yssel. The dike included sluices to allow for outflow of water and locks to accommodate shipping. The hated name Zuider Zee disappeared from the map, and perhaps the only group of people who mourned its demise were the salt-water fishermen, mainly Frisians, whose livelihood was destroyed. The highway and railroad built on the new dike provided greatly shortened transport links between western and eastern parts of the Netherlands and also reduced the mileage of exposed ocean dike to a small fraction of the former total.

The second part of the project has involved the diking and draining of four large polders from the floor of the old Zuider Zee. The *Wieringer* Polder in the far northern part was actually drained before all of the sea dike was finished, falling dry in 1931. Experimentation established the best sequence of crops to remove salinity from the soils, and soon the Wieringer Polder was being colonized by Dutch farmers. Settlement was completed in 1941, and the area is a fully integrated part of the Netherlands, largely indistinguishable from surrounding districts. The other major polders include the *Noordoost* (Northeast), drained by electric

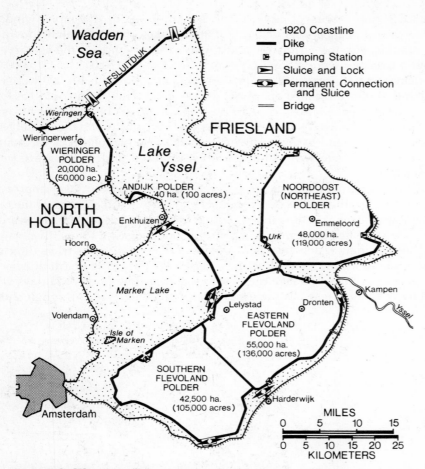

FIGURE 2.23 The Zuider Zee Project produced a dramatic change in the Dutch coastline, as well as converting what remains of the old saltwater Zee into the freshwater Lake Yssel.

pumps in 1936–1942 and colonized by the early 1960s; *Eastern Flevoland*, named for the ancient Roman lake and laid dry in 1957; and *Southern Flevoland*, pumped free of water in 1968 and today absorbing suburban spillover from the adjacent cities of Holland, as well as providing parkland. The remainder of Lake Yssel remains undrained, serving as a freshwater supply and recreational area.

With the Zuider Zee Project, the Dutch turned back the major marine encroachment on their northern coast. The other principal danger area lies in the southwestern province known as Zeeland, where the Rhine-Maas-Schelde estuary passes through six large gaps in the old sand-dune barrier. This delta country was no stranger to storm floods from the sea, but the attention of the Dutch government was finally attracted by an especially severe disaster in 1953. Between

January 31 and February 2 of that year, 160 km-per-hour (100 mph.) winds from the northwest pushed river water back up into the estuary, breaking down dikes and spilling into the farmlands and towns of the islands in the estuary. More than 80 breaches were made in the dikes, and some 150,000 ha (375,000 acres) were flooded with seawater. About 1800 persons drowned, 100,000 were evacuated, and damage reached enormous proportions. The storm could easily have been catastrophic. A strategic dike along the north bank of the Rhine-Maas channel called the Nieuwe Waterweg (New Waterway), protecting the densely settled heartland of Holland to the north, held—barely. Had it collapsed, the homeland of 3 million people would have been inundated and many more persons drowned.

To prevent such an occurrence in the future, the government approved the *Delta Project* (Figure 2.24). Four large new sea dikes closed off most of the mouths of the Rhine-Maas-Schelde estuary, with a freshwater lake on the landward side. The Nieuwe Waterweg remained open so as not to disrupt Rhine River shipping, but elaborate new water-diversion systems and storm-surge barriers directed the flow of the Rhine and Maas into the adjacent lake in case a storm tide backs up the river as in 1953. The lake can absorb the river flow for several days without spilling over its dikes, and the excess water can then escape through sluices to

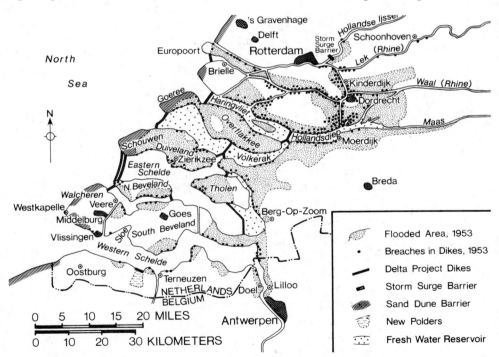

FIGURE 2.24 The Delta Project was designed to protect the southern Dutch coast and prevent another catastrophic flood like the one in 1953. (Sources: After Wagret; van Veen, with modifications.)

the sea when the storm subsides. The western Schelde estuary also remains open since it serves the major Belgian port of Antwerpen, but dikes along the estuary shore were raised and strengthened. Little land reclamation occurred in the Delta Project, only about 16,200 ha (40,000 acres), for the goal was preservation rather than expansion.

The Low Country, then, was human-made. Without the effort of the inhabitants, the seacoast would lie far to the interior, and Europe would be deprived of some of its richest farmland and largest cities (Figure 2.25).

Coastal Silting

More commonly, Europeans have modified the coastline unintentionally, especially on the three Mediterranean peninsulas. Bays have been silted up as dry land, rivers rendered unnavigable, ports made landlocked, and islands near the

FIGURE 2.25 Cattle grazing at low tide on the seaward side of the huge dike protecting the lowlands bordering the North Sea in Schleswig-Holstein province, Germany, at the far eastern tip of the Low Country. (Photo by the author, 1981.)

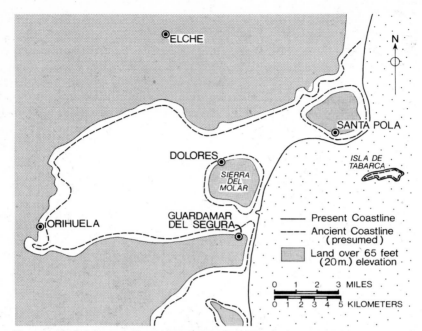

FIGURE 2.26 Coastline alteration by siltation since ancient times, Alicante district, Mediterranean coastal Spain. Materials eroded from the adjacent Bética Range have filled a sizable bay and joined several islands to the mainland. Similar siltation occurred in other Mediterranean areas. (Source: Modified from C. Delano Smith, *Western Mediterranean Europe*, London, GB: Academic Press, 1979, 332.)

coast joined to the mainland (Figure 2.26). Most of these changes occurred in historic times, some very recently.

Mediterranean people wrought these changes by destroying forests and allowing massive amounts of soil to erode. The results have been spectacular. The Greek geographer Strabo, writing about 2000 years ago, noted that the Adriatic tides reached to Ravenna in northern Italy, a city 10 km (6 mi.) inland today. Palos de la Frontera on the Odiel River, from which Columbus departed on his voyage of discovery in 1492, is now silted up for 1.5 km (1 mi.) below the former docks. Even more impressive is the silting that occurred in the area of Monte Circeo, a mountain on the western coast of Italy. According to the Homeric epic *Odyssey*, Monte Circeo formed an island, and it retained that status even as late as 300 B.C. Several centuries later siltation had joined it to the Italian mainland. Where Ulysses once sailed, farmers labor today in fertile fields. Today, the Ionian Greek isle of Levkás is in the process of being joined to the mainland.

Europeans, then, inherited and greatly altered a temperate, well-watered, forested, fertile enclave, compartmentalized by terrain and flanked on all sides by the sea and less hospitable lands where cold, aridity, and barrenness prevailed. In this comfortable niche, European civilization arose and flowered. It is tempting to attribute the human Europe to the gentle land and the isolation offered by the less-favored periphery, but that interpretation would be simplistic. Similar favored lands elsewhere in the world produced cultures fundamentally different from that of Europe. The explanation for the European culture area must also be sought elsewhere, for Europe is largely a self-written drama. The remainder, and appropriately larger part, of the book is devoted to the inter-workings of culture, economy, and ecology that contain the key to understanding Europe geographically.

Sources and Suggested Readings

David Alexander. "The Reclamation of Val-di-Chiana (Tuscany)." *Annals of the Association of American Geographers.* 74 (1984), 527–550.

Ian Y. Ashwell and Edgar Jackson. "The Sagas as Evidence of Early Deforestation in Iceland." *Canadian Geographer.* 14 (1970), 158–166.

Wilfrid Bach. "The Acid Rain/Carbon Dioxide Threat—Control Strategies." *GeoJournal.* 10 (1985), 339–352.

Brenton M. Barr and Kathleen Braden. *The Disappearing Russian Forest.* Totowa, USA: Rowman & Littlefield, 1988.

Charles F. Bennett, Jr. "Human Influences on the Ecosystems of Europe and the Mediterranean." In his *Man and Earth's Ecosystems: An Introduction to the Geography of Human Modification of the Earth.* New York, USA: Wiley, 1975, 121–144.

Hugh H. Bennett. "Soil Erosion in Spain." *Geographical Review.* 50 (1960), 59–72.

Uwe Bischoff. "Der Scirocco: Untersuchungen zur Häufigkeit und Dauer über Mittel- und Süditalien." *Erdkunde.* 46 (1992), 52–57.

Francis W. Carter and David Turnock (eds.). *Environmental Problems in Eastern Europe.* London, GB: Routledge, Chapman & Hall, 1993.

T. J. Chandler. *The Climate of London.* London, GB: Hutchinson, 1965.

T. J. Chandler and S. Gregory (eds.). *The Climate of the British Isles.* London, GB, and New York, USA: Longman, 1976.

Victor Conrad. "The Climate of the Mediterranean Region." *Bulletin of the American Meteorological Society.* 24 (1943), 127–145.

H. Clifford Darby. "The Clearing of the Woodland in Europe." In *Man's Role in Changing the Face of the Earth,* ed. William L. Thomas, Jr. Chicago, USA: University of Chicago Press, 1956, 183–216.

H. Clifford Darby. *The Draining of the Fens.* Cambridge, GB: Cambridge University Press, 2nd ed., 1956.

Gary S. Dunbar. "The Forests of Cyprus Under British Stewardship." *Scottish Geographical Magazine.* 99 (1983), 111–120.

A. M. Duncan, D. K. Chester, and J. E. Guest. "Mount Etna Volcano: Environmental Impact and Problems of Volcanic Prediction." *Geographical Journal.* 147 (1981), 164–178.

Clifford Embleton (ed.). *Geomorphology of Europe.* New York, USA: Wiley, 1984.

H. J. Fleure. "The Loess in European Life." *Geography.* 45 (1960), 200–204.

Hermann Flohn and Roberto Fantechi (eds.). *The Climate of Europe: Past, Present and Future*. Hingham, USA: D. Reidel, 1984.

Alice Garnett. "The Loess Regions of Central Europe in Prehistoric Times." *Geographical Journal*. 106 (1945), 132–143.

R. Louis Gentilcore. "Reclamation in the Agro Pontino, Italy." *Geographical Review*. 60 (1970), 301–327.

Andrew Goudie. *The Landforms of England and Wales*. Oxford, GB: Basil Blackwell, 1990.

Edward Graham. "The Urban Heat Island of Dublin City during the Summer Months." *Irish Geography*. 26 (1993), 45–57.

Michel Grenon and Michel Batisse (eds.). *Futures for the Mediterranean Basin: The Blue Plan*. Oxford, GB: Oxford University Press, 1989.

M. H. M. van Hulten. "Plan and Reality in the IJsselmeerpolders." *Tijdschrift voor Economische en Sociale Geografie*. 60 (1969), 67–76.

E. L. Jackson. "The Laki Eruption of 1783: Impacts on Population and Settlement in Iceland." *Geography*. 67 (1982), 42–50.

Jaako Jalas and Juha Suominen. *Atlas Florae Europaeae*. Helsinki, SF: Suomalaisen Kirjallisuuden Kirjapaino Oy, 1972–76.

Ljubomir Jeftic, John D. Milliman, and Giuliano Sestini, eds. *Climatic Change and the Mediterranean*. Sevenoaks, Kent, GB: Edward Arnold, 1993.

Audrey M. Lambert. *The Making of the Dutch Landscape: An Historical Geography of the Netherlands*. London, GB: Seminar Press, 2nd ed., 1985.

Vincent H. Malmström. "Influence of the Arctic Front on the Climate and Crops of Iceland." *Annals of the Association of American Geographers*. 50 (1960), 117–122.

C. Milleret. "La Forêt d'Orléans." *Annales de Géographie*. 72 (1963), 426–458.

Oleg Polunin and Martin Walters. *A Guide to the Vegetation of Britain and Europe*. Oxford, GB: Oxford University Press, 1985.

Erwin Raisz. "Physiography of Europe." In *Goode's World Atlas*, ed. Edward B. Espenshade, Jr., and Joel L. Morrison. Chicago, USA: Rand McNally, 18th ed. 1990, 132–133.

A. Scarth. "Nisyros Volcano." *Geography*. 68 (1983), 133–139.

Haraldur Sigurdson et al. "The Eruption of Vesuvius in A.D. 79." *National Geographic Research*. 1 (1985), 332–387.

S. E. Steigenga-Kouwe. "The Delta Plan." *Tijdschrift voor Economische en Sociale Geografie*. 51 (1960), 167–175.

Ch. A. P. Takes and A. J. Venstra. "Zuyder Zee Reclamation Scheme." *Tijdschrift voor Economische en Sociale Geografie*. 51 (1960), 162–167.

Arthur G. Tansley. *The British Isles and Their Vegetation*. London, GB: Cambridge University Press, 1939.

J. V. Thirgood. *Man and the Mediterranean Forest*. London, GB: Academic Press, 1981.

Sigurdur Thorarinsson. *Surtsey: The New Island in the North Atlantic*. New York, USA: Viking Press, 1966.

Harry Thorpe. "A Special Case of Heath Reclamation in the Alheden District of Jutland, 1700–1955." *Institute of British Geographers, Publication*. 23 (1957), 87–121.

Michael J. Tooley and Saskia Jelgersma, eds. *Impacts of Sea-Level Rise on European Coastal Lowlands.* Oxford, GB: Basil Blackwell, 1992. (Institute of British Geographers, Pub. No. 27).

J. Tricart and J. P. Bravard. "Le cours périalpin du Rhin, du Rhône et du Danube: aménagement fluvial et dérives de l'environnement." *Annales de Géographie.* 100 (1991), 668–713.

Johan van Veen. *Dredge, Drain, Reclaim: The Art of a Nation.* The Hague, NL: Nijhoff, 5th ed., 1962.

Paul Wagret. *Polderlands.* Trans. Margaret Sparks. London, GB: Methuen, 1968.

Carl Christian Wallén. *Climates of Northern and Western Europe.* Amsterdam, NL: Elsevier, 1970.

Michael Williams. *The Draining of the Somerset Levels.* London, GB: Cambridge University Press, 1970.

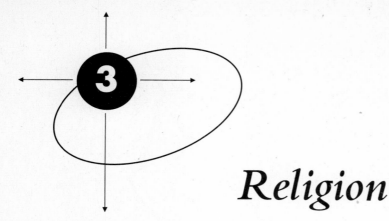

Religion

Of all the human traits mentioned in Chapter 1 that define "Europe," the single most important is Christianity. As recently as A.D. 1500, the faith and culture remained very nearly synonymous, with Christianity confined almost exclusively to Europe. Christian Europeans had been in combat with Muslims in the Mediterranean for seven centuries, strengthening their sense of cultural identity. Pope John Paul II, in 1982, expressed his opinion concerning the venerable tie between Europe and the church. European identity "is incomprehensible without Christianity," he declared, and the faith "ripened the civilization of the continent, its culture, its dynamism, its activeness, its capacity for constructive expansion on other continents." The Pope then admonished a much secularized Europe to "revive those authentic values that gave glory to your history."

The Christian heritage, more than any other single trait, still today provides the basis for the European image of "we versus they." Christianity underlies and inspires both the good and bad aspects of Europe: its great art, literature, music, and philosophy as well as its religious wars, genocides, and inquisitions. One cannot imagine European culture devoid of the magnificent cathedrals, altarpieces, crucifixes, and religious statuary. Christianity gave us the *Commentaries* of Saint Thomas Aquinas, Leonardo da Vinci's *Last Supper*, Michelangelo's *David* and Sistine Chapel, the Kremlin in Moskva and the cathedral at Chartres, Dante's *Inferno* and Milton's *Paradise Lost*. For many centuries, the church was Europe and Europe was the church. All Europeans and their overseas offspring, regardless of their present religious beliefs, bear the permanent stamp of Christianity. Even today, to depart the Christian lands and enter the bordering Muslim districts is to leave Europe (Figure 3.1).

Pagan Europe

Christianity, of course, was not native to Europe. The culture area, to a remarkable extent, is simply the result of a juxtaposition of different intrusive traits. In pre-Christian times, Europeans had a decidedly *polytheistic* culture, as was

FIGURE 3.1 Religious groups in Europe. The numbers refer to percentages of the largest group(s) within each country, and the key to abbreviations is c = Catholic, o = Orthodox, p = Protestant, u = Uniate, m = Muslim, and n = declaring no religious faith. Persons declaring a denomination but listing themselves as nonpracticing or unreligious are included as members. The figures for Russia are for lands west of the Urals. (Sources: Catholic News Service, Washington, USA, "Religious Beliefs and Practices in Twelve Countries 1991," for release June 10, 1993; Gallup Social Surveys [Gallup Poll] Ltd., Fall 1991; International Research Associates, *Eurobarometer*, Fall 1991.)

typical of all Indo-European tribes and also the more ancient, pre-Indo-European inhabitants. Most groups practiced *animism*, the belief that inanimate objects such as rocks, heavenly bodies, mountains, forests, and rivers possess souls.

A bewildering array of spirits, gods, and goddesses ruled over war, fertility, woodlands, high places, caves, harvests, death, lightning, navigation, earthquakes, volcanoes, moon, sun, winds, and a hundred other domains. The Germanic Thor hurled thunderbolts, the Greek Aphrodite governed love and fertility, and the Roman Mars assisted in warfare. Thousands of shrines and altars dedicated to these divinities dotted the ancient landscape of Europe (Figure 3.2). Some pre-Christian deities achieved more importance than others, often gaining acceptance over fairly large areas. A mother-fertility-love goddess, referred to by the Romans as *Magna Mater*—the great mother—was widely venerated throughout the Mediterranean lands, and *Mithras*, a male god derived from Persia, achieved widespread worship among the Roman military class. Especially strong in Greece, the *Mystery Cults* had a main center at Eleusis near Athínai. Their rites are little known since they occurred in secret (giving us the word *elusive*), but we

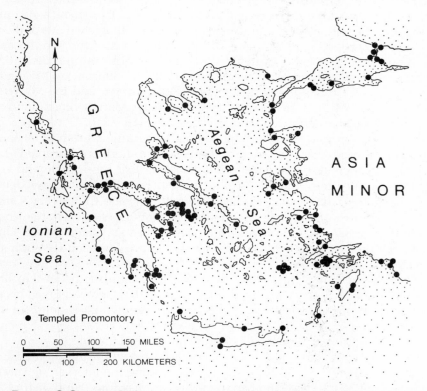

FIGURE 3.2 Templed promontories of the ancient Aegean. The seagoing Greeks placed great importance upon promontories, both as hazards to sailing and as landmarks. Temples both heightened the visibility of the promontories and allowed placation of the relevant gods. (Source: After Semple.)

do know they offered eternal life to the faithful. In the far western and northern fringes of Europe, astronomy-based religions apparently of early Indo-European origin held sway, leaving us countless *megalithic* ruins such as Stonehenge, now believed to have been a rather sophisticated observatory.

In other words, pre-Christian Europe was religiously chaotic. That virtually the entire culture area should rather rapidly have been converted to a radically different, *monotheistic* religious faith seems at first glance unlikely. Originally, the worship of a single male divinity had apparently been limited to Afro-Asiatic–speaking nomadic herders of the Near Eastern deserts. This tribal Semitic shepherd-god seemed ill suited to the agricultural, polytheistic, Indo-European lands.

Diffusion of Christianity

Perhaps the key figure in the remarkable diffusion of Christianity to Europe, the Apostle Paul, bridged the Semitic and Greek cultures; he presented monotheism in terms understandable and appealing to Europeans. Christianity also proved, throughout the centuries of conversion, adept at absorbing elements of the native religions of Europe. *Sun*day, devoted to a Roman god of the sun, became the Christian sabbath; diverse saints stood in for the old multiple divinities; the Virgin Mary annexed the devotion afforded to the Mediterranean Magna Mater; Jehovah replaced the old king of the gods, Zeus/Jupiter; and the Mystery Cult promise of eternal life was honored by Christianity. Marian veneration remains strongest in the Mediterranean lands even today (Figure 3.3).

Pre-Christian places of worship typically became Christian shrines and churches, a process that continued centuries later in northern Europe. For example, a rural church in Scotland stands atop a prehistoric artificial mound venerated since ancient times, the Alvestra monastery in south-central Sweden abuts standing stones dating from pre-Christian antiquity, and Canterbury Cathedral, seat of the Church of England, rests on the foundations of a solar-oriented pagan temple (Figure 3.4). Sacred groves from pagan times still stand protected alongside Greek monasteries, and springs holy to the pre-Christian Irish remain pilgrimage sites today.

At the same time, Christianity destroyed the animistic belief that humans were part of Nature, replacing it with the doctrine that God had given his people dominion over the environment. In this way, by removing the animistic sacredness of Nature, Christianity perhaps opened the way for the massive environmental modification that endangers European survival today.

Christian diffusion initially advanced *hierarchically* in the Roman Empire. That is, Christianity spread from city to city, leaving the intervening rural areas pagan (Figure 3.5). Indeed, the Latin word *pagus*, meaning "rural district," is the root of both the word *pagan* and *peasant*. Similarly, in much later times the isolated, unconverted dwellers of the heaths would give rise to the word *heathen*. Early Christianity in Europe remained an urban faith.

Recently, it has been proposed that one key to the concentration of the first European Christians in the cities of the Roman Empire lies in the Jewish diaspora.

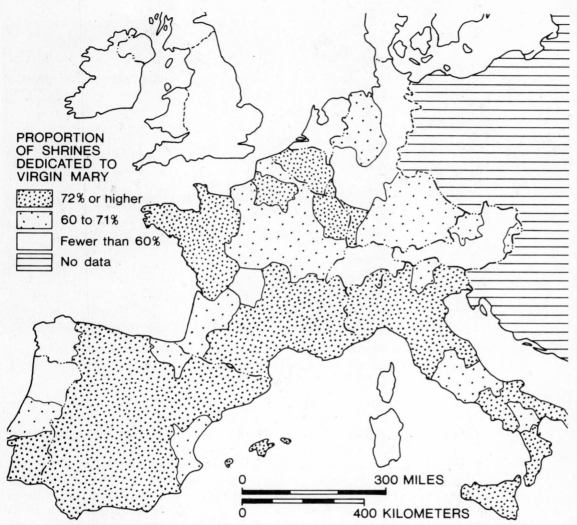

**PROPORTION
OF SHRINES
DEDICATED TO
VIRGIN MARY**

72% or higher

60 to 71%

Fewer than 60%

No data

0   300 MILES

0   400 KILOMETERS

FIGURE 3.3 Proportion of pilgrimage shrines dedicated to the Virgin Mary in modern Europe. Marian devotion is greatest in the Mediterranean lands, where the *Magna Mater* was venerated in pre-Christian times. Spain alone has some 22,000 Marian shrines. Catholic shrines dedicated to Christ and various saints are most common in the North and Alpine lands. (Source: Adapted from Nolan and Nolan, 121.)

Early in the Christian era, the Romans dispersed most Jews from Israel, in an attempt to quell their tendency to rise up against imperial authority. Jews came as refugees to almost every Roman city throughout the Empire, and they clustered in ethnic neighborhoods. Evidence now suggests that those very neighborhoods often housed the first Christian congregations. In other words, Jewish people in their diaspora, already monotheists whose holy scriptures formed half

FIGURE 3.4 Kildrummy Church positioned atop an ancient artificial mound in the northern Scottish Highlands where pagans worshipped. Such juxtapositions occur frequently in all parts of Europe. (Photo by the author, 1992).

the Bible, may have become the earliest Christians in Europe, though many or most Jews did not convert.

Whatever the case, the spread of Christianity remained slow until A.D. 313, when the Roman emperor Constantine issued an edict of toleration for Christianity, which led eventually to its status as state religion. In the centuries that followed, two major centers directed the diffusion of Christianity from its Mediterranean base—Latin Roma and Greek Byzantium (Constantinople, present-day Istanbul). The Roman Church spread rapidly in the western Mediterranean during the fourth and fifth centuries. Before the fall of the empire, Italy, France, and Iberia became converted, and the Germanic tribes who subsequently overran these areas were quickly won over to the church. From the western Mediterranean core, Roman missionaries soon spread far to the north. Patrick arrived in Ireland in 432, and a major cultural flowering occurred among the Celtic converts there. Peoples of Britain, missionised from both Ireland and the continent, converted from the 400s through the early 600s (Figure 3.5).

The pagan tribes of Germany received missionaries from Ireland and Britain, aided by others from France, in the period from the early 600s to the early 800s,

FIGURE 3.5 Diffusion of Christianity to A.D. 1400. The faith spread hierarchically in the early centuries, moving from city to city while bypassing rural areas.

and the Germans in turn carried the church to Scandinavians and Slavic Poles, missions completed by about 1100. The pivotal event in Poland occurred in 966, when the principal local ruler allowed himself to be baptized, an event duplicated in Hungary in 973. The European work of Roman missionaries ended in 1386 with the conversion of the Balts in distant Lithuania. In carrying Christianity to the heathen north of the Mediterranean core of Catholicism, missionaries of Roma also took the Latin alphabet, and the zone of Roman mission work is fairly well indicated even today by the use of Latin characters.

The impressive gains in the north were partially offset by losses to Islam in the Mediterranean area. North Africa, where the Roman church was well established, became permanently Muslim in the 700s, and much of Iberia remained under the control of the Muslims for many centuries. In general, however, Islamic invaders respected those religions that possessed a written book of beliefs, and Christianity survived in Moorish Iberia.

Greek Christians, centered in the Byzantine Empire, accomplished less missionary work than the Roman Church, confining their attention for many centuries to winning over the Slavic tribes who had spread south of the Danube River into imperial territory. These South Slavs eventually adopted Greek Christianity, except for the Croats and Slovenes, converted by Roman missionaries. Mission work north of the Danube was hindered by repeated invasions of Asiatic tribes entering Europe through the steppe corridor and Valachian Plain between 567 and 1048 (Figure 3.5). Greek missionaries sought to convert tribal rulers, who in turn spread the faith to their subjects by decree. In this manner, through conversion of a Slavic prince of Kyyiv (Kiev), Russians and Ukrainians became Christians. Greek missionaries working among the Slavs developed the Cyrillic alphabet, derived from the Greek characters, and the distribution of this script today closely parallels the extent of their church in Europe. The Greek-converted Serbs and Romanized Croats, though speaking dialects of the same language, use different alphabets because of their religious backgrounds. Greek Christianity, like its Roman counterpart, lost ground in the south while winning converts in the north. Soon after 1200 their Byzantine Empire collapsed under Turkish pressure, eventually causing the loss of Asia Minor and even the Christian center at Constantinople to Islam.

Christian Fragmentation

Religiously, as in virtually every other facet of culture, Europe displays an overarching unity, a façade partially concealing major internal contrasts. Monolithic Christianity never existed in Europe. From the very first, the more ancient contest between Greek and Roman civilizations dictated fragmentation. The claim of the Latin bishop of Roma to leadership of all Christendom never gained unqualified acceptance by the Greeks and the bishop of Constantinople. The subsequent split of the Empire into western and eastern halves, Roman and Greek, presaged a religious schism. In a separation that finally became official in A.D. 1054, the western church became Roman Catholicism, the Greek church Eastern Orthodoxy. The dividing line between Catholicism and Orthodoxy remains the most fundamental religious border in Europe today (Figure 3.1). It has changed little in a thousand years and provides the basis for many of the contrasts between west and east in Europe.

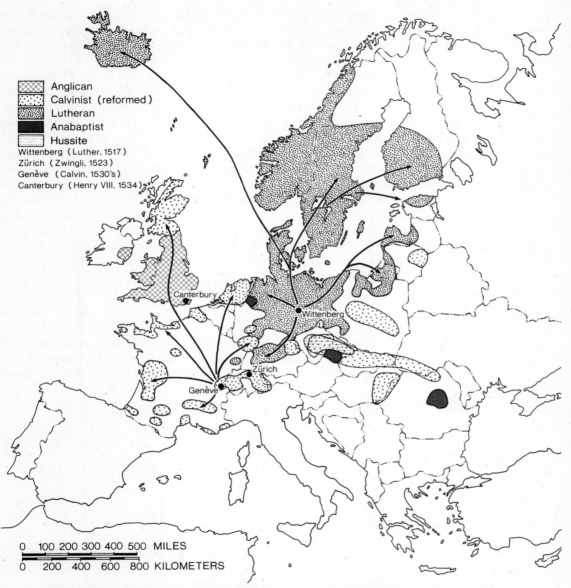

FIGURE 3.6 Diffusion of Protestantism to A.D. 1570. The Reformation spread from several different nuclei to influence most of Northern and Central Europe.

The second great schism occurred in the 1500s, when western Christianity split, the southern lands remaining Roman Catholic and the north becoming the geographical focus of Protestantism (Figure 3.6). The Protestant movement arose in different places over several centuries as various attempts to bring about reforms or changes within the Roman church. The pivotal event, the challenge to the church issued by Martin Luther at Wittenberg, Germany, in 1517, evolved into successful secession. The new church quickly spread through northern Germany and the Scandinavian lands, supported by the rulers of individual states. John Calvin furthered the Protestant cause in the mid-1500s from his headquarters at Genève (Geneva), Switzerland, dispersing Puritanism to England, Presbyterianism to Scotland, the Reformed church to the Netherlands and Germany, and the Huguenot faith to France, as well as lesser Calvinist groups to eastern Europe. In Switzerland, Ulrich Zwingli led a movement centered at Zürich. A number of Anabaptist Protestant sects also arose, including the Swiss Brethren and the Mennonites in the Netherlands. These people rejected infant baptism and offered the rite only to adult believers. An additional breakaway from Roman Catholicism came in 1534 when King Henry VIII created the Church of England.

The Protestant breakaway reinforced the great north/south cultural divide in Europe, a border that had pretty much stabilized by 1570, though the dreadful Thirty Years' War between Catholics and Protestants still lay ahead (compare Figures 3.1 and 3.6). As a result of the two Christian schisms, Europe is now divided into three major religious regions.

Roman Catholicism

About 248 million Europeans are practicing or nominal **Roman Catholics** today, roughly 36 percent of the total population (Table 3.1). Catholicism dominates a huge region stretching from Iberia and Italy in the south to Lithuania in the north

TABLE 3.1   Major Religious Groups in Europe[a] Today

Group	Number of Adherents[b]	As Percentage of European Population
Christian	475,500,000	69%
Roman Catholic	248,000,000	36%
Eastern Orthodox	130,000,000	19%
Protestant[c]	90,000,000	13%
Uniate (Ukrainian Catholic)	6,000,000	1%
Armenian Church	1,500,000	<1%
Islam	16,000,000	2%
Judaism	2,600,000	<1%
Declaring no religious faith[d]	190,000,000	27%
Other and unreported	12,200,000	2%
	696,300,000	100%

[a] In Russia includes only Ural, North Caucasus, and all other regions lying to the west; includes CY, AM, GE, M, GBZ; excludes TR north of Bosporos/Dardanelles (Rumelia and Thrace), TCY, AZ.
[b] Children are included with parents.
[c] Includes Anglicans, Mormons, and Mennonites, as well as the more obvious groups.
[d] Includes atheists, agnostics, and all others denying any religious affiliation; does *not* include persons nominally linked to a religious faith but claiming to be unreligious.
Sources: Those listed for Figure 3.16: Barrett (1982); *Eurobarometer* (1991); Catholic News Service (1991); Martyniuk (1993); Radio Free Europe/Radio Liberty (1992); Gallup Poll (1991).

and from Ireland in the west to Croatia and Hungary in the east. In some countries, such as Spain, where less than one-half of one percent of the population belongs to other churches, Catholicism is overwhelmingly prevalent, but many regions, particularly along the contact zones with Protestantism and Orthodoxy, exhibit considerable denominational variety.

Roman Catholicism has proven able to retain a unitary, central control over its European domain. It remains a truly united church largely obedient to the Roman papacy, and Vatican City is the seat of a highly centralized administration. At the same time, regional differences occur. Irish Catholicism is not the same as, say, Italian or Lithuanian Catholicism, and the church has permitted nationalistic saints and other regional qualities to persist. Individual districts and valleys often boast their own patron saints and shrines. For example, in the Bética mountains south of Granada in Spain lies the highly distinctive region of Las Alpujarras, where the town of Ugijar proudly houses the sanctuary of Our Lady of the Martirio, "patroness of Las Alpujarras." In this manner, Catholicism heightens the sense of place.

A vivid Catholic impress has been placed on the countryside in lands loyal to the Roman church. Geographers speak of *cultural landscapes*—the visual, varied trace of human presence—and much of Europe can be said to display a Catholic landscape. Among the most obvious religious contributions to the landscape are *sacred structures,* especially the church building. Europe exhibits many regional contrasts in church size, building material, and architectural style. In Roman Catholic areas, the church structures tend to be larger and more ornate than those of Protestant districts, in part because the Roman church places great value on providing visible beauty for the faithful. Catholic landscapes gain additional distinctiveness from the numerous roadside shrines and chapels that dot the countryside (Figure 3.7).

Catholicism also influenced the names people placed on the land. In Roman Catholic countries, the custom of naming towns for Christian saints became very common. Often, saintly suffixes were added to pre-existing settlements, as in Alcazar de San Juan in Spain. The frequency of such sacred names decreases to the north in Europe and rarely do they occur in Protestant lands. In Germany, about three-quarters of the towns and villages bearing the saintly prefix *Sankt* lie in the Catholic-dominated southern part of the country, including 21 percent in the province of Bayern (Bavaria) alone. Cross the religious divide into Protestant Germany (which incidentally closely parallels here the ancient northern border of the Roman Empire), and saints largely disappear from place names.

Catholicism has also had a distinctive economic imprint on its part of Europe. For example, the Catholic tradition of avoiding meat on Friday and on numerous church holidays greatly stimulated the development of the fishing industry in Europe. In particular, the church encouraged the use of fish during periods of fasting and penitence, as well as on Fridays, the latter practice having been abandoned only recently by papal decree. It is not surprising that seashore Catholics, such as Basques, Bretons, and Portuguese, are among the greatest fishing peoples of Europe. Saint Peter, the original Christian fisherman, usually holds a place of special veneration in the fishing villages of Roman Catholic Europe, as well as in those of Orthodox Greece. Catholic dietary requirements

FIGURE 3.7 A Roman Catholic wayside shrine in the Schwarzwald (Black Forest) region of Germany. Besides helping to create a distinctive German Catholic landscape, the shrine provides evidence of the surviving vitality of Christianity in this section of southwestern Germany. (Photo by the author, 1978.)

made lands such as Italy and Spain, whose adjacent seas are relatively poor fishing grounds, dependent on dried fish imports from the Atlantic front of Europe. The importance of the Roman Catholic Church to fishing is suggested by the economic crisis that occurred in English fishing when Roman Catholic dietary restrictions were removed as a result of the Anglican breakaway in the 1500s. Many fishermen were obliged to become sailors, perhaps leading to the great era of English naval exploration, piracy, and overseas colonization.

Pilgrimages

An even more profound economic influence of Catholicism results from the Church's enduring practice of religious pilgrimages. Millions of European Catholics visit literally thousands of holy places scattered through the countryside (Figure 3.8). Pilgrimage possesses an enormous economic impact, which tends to be concealed by the infrastructure supporting tourism at large, and

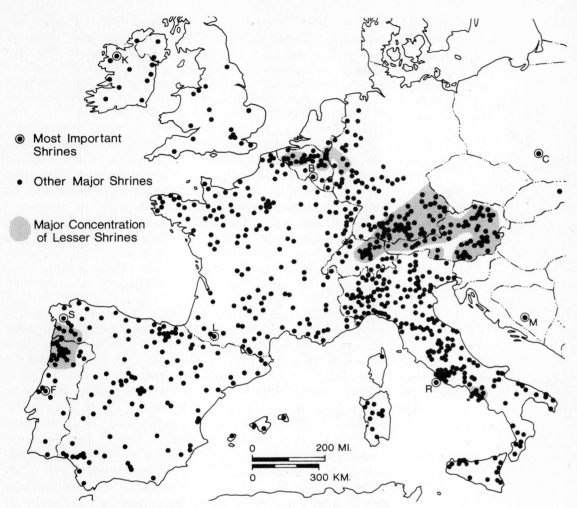

FIGURE 3.8 Pilgrimage shrines in Western Europe. Each dot represents a shrine that is the most important in its diocese and/or draws at least 10,000 pilgrims per year. In the shaded areas, remarkable concentrations of lesser shrines occur. Pilgrimage is largely a Catholic phenomenon, as the distribution suggests. Only a small selection of eastern European shrines is shown. Key to symbols for most famous shrines: B = Beauraing; C = Częstochowa; F = Fátima; K = Knock; L = Lourdes; M = Medjugorje; R = Roma; S = Santiago de Compostela. (Source: Adapted from Nolan and Nolan, 29, 31, 32.)

favored holy sites derive considerable financial benefit. In Catholic Europe, tens of millions of pilgrims travel to holy places each year. Pilgrimage sites vary in importance, ranging from small shrines that attract only the faithful from the immediate surroundings to internationally known places sought out by Catholics from all over Europe and America. Pilgrimage sites are unevenly distributed in Europe, even within Roman Catholic areas. In France, for example, pilgrimage sites devoted to the Virgin Mary lie mainly in the south and west, with a few isolated clusters elsewhere in the country (Figure 3.3). Contrary to what might be expected, the sites are not concentrated in areas of densest population. The flow of pilgrims to the major Marian shrines is of much greater economic benefit to southern France than to other parts of the country. Similarly, a passion play held every ten years at Oberammergau, a small town in the German Alps of southern Bayern, developed into a major financial boon to the entire district.

Vatican City draws millions of Roman Catholic visitors to Roma each year, adding to the already important tourist trade based on antiquities. As recently as the 1700s, almost all of the long-distance travel of people within Europe involved pilgrims going to Roma and a few other religious centers. Many roads developed mainly for pilgrim traffic, complete with hospices at difficult places such as mountain passes. Monks built bridges along these routes. Even the directional trend of many European roads was influenced by their function as pilgrimage routes. For example, the ancient route in southwestern France, leading toward Spain, left the banks of the Loire at the town of Amboise, but in later centuries the attraction of the tomb of Saint Martin caused the road to detour along a less advantageous route through the city of Tours, a change reflected in the road map of France still today.

The major present-day pilgrimage sites in addition to Roma, include *Lourdes,* a French town at the foot of the Pyrenees in the Basin of Aquitaine where the Virgin Mary supposedly appeared in a vision; *Fátima,* north of Lisboa in Portugal; *Beauraing,* a small place in French-speaking southern Belgium near the border of France; *Knock,* in the hilly west of Ireland; *Częstochowa,* where the greatest icon of Polish Catholicism, the miraculous Black Virgin, is housed; *Medjugorje,* in the Croatian Catholic district of Bosnia-Herzegovina, where the faithful believe the Virgin Mary appeared repeatedly beginning in 1981; and *Santiago de Compostela* in Spanish Galicia, a medieval site associated with St. James that has recently experienced a revival (Figures 3.8, 3.9). Fátima alone attracts over 4 million pilgrims annually and Lourdes about 5 million. In the centennial year of the miracle at Lourdes in 1958, an astounding 8 million visitors came. Small wonder that this small town of 16,300 ranks second in France only to Paris in number of hotels.

Protestantism

Protestantism is the traditional faith of the European north in the lands around the shores of the North and Baltic seas (Figure 3.1). About 90 million persons presently claim Protestant affiliation, forming roughly 13 percent of the total population.

In marked contrast to Catholicism, the most profound geographical feature of European Protestantism is its fragmentation into separate denominational regions, a splintering present from the very first, due to the work of multiple Reformation leaders (Figure 3.6). *Lutheranism* has the largest geographical distribution, including the Scandinavian countries, Iceland, Estonia, Latvia, and half of Germany (Figures 3.1, 3.10). In several of these countries, such as Sweden and

FIGURE 3.9 Procession at the pilgrimage shrine of the Virgin Mary in Altötting, province of Bayern, southern Germany. Catholic pilgrimages are very common in Bayern. (Photo 1985, courtesy of Prof. Mary Lee Nolan.)

Norway, Lutheranism is the established state church. No central Lutheran authority exists in Europe, and the faith is divided into a series of independent national churches.

The *Anglican* denomination remains the official established church in England, with lesser branches in the other British provinces, as well as in Ireland, and *Presbyterianism,* derived from Calvinism, enjoys the status of official Church of Scotland, with an adult communicant membership of about 800,000. Also in the United Kingdom are an array of so-called "free churches," lacking official status but nevertheless traditional denominations of long standing. The largest of these is *Methodism,* with a community of about 1,300,000, with lesser numbers of *Baptists, United Reformed,* and many others. The *Dutch Reformed* Church, another Calvinist-derived body, is centered in the northern Netherlands and has about 2 million adherents today. In Switzerland, the Protestant majority belongs to a church that combines Lutheran and Zwinglian influences. All that remains of the work of Jan Hus, the first Reformation leader, is a tiny community of about 200,000 *Brethren* in the Czech Republic and one parish at Herrnhut in Germany. A small population of *Mennonites,* descendants of the Anabaptist movement, survives in Ukraine and Russia.

All of these traditional Protestant groups in Europe have experienced sharp declines, particularly since about 1900. *Neo-Protestantism* provides an exception. In the past several decades, evangelical-fundamentalist groups, often based in the United States, have begun actively missionizing Europe, especially the

FIGURE 3.10 A rural Lutheran church in southwestern Iceland. This modest, Gothic-influenced structure is typical of the Protestant cultural landscape in Iceland, a barren European outpost island in the North Atlantic. (Photo by the author, 1971.)

Protestant north, and their activities have now expanded in the formerly Communist east (Figure 3.11). Pentecostals, Jehovah's Witnesses, Seventh-Day Adventists, and Baptists have been especially active. Ethnic minorities such as the Sami (Lapps) in Scandinavia and South Asians in the United Kingdom have been particularly attracted to neo-Protestantism. Romania, perhaps typical of Eastern Europe, now has about 160,000 converts. In Russia, neo-Protestantism has won many new members since 1992 and continues to grow rapidly.

As a result of the diversity of European Protestantism, no single religious landscape has been produced. As a rule, however, Protestantism appears far less visibly in the landscape than Catholicism. Church buildings tend to be smaller and far less ornate, pilgrimage places are absent, and no wayside shrines line the roadsides (Figure 3.10). Some Protestant groups have traditionally rejected all visible ostentation, rendering their presence almost invisible. For example, the modest Methodist chapels of Wales, lacking steeples and stained glass, often prove difficult for the uninitiated even to identify as places of worship (Figure 3.12).

Instead, Protestant influences should be sought in other aspects of European culture. Some scholars have suggested that *individualism*, so central a trait in modern European culture, has its roots in the Protestant Reformation. Others feel that the far-reaching *Industrial Revolution* (see Chapter 11), which so profoundly reshaped European culture, also derives from Protestantism. According to this

FIGURE 3.11 Neo-Protestant church in Ivalo, Finland, a Sami region. The sign above the door reads "Pentecostal Congregation" and on the bus "Live in Jesus." Neo-Protestantism has gained a modest foothold in some parts of Europe and is growing. (Photo by the author, 1985.)

view, the inherently dynamic character of Protestantism, the willingness of its adherents to accept change and strive for self-improvement, coupled with the Protestant ethic of hard work and the rejection of Catholic restrictions on lending money for interest, provided necessary social precedents for the Industrial Revolution. Indeed, modern industrialism arose in Protestant lands and only belatedly spread into Roman Catholic and Orthodox areas, though nonreligious factors such as the location of coal deposits help explain industrial origin and dispersal. Earlier, Roman Catholic persecution of French Calvinists (or *Huguenots*) and Protestant Flemings, including many skilled artisans, caused an emigration of these craftsmen to England, northern Germany, and Holland. The dominantly Protestant countries thereby gained a valuable industrial impetus, while the Catholic lands, particularly France, suffered a setback.

Given such attitudinal and cultural contrasts, it is not surprising that the Protestant/Catholic border, helping divide Europe into north and south, witnessed much strife over the centuries. The Thirty Years' War (1618–1648), a Protestant/Catholic contest for possession of the core of Europe, devastated large areas of Germany and the Czech Republic and caused enormous loss of life (look ahead to Figure 6.5). Two centuries earlier the Hussite war, a similar contest, also caused much grief. Most of the religious border has since fallen quiet, and the two groups learned to live in peace and mutual respect. Only in Northern

FIGURE 3.12 This Methodist chapel in the Lleyn Peninsula of Celtic Wales reflects the architectural simplicity preferred by British "free" churches and helps produce a very subdued religious landscape. (Photo by the author, 1974.)

Ireland, where the population is 52 percent Protestant and 42 percent Catholic, does the feud persist. An intrusive Protestant conquest and colonization occurred in Northern Ireland in the 1600s, followed by centuries of overlordship and attempted conversion by the Protestants. In recent decades, the province suffered from terrorist activity by extremists of both religious groups, with the result that Protestants and Catholics now live mainly apart in segregated neighborhoods (Figure 3.13).

Eastern Orthodoxy

As its name implies, **Eastern Orthodox** Christianity prevails in the eastern part of Europe, especially in Greece, most of the Balkans, Ukraine, Belarus, and Russia, as well as Georgia in the Caucasus (Figure 3.1). Perhaps about 130 million Europeans profess this faith, roughly 19 percent of the total population of the culture area (Table 3.1). The Patriarch of Constantinople, nominal leader of Orthodoxy, enjoys none of the central authority of the Roman papacy. Orthodoxy long ago splintered into an array of 13 national churches, most of

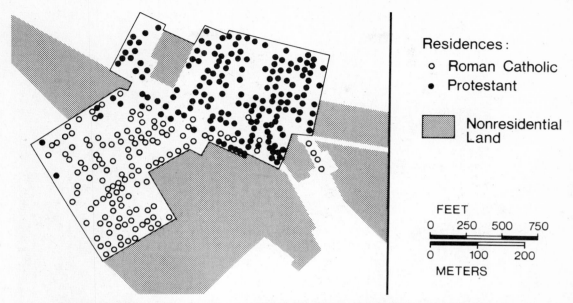

FIGURE 3.13 On the Protestant/Catholic divide, in Belfast, Northern Ireland.
Only here does strife continue on the great north/south religious border in Europe, with the result that people have become residentially segregated along denominational lines. This pattern, mapped in the late 1950s, persists today. (Source: After Boal 1969, 37.)

which survive today, including Greek, Serbian, Bulgarian, Romanian, Russian, Cypriot, Georgian, and Ukrainian Orthodoxy. The leadership at Constantinople, or Istanbul, was permanently weakened when this capital of eastern Christendom fell to the Turks in 1453. In the various Orthodox countries, the local patriarch of the national church often also served as the head of the government, firmly linking state and church.

Splintering occasionally extended still further. In Russia, the ultraconservative *Old Believers* separated from Orthodoxy in the late 1600s, and some 10 million followers lived in different parts of Russia by 1910. Today, only about 70,000 remain, centered in Belarus, Latvia, Lithuania, and Russia, though a revival appears to be underway. Another conservative splinter group, the *Molokans*, dating from the 1700s, once had 1,200,000 followers, and today surviving parishes can be found in the Caucasus, south Russia, Ukraine, and Moldova.

The Orthodox religious landscape shares with that of Catholicism a beauty and vividness, while at the same time being both highly distinctive and regionally varied. Balkan church buildings, borrowing from the colorful and decorative Byzantine architectural style of the Greek south, attract the eye with abundant reds and yellows (Figure 3.14). Russian churches and monasteries display their own style, often built in wood with onion towers (Figure 3.15).

The Orthodox church today is experiencing a revival in the Slavic north, after seven decades of governmental oppression. Churches and monasteries reopen while leaders seek to provide enough clergy. In Russia, the Orthodox Church

FIGURE 3.14 Greek Orthodoxy in the cultural landscape of Kriti (Crete). Compare this religious landscape found in the southernmost extremity of Europe with that in Figure 3.10 at the opposite territorial end of the culture area. (Photo by the author, 1971).

FIGURE 3.15 A Russian Orthodox religious landscape, on Kizhi Island in Lake Onezh (Onega), Karelian Republic. The spectacular churches are built of notched logs. (Photo by the author, 1992.)

may well become a major element of the rising Russian nationalism. Religiously, most of Eastern Europe is presently in a state of flux.

Uniate and Armenian Churches

A fourth, minor division of European Christianity consists of the **Uniate** Church, centered in western Ukraine and adjacent parts of Romania, Slovakia, Hungary, and Poland. Also referred to as "Greek Catholic" or "Ukrainian Catholic," this church claims about 6 million adherents. The Uniate Church derives from the long former Polish rule of the area, when Catholic Poles demanded that the local Orthodox population acknowledge the authority and supremacy of the Roman pope. Beneath that façade of Catholicism, the church retained most Orthodox rites and practices, such as a married priesthood. When Polish rule ended, the Uniate Christians suffered persecution by czarist Orthodoxy and, later, Communists. Many outsiders believed the Uniate Church in Ukraine to be dead, but when freedom of religion was restored in 1990, the church reemerged vigorously in the western part of the country, becoming one statement of Ukrainian identity. Some 2000 parishes reopened, and Orthodoxy found itself challenged in western Ukraine. The future of the revitalized Uniate Church seems secure.

The **Armenian** Church, while regarded as a branch of Eastern Christianity, is independent of Orthodoxy and never acknowledged the supremacy of Constantinople. This ethnic church, with perhaps 1.5 million adherents, is one of the oldest branches of Christendom and today survives in refuge in independent Armenia, the embattled southeasternmost outpost of Europe and Christianity.

Dechristianization

A substantial part of the European population, about 27 percent, has become secularized (Table 3.1). These people, some 190 million in all, usually claim atheism or agnosticism. If affiliated with churches, they declare themselves "unreligious" in surveys. The geographical pattern of **dechristianization** appears quite uneven (Figure 3.16) and difficult to generalize. The most disaffected areas, where over half of the population is secularized, lie in the north and east, with notable outliers in eastern Germany, Čechy (Bohemia), parts of Hungary, the Netherlands, and Mediterranean France. By contrast, refuge regions of surviving Christian vitality include a belt from Poland through western Ukraine to Romania, nearly all of Greece, southern Italy, western Iberia, the Irish west, and an area overlapping parts of the Alps and the Po-Veneto Plain.

The decades-long persecution of the church under Communist regimes clearly helps explain the pattern, though it does not address the issue of how or why Polish Catholicism, Romanian Orthodoxy, or the Ukrainian Uniate Church so successfully resisted that oppression. Arguably, the far north never became thoroughly Christianized, lying remote from the centers of church authority. Of the

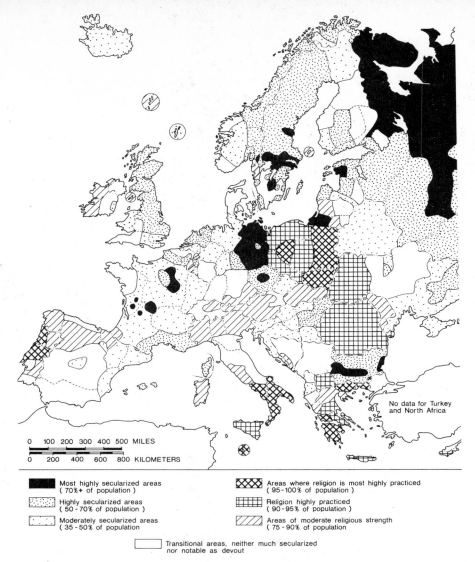

Legend:

- Most highly secularized areas (70%+ of population)
- Highly secularized areas (50-70% of population)
- Moderately secularized areas (35-50% of population)
- Areas where religion is most highly practiced (95-100% of population)
- Religion highly practiced (90-95% of population)
- Areas of moderate religious strength (75-90% of population)
- Transitional areas, neither much secularized nor notable as devout

No data for Turkey and North Africa

0 100 200 300 400 500 MILES
0 200 400 600 800 KILOMETERS

FIGURE 3.16 Secularization and religious vitality in Europe. *Secular* is defined as some combination of the responses "atheist," "agnostic," "unreligious," "no religious faith," and "never attend church." The belt of greatest Christian vitality stretches from the Baltic to the Black Sea through Poland, Lithuania, Slovakia, western Ukraine, Romania, and Moldova. Other Christian refuges include the Greek lands, southern Italy, and western Iberia. The Protestant north and Orthodox east reveal the highest levels of secularization. (Sources: Based principally upon *Eurobarometer*, unpublished public-opinion survey carried out in both Western and Eastern Europe by Gallup Poll Social Survey for the Commission of the European Communities in 1991/1992; as well as upon Catholic News Service, unpublished "Religious Beliefs and Practices in Twelve Countries [1991]," Washington, USA, released June 10, 1993; unpublished survey conducted in UKR, 1992, by Media & Opinion Research Dept. of Radio Free Europe/Radio Liberty Research Institute, Washington, USA; Gustafsson, 145; Boulard, 48, 79, folded map at end; Gay, 264–265, 273; Duocastella, 281–282; Knudsen, 7; David B. Barrett, ed., *World Christian Encyclopedia*, New York, USA: Oxford University Press, 1982; Ferdinand Mayer, ed., *Diercke Weltatlas*, Braunschweig, D: Georg Westermann, 1974, 95; Nolan and Nolan, 1989, 31–32.)

three main divisions of Christianity, Catholicism has clearly resisted secularization most successfully, while Protestantism has suffered the greatest losses. In formerly Lutheran-dominated Latvia, only 7.5 percent of the people today claim to be practicing Protestants, while in the United Kingdom, almost half the adult population never attends church.

Some apparent dechristianization may, instead, be reaction against the established churches, particularly since these groups often have status as official state churches and are supported by tax revenues. The success of the neo-Protestant movement suggests as much. It works the other way, too. Some professed devotion to the church could be the reaction to governmental suppression, as in Poland. For these reasons, a better measure of secularization might be the proportion of the population that believes the Christian Easter promise of eternal life (Table 3.2). By this measure, Greece and Poland appear far less religious, as do Denmark and Slovenia. Major regional differences still remain evident. Of interest

TABLE 3.2   Christian Belief in Selected European Countries

	Percent expressing belief in life after death			
	1948	1968	1981	1991
Dominantly Catholic countries				
Belgium	—	—	37	—
France	58	35	35	—
Ireland	—	—	76	80
Italy	—	—	47	66
Poland	—	—	—	61
Slovenia	—	—	—	33
Spain	—	—	55	—
Dominantly Protestant countries				
Denmark	—	—	26	—
Finland	69	55	49	—
Great Britain[a]	49	38	45	51
Norway	71	54	44	60
Sweden	49	38	—	—
Mixed Catholic/Protestant countries				
Germany, western	—	41	39	53
Hungary	—	—	—	26
Netherlands	68	50	42	53
Northern Ireland	—	—	72	78
Predominantly Orthodox country				
Greece	—	57	—	—

[a] Excluding Northern Ireland.
Sources: *The Gallup Report,* for release Thursday, December 26, 1968, published by the American Institute of Public Opinion; *PRRC Emerging Trends,* published by the Princeton Religious Research Center, 7:6 (June 1985), and 7:7 (Sept. 1985), using data collected by the Gallup International Research Institutes for the Center for Applied Research in the Apostolate and European Value System Study Group; Catholic News Service, Washington, USA, "Religious Beliefs and Practices in Twelve Countries," unpublished news release, June 10, 1993.

is the upward swing of belief suggested by comparison of the 1991 responses with those of a decade earlier.

Though many Europeans hold secular views, the influence of a Christian heritage still permeates the culture of Europe. An entire mindset, a way of thinking and viewing the world, was shaped by Christianity. That cornerstone of the culture area will persist as long as Europe exists. The two are inseparable. True, some say that secularized Europe lives on "old capital" inherited from Christianity and therefore represents a culture in decline, its basic institutions supported only by inertia, but others counter that agnostic intellectual freedom, unfettered by religious dogma, represents the logical culmination of the European experiment in individualism.

Non-Christian Minorities

The diffusion of Christianity through Europe proved almost complete, leaving virtually nothing in the way of a religious residue. Today, the only substantial non-Christian presence is intrusive and consists of Muslims, or **Islamic** peoples. For the past 1200 years, the southern and southeastern borders of the European culture area have coincided with the Christian/Muslim religious divide, a boundary that has shifted back and forth amid frequent warfare (Figure 3.1). In modern times, the border has taken on a First World/Third World meaning. Christianity in the Eastern Hemisphere correlates geographically with Europe, prosperity, and high living standards, while Islam connotes non-Europe, the "other," widespread poverty, and increasing resistance to dominance by Europeans. A much higher birth rate in most Islamic areas provides an additional basis for continuing culture conflict.

As is true of nearly every cultural border, the Christian/Islamic line is in many areas not a sharp one. Only Gibraltar offers a clear-cut division, achieved by systematic ethnic cleansing centuries ago. In fact, some 16 million Muslims reside in modern Europe. Most of these live in ancient ancestral homelands, including the *Bosnians* (Muslim Slavs of the Dinaric region); *Pomaks* (Muslim Slavs of Bulgaria and Macedonia); *Albanians*; *Turks*; assorted minorities living in the Caucasus, in particular the *Abkhazis* and *Adzhars* of Georgia and the *Chechens* and *Ingushis* of south Russia; and various Turkic groups, such as the *Tatars*, living on the margins of the East European Plain (Figure 3.17).

Many other Muslims, at least 6 million in all, are recent immigrants to Europe, particularly from Turkey, North Africa, and Pakistan. France, with 2.5 or 3 million such immigrants, largely Arabs, and Germany with 1.7 million, mainly Turks, house the largest populations. The almost instinctive European reaction to such minorities is prejudice, hatred, or worse. A French politician recently spoke of "the smell of Islam" permeating certain urban neighborhoods in his country. Clearly, many Europeans view Muslims as a threat to their cultural identity. The Medieval bigotry and hostility persist. Muslims cannot, given this bias, be Europeans.

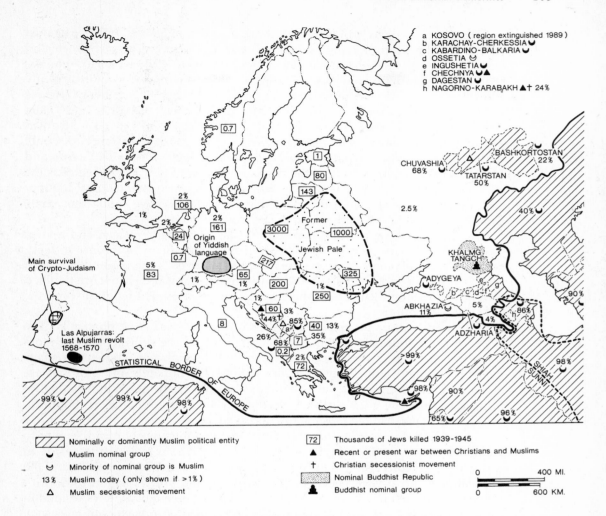

a KOSOVO (region extinguished 1989)
b KARACHAY-CHERKESSIA ☾
c KABARDINO-BALKARIA ☾
d OSSETIA ☾
e INGUSHETIA ☾
f CHECHNYA ☾▲
g DAGESTAN ☾
h NAGORNO-KARABAKH ▲† 24%

FIGURE 3.17 The non-Christian periphery and former Jewish diaspora. Islam and Judaism both present Europe with a perceived challenge to the very essence of its culture. Both minorities have been handled harshly. Within YU, separate Muslim data are shown for Kosovo and Crna Gora; the figure shown in YU is for the remainder of Serbia, including Vojvodina. The Jewish element has been diminished by 73% since 1939 by genocide and emigration. The Jewish dead total shown on the border of UKR and BY is the Soviet Union total, less EW, LT, LR, and MD. Of this total, about 625,000 occurred in UKR. (Sources: Cecil Roth, *A History of the Marranos*, New York, USA: Hermon Press, 4th ed., 1974, 368–373; Robert D. King, "Migration and Linguistics as Illustrated by Yiddish," in *Reconstructing Languages and Cultures*, ed. Edgar C. Polomé and Werner Winter, Berlin, D: de Gruyter, 1992, 419–439.)

Hostility is directed not just toward the Islamic immigrants, but also against certain Muslim peoples living in their ancestral homelands. Catholic Croats and Orthodox Serbs battered Bosnian enclaves in the 1990s with a ferocity reminiscent of the Crusades. On Europe's southern cultural frontier, Armenians recently warred against Muslim Azeris; Georgians against Abkhazis; and Greek Cypriots against Turkish Cypriots (Figure 3.17). Muslim Chechens, Ingushis, and Tatars defy Russian rule today. Yugoslavia would like to cleanse Kosovo of Albanian Muslims, and Bulgaria, as recently as 1989, expelled 350,000 Muslim Turks, only perhaps half of whom later returned. Tensions between Orthodox Greece and Muslim Turkey never relax, and the two countries went to war as recently as the 1920s. Clearly, Islam simultaneously gives focus to European cultural identity and, in the European mind, threatens that very identity. We should not, then, expect an early entry of Turkey into the European Union.

Contrary to some popular perception, Islamic fundamentalism and revival have generally not caught hold among most European Muslims. Indeed, Bosnians and Albanians had become rather secularized, even before the advent of Communism in the 1940s. We often witness, improbably, dechristianized Europeans battling secularized Muslims. Ethnicity succeeded religiosity and the old struggle continues.

Islam announces its presence in the cultural landscape emphatically. The minarets of mosques pierce the sky as aggressively as the spires of Christendom (Figure 3.18). One does not "need a program to tell the players." When Christians overrun and ethnically cleanse Muslim regions, the minarets and mosques are either quickly destroyed, as in Bosnia, or else converted into churches (Figure 3.19). Likewise, the great Orthodox cathedral of Constantinople, St. Sophia's, became a minaret-flanked mosque in Turkish Istanbul.

The other sizable religious minority in Europe consists of adherents to **Judaism,** today numbering about 2.6 million, of whom over a fifth reside in Ukraine. As recently as 1939, Europe was the principal Jewish homeland and the population stood at 9,500,000, about 60 percent of the world total. In 1880, prior to the great Jewish migration to America, about 90 percent of all Jews resided in Europe. Not only was Europe the principal homeland of Judaism, but Jews such as Albert Einstein, Felix Mendelssohn, Benjamin Disraeli, Sigmund Freud, and Heinrich Heine had contributed greatly to the development of European history and civilization.

Jews reached Mediterranean Europe in Roman times, after their forced dispersal from Palestine. One major early concentration developed in Muslim Arabic Iberia, where Judaism won toleration, flourished, and eventually claimed perhaps as much as one-fifth of the total population. These Iberian Jews, or *Sephardim,* later faced eviction or forcible conversion to Roman Catholicism after the Christian reconquest, leaving behind only "secret Jews" (*Marranos*), and empty *judarias* (ghettoes). Their fine synagogues became churches. To the present day, in certain mountain towns of northern Portugal, Marranos still practice Jewish ritual while outwardly adhering to Roman Catholicism (Figure 3.17). Many Sephardic Jews fled Iberia and found new homes, particularly in Protestant countries such as Britain and the Netherlands. Another major Jewish

FIGURE 3.18 A Village mosque and minaret amid the ripened wheat fields of Rodos (Rhodes) announce the presence of the Muslim minority on this Greek Aegean island. Rodos is one of the few European areas where Christians and Muslims co-exist peacefully. (Photo by the author, 1971.)

concentration developed in medieval times in western and southern Germany, where the German-derived *Yiddish* ("Jewish") language originated. These became the *Ashkenazim*, the second major division of European Jewry. In the late Middle Ages, Ashkenazic Jews, responding to an edict of tolerance and invitation to settle by the Kingdom of Poland, began the migration that created the great concentration in eastern Europe. This second refuge, the *Jewish Pale* (Figure 3.17), fell victim to the Nazi genocide.

Everywhere in Europe the vestigial Jewish identity is perishing. It will play little if any role in twenty-first-century Europe. In the final analysis, the pervasive Christian identity and heritage of Europe prevented enduring toleration of this small, creative religious minority. Any self-claim of Europe's cultural superiority, and these are not hard to find, must always be measured against the treatment Europeans have afforded religious minorities over the centuries and down to the present day.

FIGURE 3.19 The Giralda, a tower on the Roman Catholic cathedral at Sevilla (Seville) in southern Spain, was originally the minaret of the Great Mosque when the city was Arabic and Muslim. After the reconquest and forced expulsion or conversion of the Muslims, victorious Christians added the bell chamber to the top. In this manner, a Muslim element was retained in the religious landscape. (Photo by the author, 1986.)

Christianity, then, is the essential feature of European culture. Even in an age of secularism and science, a Christian heritage still identifies Europe and all it represents. Still, there is more to understanding the distinctiveness of Europe than religious faith. Language provides the second key trait, and the following chapter, accordingly, is devoted to geolinguistics.

Sources and Suggested Readings

James Anderson. "Regions and Religions in Ireland: A Short Critique of the Two Nations Theory." *Antipode.* 11 (1980), 44–53.

Yoram Bar-Gal. "The Shtetl—the Jewish Small Town in Eastern Europe." *Journal of Cultural Geography.* 5:2 (1985), 17–29.

H. Bleibrunner. "Der Einfluss der Kirche auf die niederbairische Kulturlandschaft." *Mitteilungen der Geographischen Gesellschaft in München.* 36 (1951), 7–196.

directions as the population of farmers grew and more fields and pastures were needed. They began to lose contact with each other as they dispersed, and *linguistic drift*—the gradual change of language generation after generation in the absence of a standard written form—caused their speech to diverge. Also, they encountered and absorbed indigenous hunter-gatherers who spoke different languages, and in the process some words and pronunciations were borrowed.

TABLE 4.1   Comparative Vocabularies of Selected Indo-European and Non-Indo-European Languages

Language family	Division	Group	Language	Word meaning "three"	Word meaning "mother"
Indo-European	Western	Hellenic	Greek	tría[a]	mitéra[a]
"	"	Celtic	Erse	tri	mathair
"	"	Romance	Latin	tres	mater
"	"	Romance	Italian	tre	madre
"	"	Romance	Spanish	tres	madre
"	"	Romance	French	trois	mère
"	"	Romance	Romanian	trei	mama
"	"	Germanic	English	three	mother
"	"	Germanic	German	drei	mutter
"	"	Germanic	Swedish	tre	moder
"	"	Germanic	Icelandic	thrír	módir
Indo-European	Eastern	Thracian	Albanian	tre	motrë
"	"	Slavic	Russian	tri[a]	maht[a]
"	"	Slavic	Czech	tri	matka
"	"	Slavic	Polish	trzy	matka
"	"	Slavic	Serbo-Croatian	tri	mati
"	"	Baltic	Lithuanian	trys	motyna
Uralic	Finnic	Northwest	Finnish	kolme	äiti
"	Ugrian	—	Hungarian	három	anya
Altaic	Southwest	Turkic	Turkish	uç	anne
Afro-Asiatic	—	Semitic	Maltese	tlieta	omm
Caucasic	Southern	—	Georgian	sami	déda
Euskara	—	—	Basque	iru	ama

[a] Transliterated from non-Latin alphabet.

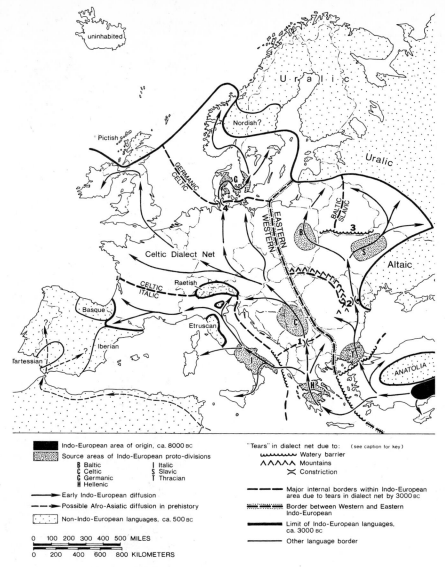

FIGURE 4.2 Origin, diffusion, and fragmentation of the Indo-European languages. 8000 to 3000 B.C.: a geographical speculation. The dialect net was "torn" whenever the advancing Indo-European farmers split around an obstacle, losing contact with their former neighbors. Such tears soon produced separate languages, due to linguistic drift in isolation. It is possible that other, now extinct Indo-European groups developed in southern France and the British Isles, due to the Alpine and English Channel obstacles. The prehistoric diffusion of Afro-Asiatic-speaking farmers into Iberia is speculative. Indeed, the entire map is speculative. Residual non–Indo-European speakers survived best in border areas between languages and in harsh environments marginally suited to agriculture. Key to nonobvious obstacles: **1** = Vardar-Morava rift valley; **2** = constriction between Carpathians and steppes; **3** = Pripyat Marsh; **4** = Jylland narrows, a wedge of good land between marshes and outwash plains on the west and the Schlei Fjord on the east. (Sources: Krantz; Renfrew 1988, 1989; with very substantial modifications.)

In these ways, Nostratic fragmented into: (1) Indo-European, on the northern farming frontier of Anatolia, part of modern Turkey (Figure 4.2); (2) the Afro-Asiatic language to the south, parent of the present Semitic and Hamitic tongues; and (3) the Dravidian languages to the east.

Indo-European Diffusion

In the formative stage of Indo-European speech in Anatolia, after about 8000 B.C., different dialects developed, due to continued linguistic drift and mixing with alien peoples. A *dialect net* took shape, a linguistic continuum in which the speakers of each dialect could understand the neighboring ones but not those spoken farther away in regions with which they had no regular contact. Further fragmentation into separate, mutually unintelligible *languages,* in which adjacent Indo-European peoples could not understand each other, seems to have occurred whenever the dialect net was "torn." That likely happened where the farming frontier, spreading slowly west and north from Anatolia, encountered physical geographical obstacles. Indo-Europeans must have branched around these obstacles, some going one way and some the other. When that occurred, the two groups lost contact with each other for centuries and their speech drifted apart. Generations later, when they coalesced beyond the obstacle, they could not understand each other.

The first such tear, a profound one, apparently occurred about 6000 B.C. when one branch of the Indo-Europeans spread westward from Anatolia into the Aegean isles and beyond, onto the Greek mainland, while the other went north to the Bosporos and Dardanelles (Figure 4.2). This Aegean tear seems to have produced the divide between **Western** and **Eastern** (formerly called *Centum* and *Satem*) Indo-European, a divide that would later extend all the way to the Baltic Sea, for when the two branches met again to the north in the Balkans, their speech had drifted too far apart to be understood.

Fragmentation continued. The Eastern branch divided at the crossing of the Bosporos-Dardanelles, perhaps about 5500 B.C., with *Thracian* developing on the European side of the straits, distinct from its Anatolian parent. To the north, a second division occurred when some agriculturists crossed over the narrows of the steppe grasslands and entered the East European Plain. They apparently became the ancestral Balto-Slavs. In their continued northward thrust, they must have divided around the Pripyat Marsh, separating the *Baltic* and *Slavic* languages. The Slavs drove east and north, populating a wedge between the 120-day growing season on the north and the steppes to the south, pushing agriculture as far as the prehistoric technology would allow and providing, in the short run at least, a satisfactory eastern border for "Europe" (Figure 4.2).

Equally profound tears in the dialect net happened at obstacles in the west. From Greece, where *Hellenic* speech had developed, some Indo-Europeans migrated about 5500 B.C. across the Strait of Otranto to Italy, giving rise to the *Italic*-speaking group, while others pressed north about the same time through the Vardar-Morava rift valley, a narrows that restricted contact with the Hellenes to the south. Emerging into the Hungarian Basin, they became the proto-*Celtic* people. Much later, this group divided again, when some went north into Scandinavia by way of the Jylland peninsula of modern Denmark, crossing the infertile outwash plain and following a narrow strip of fertile land along the fjorded east coast of Jylland (Figure 4.2). Those venturing north along this route after about 3500 B.C. apparently became the *Germanic* peoples.

What happened in Iberia remains even less clear. The substantial survival of non–Indo-European languages there into historic times suggests a different linguistic order prevailed. Perhaps Afro-Asiatic farmers had spread from the Fertile Crescent across North Africa, entered Iberia at Gibraltar, and continued northward until they met their fellow agriculturists, the Indo-Europeans, somewhere near the Pyrenees or in the Ebro Valley (Figure 4.2). If so, "Africa begins at the Pyrenees" describes an ancient condition, and the now extinct Tartessian and Iberian tongues were Afro-Asiatic. Basque, apparently unrelated to either Indo-European or Afro-Asiatic, can perhaps best be viewed as an indigenous tongue that survived along the contact zone of the two immigrant farming peoples.

A comparison of the diffusion of the Indo-European languages with that of Christianity reveals similarities as well as differences. Both of these cultural traits, so essential in shaping and defining Europe, arose in very nearly the same place in the Near East, well outside the present limits of the European culture area. Both spread from southeast to northwest, reaching Europe by way of the Aegean lands, and both split into eastern, western, and northern divisions. Indeed, the patterning is strikingly similar. Catholicism prevails in the Romance language region, Protestantism in the Germanic areas, and Orthodoxy in the Slavic lands, though exceptions to this generalization abound. Both religiously and linguistically, then, Europe falls into three major, spatially correlated components.

The two diffusions also differed in fundamental ways. Spread of Indo-European occurred much earlier, in prehistoric times. It proceeded wavelike instead of hierarchically from city to city and took far longer to complete—over 5000 years for Indo-European and just over a millennium for Christianity. Too, the Christian diffusion left essentially no indigenous survivors and no religious equivalents of the Uralic or Basque speakers. Both diffusions demonstrate that in Europe we deal, to a considerable extent, with an imported rather than a native culture.

Many geolinguistic changes have occurred in Europe since 3000 B.C. when the Indo-European diffusion had largely run its course, though some features have displayed remarkable durability, such as the western/eastern divide and the tenacious survival of indigenous Basque and Uralic minorities. One notable change has been the continued tearing of the several dialect nets to form more and more languages. Over 90 percent of all Europeans are accounted for by three Indo-European divisions—Germanic, Slavic, and Romance, but each of these now contains multiple languages (Figure 4.1).

Romance Languages

The **Romance** languages, western Indo-European in affiliation and forming one of three major divisions of the family, today claim about 186 million speakers in Europe, roughly one-fourth of the total population. Romance languages derive from the ancient Italic division of Indo-European (Figure 4.2). One Italic tongue, *Latin*, originally spoken only in the district of Lazio (Latium) around Roma, rose to dominance and achieved a remarkable dispersal. When a language successfully expands in this manner, its speakers possess some cultural/technological advantage. In the case of Latin speakers, this advantage came in the form of superior political organization, which permitted empire building. Latin, of course, was the language of the Roman Empire. It spread with Roman victories, slowly at first, for the conquest of Italy alone required two centuries. About A.D. 100 the Roman Empire, and with it Latin, reached its greatest territorial extent, and the Romance tongue was heard on the banks of the Thames, Rhine, and Danube, as well as in North Africa. Few of the cultural groups ruled by the empire resisted linguistic assimilation, though the Greeks did because of their high culture. In fact, many Greek words found their way into Latin. The *Etruscans*, a highly civilized non–Indo-European group living just north of Roma, succumbed linguistically to Latin, but not before giving it the parent words for "people," "public," "military," "autumn," and other vocabulary that later passed from Romance into English speech. In Iberia, the Romans likely achieved the decisive introduction of Indo-European, wresting it away from the Afro-Asiatic peoples and a scattering of Celts. Indeed, the Celts fared poorly against Latin almost everywhere, especially in Gaul ("Celt's land"), which is modern France.

When the Empire collapsed, the Romance languages retreated but survived remarkably well. Germanic invaders brought their own language to Britain, the west bank of the Rhine, and the Alps, while Slavs and Magyars surged into the Balkans, leaving a lonely linguistic outpost in Romania as a reminder of the former eastern greatness of the Romans (Figure 4.1). In these forfeited areas, only place names survive today as remnants of the Latin tongue. In England for example, *-caster* and *-chester* suffixes, as in Lancaster or Manchester, derive from *castra*, Latin for "military camp." Later, when the Moors invaded Iberia beginning in the 700s, the Afro-Asiatic languages, especially Arabic, regained a foothold there, though the Latin-derived *Mozarabic* tongue survived as the language of Christians under Moorish rule. The subsequent defeat of the Moors by the Spaniards and Portuguese reclaimed nearly all of Iberia for the Romance languages and completely extinguished Arabic. Only abundant place names survive as reminders of the former Arabic presence (Figure 4.3).

The collapse of the Roman Empire accelerated the fragmentation of Latin into many separate languages. Mozarabic, now like Latin extinct, was only one of these. All of the surviving Romance tongues in modern Europe represent the fragmented legacy of Latin. Today the Iberian peninsula is home to three of these languages. Dominating the nation of Spain from the Meseta interior is *Castilian Spanish*, spoken by some 25 million people. Speakers of the *Catalan* language, numbering 9 million and found in the eastern coastal fringe of Spain, the Baleares (Balearic) Islands, a tiny corner of southern France, Andorra, and a foothold on Sardegna, preserved their speech against the inroads of politically more powerful groups (Figure 4.4). Even France, which historically extended few rights and privileges to linguistic minorities, now permits bilingual French-Catalan roadsigns in its southern region, where Catalan is spoken. The Atlantic front of Iberia is home to *Portuguese/Gallegan*, a dialect net with some 12 million

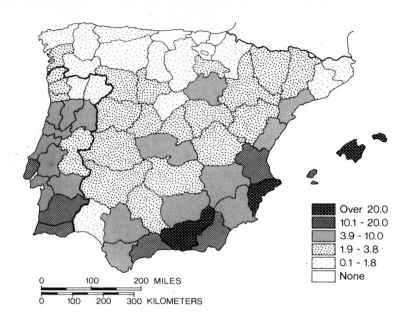

FIGURE **4.3 Number of Arabic and Arabized topographic names** per thousand sq km (386 sq. km.) in Iberia. "Africa begins at the Pyrenees," according to a French saying, and a thousand years ago, that was almost literally true. Arabic and the Islamic faith had pushed European culture northward, almost to the Pyrenees. The subsequent Indo-European–Christian reconquest of Iberia left behind, as a reminder, many place names derived from the Arabic tongue. (Source: After Lautensach.)

speakers. The survival of Portuguese seems guaranteed by political independence, and Gallegan has so far withstood the same Castilian pressure as Catalan within the Spanish nation.

Northward from Iberia, beyond the Pyrenees, is found *French,* the speech of the large majority of France's population as well as of the southern Belgians, or Walloons, the western Swiss, and residents of the Valle d'Aosta in northwest Italy, a total of some 54 million persons. The southern of two principal French tongues, *langue d'oc* (or Occitan), gives way to *langue d'oïl,* originally found only in the Parisian north. *Italian,* with more speakers than French, some 60 million, is spoken not only in Italy but also on the island of Corsica, which belongs to France, Canton Ticino in southern Switzerland, and the Nice district on the French Riviera. The Tuscan dialect has become standard Italian speech, a heritage of the cultural greatness of Firenze. Italian has the third largest (after Russian and German) number of speakers among the languages of Europe (Table 4.2).

Along the northern fringe of Romance speech, sheltered in Alpine valleys, are found several minor, dying tongues—*Romansh* in eastern Switzerland, *Ladinic* in Italian South Tirol, and *Friuli* in the easternmost end of the Po-Veneto Plain. Collectively, these three constitute the Raeto-Romanic group. *Sardegnan,* with about 1,600,000 speakers, survives on a Mediterranean island and is distinct from Italian.

FIGURE 4.4 Bilingual Castilian-Catalan sign announcing highway work in northern Catalunya (Catalonia), Spain. The sign illustrates both the difference between the two languages and the central government's acknowledgment of the cultural rights of Catalan speakers. On many such signs in Catalunya, the Castilian version has been defaced. (Photo by the author, 1986.)

Romanian represents an eastern outlier of the Romance languages, separated from the larger western area by the interposed South Slavs. This language, spoken by 24 million persons in Romania and adjacent Moldova, has survived in spite of invasions by Slavs, Magyars, and other groups, though the vocabulary is infiltrated with Slavic words. Closely related to Romanian is *Vlakh*, presumably derived from Valachia (Wallachia) in southern Romania but today spoken by a few nomadic herding tribes in interior northern Greece and adjacent countries. The Vlakhs apparently descend from Romanians who migrated southward after the collapse of the Roman Empire to find refuge in the Dinaric-Pindhos mountain region. Still today the crude shelters of the Vlakh nomads may be seen at the foot of Mount Ólimbos (Olympus) in Greece and elsewhere.

The northern border of the Romance languages today, stretching from the English Channel to the head of the Adriatic Sea (Figure 4.1), displays a diverse character that relates to physical geography. Generally, where the border crosses plains, as in Vlaanderen and the upper Rhône Valley of Switzerland, it tends to be unstable and mobile. French advances against Dutch in the former and retreats before German in the latter. But where the language border follows ridges, as in the St. Gotthard Pass region in the western Alps, it has remained unchanged for more than a thousand years. To cross St. Gotthard going north

TABLE 4.2   Languages with 10 Million or More Speakers in Europe

Languages	Millions of Speakers	As a Percentage of Europe's Population
Russian (Great Russian)	100[a]	14
German	90	13
Italian	60	9
English	59	8
French	54	8
Ukrainian	42	6
Polish	35	5
Spanish	25	4
Romanian	24	3
Dutch/Flemish	20	3
Scandinavian[b]	18	3
Serbo-Croatian	14	2
Czech/Slovak	14	2
Hungarian	13	2
Portuguese/Gallegan	12	2
Bulgarian/Macedonian	11	2
Greek	10	1

[a] Eurorussia only.
[b] Danish, Norwegian, Swedish.

today, as in the Dark Ages, is to leave Romance speech and enter the Germanic lands.

Germanic Languages

The second of the three major Indo-European groups, also belonging to the western division of the family, consists of the **Germanic** languages, with about 190 million speakers in Europe, almost exactly the size of the Romance population. One of every four Europeans speaks a Germanic language, and these tongues dominate most of Northern and Central Europe (Figure 4.1).

Geographical development of the Germanic languages over the past 5,000 years has been volatile. The Germanic branch probably arose, as described earlier, in the isolation of Jylland (Figure 4.2), and from there it spread through the Danish isles and into Scandinavia, absorbing a non–Indo-European coastal race of hunters and fishers, a tall, blond people skilled in longboat building and sometimes referred to as *Nordish*. From them the early Germanic people apparently adopted a sizable vocabulary, with the result that perhaps a quarter or even a third of all Germanic words today are not Indo-European in origin. *Bear* provides an example. The Germanic speakers, in the process, also took on many of the tall, blond racial traits of the indigenous hunter-fishers, as well as their seagoing abilities. In the colder conditions of the north, their grain crops developed into faster-maturing varieties to accommodate the shorter growing season, but the Germanic advance apparently halted at about the northern limits of the humid continental and marine west coast climates (Figures 2.7, 4.2).

There, in the north, the Germanic people remained for millennia on the outer margins of the agricultural, Indo-European world. Then, about 500 B.C., the climate of Scandinavia became colder, in a deterioration that continued to the beginning of the Christian era. Their response was remarkable. If we are to believe the archaeological record, most Germanic people evacuated the north, boarding longboats and crossing the seas to resettle in the river valleys of northern Germany. These valleys, due to a pattern of springtime flooding which delayed planting and effectively shortened the growing season, had apparently remained largely uncolonized by the resident Celtic Indo-Europeans. The Germanic folk, with their fast-ripening grains, could occupy this riverine environment. Their southward advance continued, eventually displacing the Celts from Germany, leaving behind only a scattering of Celtic place names such as *Alp* ("mountain"), *Halle* ("salt"), and *Rhine* ("river"). With the collapse of the Roman Empire, Germanic tribes such as the Franks, Goths, Burgundians, and Lombards pressed far into Romance territory but usually failed to achieve a permanent implantation of their languages.

Elsewhere, the Germanic longboat invasions continued, bringing Anglo-Saxons to England and, after warmer climatic conditions resumed, accomplishing much agricultural recolonization in Scandinavia. From there, Viking longboats eventually reached the Faeroes, Iceland, and Greenland. For 1500 years, Germanic longboats had assisted the dispersal of these peoples.

In Central Europe, about A.D. 700, the Germans developed an innovative, more intensive form of agriculture known as the *three-field system* (see Chapter 8) and an effective system of organized government, the *feudal system.* Armed with those new technologies, they began expanding east at the expense of the Slavic peoples about A.D. 800, pushing the German language frontier well into present Poland and also eventually creating the eastern diaspora of Germans that recently returned home. Only a residue of Slavic place names survived in some parts of the North German Plain and Danube Valley as reminders of their former presence (Figure 4.5).

The single most important Germanic language, both in terms of the population of speakers and the number of countries where it serves as mother tongue, is *German.* About 90 million people speak this language, including majorities not just in Germany, but also in Austria, Switzerland, Liechtenstein, and Luxembourg. In addition, German-speaking provinces can be found in Italy (South Tirol, or Aldo-Adige), eastern Belgium, and France (Alsace). Until very recently, large German minorities remained in many Eastern European countries, especially Russia, Hungary, Romania, and Poland, though all of these groups have been greatly depleted by recent *return migration* to Germany after an absence of centuries. During the 6-year span from 1986 through 1992, over 1.5 million ethnic Germans departed Eastern Europe, including the former Soviet Union, and went to Germany, where automatic citizenship awaited them. Romania's German minority dwindled from 360,000 in 1977 to only 50,000 by

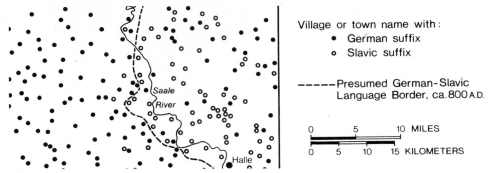

FIGURE 4.5 An archaic language border in Germany. About the year A.D. 800, the Germanic-Slavic boundary in central Europe lay roughly along the line of the Elbe and Saale rivers. German-speaking settlers, in the 800–1300 period, surged eastward across this border, changing the linguistic pattern as they carried their speech far into Slavic territory. But even today, evidence of the old border of A.D. 800 remains in the form of Slavic place names. Villages with name suffixes such as *-itz, -in,* and *-zig* are of Slavic origin. Europe abounds with such archaic linguistic features.

1992. At border crossings leading into Germany's Bayern province, busloads of Romanian Germans, or *Siebenbürger-Sachsen,* still arrived in the spring of 1993. The German diaspora in eastern Europe has, for all practical purposes, ceased to exist in the course of the past decade, though many remain in Russia.

In spite of the multinational distribution of German, a standardized form based on Luther's Bible translation is now spoken throughout the German language region. However, some dialects survive, in effect as second languages, in some areas. Taken out of the context of the former German dialect net of Low, Middle, and High German (Figure 4.1), these have now become proper languages, unintelligible to other speakers of standard German. Most notable are *Letzeburgish,* which is gaining increased usage in Luxembourg; *Alsatian,* the declining German dialect of eastern France; and *Swiss-German,* spoken as a second language by most citizens of Switzerland. Both Letzeburgish and Swiss-German serve to support nationalistic sentiment.

Dutch, spoken by 20 million in the Netherlands, northern Belgium, and extreme northern France, also developed as a separate language out of the former German dialect net in the Low German region but with the difference that its speakers never adopted standard German. Also derived from Low German is the *Frisian* language, spoken by about 300,000 people, mainly in the northeastern Netherlands.

English, the closest Germanic relative of Frisian, also derives from Low German and is spoken by some 59 million persons in the United Kingdom, Ireland, and Gibraltar. As a result of the Norman-French conquest of England almost a thousand years ago, English absorbed a great many Romance words, totaling perhaps 30 percent of the present English vocabulary. This mixing of Germanic and Romance, with the resultant richness of vocabulary, provides the distinctiveness of English. Since World War II, English has become the *lingua franca*, or language of international contact, of the western half of Europe and may soon play that role throughout the culture area.

The northern part of the Germanic language region is dominated by the *Scandinavian* dialect net (Figure 4.1). The independent countries of that part of Europe would have us believe that separate Danish, Norwegian, and Swedish, languages exist, but in fact these are mutually intelligible dialects, even in the standard forms promoted by the three governments. For example, some 64 percent of Norwegians understand "all but a few words" of standard Swedish, and the same is true of 58 percent of all Danes concerning the *Bokmål* form of Norwegian, one of two government-recognized dialects in that country (Figure 4.1). In local areas along international borders within Scandinavia, mutual intelligibility is virtually universal. *Isoglosses,* or word boundaries, crisscross Scandinavia without regard to political borders. Only *Icelandic,* where the Scandinavian dialect net was "torn" by the intervening sea, is properly regarded as a separate language. The Scandinavian dialect net encompasses about 20 million speakers and Icelandic about 260,000. *Faeroese,* spoken in a small island group between Iceland and Norway, should perhaps also be regarded as a separate Scandinavian language, but long rule by Denmark has altered the local speech of these islands to the extent that Faeroese might best be regarded as part of the Scandinavian dialect net.

Slavic Languages

The third of the three major Indo-European divisions, and the largest, consists of the **Slavic** languages, which belong to the Eastern branch of the family. About 237 million people west of the Urals speak a Slavic language, over one-third of the population of Europe. Together, the Romance, Germanic, and Slavic divisions account for almost 9 of every 10 Europeans.

The origins of the Slavic languages probably lie somewhere on the margins of the Pripyat Marsh (Figure 4.2) in dim prehistory. The proto-Slavs, who called themselves Sorbs or Serbs, achieved the agricultural colonization of the central section of the East European Plain, wedged between alien peoples belonging to the Uralic and Altaic language families. Slavs might have remained a minor and peripheral linguistic group, had they not, about A.D. 200, invented a new type of curved-blade plow, equipped with a moldboard, that lifted the topsoil and turned it over. Mounted on wheels and pulled by multiple teams of oxen, this plow allowed for the first time the cultivation of heavy clay soils and greatly increased crop production. With this innovation they expanded west and south, entering the mollisol prairie regions. When the Roman Empire collapsed, they pushed deep into the Balkans.

The Slavic region is today separated into a large northern part and a much smaller southern area, divided by a corridor of non-Slavic languages (Figure 4.1). In the north, *Polish* claims about 35 million speakers, the *Czech/Slovakian* dialects net 14 million, and the *Russian* dialect net about 159 million from the Urals westward. Most sources recognize *Ukrainian* (Little Russian, 42 million speakers),

Belarussian (White Russian, 10 million), and *Great Russian* (107 million) as three separate languages, and they are now being promoted as such for nationalistic purposes, but in fact these three form a multi-ethnic Russian dialect net that encompasses virtually the entirety of the East European Plain. The Great Russian component, until recently strewn widely through the former Soviet Union, includes about 14 million persons in newly independent European countries. Another 10 million or so Russian speakers live in the former Soviet Central Asian republics, also now independent. By 1993 well over a million Russians had emigrated from Central Asia to Russia, and at least another 1.5 million reportedly planned to follow by 1996. Some 300,000 moved to Russia from Kazakhstan alone in 1994.

Stretching from the Adriatic to the Black Sea in the Balkan Peninsula, the southern Slavic languages fall into three groups: *Slovenian,* with 2 million speakers, the *Serbo-Croatian* dialect net with 14 million, and the *Bulgarian-Macedonian* dialect net with 11 million. Further complicating the pattern of Slavic languages is an alphabet divide, a fundamental cultural boundary in Europe that separates users of the Latin characters from those employing Greek or Greek-derived Cyrillic letters (Figure 4.1). This literary divide cuts right through the Slavic lands, both northern and southern.

Celtic Languages

All of the other Indo-European groups are small in population and peripheral in location. Most have experienced retreat and some face possible extinction. That is certainly true of the **Celtic** division of Western Indo-European. Today, the Celts cling to dying refuges in the hilly, cloudy, tattered periphery of northwestern-most Europe (Figures 4.1, 4.6). *Welsh,* one of the surviving Celtic tongues, retains about 500,000 speakers in the hills of Wales, a fragmenting refuge area called the *Bro gymraeg.* As recently as 1911 Welsh had almost a million speakers, but today those who remain, virtually all of whom also speak English, can foresee "a land where children will not be able to pronounce the names of the places where they live." Indeed, some Celtic languages died in recent times, including *Manx* on the Isle of Man and *Cornish* in Cornwall.

Breton, a Celtic language of western France, faces a fate similar to Welsh and retains about the same number of speakers. French inroads increase with each passing decade, and the decline of Breton accelerated after 1945 when the Catholic clergy switched to preaching in French. Literacy in Breton has virtually disappeared. Yet in the late nineteenth century, almost a million and a half persons spoke Breton.

The situation of *Gaelic* in the *Gaidhealtacht* refuge of the northern highlands and islands of Scotland has become even more desperate. Bilingual Gaelic/English road markers conceal the fact that only about 85,000 persons, mainly elderly, still speak the language. *Erse,* or Irish Gaelic, has enjoyed govern-

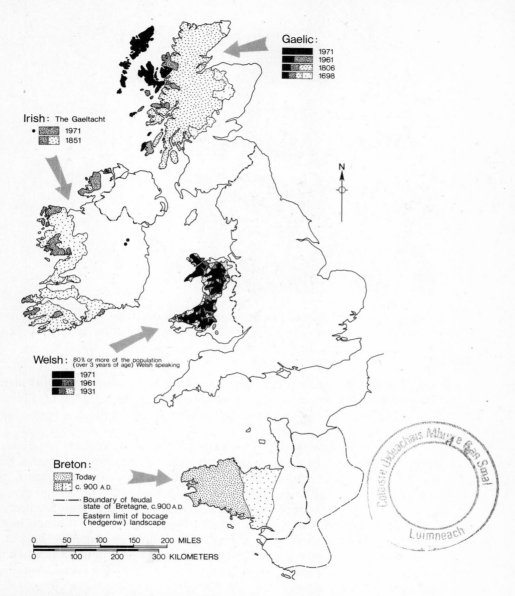

FIGURE 4.6 Retreat of the Celtic languages, as represented by Erse, Breton, Scottish Gaelic, and Welsh. The refuge areas fragment in the final stage of linguistic death, speeding the process of deterioration. (Source: After Withers 1984, 47, 81, 233, 234; D. Williams; Jones and Griffiths; Bowen and Carter; and Kearns, 84.)

mental protection and support since the independence of Ireland in the 1920s, but it, too, has declined severely. Its *Gaeltacht* refuge area continues to shrink,

FIGURE 4.7 Defacing of English language on highway signs in the Connemara *Gaeltacht*, Republic of Ireland. The official bilingual policy of the republic is unpopular in both English and Erse areas. (Photo by the author, 1974.)

and mandatory teaching of Erse in schools ceased in the 1980s. Only about 60,000 persons still use Erse as the language of the household. Some Erse speakers protest desperately by defacing the English parts of bilingual signs (Figure 4.7), but the issue seems decided.

Why do languages die? The geographer Charles Withers, studying Scottish Gaelic, listed four basic processes by which minority linguistic areas shrink and perish. Each is directly or indirectly spatial. First is a *clearance model,* or decline caused by emigration of speakers to places outside the refuge area, leaving behind a much smaller population to perpetuate the language. Similarly, second, a *changeover model* brings about reduced linguistic viability through immigration by an alien population. A third process encouraging linguistic simplification is the *economic development model.* New modes of production, particularly industrialization, accompanied by urbanization, can break up the social structure needed to perpetuate a language. The transition from subsistence farming to working in a factory, even if made within the ethnic area, can be quite destructive in the linguistic sense, particularly if the language of the work place is not that of the farm. In this context, the geographer Keith Buchanan has referred to the decline of the Celtic tongues as a "liquidation" carried out by the English in order to produce a loyal and obedient work force for the mines and factories. Finally, a *social morale model* describes the process by which an ethnic minority, over time, loses pride in its language and voluntarily abandons it. An educational system using solely the majority language produces bilingualism and, indirectly, fosters illiteracy in the minority tongue. Depriving the language of legal and religious status helps convey the same message—the minority tongue is inferior and its use socially degrading. Denying the language access to the printed and broadcast media can hasten the process.

All four of these processes have been at work in the twentieth century to destroy the Celtic languages and others in Europe, as well. One basic problem that faced most of the Celts is their lack of political independence, the only exception, and belated, being the Irish. The day of the Celts nears an end.

Their demise is all the sadder because of their former greatness. The first Celts apparently arose somewhere in the western Hungarian Basin and eventually established a dialect net extending from the Alps to the North Sea (Figure 4.2). By the time the Celts, who called themselves the Galls, can be identified in the archaeological record, about 700 B.C., they exhibited a high culture at places such as Hallstatt in Austria and Lake Neuchâtel in Switzerland, excelling in metalworking and art.

The Celtic decline began when the Germanic peoples surged southward out of Scandinavia about 500 B.C., displacing them from Germany and creating a Celtic diaspora over much of Europe. Perhaps, too, the same colder conditions that prompted the Germanic shift also prompted the Celts to seek warmer conditions. *Gal*icia, a region in southern Poland, derives its name from these prehistoric Celtic refugees, as does *Gal*atia in faraway interior Turkey, another *Gal*icia in northwestern Iberia, nearby *Gal*ache in western Spain, and *Gal*ul (ancient France and Po-Veneto Plain). Most of these refugees soon fell victim to the northward advance of the Romans, which occurred as warmer conditions returned. Pinched between the Romance and Germanic speakers, the Celtic languages retreated west to the remote refuges where we find them in their present predicament.

Other Indo-European Groups

The ancient **Hellenic** branch of the Indo-European languages is parent to modern *Greek,* spoken by about 10 million people in Greece and Cyprus. Minorities can be found in surrounding countries such as Albania. While a minor tongue, accounting for less than 1.5 percent of all Europeans, Greek is not an endangered language. The social morale of its speakers has always been very high, and Greeks still take justifiable pride in the cultural achievements of their ancient ancestors. Greek Orthodox Christianity has also played a major role in the survival and vigor of Greek culture. Self-pride allowed the Greeks to preserve their language even during lengthy periods of rule by the Romans and Turks. Modern Greek is spoken in almost precisely the same region as in the Mycenean Age 13 centuries before Christ and, indeed, precisely in the area where the dialect net tear apparently produced proto-Hellenic some 8500 years ago. The language changed—modern Greek is roughly as different from Classical Greek as Italian is from Latin—but remained astoundingly stable geographically.

Neighbors to the Greeks are the speakers of the **Thracian** group, today represented only by *Albanian.* They number over 5 million and reside in Albania, Kosovo province in Yugoslavia, and western Macedonia. A scattering of

Albanian villages can also be found in southern Italy, Crna Gora (Montenegro), and Greece. In the main, contiguous Balkan area of Albanian speech, a dialect net survives, mutually unintelligible in extreme forms. One of the northern, or *Tosk* dialects, has become the standardized form of the language. The ancestral Thracian group, belonging to the Eastern Indo-European division, apparently originated on the European side of the Bosporos-Dardanelles from northwestern Anatolian parentage (Figure 4.2), but the ancient geographical development remains very poorly understood. Apparently the Thracian speakers evolved at some point into a mountain people, diffusing through the Stara Planina and Rodopi Range. This could have led them over into the Dinaric Range, the present seat of the Albanian language. Eventually, Thracian died out altogether in the eastern Balkans, and modern Albanian occupies a refuge not unlike that of the Celtic, though less endangered.

Another minor group of Eastern Indo-European consists of the **Baltic** languages, *Lettish* (Latvian) and *Lithuanian,* spoken in two small independent states on the eastern shore of the Baltic Sea (Figure 4.1). Together, these languages have about 4 million speakers. Baltic speech survives close to its presumed area of origin west of the Pripyat Marsh (Figure 4.2). Territory was later lost to both Germanic and Slavic languages, but the Balts have held out in a northern refuge. The recent achievement of political independence by Latvia and Lithuania bodes well for these two endangered languages.

Romany, the eastern Indo-European speech of many or most of the 6.5 million or so Gypsies (properly, Roma), is spoken widely, especially in Eastern Europe, though not in contiguous or sizable areas. The ancestral speech of the Roma has split into three separate languages and 13 dialects, due to the strewn distribution of the group and the largely nonliterate status of Romany. The Roma apparently entered Europe in the 1300s as a caste of itinerant Hindu peddlers from the Indus Valley of present Pakistan. In almost every European country, they are despised and persecuted.

In distant Armenia, an embattled outpost of Europe in the trans-Caucasus region (Figure 1.6), is found the final notable Indo-European language, also belonging to the eastern branch. Almost 5 million people speak *Armenian.* Much dispersed, the Armenians are today engaging in return migration to their ancient, newly independent homeland, amid warfare and chaos. Near kin of the Armenians are the *Kurds,* 400,000 of whom have immigrated to Germany in recent decades.

Non-Indo-European Languages

The Indo-European languages, as earlier suggested, represent one of the defining human traits of Europe. In that context, it is not surprising that non-Indo-European tongues are both rare, accounting for only 5 percent of the population, and peripheral in Europe (Figures 1.6, 4.1).

On the northeastern periphery of Europe live speakers of the **Uralic** language family, an indigenous group whose ancestors retreated to cold, marshy refuges as the Indo-Europeans advanced. Today they live in a chain of independent countries and autonomous Russian regions from Finland and Estonia eastward through the Karelian and Komi republics, among others, as far as Mordvinia (Figure 1.6). Essentially these are peoples of the taiga, a land Indo-Europeans never found attractive. Many, particularly the speakers of *Estonian* (1 million) and *Finnish-Karelian* (5 million), adopted agriculture in ancient times from the Indo-Europeans and carried it into the taiga, but certain other Uralic groups, such as the *Sami* (or Lapps, 59,000) and *Nenets* never became farmers. The Uralic peoples still display a deep veneration for forests, and their graveyards often take on a wooded, wild appearance. These reflect ancient memories from the time they were hunters in the forests, before the Indo-Europeans came. A formidable belt of marshes marks the Uralic/Indo-European border along the present Estonia/Latvia boundary, a line beyond which the Baltic speakers apparently never progressed.

Among the Uralic speakers, only the *Hungarians,* or Magyar, do not live in a peripheral area. Instead, 13 million strong, they occupy the heart of the structural basin that bears their name, almost in the very center of Europe (Figure 4.1). Most live in Hungary, but sizable minorities can also be found in Romania, Slovakia, northern Yugoslavia, and western Ukraine. By their own tradition and historical evidence, the ancient Hungarians, a herding people of the east, entered Europe as invaders in the year A.D. 895 and found a permanent foothold in areas where a prairie vegetation had been created by earlier human activity in the Central European biotic province.

On the southeast, the Indo-Europeans border the **Altaic** language family, mainly Turkic groups. The *Osman Turks* of Anatolia long ago attained footholds in Cyprus and north of the Bosporos-Dardanelles. In addition, their long rule of the Balkans left behind minorities in countries such as Bulgaria, where perhaps one in ten persons speaks Turkish, in spite of two attempts in the past fifty years to expel them. Another 1.5 million Osman Turks reside in Germany. *Tataric,* also a major Turkic language, is centered in Tatarstan, Bashkortostan, and, as a minority, in Krym (Crimea), a part of Ukraine (Figure 1.6). About 6 million Tatars live in Europe. In small pockets of Moldova, Bulgaria, and southern Ukraine live over 200,000 *Gagauz* speakers, who are Christians and belong to the Oguz branch of Turkic. Europe abounds with such tiny minorities, most of which have not been mentioned here. As always, the cultural complexity of Europe proves to be profound.

The **Caucasic** language family, including most notably *Georgian,* also help bound Indo-European on the southeast (Figure 1.6). To the south, across the Mediterranean Sea, **Afro-Asiatic** languages such as *Arabic* and *Maltese* mark the cultural border of Europe and remind us that the desert lies not far away in that direction.

The non-Indo-European periphery of Europe is completed by *Basque,* or Euskara, in the southwest, on the Pyrenean borders of Spain and France. Perhaps

650,000 speakers remain, but the language has been in decline for over a century and may soon reach a desperate condition. In Spain, establishment of the Basque Autonomous Province offers some hope for the survival of this unique language.

Closer inspection, then, has revealed that Europe possesses neither Indo-European homogeneity nor linguistic chaos. We have discerned a core, where three major Indo-European divisions prevail, surrounded by an inner periphery of lesser Indo-European groups and an outer periphery of altogether alien tongues. Moreover, east-west linguistic contrasts are reflected in the major, most ancient division within the Indo-European family and by two different alphabets. The Romance/Germanic divide and the split of Slavic into two geographically separate areas provide a significant north/south patterning.

Sources and Suggested Readings

J. W. Aitchison and Harold Carter. *The Welsh Language 1961–1981: An Interpretive Atlas*. Cardiff, GB: University of Wales Press, 1985.

J. W. Aitchison and Harold Carter. "The Welsh Language at the 1981 Census." *Area*. 17 (1985), 11–17.

Mario Alinei et al. *Atlas Linguarum Europae*. Assen, NL: van Gorcum, Vol. 1, 1983.

Hans Becker. "Die Volksgruppen der italienischen Ostalpen: Begleitworte zum Versuch einer Kartendarstellung." *Kölner Geographische Arbeiten*. Sonderband D. : Festschrift für Kurt Kaiser, 1971, 256–270.

Erdmann D. Beynon. "The Eastern Outpost of the Magyars." *Geographical Review*. 31 (1941), 63–78.

Y. E. Blomkvist. "Settlements of the Eastern Slavs." *Soviet Geography*. 26 (1985), 183–198, 268–283.

E. G. Bowen and Harold Carter. "The Distribution of the Welsh Language in 1971: An Analysis." *Geography*. 60 (1975), 1–15.

Keith Buchanan. "Economic Growth and Cultural Liquidation: the Case of the Celtic Nations." In *Radical Geography: Alternative Viewpoints on Contemporary Social Issues*, ed. Richard Peet. Chicago, USA: Maaroufa Press, 1977, 125–143.

Carl D. Buck. *A Dictionary of Selected Synonyms in the Principal Indo-European Languages*. Chicago, USA: University of Chicago Press, 1949.

Vaughan Cornish. *Borderlands of Language in Europe and their Relations to the Historic Frontiers of Christendom*. London, GB: Sifton, 1936.

Jovan Cvijić. "The Geographical Distribution of the Balkan Peoples." *Geographical Review*. 5 (1918), 345–361 (includes large color map).

Aldo Dami. "Les Rhetoromanches." *Le. Globe*. 100 (1960), 25–71.

Leon Dominian. *The Frontiers of Language and Nationality in Europe*. New York, USA: American Geographical Society, Special Publication No. 3, 1917.

J. S. Dugdale. *The Linguistic Map of Europe*. London, GB: Hutchinson University Library, 1969.

François Falc'hun. *Histoire de la langue bretonne d'après la géographie linguistique*. Paris, F: Presses Universitaires de France, 1963.

John Geipel. *The Europeans: An Ethnohistorical Survey.* London, GB: Longmans, 1969.

Walter Geisler. "Die Sprachen- und Nationalitätenverhältnisse an den deutschen Ostgrenzen und ihre Darstellung." *Petermanns Mitteilungen Ergänzungsheft* No. 217. Gotha, D: Justus Perthes, 1933.

Josef Grüll. "Entwicklung und Bestand der Rätoromanen in den Alpen." *Mitteilungen der Österreichischen Geographischen Gesellschaft.* 107 (1965), 86–103, 117.

Chauncy D. Harris. "The New Russian Minorities: A Statistical Overview." *Post-Soviet Geography.* 34 (1993), 1–27.

Einar Haugen. *The Scandinavian Languages.* Cambridge, USA: Harvard University Press, 1976.

Marvin I. Herzog. *The Yiddish Language in Northern Poland: Its Geography and History.* The Hague, NL: Mouton, 1965.

Reg Hindley. *The Death of the Irish Language: A Qualified Obituary.* London, GB: Routledge, 1990.

Emrys Jones and Ieuan L. Griffiths. "A Linguistic Map of Wales, 1961." *Geographical Journal.* 129 (1963), 192–196.

Philip Jones and Michael T. Wild. "Western Germany's 'Third Wave' of Migrants: The Arrival of the Aussiedler." *Geoforum.* 23 (1992), 1–11.

Kevin C. Kearns. "Resuscitation of the Irish Gaeltacht." *Geographical Review.* 64 (1974), 83–110.

John M. Kirk, Stewart F. Sanderson, and John D. A. Widdowson (eds.). *Studies in Linguistic Geography: The Dialects of English in Britain and Ireland.* London, GB: Croom Helm, 1985.

Grover S. Krantz. *Geographical Development of European Languages.* New York, USA: Peter Lang, 1988.

Hermann Lautensach. "Über die topographischen Namen arabischen Ursprungs in Spanien und Portugal." *Die Erde.* 6 (1954), 219–243.

Thomas Lundén. "The Finnish-Speaking Population of Norrbotten (Sweden)." *Europa Ethnica.* 3 (1966), 98–102.

Thomas Lundén. "Language, Geography and Social Development: The Case of Norden," in Colin H. Williams, ed. *Language in Geographic Context.* Clevedon, GB: Multilingual Matters, 1988, 47–72.

Olinto Marinelli. "The Regions of Mixed Populations in Northern Italy." *Geographical Review.* 7 (1919), 129–148 (includes large color map).

Ian M. Matley. "Demographic Trends and Assimilation Among the Finnic-Speaking Peoples of North-Western Russia." *Ural-Altaische Jahrbücher.* 48 (1976), 167–185.

Roy Mellor. "A Minority Problem in Germany." *Scottish Geographical Magazine.* 79 (1963), 49–53.

Christopher Moseley and R. E. Asher (eds.). *Atlas of the World's Languages.* London, GB: Routledge, 1993, Sections 5 ("Northern Asia and Eastern Europe," 219–244, by B. Comrie) and 6 ("Western Europe," 245–261, by J. L. MacKenzie).

Alexander B. Murphy. *The Regional Dynamics of Language Differentiation in Belgium: a Study in Cultural-Political Geography*. Chicago, USA: University of Chicago, Geography Research Paper No. 227, 1988.

Hallstein Mycklebost. "Armenia and the Armenians." *Norsk Geografisk Tidsskrift*. 43 (1989), 135–154.

Cathal O'Luain. "The Irish Language Today." *Europa Ethnica*. 46:1 (1989), 1–10.

Harold Orton and Nathalia Wright. *A Word Geography of England*. London, GB: Seminar Press, 1974.

W. T. R. Pryce. "Migration and the Evolution of Culture Areas: Cultural and Linguistic Frontiers in North-East Wales, 1750 and 1851." *Transactions of the Institute of British Geographers*. 65 (1975), 79–108.

Colin Renfrew. *Archaeology and Language: The Puzzle of Indo-European Origin*. Cambridge, GB: Cambridge University Press, 1988.

Colin Renfrew. "The Origins of Indo-European Languages." *Scientific American*. 261:4 (1989), 106–114.

André-Louis Sanguin (ed.). *Les minorités ethniques en Europe*. Paris, F: L'Harmattan, 1993.

Joachim H. Schultze. "Zur Geographie der altgriechischen Kolonisation." *Petermanns Geographische Mitteilungen*. 87 (1941), 7–12 plus map.

Lee Schwartz. "USSR Nationality Redistribution by Republic, 1979–1989." *Soviet Geography*. 32 (1991), 209–248.

David E. Sopher. "Arabic Place Names in Spain." *Names*. 3 (1955), 5–13.

Manfred Straka. "Karte der Völker und Sprachen Europas unter besonderer Berücksichtigung der Volksgruppen." Graz, A: Akademische Druck- u. Verlagsanstalt, 1979, 15pp. plus map.

Alan R. Thomas. *The Linguistic Geography of Wales*. Cardiff, GB: University of Wales Press, 1973.

J. G. Thomas. "The Geographical Distribution of the Welsh Language." *Geographical Journal*. 122 (1956), 71–79.

Henry R. Wilkinson. *Maps and Politics: A Review of the Ethnographic Cartography of Macedonia*. Liverpool, GB: University Press, 1951.

D. Trevor Williams. "A Linguistic Map of Wales According to the 1931 Census, With Some Observations on Its Historical and Geographical Setting." *Geographical Journal*. 89 (1937), 146–151.

Charles W. J. Withers. *Gaelic Scotland: The Transformation of a Culture Region*. London, GB: Routledge, 1988.

Charles W. J. Withers. *Gaelic in Scotland, 1698–1981: The Geographical History of a Language*. Edinburgh, GB: Donald, 1984.

Ronald Wixman. "Demographic Russification and Linguistic Russianization of the Ukraine, 1959–1979." In *Geographical Studies on the Soviet Union*, ed. George J. Demko and Roland J. Fuchs. Chicago, USA: University of Chicago, Department of Geography, Research Paper No. 211, 1984, 131–156.

Ronald Wixman. *Language Aspects of Ethnic Patterns and Processes in the North Caucasus*. Chicago, USA: University of Chicago, Department of Geography, Research Paper No. 191, 1980.

Ronald Wixman. "Territorial Russification and Linguistic Russianization in Some Soviet Republics." *Soviet Geography.* 22 (1981), 667–675.

Bogdan Zaborski. "Europe Languages" (map). In *Goode's World Atlas,* ed. Edward B. Espenshade, Jr., and Joel L. Morrison. Chicago, USA: Rand McNally, 18th ed., 1990 134–135.

Wilbur Zelinsky and Colin H. Williams. "The Mapping of Language in North America and the British Isles." *Progress in Human Geography.* 12 (1988), 337–368.

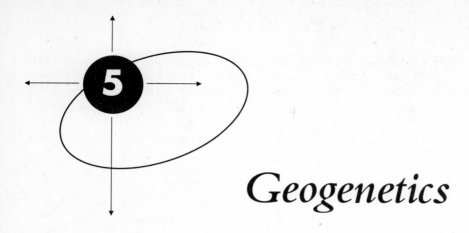

Geogenetics

While far less important than religion and language in defining the European culture area, **race**—here defined as the *genetic* characteristics of people—does represent one of the three basic traits. The *Caucasian* (or *Caucasoid*) race readily distinguishes Europeans from *Negroid* Africans and *Mongoloid* Asians. One might well argue that genetics, acultural in nature, should play no role in the defining of Europe as a *culture* area. The reply must be that all Europeans have racial perceptions. Many harbor racial prejudices. Such perceptions and biases help shape the phenomenon of we-versus-they that underlies perceived European-ness. Moreover, human physical traits differ greatly *within* Europe, prompting additional biases and perceptions. Recently, for example, swarthy vendors from the Caucasus region faced possible expulsion from the public markets in Moskva because of racial prejudice, and Africans have been attacked by "Skinheads" in Germany and certain other countries. Simply ignoring the issue of race will not make neo-Nazis and Skinheads disappear, nor will it expunge the widely held racial perceptions. Inexorably bound up with the very concept of Europe, race became part of culture when it helped shape the European self-image, both at the scale of the culture area and regionally within Europe.

Moreover, as we will see, valuable insights concerning such diverse cultural matters as the spread of languages and the diffusion of agriculture have recently been achieved through human genetic analysis. We should not hesitate to utilize such findings just because race is no longer "politically correct." Let us, then, consider the racial/genetic aspects of both Europe-versus-non-Europe and internal European diversity. The geographical approach to this subject might best be called *geogenetics*.

Pigmentation

Traditionally, scholars who study human genetic traits concentrated on readily visible physical characteristics, such as **pigmentation**—the color of the skin, hair, and eyes. While Caucasians form the "white" race, they exhibit a considerable range of coloration.

In the lands around the shores of the North and Baltic seas, including most of Scandinavia, northern Germany, Poland, Finland, Estonia, Latvia, Belarus, the Netherlands, and eastern Great Britain, most of the population is light complected (Figure 5.1). The same is true of Iceland, eastern Ireland, and parts of northwestern Russia. Belarussians—literally, "white Russians"—derive their very name from light complexion. In these northern regions, hair is blond, red, or light

Hair Color:

- Light Prevalent (Blond, Red, Light Brown)
- Mixture of Light and Brown
- Brown or Dark Brown Prevalent

0   100 200 300 400 500 MILES

0   200   400   600   800 KILOMETERS

FIGURE 5.1 Hair color. (Source: After Günther and Biasutti.)

brown; eyes are blue, gray, or hazel; and the skin is unusually fair. Some experts divide the depigmented north into two subregions. In the west, including Scandinavia, the Netherlands, northwestern Germany, and the British Isles, golden blond hair and blue eyes are the commonest forms of light coloring, while to the east, in Finland and the lands of the northern Slavs, grayish eyes and ash blond hair are more typical. Red hair occurs most often in the Scottish Highlands, but even there only about 10 percent of the population exhibits that trait. The fairest-skinned Europeans live east of the Baltic Sea and in certain Norwegian valleys. Nowhere else in the world is depigmentation of hair, eyes, and skin so common as in Northern Europe.

Dark-complected people dominate the Iberian Peninsula, the Balkan Peninsula, Italy, southern France, and Wales (Figure 5.1). Dark brown or brown hair and eyes together with swarthy skin appear most commonly in these Southern European areas. The darkest-skinned Europeans are the Portuguese, southern Spaniards, Romanians, and southern Italians. Beyond the limits of Europe, in North Africa, the Middle East, and central Asia live even darker-complected peoples, though most of these peripheral populations are still regarded as Caucasoid.

Between the northern region of depigmentation and the southern brunet zone stretches an east-west belt of medium complexion. Overall, pigmentation tends to decrease steadily to the north through Europe, with some local irregularities. No sharp pigmentation borders exist, and complexion lightens gradually with increasing latitude. A geographical transition of this type, from lower to higher incidence of a human physical trait, is called a *cline*. All physical differences among Europeans are clinal in character.

While the pigmentation averages compiled for the various peoples of Europe do reveal a clinal distribution, a continuum, we should recognize that blond *individuals* can be found in southern areas such as Spain, Italy, and Greece, while some brunet persons live in Sweden, Iceland, or Norway. Brunet pigment survives in nearly all northern areas of depigmentation. Even at the blond extreme, in certain eastern valleys of Norway, only about half of the population is wholly blond. Moreover, the incidence of brunet traits has increased in recent times in countries such as Sweden.

Depigmentation represents a response to reduced sunlight. The pigment map of Europe closely resembles the climatic distribution of cloudiness. Sunny climates such as the Mediterranean appear to be more conducive to brunet populations, while cloudy climates, including the marine west coast, induce depigmentation. The key to this cause-and-effect relationship, a dark-colored chemical substance called *melanin*, is deposited in the lower strata of the epidermis. Melanin production is stimulated by exposure to ultraviolet light, as the body seeks to deposit a barrier to protect itself from ultraviolet rays, which can damage living cells. Pigmentation of the hair and eyes evolves in the same way as that of the skin. Depigmentation may also be a result of the greater use of clothing for thousands of years in the colder lands of the north. Northern Europeans, representing the world's only important nucleus of blond people, then, probably reflect an ancient mutation that reduced melanin. The central zone of medium pigmentation in Europe, perhaps the product of mixing between southern brunets and northern blonds, more likely represents a response to a climate intermediate in degree of cloudiness.

Stature

A second traditional standard for physical comparison of Europeans is **stature,** or height. Taller Caucasoids populate the lands bordering the Baltic and North seas, the Dinaric Range, and Ukraine (Figure 5.2). The Po-Veneto Plain and middle Rhine districts also have relatively tall populations. Tallest of all are highlanders and island folk from parts of western Scotland. Short stature characterizes parts of Spain, southern Italy, France, central Poland, and inland northern Scandinavia. The Sami (Lapps) of northern Scandinavia are the shortest Europeans. Stature, like pigmentation, varies in a clinal manner, with transition areas of medium stature between regions of tall and short peoples.

Stature partially results from a genetic reaction to temperature, for the tallest Europeans tend to live in the north. The larger and heavier representatives of many animal species live in colder regions. The cause seems to lie in the fact that for a large body, the ratio of surface area to volume is lower than for a small body, making it easier for a large person to keep warm in the northern climate. Stature can also be influenced by nutrition. Average stature increased in many countries after World War II, presumably as a result of a more satisfactory diet. Spanish males, for example, today average about 173 cm (5 ft. 8 in.) in height, far taller than suggested in Figure 5.2. Similarly, a decline in stature noted in Iceland between A.D. 1200 and A.D. 1700 during a period of colder climate likely resulted from crop failures and food shortages caused by decreased temperatures.

Cephalic Index

Yet another traditional measure of human physical differences, the **cephalic index,** measures the breadth of the head as a percentage of the length. An oblong skull, then, has a low cephalic index, in which case the individual is referred to as *dolichocephalic.* Zones of dolichocephalic averages are found in both Northern and Southern Europe, particularly in Scandinavia, the British Isles, Iceland, Iberia, southern Italy, and the southeastern Balkan Peninsula (Figure 5.3). In these areas the population averages less than 79 in cephalic index, reaching the lowest averages in northern Portugal and in central Sardegna. Broad-headed, or *brachycephalic,* people are found in central Europe, in a belt stretching from Atlantic coastal France eastward into Ukraine and Russia. Cephalic indexes of 83 or more occur in this zone, reaching extremes of 87 or more in parts of southern France and Albania. Another brachycephalic cluster appear in northern Scandinavia. *Mesocephalic* averages, ranging from 79 to 83, characterize the transition zones between broad- and narrow-headed peoples.

While brachycephalic people have lived in Europe since pre-Neolithic times, including one specimen 30,000 years old found in the Balkans, a pronounced increase in cephalic index occurred throughout most of Europe in more recent times. Since about A.D. 600, and particularly since the year 1000, the cephalic

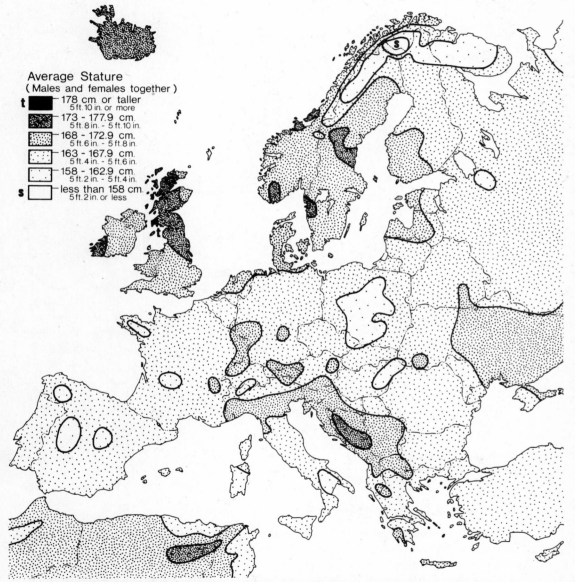

Average Stature
(Males and females together)

t ▉ 178 cm. or taller
    5 ft. 10 in. or more
    173 - 177.9 cm.
    5 ft. 8 in. - 5 ft. 10 in.
    168 - 172.9 cm.
    5 ft. 6 in. - 5 ft. 8 in.
    163 - 167.9 cm.
    5 ft. 4 in. - 5 ft. 6 in.
    158 - 162.9 cm.
    5 ft. 2 in. - 5 ft. 4 in.
s   less than 158 cm.
    5 ft. 2 in. or less

FIGURE 5.2 Average stature of the population, including both males and females. These measurements were made mainly in the 1930s, or even earlier, and improved nutrition has substantially increased averages in every country. (Source: After Biasutti.)

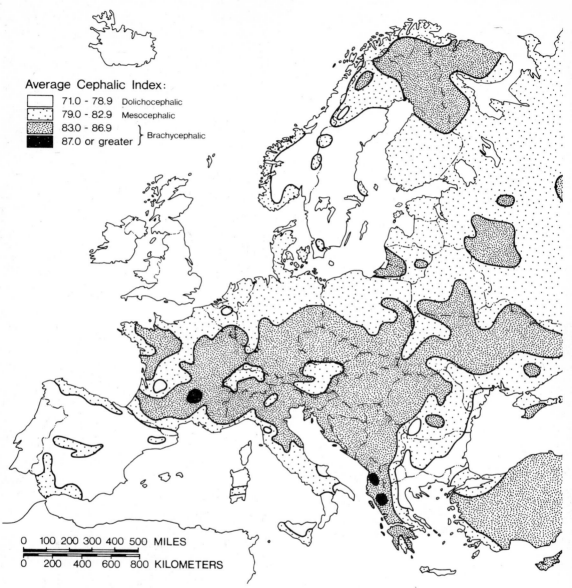

Average Cephalic Index:

☐	71.0 - 78.9 Dolichocephalic
⬚	79.0 - 82.9 Mesocephalic
▨	83.0 - 86.9 ⎫
■	87.0 or greater ⎬ Brachycephalic

```
0  100 200 300 400 500  MILES
0    200  400  600  800  KILOMETERS
```

FIGURE 5.3 Cephalic index. (Source: After Biasutti.)

index has risen significantly, especially in Central Europe. During the same peri-od, dolichocephalism retreated almost everywhere. Most Europeans are now either brachycephalic or mesocephalic.

Areal differences in cephalic index and the changes that occurred in the past 1500 years or so can be explained in various ways. The brachycephalic trait may be the result of racial mixture with Mongoloid peoples, most of whom have high indexes. The brachycephalic zone of Europe lies astride the historic axis of invasion by Avars, Tatars, Magyars, Huns, and other possibly Mongoloid groups. Moreover, since many of these invasions occurred after A.D. 600, Asian intrusion could explain the recent increase of brachycephalism. Detailed studies, however, failed to establish that the Asiatic invaders were broad-headed. Rather, many of these groups seem to have been rather diverse in head shape. Moreover, the invasion explanation would lead us to expect an increase in brachycephalism to the east, toward the source region of the invaders, but the map reveals no such cline. Some of the highest cephalic indexes occur in France, near the *western* end of the zone. In addition, a pronounced Mongoloid contribution to cephalic index should have been accompanied by the implantment of other Mongoloid traits, but such was apparently not the case.

Perhaps more plausible is the suggestion that brachycephalism represents a mutation within the Caucasoid population, the result of an evolutionary process. A broad head may provide a more efficient container for the brain, one better able to withstand a blow. The spread of brachycephalism might be viewed as the result of this inherent superiority. Some racists earlier in the twentieth century concluded that dolichocephalic people were mentally superior to those with broad heads, but no evidence whatever exists to support the notion that intelligence is in any way related to shape or size of the skull.

Other Traditional Indices

Closely related to the cephalic index is the **facial index**, an attempt to distinguish broad-faced persons from those with elongated faces. The index takes the height of the face—measured as distance from the bridge of the nose to the chin—as a percentage of the *bizygomatic diameter*—the straight-line distance between the extreme outer sides of the cheekbones. Lower indexes, less than 83, describe broad-faced people, while higher figures, 86 or more, indicate a long face. In Europe, long-faced populations occur in both north and south, separated by a fragmented zone of broad-faced people (Figure 5.4). The highest facial indexes occur in the British Isles and eastern Spain, while the lowest are found in the Hungarian Basin, Massif Central, western Alps, and far northern regions of Europe.

As with cephalic index, the geographical distribution points to possible influences by broad-faced invaders from Asia. The Hungarian Basin, for example, remains the homeland of the descendants of Magyar invaders, the modern Hungarians. Even today the *Mongol spot,* a small, temporary bluish area near the base of the spine, occurs in some Hungarian infants, though the population of the area otherwise exhibits Caucasian traits.

Many other traits have traditionally been used to classify people into racial groups. One is the **nasal index,** a measure of the width of the nose as a percentage of length. Northern Europeans and Iberians have very low indexes, less than 67, while Central and most of Southern Europe fall in the 67-to-72 category. Another commonly measured physical trait is *head size.* The Europeans having

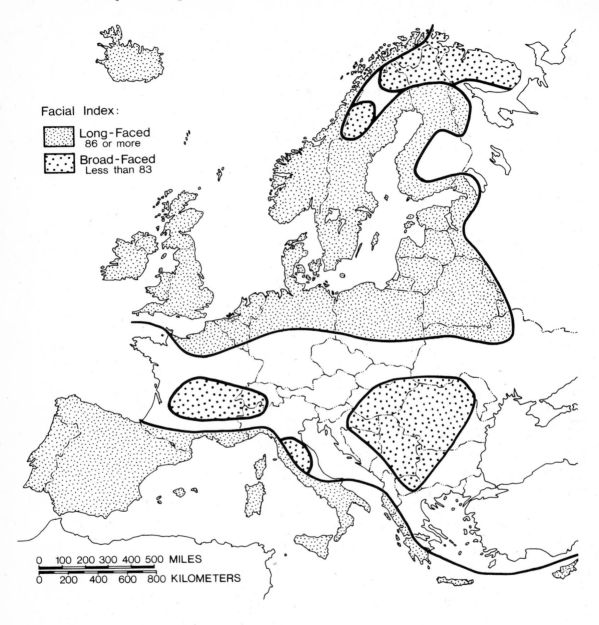

FIGURE 5.4 Facial index. (Source: After Günther, p. 105.)

the largest head size live mainly in northwestern areas and in the Dinaric Ranges of the Balkan Peninsula, regions also characterized by tall people, as well as in

Dordogne area of southwestern France. Other traits that differ regionally in Europe include hair form (straight, wavy, or curly), nasal profile, and eyelid shape.

Subraces

Traditionally, traits such as pigmentation, cephalic index, and stature were used to devise racial classifications. Scholars who studied human physical traits designated not just races but also **subraces,** groups possessing *an aggregate* of common physical traits, that distinguished them individually and collectively from other races or subraces. Properly used, the term *race* refers only to physical traits, not to cultural characteristics such as language, religion, or nationality.

In recent years the concepts of race and subrace have been discarded by geneticists. Races, they say, do not exist. Their objection centers on the fact that the various physical variations in humans are not areally concordant, that the distribution of cephalic index, for example, does not match the distribution of head size, pigmentation, or any other trait. No aggregates of physical traits have the same areal distribution, and the entire concept of race and subrace rests on the assumed existence of such inherited aggregates. Each trait varies areally in a unique way. At best the grouping of peoples into races or subraces serves the purposes of generalization, and any racial classification is arbitrary. Literally an infinite number of such classifications is possible, depending on which traits are chosen for inclusion and what numerical limits are arbitrarily selected on the cline, or continuum, as dividing points. One classifier of races may choose to emphasize pigmentation and stature, while another prefers cephalic index and head size. One may set 82 as the breaking point between cephalic index types, while another may prefer 81, 83, or some other percentage.

Five traditional Caucasian subraces are described below (Figure 5.5). But the number could just as well be 30 or 300. We must recognize that these subraces do not represent concrete, separate entities, but rather artificial and arbitrary groupings to serve the purposes of generalization. Many Europeans *believe* these subraces exist and at times have let this belief influence their behavior toward fellow Europeans. For that reason, if no other, we need to consider the traditional subracial classification.

The **Nordic** subrace, as the name implies, is centered in Northern Europe, especially southern and central Scandinavia, the British Isles, and Iceland. Nordic people tend to be light complected, tall, and dolichocephalic to mesocephalic. The nasal index is usually low, 65 or less, and the head is large. Overall, the Nordics are a big-boned people, physically larger than most of their southern neighbors.

In the southern extremities of Europe lives the **Mediterranean** subrace, a group characterized by relatively short stature, low to very low cephalic index, long face, and fairly dark complexion. Most often, Mediterranean people have a slender body build, narrow face, straight and prominent nose, small jaw, and small to medium head size. The form of the hair varies but is often curly, and in

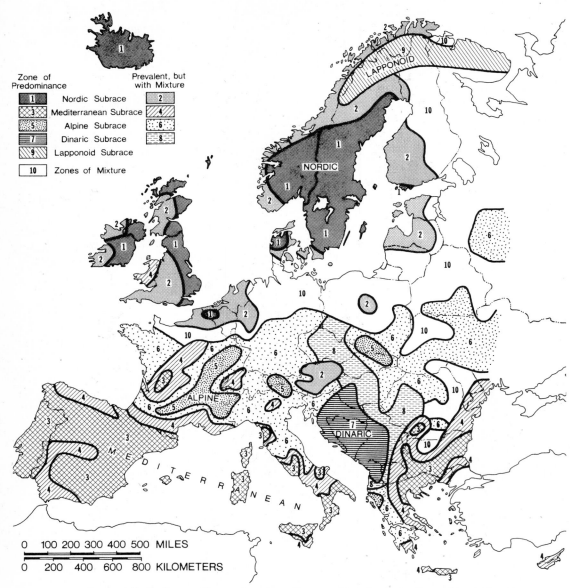

FIGURE 5.5 Caucasian subraces. (Source: Based principally on Biasutti.)

most cases the upper face is relatively long in proportion to the total face height. Iberia is the principal Mediterranean subrace area, but such people also reside in southern Italy, parts of Greece and the eastern Balkans, southern France, and Wales. Mediterranean people are also typical of North Africa, the Middle East, and northern India.

Mediterranean types have lived in Europe for at least 10,000 years, but a more recent infusion apparently occurred in Neolithic times with the coming of agriculture to Southern Europe. Iberia received an additional influx of Mediterraneans with the Moorish invasion in historic times. Sculpture from the period of classical Greece and the Roman Empire most often portrays individuals with Mediterranean traits. Some link the influx of the Mediterranean subrace to the rise of higher civilization in Europe. They have been portrayed as bearers of technology from Mesopotamia, Anatolia, and Egypt, who established the first high civilization in the European culture area.

Much of the central section, wedged between the Nordic and Mediterranean zones, is dominated by the **Alpine** subrace. The traditional term *alpine* is somewhat misleading, for members of this alpine subrace appear all the way from Bretagne on the Atlantic coast of France to the interior provinces of China. However, Alpine peoples are more common in mountainous or hilly areas than on the adjacent plains. The principal distinguishing trait of the Alpines is a high cephalic index, in excess of 83 generally. They are of medium stature and stocky build, with short arms and legs, and large hands and feet. The face is broad or round, and the nose usually has a low bridge.

The **Dinaric** subrace, like the Alpine, consists mainly of mountain-dwelling people. Their home lies principally the Dinaric Mountain Range along the eastern shore of the Adriatic Sea. Similarity to the Alpines is also seen in the brachycephalism of the Dinarics, but in most other ways they remain distinct from the Alpines. The face is usually somewhat triangular in shape, with a broad forehead, narrow jaw, and long, narrow, convex nose. Still more distinctive is the tall stature of the Dinarics, the major trait that distinguishes them from neighboring Mediterraneans and Alpines. The Dinarics may be the result of a mixture between round-headed, broad-faced people and others who were long-headed and narrow-faced. Their brachycephalism results partly from cultural practices, in particular the traditional use of cradle boards for infants, which tends to flatten the occipital area of the skull. Dinaric types have lived in the mountains of Albania for at least 2500 years, and similar people live far to the east in Armenia and the Caucasus.

One of the most distinctive groups in Europe, the **Lapponoid** subrace, lives in the northern parts of Sweden, Norway, Finland, and the Kola Peninsula in Russia. These people, called the Sami, are of short or very short stature, with small hands and feet. Normally brachycephalic, they have broad faces, widely separated eyes, pointed chin, small teeth, and straight hair. Lapponoids have snub noses with a nasal index of 70 or more. Their complexion is somewhat darker than that of the Nordics to the south, and they are more likely to be *mesognathous*, meaning that some projection of the lower face occurs. The Lapponoids, small people, have short arms and legs, and their origins remain disputed. The traditional view, that these people were partially or even largely Mongoloid, has given way to the belief that they represent a survival of a very early, indigenous Caucasoid group.

This fairly simple subracial classification and the resultant map (Figure 5.5) conceal a great many local, even intraprovincial contrasts. In western Kriti, for example, many of the people called Sfakians better fit the Nordic classification, even though they live among Mediterranean types. Another example can be drawn from Norway, where, in the province of Möre og Romsdal, two rather different genetic groups live side by side (Figure 5.6).

No sooner had this classification of Europe's subraces appeared about 1900 than various writers began attaching *behavioral* images to each group, so repeatedly that the images became stereotyped. The Nordics supposedly possessed genius for leadership and were work-loving, efficient, and militaristic, while the Mediterraneans were labeled as artistic, lazy, inefficient, and hot-blooded. The Alpines were said to be unimaginative, plodding, and reserved. A satirical poem by Hilaire Belloc sums up these popular images quite well:

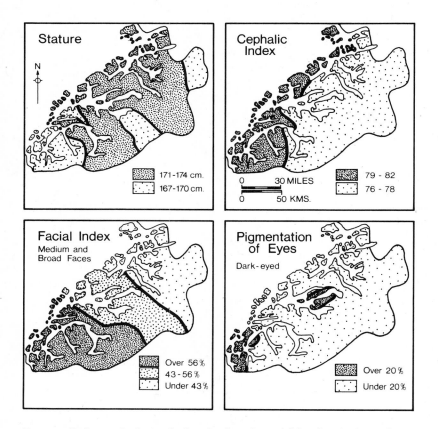

FIGURE 5.6 Variation of physical traits within the Norwegian province of Möre og Romsdal. The human complexity of Europe is well illustrated in this small area, where a relatively short, dark, mesocephalic, and broad-faced group lives in the west and a tall, fair, dolichocephalic, long-faced element occupies the east. Note, too, that no two of these racial traits have the same geographical distribution. (Source: After Günther, 5, with modifications.)

Behold, my child, the Nordic man,
And be as like him as you can.
His legs are long—his mind is slow;
His hair is lank and made of tow.

And here we have the Alpine race,
Oh! what a broad and brutal face.
His skin is of a dirty yellow.
He is a most unpleasant fellow.

The most degraded of them all
Mediterranean we call.
His hair is crisp and even curls
And he is saucy with the girls.*

These stereotypes have no basis in scholarship, and Belloc rightly pokes fun at them, but they nevertheless appear again and again, and their imagined truth and importance reached absurd and tragic proportions in Nazi Germany. Nordic persons were favored, while people displaying the "wrong" physical traits, such as dark-complected Gypsies, faced slavery, imprisonment, or extermination. To a degree, German nationalism became identified with a specific subracial type, and persons who did not fit the "ideal" Nordic stereotype found it difficult to be accepted as rightful citizens of the Nazi state. Strangely, the most influential advocates of Nordic supremacy, Adolf Hitler and his propaganda minister, Josef Göbbels, were both short and dark-complected. No "master" race or subrace exists.

Blood Chemistry

The study of racial traits such as pigmentation, cephalic index, and stature, as well as the formulation of subracial classifications has fallen completely from favor in recent decades. The Nazi abuse formed only part of the problem. Stature varied with nutrition and was less of a genetic trait than had been assumed. Cephalic index could be greatly influenced by the use of infant cradle boards, and depigmentation occurred with diminished sun exposure.

Today, all research focuses upon **blood chemistry**, which has proven to be highly complex, regionally varied, and enormously revealing. Initially, most findings were linked to the basic blood "factors" *A* and *B*. Presence or absence of factors A and B led to the designation of four *blood types:* type A, containing only factor A; type B, containing only factor B; type O, in which neither factor A nor B is present; and type AB, containing both factors. This classification was further refined by the presence or absence of the *Rhesus* factor, the shorthand for which is *Rh+* and *Rh-*.

These particular blood factors display uneven distributions in Europe (Figure 5.7). Type A occurs more commonly in Western Europe than elsewhere, accounting for 30 percent or more of the population in parts of western Iberia,

*Reprinted by permission of A. D. Peters & Co. Ltd.

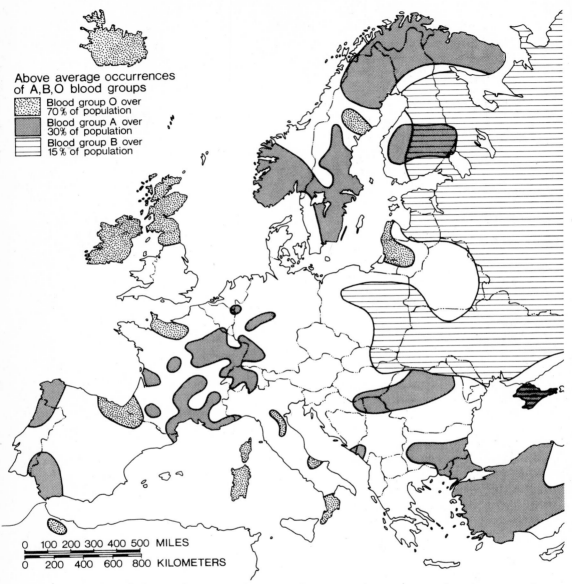

FIGURE 5.7 Distribution of A-B-O blood groups. (Sources: After Mourant; Vallois and Marquer.)

eastern France, Scandinavia, northern Italy, and the Carpathians. The concentration of type A in marginal and highland areas suggests that it may be a very old blood trait in Europe. One of the highest rates of occurrence of type A, for example, occurs in the Aran Islands, on the far western fringe of Ireland, where 40 percent of the people have this kind of blood.

In contrast, type B, less common than type A, appears usually in Eastern Europe. Type B is dominant among the Mongoloid peoples of Asia, and the greater occurrence in eastern Europe may be the result of fairly recent Mongoloid mixture with Caucasoids there. Nowhere in Europe does type B account for more than one fifth of the population. By far the most common blood type in Europe, O, reaches greatest frequencies in the coastal periphery of Western and Southern Europe. In Iceland, Scotland, Ireland, Corsica, Sardegna, and the Basque area of the Spanish-French borderland, more than 70 percent of the population have type O. Nearly all parts of Europe have at least half of the population with this type blood. The dominance of type O in the far-western peripheries of Europe has led some geneticists to regard it, rather than type A, as the oldest European blood type. Interestingly, residents of Wales who have Welsh surnames have a higher frequency of blood type O than those in the same area with English family names. Europe abounds with such puzzling and intriguing genetic correlations. For example, Icelanders are more closely related in blood chemistry to the Irish than to their linguistic ancestors, the Norwegians.

The Rh factor also displays an interesting geographical pattern. Northwestern Europeans have the greatest Rh– presence, and among the Basques its occurrence is the highest in the world. Some believe that the preagricultural, Mesolithic hunter-gatherer population of Europe was largely Rh–, and that Rh+ entered from the southeast with Neolithic farmers.

Even more revealing geographic patterns have been detected through multivariate analysis of different blood gene forms, including not only A-B-O and Rh, but also many others. Applying *principal components analysis,* a type of factor analysis, a team of scholars took 39 of these blood-gene forms for some 400 geographical locations in Europe, reduced them to weighted means that summarized all gene frequencies at each given place, and mapped the results (Figure 5.8). Their maps revealed several blood chemistry clines, the most notable of which is a striking southeast-to-northwest pattern. The implication of this cline is profound since the migration thrust it suggests parallels very closely the proposed ancient diffusion of the Indo-European languages, as presented in Chapter 4. In other words, the geographies of blood chemistry and linguistic spread correlate. Moreover, as we will see in Chapter 8, the diffusion of agriculture also coincided with this same southeast-to-northwest movement. Other clines revealed through this multivariate analysis suggest (1) an east-to-west migration that may commemorate the repeated Asiatic invasions, and (2) a southwest-to-northeast thrust paralleling historic (and perhaps also ancient) Semite-Hamite entries into Iberian Europe.

Racially Exotic Immigration

European geogenetics became still further complicated by an influx of exotic racial strains during the post–World War II economic boom. Most came from the extensive colonial empires of the British, French, Portuguese, and Dutch.

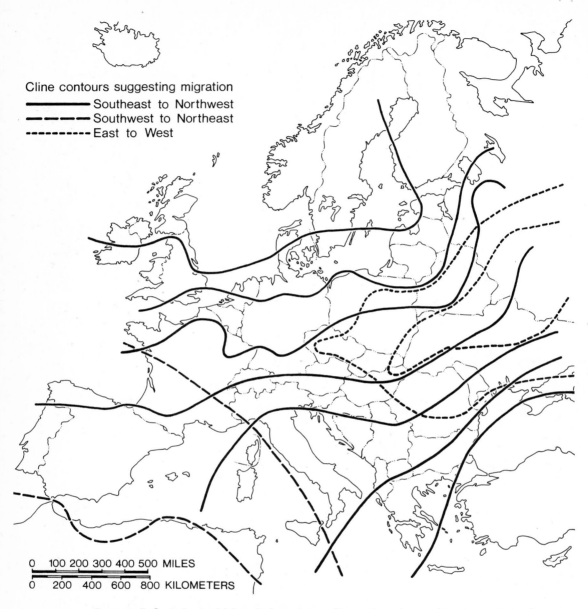

FIGURE 5.8 Selected blood chemistry clines. Based on multivariate principal components analysis of 39 blood-gene forms at 400 sites, these clines suggest migrations, some of which are quite ancient, from southeast to northwest, east to west, and southwest to northeast. The first of these migrations is apparently linked to the spread both the Indo-European languages and agriculture (see Chapters 4, 8). (Sources: Adapted with modifications from Ammerman and Cavalli-Sforza, 105–107; Menozzi et al., 788–790, plus cover illustration.)

Darker-skinned people from the tropics formed the bulk of these racially distinctive immigrants.

In the United Kingdom, the principal groups are South Asians, derived mainly from India, Pakistan, and Bangladesh, including many persons who lived in East Africa prior to migrating to Britain. These Asians now number about 1,400,000 in the United Kingdom, forming over 2 percent of the national population. They live mainly in major industrial and commercial centers, such as London, Bradford, Birmingham, and Coventry (Figure 5.9). This selective urban concentration means that South Asians often form a substantial part of the city population. While these people from the Indian subcontinent should be classified as Mediterranean Caucasians, they are sufficiently dark-complected to be regarded by the indigenous British as "coloured." One can easily distinguish them from the tall, fair Britons. Chinese, almost all from Hong Kong, form the other major Asiatic group in the United Kingdom, numbering about 140,000. The Chinese

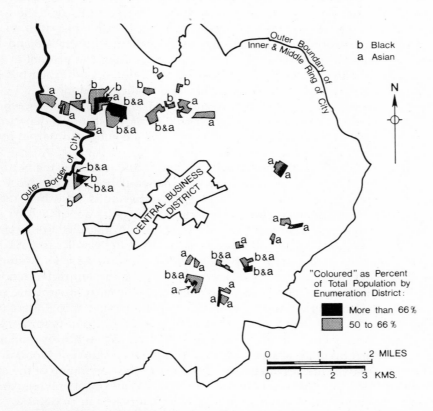

FIGURE 5.9 Negroid and Asian population concentrations in central sections of Birmingham, England. Racial minorities and residential segregation have become common in parts of Western Europe since 1950. At times these ghettoes have erupted into violence, as in Birmingham in 1985. (Source: Adapted from Jones, 1976, 91.)

generally do not live in urban ghettoes, and in fact only half live in the large cities. They have scattered through the country and achieved considerable economic success.

The other major racial minority in Britain consists of Negroid, or black, immigrants. Afro-Caribbeans form the large majority of Britain's black population, about 77 percent. Blacks now number about 607,000 and remain concentrated in urban ghettoes. Their migration, like that of the South Asians, was facilitated by the fact that they hold British citizenship, a legacy of the Empire. The tiny Caribbean island of Montserrat sent nearly one-third of its total population to Britain between 1955 and 1961. While exceptional in proportion, the emigration from Montserrat symptomized the economic troubles in the West Indies. Much larger and more populous Jamaica sent nearly one in every ten of its citizens to Britain in the 1953–1961 period, forming by far the largest West Indian contingent.

Residential segregation, less intense than in the United States, characterizes both South Asian and black elements in British cities (see Chapter 10) (Figure 5.9). In the words of the geographers T. P. Jones and D. McEvoy, "The ghetto must now be recognized as an established feature" of British inner cities. In spite of civil rights legislation, most notably the Race Relations Acts of 1968 and 1976, racial discrimination persists in the United Kingdom. For the present at least, such racial minorities, particularly the blacks, continue, as Ceri Peach put it, to fill "gaps at the lower end of the occupational and residential ladder."

France, similarly, is today home to almost 300,000 Afro-Caribbeans, who are French citizens due to France's continuing rule of its West Indies departments and Guiana. Other blacks who are resident in France come mainly from former colonies within the French economic community in sub-Saharan Africa. They, too, remain confined to racial neighborhoods and work at or near the bottom of the occupational ladder in semi- or unskilled manual labor jobs vacated by the increasingly prosperous native French. The Netherlands absorbed 180,000 Eurasians and 35,000 Moluccans from Indonesia, as well as about 200,000 Afro-Caribbeans immigrants from Surinam and the Dutch Antilles. In Rotterdam by 1972, some 12,000 Surinamese and lesser numbers from the Antilles formed about 2 percent of the population, a proportion today accounted for by Moluccans alone. Following the British and French models, the Rotterdam racial minorities generally live in older residential sections adjacent to the city center. Amsterdam, 's Gravenhage (The Hague), and Utrecht display patterns similar to Rotterdam.

Portugal, too, inherited a sizable Negroid population from its former slave trade and African empire, a total of about 100,000 persons. In nearby Andalucía, part of southern Spain, black African slaves introduced during Moorish rule remained common centuries later. Over 7 percent of the population of the city of Sevilla consisted of African slaves in the early 1500s. While most of these Africans were sent to the American colonies, a racial legacy survived in Andalucía, where a few villages still have populations displaying partially Negroid traits.

Germany also has immigrant racial minorities, though not on the scale of the former empire-ruling countries, and it acquired a small population of mulattoes as a result of the American military presence. About 95,000 Vietnamese reside in Germany, mainly in the eastern part of the country, where 15,000 natives of

Mozambique in southern Africa also live. Some 57,000 Asian Indians and Sri Lankans had come to western Germany by 1990. Iceland forbade residence by non-Caucasians, even excluding black military personnel at the United States base at Keflavik. On a brighter note, numerous Swedes and other Scandinavians have adopted dark-skinned children from impoverished Third World countries. Reared in northern affluence and thoroughly assimilated, these children often find it difficult to gain full acceptance into society as adults.

Europeans of many nationalities have established so many ties to the rest of the world since the Age of Discovery that virtually every racial strain has found its way into Europe. Indeed, such infusions go back at least to Roman times, when black slaves were introduced. The immigration of the Roma (Gypsies) in the late Middle Ages represented the earliest infusion of darker-complected peoples from the Indian subcontinent, long predating the more recent influx. Clearly, European racial purity or homogeneity has always been a myth.

This chapter and the two preceding it dealt with the basic defining traits of Europe—religion, language, and race. We next turn to other, equally important characteristics of the European people. Demography, the social study of population, provides our next subject.

Sources and Suggested Readings

J. M. M. van Amersfoort and C. Cortie. "Het Patroon van de Surinaamse Vestiging in Amsterdam in de Periode 1968 t/m 1970." *Tijdschrift voor Economische en Sociale Geografie.* 64 (1973), 283–294.

Albert J. Ammerman and L. L. Cavalli-Sforza. *The Neolithic Transition and the Genetics of Populations in Europe.* Princeton, USA: Princeton University Press, 1984.

Hilaire Belloc. "Talking (and Singing) of the Nordic Man." In *Hilaire Belloc: An Anthology of His Prose and Verse,* ed. W. N. Roughead. Philadelphia, USA, and New York, USA: Lippincott, 1951, 253. (Poem reprinted by permission of A. D. Peters & Co. Ltd., 10 Buckingham St., London, GB).

Erdmann D. Beynon. "Isolated Racial Groups in Hungary." *Geographical Review.* 17 (1927), 586–604.

Renato Biasutti et al. *Le Razze e i Popoli della Terra,* Vol. 2, *Europa-Asia.* Torino, I: Unione Tipografico-Editrice Torinese, 4th ed., 1967.

V. Bunak. "Genetic-Geographical Zones of Eastern Europe by ABO Blood Groups." In *Soviet Ethnology and Anthropology Today,* ed. Y. Bromley. The Hague, NL: Mouton, 1974, 331–358.

P. B. Candella. "The Introduction of Blood Group B into Europe." *Human Biology.* 14 (1942), 413–444.

John Cater and Trevor Jones. "Ethnic Residential Space: the Case of Asians in Bradford." *Tijdschrift voor Economische en Sociale Geografie.* 70 (1979), 86–97.

Stephanie A. Condon and Philip E. Ogden. "Afro-Caribbean Migrants in France: Employment, State Policy and the Migration Process." *Transactions of the Institute of British Geographers.* 16 (1991), 440–457.

Carleton S. Coon. "The Mountains of Giants: A Racial and Cultural Study of the North Albanian Mountain Ghegs." *Papers of the Peabody Museum of American Archaeology and Ethnology.* 23:3 (1950).

Carleton S. Coon. *The Races of Europe.* New York, USA: Macmillan, 1939.

Josef Deniker. *The Races of Man.* New York, USA: Scribner, 1900.

P. Drewe, G. A. van der Knaap, G. Mik, and H. M. Rodgers. "Segregation in Rotterdam." *Tijdschrift voor Economische en Sociale Geografie.* 66 (1975), 204–216.

Martin Eaton. "Foreign Residents and Illegal Immigrants: os Negros em Portugal." *Ethnic and Racial Studies.* 16 (1993), 536–562.

Herbert J. Fleure. *The Races of England and Wales: A Survey of Recent Research.* London, GB: Benn, 1923.

John Geipel. *The Europeans: An Ethnohistorical Survey.* Harlow, Essex, GB: Longmans, 1969.

Hans F. K. Günther. *The Racial Elements of European History.* Trans. G. C. Wheeler. Port Washington, USA: Kennikat Press, 1970.

Ellsworth Huntington. *The Character of Races as Influenced by Physical Environment, Natural Selection and Historical Development.* New York, USA: Scribner, 1927, chaps. 14–20.

Peter Jackson. "The Racialization of Labour in Post-War Bradford." *Journal of Historical Geography.* 18 (1992), 190–209.

Philip N. Jones. "Colored Minorities in Birmingham, England." *Annals of the Association of American Geographers.* 66 (1976), 89–103.

Philip N. Jones. "The Distribution and Diffusion of the Coloured Population in England and Wales, 1961–1971." *Transactions of the Institute of British Geographers.* 3 (1978), 515–532.

Philip N. Jones. "Some Aspects of the Changing Distribution of Coloured Immigrants in Birmingham." *Transactions of the Institute of British Geographers.* 50 (1970), 199–218.

T. P. Jones and D. McEvoy. "Race and Space in Cloud-Cuckoo Land." *Area.* 10 (1978), 162–166.

Geoffrey W. Kearsley and Sheela R. Srivastava. "The Spatial Evolution of Glasgow's Asian Community." *Scottish Geographical Magazine.* 90 (1974), 110–124.

Trevor R. Lee. *Race and Residence: the Concentration and Dispersal of Immigrants in London.* Oxford, GB: Clarendon Press, 1977.

Frank B. Livingstone. "On the Non-Existence of Human Races." *Current Anthropology.* 3 (1962), 279–281.

P. Menozzi, A. Piazza, and L. L. Cavalli-Sforza. "Synthetic Maps of Human Gene Frequencies in Europeans." *Science.* 201 4358 (Sept. 1, 1978), 786–792.

Ashley M. F. Montagu (ed.). *The Concept of Race.* New York, USA: Free Press, 1964.

A. E. Mourant. *The Distribution of Human Blood Groups.* Springfield, USA: Thomas, 1954.

A. E. Mourant, A. C. Kopec, and K. Domaniewska-Sobczak. *The ABO Blood Groups.* Oxford, GB: Blackwell, 1958.

Martin P. Nilsson. "The Race Problem of the Roman Empire." *Hereditas*. 2 (1921), 370–390.

Ceri Peach. *West Indian Migration to Britain: A Social Geography*. London, GB: Oxford University Press, 1968.

G. C. K. Peach. "Factors Affecting the Distribution of West Indians in Great Britain." *Institute of British Geographers, Transactions and Papers*. 38 (1966), 151–164.

William Z. Ripley. *The Races of Europe*. New York, USA: Appleton, 1899.

Vaughan Robinson. *The Segregation of Asians within a British City: Theory and Practice*. Oxford, GB: Oxford University School of Geography, Research Paper No. 22, 1979.

Giuseppe Sergi. *The Mediterranean Race: A Study of the Origins of European Peoples*. London, GB: Walter Scott, 1901.

Robert R. Sokal, Neal L. Ogden, and Chester Wilson. "Genetic Evidence for the Spread of Agriculture in Europe by Demic Diffusion." *Nature*. 351 (May 9, 1991), 143–145.

T. Griffith Taylor. "Race and Nation in Europe." *Australian Journal of Psychology and Philosophy*. 4 (1926), 1–7.

T. Griffith Taylor. "Racial Geography." In *Geography in the Twentieth Century*, ed. T. Griffith Taylor. New York, USA: Philosophical Library, and London, GB: Methuen, 1951, 433–462A.

H. V. Vallois and P. Marquer. "Le Répartition en France des Groupes Sanguins A B O." *Bulletins et Mémoires de la Société d' Anthropologie de Paris*. 11th series, 6:1 (1964), 1–200.

Franz Weidenreich. "The Brachycephalization of Recent Mankind." *Southwestern Journal of Anthropology*. 1 (1945), 1–54.

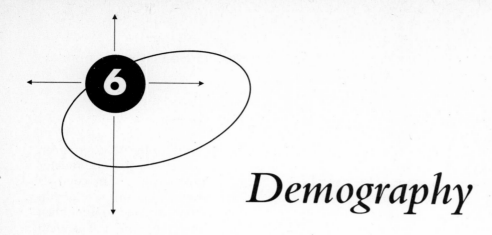

Demography

Europe possesses a highly distinctive demography, and various traits of its population help both to define and to differentiate the culture area. Numbers, densities, fertility, mortality, health, education, mobility, and living standards of the European people all reveal unique characteristics and geographical patterns. Religion, language, and geogenetics do not provide a full understanding of the human Europe; demography allows us to refine our view of the culture area.

Numbers

Europeans are very numerous, forming one of the largest population groups in the world. Within the confines of the traditional Uralian border live some 700 million people, a total surpassed only by Asia. About one of every eight persons in the world is a European. If Eurorussia, the Caucasus states, and cis-Bosporos Turkey are subtracted, the remaining total, 565 million, is still double the population of the United States and Canada combined.

Six independent European states have populations in excess of 50 million, including Eurorussia with 116; Germany, 81; Italy, the United Kingdom, and France, each with 58; and Ukraine, 52. Nine other European countries have at least 10 million inhabitants. European Russia, if separate, would form the ninth most populous country in the world.

Humankind did not originate in Europe, but prehistoric migration to Europe from ancestral Africa began very early. People multiplied slowly over many millennia. By the beginning of the Christian Era, about 33 million people lived in Europe, but the disruption associated with the collapse of the Roman Empire caused the total to fall to only 18 million by the year 600. The Medieval Age witnessed great population growth, to about 70 million by 1340, but then the ravages of the Black Death led to another major decline. Rebounding rapidly after about 1450, the European population reached 100 million by 1650, 200 million by shortly after 1800, 400 million by about 1900, and 600 million by 1960. During the last 2000 years, the major center of population shifted northward from the Mediterranean to Central Europe.

Density and Distribution

If the people presently living west of the Urals and north of the Mediterranean were evenly distributed over the land area of Europe, each square kilometer would contain about 71 persons (184 per sq. mi.). However, this figure conceals the fact that population density varies greatly from one part of Europe to another, ranging from the totally uninhabited glaciers of interior Iceland to more than 500 per sq km (1300 per sq. mi.) in some favored districts. Among independent states, densities range from Iceland's 2½ persons per sq km to Malta's 1,094 and Monaco's 16,550.

The pattern of population distribution can even help provide boundaries for Europe. The culture area represents one of four major population clusters in the world, each of which is surrounded by areas of lower density. One way to display this pattern is through the concept of *continuous* and *discontinuous* settlement, the former including all areas in which habitations and transport routes form a dense network (Figure 6.1). Defined in this manner, Europe stands separate, bounded by sparsely settled deserts and subarctic wastes, which serve to isolate it from the peoples of sub-Saharan Africa and the great cultures of India and the Orient. To leave Europe requires passage through thinly peopled, harsh lands. Encapsulated in their isolated "bubble" of continuous settlement, Europeans developed as a distinct people and culture.

Measured and mapped in another way, the pattern of population density in Europe presents a core/periphery configuration (Figure 6.2). Most densely populated districts—those having 200 or more persons per sq km—lie in or near the center of Europe, while regions of sparse settlement, with fewer than 50 persons per sq km, usually appear around the perimeter of the culture area, forming the transition into the deserts and boreal wastelands that border Europe. In the core, a corridor or axis of dense settlement reaches from England into Italy, including the Netherlands, Belgium, and Germany. In recent times, the core/periphery contrast grew even more pronounced in Europe, due to migration. In countries such as Sweden, many people have abandoned the sparsely settled north to relocate in the more populous south.

Explaining Distribution: The Environment

Many causal forces interact, over centuries, to produce the pattern of population distribution. Some of these forces reside in the physical environment. For example, most areas of densest population lie in the lowland plains regions, especially in the fertile, loessial parts of the Great European Plain, while European moun-

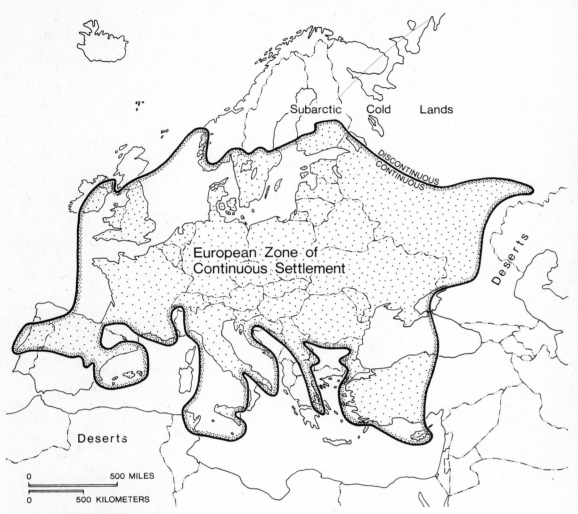

FIGURE 6.1 Europe forms one of four major or "primary" clusters of "continuous" settlement in the world. Continuous settlement, a term devised by geographer Kirk Stone, means that all habitations lie no more than 5 km (3 mi.) from other habitations in at least six different directions and that roads/railroads lie no farther than 16 to 32 km (10 to 20 mi.) away in at least three directions. In other words, the term describes a densely inhabited land, served by a transport network. (Sources: Adapted from Kirk H. Stone, personal communications, 1993; Stone, "The World's Primary Settlement Regions" [map], *GeoJournal,* 2:3, 1978, 196; Stone, 1962, 1966, 1971.)

tain ranges stand out as zones of sparser settlement. Also, Europeans have tended to avoid the colder climates, and the northern border of continuous settlement

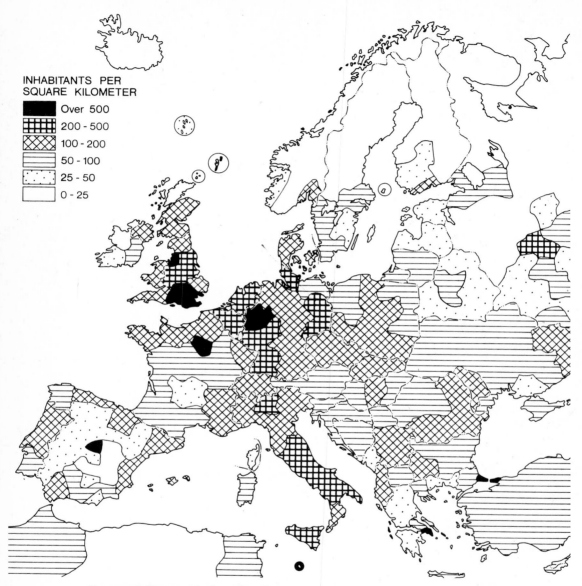

FIGURE 6.2 Population density in Europe. A distinct core/periphery pattern is evident. A core area of over 200 persons per sq km reaches southeast from the Anglican Plain through the Low Country and Germany to Sicilia, forming an English-Rhenish-Italian axis of dense population. Peripheral regions, especially the subarctic north, are far more sparsely settled. (1 sq km = 0.386 sq. mi.)

in Scandinavia follows very closely the line between humid continental and subarctic climate types.

People respond not only to severity of climate, but also to changes. Long-range climatic fluctuations can contribute to modification of population density, especially in marginal areas. During the "Little Ice Age" from the 1200s into the 1800s, the permanent snow line on the south side of the great glacier in Iceland called Vatnajökull moved ever lower, a good indicator of cooling climate. During this same period, the Icelandic population declined almost 30 percent, and the average height of males was reduced by 5 cm (about 2 in.), presumably in large part as a result of a diminished food supply caused by climatic deterioration. By the 1700s, humans neared the verge of extinction in Iceland. The population of the country rebounded in the last 200 years in a period of milder climate to reach an all-time high of 262,000.

Insolation, or exposure to sunlight, can also influence people's selection of a place to live. In the Alps of Switzerland, northern Italy, and Austria, where the mountain ridges run in an east-west direction, south-facing slopes receive much more sunlight than do the shadowy, north-facing slopes. The local inhabitants have long recognized this contrast, and the Alpine French coined the words *adret* for sun slope and *ubac* for shade slope. Adret sides of the longitudinal valleys in

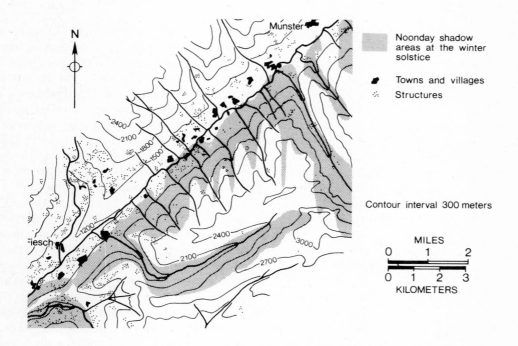

FIGURE 6.3 Concentration of settlement on the *adret* of the Rhône Valley, Swiss Alps. The shaded area is in shadow at noon at the winter solstice. Villages and scattered dwellings are shown in black. Elevations are shown in meters. (Source: After Garnett, 1935.)

the eastern and western Alps contain more population than the ubac, in some instances twice as many people (Figure 6.3). North-facing slopes commonly remain forested, for the local farm folk know that crops that ripen early on the sunny slopes may fail to ripen at all on the opposite side of the valley. So strong is the distinction between the adret and ubac in some districts that the residents of the former long considered themselves socially superior to the "shady characters" from the *ubac* and frowned upon intermarriage. Many different insolation characteristics influence the choice of settlement site, including the area in noon-day shadow at the winter solstice, the number of hours of potential sunlight, and the *intensity* of insolation, which varies with degree of slope. Through centuries of trial and error, the inhabitants of these mountains discerned the areas of optimum insolation and distributed themselves accordingly. Even so, members of different cultures interpreted the Alpine adret and ubac in contrasting ways. The southern ridge of the Alps is home to both Germanic and Romance-speaking peoples. Latins, reluctant to abandon warmth-loving crops such as maize and the grapevine, established their highest permanent adret settlements considerably *lower* than those of German dairy-cattle raisers, called *Walser*, living on the inferior ubac over the ridge to the north. The more complete German utilization of the mountain environment in part results from their greater reliance on hearty crops such as hay and oats.

Natural resources can also influence population distribution. Human perceptions of what constitutes a resource changed many times in the past, causing people to move about as technological changes occurred. To the preagricultural hunters of Europe, the great natural resources were wild game and the raw materials for making weapons of the hunt. The location of wild animal herds or of types of wood well suited for spears and bows attracted them. Modern Europeans, having created a different form of economy, became seekers of coal and iron ore; these resources influenced their settlement distribution just as herds of deer attracted their ancestors. As a consequence, every area with sizable deposits of high-grade coal acquired in recent centuries a large population, and the correlation between the distribution of coal and people is striking.

The environmental contrast of seacoast and interior has been evaluated variously in different parts of Europe. In the Mediterranean peninsulas and Scandinavia, which are mountainous or cold, people have more often chosen to settle on or near the coasts, while in the remainder of Europe, the bulk of the population is in the interior. The coastal rim of Iberia is more densely peopled than the Meseta, while in Norway almost all of the population is clustered in or near port settlements. In the Mediterranean, Scandinavian, and Baltic countries, 77 percent of all cities of 500,000 or more population are on or within 40 km (25 mi.) of the seashore, while for the remainder of Europe, excluding Russia, only 30 percent are so situated. The Greeks, Portuguese, and Norwegians traditionally turned to the sea for a livelihood as traders and fishers, and the merchant marine of Norway has been one of the largest in the world. In contrast, most of the French, Germans, and Irish, in spite of ample coastlines, concentrated in the interior.

Natural disasters such as volcanic eruptions and earthquakes can alter the population of small areas over short periods of time. The 1783 eruption of the

volcano Laki in southern Iceland, when ash was deposited on pastures and cropland, caused famine and a population reduction of 20 percent to only 38,000 by
1784. The spread of major diseases also altered the numbers and distribution of
population in Europe. Among the exotic Oriental exports that moved westward
over newly opened caravan routes between China and Europe in the late Middle
Ages came the *bubonic plague*. Together with silks and tapestries, it reached
Constantinople (modern Istanbul) in 1347, spreading quickly on beyond to Kriti,
Genova, and southern France (Figure 6.4). In the following year, the plague made
major inroads into Greece, Italy, Spain, and the remainder of France before entering the Germanic lands and Hungary. Epidemics recurred through much of the
remainder of the fourteenth century, and eventually the plague became endemic.
Some believe that the Black Death claimed 25 million victims in the 1300s, including two-thirds of the people in parts of Italy. The English population declined
from 3.7 million in 1350 to only 2 million by 1377. Less spectacular but still significant, *malaria* spread into the lowlands of the European Mediterranean in the
third and fourth centuries B.C., presumably from North Africa. Eventually malaria afflicted the Campagna, a large plain of about 2000 sq km (800 sq. mi.) between
the city of Roma and the Mediterranean coast. Intensively cultivated in antiquity,
the Campagna reached a peak of productivity at the height of the Roman
Empire. Then the elaborate system of drainage ditches built by the Romans fell
into neglect, cropland became abandoned, and marshes spread. Malaria entered
the Campagna and became endemic, particularly in the 1600s and 1700s. In consequence, the once-thriving Roman province became a thinly populated wasteland by 1800, a curious empty area on the outskirts of one of Europe's great
cities. The view to the west from the hills of Roma was bleak indeed, perhaps not
duplicated in desolation by the fringes of any other city in the world.
Reclamation and resettlement of the Campagna followed eradication of malaria
early in the present century. In certain other parts of Italy, hilltop towns and villages reveal the desire to escape malarial lowlands.

Cultural Factors in Distribution

The physical environment and its evaluation by humankind provides only part
of the explanation for population distribution. For a more complete answer, we
must turn to internal contrasts of European culture. Inheritance laws provide an
example. Traditionally, Southern Europe's legal systems derived from the
Romans, and in areas once part of the Roman Empire, their practice of divided
inheritance long remained dominant. In this tradition, landholdings and other
possessions were divided equally among all heirs. Farms thus became ever
smaller, in some instances producing landholdings too small to support the families living on them. Roman law, then, tended to produce very dense rural population.

In Northern Europe, by contrast, Germanic law and its English common law
offspring supported the principle of *primogeniture* or some other means of undivided inheritance. Land passed intact from parent to one child, with the remaining

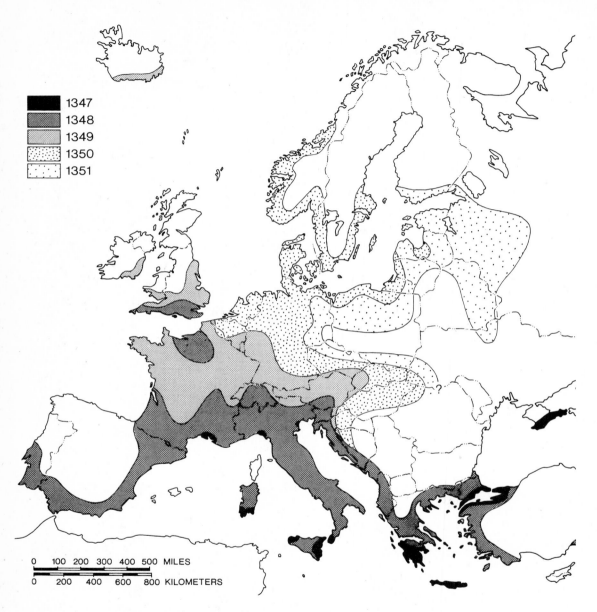

FIGURE 6.4 Diffusion of the Black Death, 1347–1351. Before the century ended, the disease had killed perhaps 25 million persons in Europe, causing a major population decline. The political borders shown are modern. (Sources: Adapted from Norman J. G. Pounds. *Hearth & Home,* Bloomington, USA: Indiana University Press, 1989, 225; E. Charpentier, "Autour de la peste noire," *Annales: Economies/Sociétés/Civilisations,* 17 (1962), 1062–1092; Colin McEvedy, "The Bubonic Plague," *Scientific American,* 258:2 (Feb. 1988), 121.)

offspring gaining compensation in other ways, if at all. Often the landless children emigrated or, in more recent times, moved to the cities, though many remained as tenant farmers. Germanic law, then, held down rural population growth. Germany lies directly astride the ancient legal divide between Southern and Northern Europe. In the provinces along the Rhine, Lahn, Main, Neckar, and Mosel rivers, once under Roman rule, including Baden-Württemberg, Rheinland-Pfalz, and parts of Hessen, farm miniaturization reached a critical degree by the 1840s, and rural overpopulation became a major problem, while in the North German Plain, a traditional stronghold of Germanic law never conquered by the Romans, rural population densities even in the fertile loess districts remained lower.

Warfare, another cultural phenomenon, can greatly alter population density. Numerous European wars had catastrophic demographic effects, perhaps none as destructive of human life as the Thirty Years' War, fought from 1618 to 1648 in Central Europe. The population of some German districts declined by two-thirds

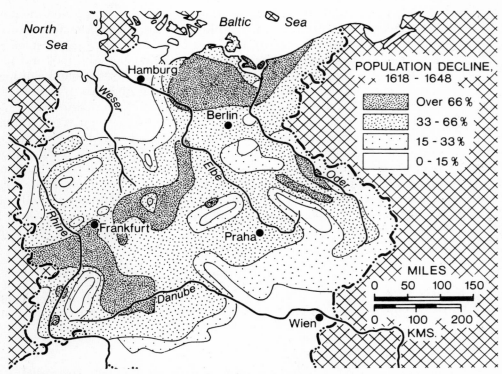

FIGURE 6.5 Population loss owing to warfare and disease in central Europe, 1618–1648. The Thirty Years' War and associated epidemics drastically reduced the number of people in parts of Germany and the present Czech Republic, producing a major change in population density and distribution. (Source: After Franz and Keyser in *Westermanns Grosser Atlas zur Weltgeschichte*, Braunschweig, D: Georg Westermann, 1956, 107.)

or more in that war, and major losses of life also occurred in Čechy (Bohemia) (Figure 6.5). More recently the estimated 20 million casualties suffered in World War II by the former Soviet Union, representing about 10 percent of its inhabitants, caused a decline in population that required decades to overcome. Germany counted almost 6 million soldiers and civilians dead in the same war, more than 8 percent of its people, and the former Yugoslavia lost fully 11 percent of its population, some 1.7 million persons.

Emigration

The most potent force influencing population density is migration, and Europeans have always proven remarkably mobile, especially during the past three centuries. The choice to migrate rests in culture, and a great many "push" and "pull" factors work to prompt the decision to leave one's home and seek another.

From about 1500 to 1950, emigration from Europe constituted the dominant flow. During that period, many millions of Europeans departed for Anglo-America, Latin America, Australia, New Zealand, South Africa, Israel, Siberia, and Algeria. Iberians began the exodus in the 1500s. Between 1600 and 1880, this greatest emigration in all history involved mainly northwestern Europeans of Germanic and Celtic background seeking better economic opportunity abroad. After about 1870 the exodus spread to Southern and Eastern Europe.

Some countries lost substantial parts of their total populations in this manner, causing major changes in densities. The island of Ireland provides a good example. In 1841 the census listed more than 8 million Irish, a density of more than 97 per sq km (250 per sq. mi.), and by the middle of the decade the Irish population had reached an all-time high of almost 8.5 million (Table 6.1). Then came the great famine of the mid–1840s, bringing death to hundreds of thousands, and in its wake a massive and persistent out-migration to Great Britain and overseas. In a five-year span from 1846 to 1851, some 800,000 Irish starved or

TABLE 6.1   The Irish Population, 1800–1992

Year	Population	Density of population per square kilometer
1800	5,000,000	59
1841	8,175,000	97
1845	8,450,000	100
1851	6,552,000	78
1861	5,765,000	68
1968	4,400,000[a]	52[a]
1992	5,113,000[a]	60[a]

[a] The Republic of Ireland plus Northern Ireland.

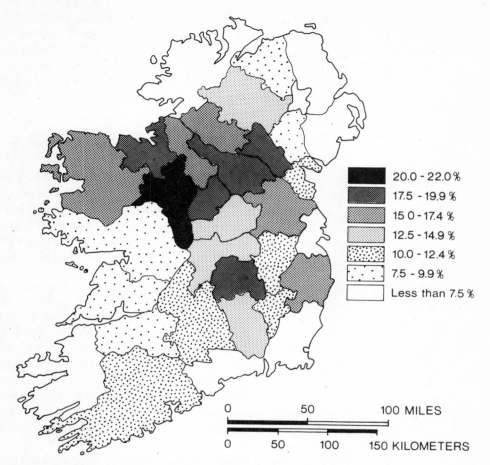

FIGURE 6.6 Emigration from Ireland, 1846–1851, As a percentage of the 1841 population. (Source: After S. H. Cousens, "The Regional Pattern of Emigration During the Great Irish Famine, 1846–51," *Institute of British Geographers, Transactions and Papers,* 28 (1960), 121; see also: James H. Johnson, "The Distribution of Irish Emigration in the Decade Before the Great Famine," *Irish Geography,* 21:2 (1988), 78–87.)

perished from disease, and another million emigrated to foreign lands. Hardest hit was interior Ireland, where one county lost more than 20 percent of its population through emigration (Figure 6.6). A century later, a little more than half as many resided in Ireland as in 1841. By 1990, 8½ times as many persons claiming Irish ancestry lived in the United States as remained in Ireland, and even Canada had a fourth as many Irish as the home country.

Germans, too, departed their native land in enormous numbers, settling mainly in the United States but also in southern Brazil, Canada, and South Africa. Persons of German ancestry constitute the largest national origin group in the United States numbering some 58 million in 1990, about 73 percent of the present population of Germany. Sweden and Norway experienced the highest proportional losses. Between 20 and 25 percent of the total population of those two Scandinavian countries emigrated overseas in the nineteenth century. Imagine what the density of people in Europe would be had mass emigration not occurred.

Immigration

About 1950 Europe rather suddenly changed from a land dominated by emigration to one of immigration, and that pattern has prevailed to the present. A booming economy attracted foreign workers, and growing affluence left many Europeans unwilling to engage in menial jobs. Among the immigrants drawn into Europe to supply needed labor were the West Indians, Africans, and Asians mentioned in Chapter 5, who came mainly to the United Kingdom, France, and the Netherlands.

Another major immigrant flow brought about 1 million Muslims from the formerly French-ruled **Maghreb** countries of North Africa—Morocco, Algeria, and Tunisia (Figure 6.7). Following on the heels of numerous ethnic French fleeing Algeria after that country overthrew rule by France in 1962, the Maghreb Muslims came mainly to France. In addition, many Moroccans went to Belgium and the Netherlands. The Maghreb immigration peaked in the 1970s, after which entry became more difficult. By the middle 1980s, Italy and Spain became the major destinations of Maghreb immigrants, and most now enter Europe illegally, crossing by small boats at the Strait of Gibraltar. Morocco has become the main source country, but even sub-Saharan Africans now reach Europe by the Gibraltar route.

Paralleling the Maghreb immigration, another 2 million persons or more entered Europe from **Turkey**; three-quarters of them headed to Germany (Figure 6.7). Turks also became the largest non-European immigrant group in Switzerland and Sweden. While this influx has largely ended, a steady flow of illegal Middle Eastern immigrants, including Kurds, Iranians, and Iraqis, still enters Europe. They come mainly by way of Turkey and Greece, the latter a country swamped by 400,000 to 600,000 illegal residents in 1993.

With the collapse of the Soviet Union in 1991, a new type of immigration to Europe began. Ethnic Russians residing in the former Central Asian Soviet Republics, particularly Kazakhstan, began moving to Russia, reversing a generations-old diaspora and overwhelming the supply of jobs, housing, and social services. This movement received attention in Chapter 4. It differs from typical European immigration in that it involves the return of a European-derived population to Europe, rather than the intrusion of ethnically alien foreigners. As such, the Russian migration can be compared to the movement of ethnic French out of Algeria in the 1960s.

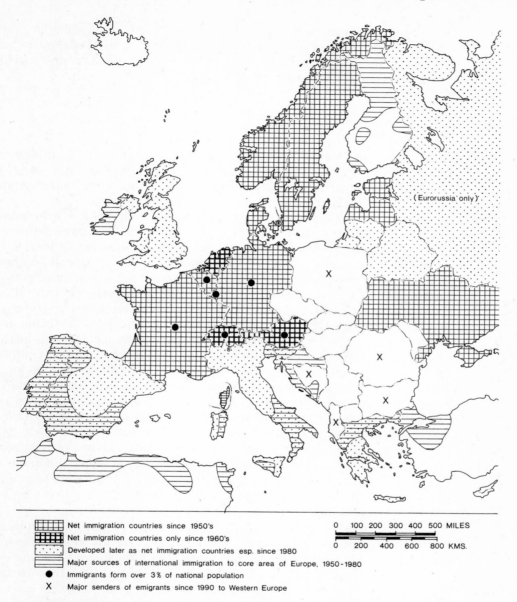

Net immigration countries since 1950's
Net immigration countries only since 1960's
Developed later as net immigration countries esp. since 1980
Major sources of international immigration to core area of Europe, 1950-1980
● Immigrants form over 3% of national population
X Major senders of emigrants since 1990 to Western Europe

0 100 200 300 400 500 MILES
0 200 400 600 800 KMS.

FIGURE 6.7 Migration in Europe since 1950. Prior to 1950, Europe lost more people through migration than it gained, but since then the greater part of the culture area has become a new immigration zone (immigrants outnumber emigrants). (Source: Adapted from King, 1993, 24, 209.)

The long-term mass immigration of non-Europeans, while initially welcomed and even encouraged, now causes alarm in many nations of Europe.

Restrictive new laws make legal immigration virtually impossible in countries such as Germany. Europeans feel threatened today; they fear being overwhelmed by throngs of poor people from the Third World. In the world's most cosmopolitan culture area, xenophobia ascends.

Internal Migration

Equally profound mass migration has occurred *within* Europe, a movement centuries old. One prevalent flow that began in the nineteenth century and still has not run its course everywhere is rural-to-urban migration. This important subject will be treated in Chapters 8 and 10.

Other internal migration generally falls in the category of **periphery-to-core**, though several distinctly different flows can be detected. Perhaps the prototype for this sort of migration involved the large-scale movement of Irish to Great Britain in the nineteenth century, a movement that has greatly diminished but never ceased, even to the present day. Of far greater magnitude in the periphery-to-core shift was the *south-to-north* migration in the period 1950 to 1975. Spain, Portugal, Italy, Greece, Croatia, and Slovenia became the major senders, with destinations lying mainly in France, Germany, Belgium, the Netherlands, and the Alpine countries (Figure 6.7). Some 5 million persons took part in this migration, including 1.7 million Italians, mainly from the impoverished southern part of that country, and 1.1 million Portuguese. They blazed a trail to the north in the 1950s and early 1960s that would later be followed by the Maghreb Africans and Turks. As late as 1970 in Germany, Yugoslavs and Italians ranked as the two largest immigrant groups. Portugal and Spain contributed disproportionately to France, and the Low Countries also received large contingents of Spaniards. A great many Southern European emigrants eventually returned to their native lands.

The northern periphery of Europe, far more thinly populated than the south, could not send mass migration to the core. Even so, a sizable proportion of the northerners went south, most notably Finns from subarctic districts who sought employment opportunities in central and southern Sweden.

At present, the largest periphery-to-core movement under way involves **east-to-west** migration. Long dammed up by the Iron Curtain, this new avenue of mobility opened in earnest in the late 1980s. The former East Germany experienced a population decline of 1 million between 1989 and 1994. Dire predictions of uncontrollable mass migration from the east appeared, including speculation that as many as 46 million Russians desired to move west. The influx of a mere 43,000 desperate Albanians to Italy in 1991 led a newsweekly there to editorialize that "well-to-do Europe intends to defend itself from the invasion of the new barbarians who come from the East." In the same year, the French similarly recoiled at the sight of thousands of Eastern Europeans camped in tents in the Bois de Boulogne park in Paris, and the government acted to evict them. As early as 1989, about 1 million Eastern Europeans, excluding emigrants from East Germany, resided in Western Europe. About a third of these consisted of ethnic Germans from countries such as Romania, who enjoy the legal right to come to Germany.

So far the predicted tidal wave of east-to-west migration has not materialized, in part because of more restrictive immigration policies. Only Germany, which housed one million Eastern Europeans by 1990, and Austria, home to 600,000 foreigners by 1992, felt serious impacts, and many of their immigrants are Balkan war refugees or ethnic Germans. Emigration from Russia and other former Soviet republics apparently peaked in 1990 at 454,000. Many Eastern European states have a larger volume of immigration than emigration (Figure 6.7). Barring total economic collapse in the east, migration seems unlikely to get out of control. However, the great disparity in wealth and living standards between the two halves of Europe will continue to exert a powerful westward pull, and an even more profound contrast along Europe's Mediterranean frontier likewise produces continuing instability. Can the rich nations of Europe maintain their enviable standards of living, admitting just enough disadvantaged foreigners to supply labor needs?

Ethnic Cleansing

The sinister twin of voluntary migration is forced population movement, usually carried out in Europe to remove undesired ethnic minorities. Indeed, Europeans, who often take on airs of cultural superiority, perfected large-scale ethnic cleansing and developed it practically into an art form. The peak period of these forced migrations occurred between 1920 and 1950, when an astounding total of 33 million Europeans were forcibly expelled from their homelands, a violation of what that most civilized of all Europeans, Albert Schweitzer, called "the most basic of all human rights"—to live in one's ancestral homeland (Figure 6.8). Sudden, drastic changes in population density and cultural patterns resulted.

The precedent for this ugly business came in the Greek-Muslim exchange of the early 1920s. The century-long war of Greek liberation from Turkish rule ended, leaving the large ethnic Greek populations in Asia Minor and the Istanbul area still in Turkey. At the same time many Muslims lived in the liberated regions. A population exchange brought ethnic and political boundaries into agreement. More than 1 million Greeks left Turkey, in exchange for hundreds of thousands of Turks, Pomaks, and other Muslims. From that time on, millions of Europeans, whose only fault was residence on the wrong side of an artificially created political border, lost the right to continue to live in the land of their ancestors.

Nazi Germany instigated the next series of ethnic cleansings. Contrary to what might be expected, the people involved were often ethnic Germans, Teutonic minorities from the Alps and plains of Eastern Europe "called home" by Hitler. Altogether, some 600,000 ethnic Germans left ancestral homes in Italy, Estonia, Latvia, Lithuania, eastern Poland, Croatia, Romania, and Hungary. The Nazis expelled even greater numbers of Jews, Poles, Russians, and other Eastern European groups from their homelands and a great many of them perished in concentration camps. The Nazis achieved an immense restructuring of the ethnic geography of Eastern Europe.

Germans
B   Balts
C   Czechs and Slovaks
F   Finns
G   Greeks
H   Hungarians
I   Italians
M   Macedonian Slavs (Pomaks)
P   Poles
R   Russians, etc.
S   Serbs and Croats
T   Turks
U   Ukrainians

to Germany

from
Dodecanese

Number of migrants:
■   25,000
■   125,000
■   500,000
■   2,000,000

FIGURE 6.8 Selected forced migrations, or "ethnic cleansing," in Europe, 1920–1980. Jewish deportations are excluded (see Figure 3.18), as is recent ethnic cleansing in Bosnia-Herzegovina and the abortive renewed removal of Turks from Bulgaria in 1989. (Sources: Joseph B. Schechtman, *Postwar Population Transfers in Europe,* Philadelphia, USA: University of Pennsylvania Press, 1963; Guido Weigend, "Effects of Boundary Changes in the South Tyrol," *Geographical Review,* 40 (1950), 364–375; Velikonja 1958; Blanchard 1925; Kostanick 1957.)

Soon the Germans were abundantly repaid for these abuses. As the *Third Reich* collapsed, large eastern territories were annexed by Poland and Russia. Between 1944 and 1951, in the largest forced migration ever to occur, 9 million people were expelled from these areas, amounting to 90 percent of the total population in an area of 130,000 sq km (50,000 sq. mi.), approximately the size and population of present-day Pennsylvania. The catastrophic effect on population density persisted for decades (Figure 6.9).

Simultaneously, Czechs expelled 3 million more Germans from their centuries-old ethnic stronghold in the Sudetenland, the highland rim of the Czech Republic. Elsewhere, the ethnic housecleaning following World War II involved a great variety of groups other than Germans. An exchange of Slovaks and Hungarians occurred, as well as a Soviet-Polish trade involving more than 2 million persons. In the early 1950s and again in 1989, Bulgaria transferred additional Turks "back" to Turkey, continuing an expulsion begun in the 1920s. Finland, which shared Germany's wartime defeat ceded certain eastern territories to Russia, causing a flood of 500,000 displaced Finns to enter the remnant Finnish nation. More recently, 260,000 Greeks and Turks suffered ethnic cleansing in Cyprus in the 1970s, and the present Balkan war brought renewed ethnic cleansing to Europe. Bosnians and Croats suffered most in this latest episode of forced migration, with perhaps as many as 1 million refugees by 1994.

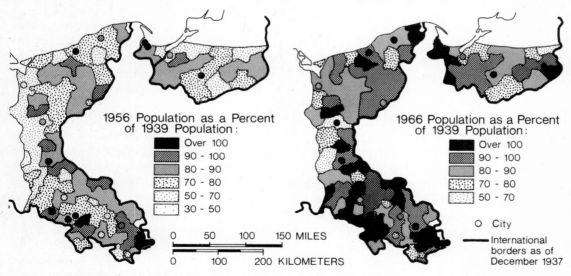

FIGURE 6.9 Population density changes in the former eastern German territories now part of Poland, 1939–1966. From the old German provinces of Schlesien, Pommern, and Ostpreussen, as well as the area of Danzig (modern Gdańsk), some 8 million people were forcibly expelled in the 1944–1951 period as a result of border changes. These maps reveal the Polish difficulty in replacing the expelled people with ethnic Poles over a period of 20 years. (Source: Ekkehard Buchhofer, "Der Aufsiedlungsgrad der polnisch verwalteten deutschen Ostgebiete von 1946–1966," *Geographische Rundschau*, 20, 1968, 368–369.)

Fertility

The size and distribution of population in Europe has also been greatly influenced by birth and death rates; these have varied both through time and through geographical area. One of the distinguishing human traits that sets Europeans apart from most other inhabitants of the Eastern Hemisphere has been their mastery over both fertility and mortality. A phenomenon known as the **demographic transition** originated in Europe in the nineteenth century. Prior to this far-reaching change, both birth rates and death rates remained high, producing at best a slowly growing population. Then, initiating the transition, Europeans lowered the death rate through improved health care and the elimination of famine, causing a major population explosion in the short run since birth rates stayed high.

The second stage of the demographic transition also began in Europe. It involved a gradual, persistent fall in the birth rate, leading to *sustained fertility decline* and to a situation in which both birth and death rates were low. The European population explosion had ended, ushering in another period of slow growth.

The transition initially revealed a vivid geography. Sustained fertility decline first appeared in France about 1820, perhaps as an after-effect of the personal freedoms achieved through the French Revolution (Figure 6.10). Ethnic minorities in France and people in other countries were initially slow to follow the French example, with the result that France fell behind major neighboring countries in size of population (Table 6.2). In the 1700s, when 1 of every 6 Europeans was French, and even as late as 1850, the French outnumbered the Germans, Italians, and British, but by 1970 they had become the smallest of these four nations, even though far more Germans died in wars and a much smaller flow of emigration emanated from France.

Eventually, though, sustained fertility decline spread. By 1900 about half of all European provinces had been affected (Figure 6.10), and today birth rates have become remarkably uniform and low throughout the culture area. In Europe as a whole, the annual rate of population growth now stands at +0.2 percent, a startling contrast to Africa's +3.0 percent or even Turkey's +2.1 percent and Turkish Cyprus' +1.3 percent.

Achievement of sustained fertility decline came last to the fringe areas of Europe, and remnants of a core/periphery pattern can still be detected in the map of annual natural population change (Figure 6.11). Communist rule in Eastern Europe somewhat retarded the decline of birth rates there before about 1990, especially in Romania, but a major decline in fertility recently began there. In Russia, for example, the annual birth rate fell from 17.2 per thousand inhabitants in 1987 to only 10.8 in 1993. Eastern Germany's birth rate declined from 11.1 in 1990, at the time of reunification, to only 5.1 by 1993. Some peripheral European areas remain anomalous in fertility, as, for example, Iceland, the Arctic fringe, and Muslim sections of the Balkans. The southern and eastern borders of the European culture area, where it touches the Islamic world, stands out very

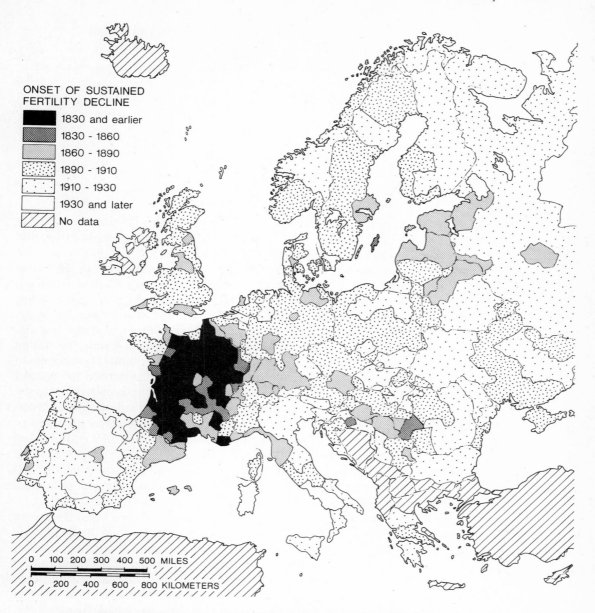

ONSET OF SUSTAINED FERTILITY DECLINE

- ■ 1830 and earlier
- ▨ 1830 - 1860
- ▦ 1860 - 1890
- ⠿ 1890 - 1910
- ⠂ 1910 - 1930
- ☐ 1930 and later
- ▧ No data

0 100 200 300 400 500 MILES

0 200 400 600 800 KILOMETERS

FIGURE 6.10 Advent of sustained fertility decline in Europe, as measured by an index of married women. The French-speaking part of France provided the prototype for diminished fertility. People in other countries were slow to emulate the French, but diffusion to the various peripheries of Europe eventually occurred. Today, nearly all areas have birth rates far below the world average. (Source: Adapted from Coale and Watkins 1986, follows 484.)

TABLE 6.2   The Growth of the French, German, British, and Italian Populations, 1720–1970 (in Millions)

Nation	1720	1800	1850	1900	1930	1970
France	19	27	36	38	42	50
Germany	14	25	35	56	64	77[a]
Italy	13	18	23	32	41	53
Great Britain and Northern Ireland	7	11	27	37	46	55

[a] East and West Germany together.

clearly on the map of annual population change. Within Tatarstan, a Turkic Muslim republic in Russia, the Tatar birthrate stands 40 percent higher than that of ethnic Russians living among them.

Parts of Europe, in fact, have experienced what some experts call the *second demographic transition,* in which the birth rate falls and remains below the death rate, leading within a generation to population decline. In this case western Germany provided the prototype, quickly followed by Austria and Hungary. Fertility dropped below replacement level there about 1965, with actual population decline setting in by 1980 or 1985. In fact, Europe as a whole had fallen below the replacement level as early as 1985, presaging a declining population in the very near future for the entire culture area. Russia experienced the second demographic transition with surprising rapidity; deaths exceeded births by 200,000 there in 1992 and by 800,000 the following year. In the long run, an average of 2.1 children must be born to each woman for population numbers to remain stable, but the average in Europe by 1985 had fallen to 1.69 and in western Germany to 1.28. In Russia the average declined to 1.4 by 1993. Europe entered what some called a "demographic crisis" or even "catastrophe" or "collapse." A greater contrast to the Third World, with its exploding populations, could not be imagined.

The result of both these demographic transitions has been a rapid decline of the European proportion of the world population. In the year 1900, Europe accounted for 25 percent of the world total, but by 1995 only about 12 percent of all humans lived in Europe, and the proportion continues to decline rapidly. Should the present trend continue, Europeans will constitute an insignificant part of the world population by the year 2025, making the culture area an even more enticing goal of mass immigration from the impoverished Third World. Europeans could well breed themselves out of existence.

The Europeans achieved their remarkable level of fertility control through diverse techniques. In the formative stage in early-nineteenth-century France, infanticide—the killing of the newborn—apparently occurred widely. Abortion, early achieved with various folk methods and later through state-supported medical systems, represents another favored European method, though now in

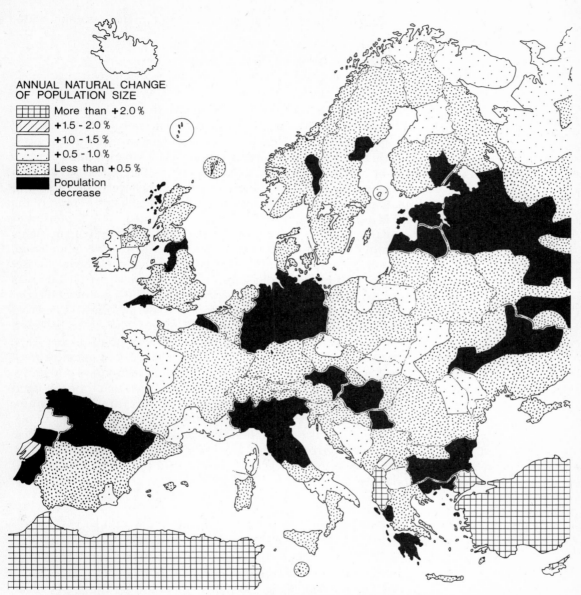

FIGURE 6.11 Annual natural population change, about 1990, as a percentage of total population, by province. This rate is achieved by comparing the number of births and deaths in a year, calculating the difference (either + or –), and taking it as a percentage of population. A faint core/periphery pattern can be detected. Since 1990 nearly all of Eastern Europe has reportedly fallen into the "decrease" category, but reliable provincial statistics remain unavailable. Gains or losses through migration are not reflected here. (Sources: Various national censuses and statistical yearbooks.)

decline (Figure 6.12). Sterilization and diverse contraceptive devices enjoy widespread acceptance.

Age Structure

Because of fertility control and the reduction of the death rate, Europe's population is the world's oldest. The 18 countries with the greatest proportion of people aged 65 or older all lie in Europe, led by Sweden and Norway. Many provinces, especially in Scandinavia and the European Union (E.U.), have an aged population of 16 percent or more; a few even exceed 20 percent (Figure 6.13). With each passing year, these proportions grow higher. The contrast between the aging European population and the overwhelmingly youthful inhabitants of most of the rest of the world is quite striking. In 1990, the E.U. accounted for 6 ½ percent of the world's population and 15 percent of those 65 and older. Major problems loom concerning provision of health and welfare services to an older population, since such a large demographic sector has reached retirement age. The later onset of profoundly diminished fertility in Eastern Europe and most peripheral areas yields noticeable east/west and core/periphery patterns. The most obvious contrasts, however, separate Europe from North Africa, Turkey, and the Middle East.

The more affluent among Europe's elderly often migrate to selected provinces, helping to shape the map of aging. Many retired people seek to escape cities and colder regions. In Great Britain, for example, southern England's coast remains a preferred destination for retirees; the south of France enjoys popularity within that country; and the south coast of Norway lures many of the aged Norse. Some even leave their native country and migrate to the sunny Mediterranean, at least for part of the year. By the middle 1980s, for example, some 2500 elderly Norwegians resided in the Benidorm district south of Valencia in Spain. In Eastern Europe, by contrast, the elderly usually move to the cities, where their children often live and health care amenities are better. Poland has such a migration pattern.

Education

Another distinctly European demographic trait is a very high level of education. By any measure, Europe possesses the best-educated population of any sizable area in the world. To understand the enormous global impact Europe has had, we must recognize that we deal here with 700 million skilled, educated people, not with poorly schooled or illiterate masses. As a result Europe has functioned as the world center of research, progress, and innovation.

Access to basic education for the great majority of Europeans came about in the nineteenth and early twentieth centuries, beginning in northwestern Europe and spreading southward and eastward. German peasants learned to read and write in the first half of the 1800s, while most Russians, Italians, and other Mediterranean and Slavic farm folk remained illiterate. Only after the

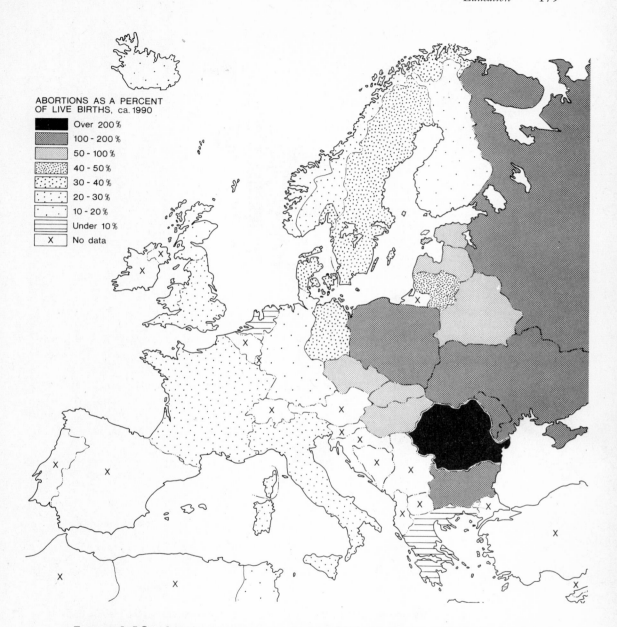

FIGURE 6.12 Abortions as a percentage of live births, ca. 1990. The legality of abortion varies within Europe, as does its application. It appears to be the principal device for fertility control in eastern Europe. Poland instituted very restrictive abortion laws after 1990, and in the former East Germany, the abortion rate fell by 40% between 1989 and 1992. Internal differentiation is shown only for Norway and the United Kingdom; western and eastern Germany are also separated. (Sources: U.N. Demographic Yearbook and various national statistical yearbooks.)

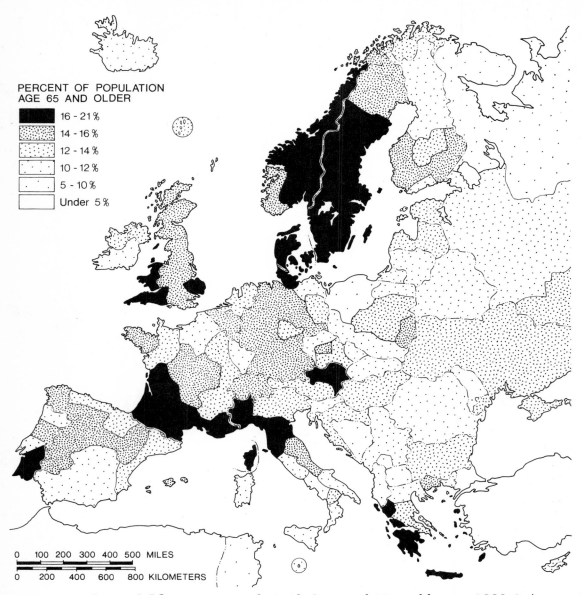

PERCENT OF POPULATION
AGE 65 AND OLDER

- 16 - 21 %
- 14 - 16 %
- 12 - 14 %
- 10 - 12 %
- 5 - 10 %
- Under 5 %

0 100 200 300 400 500 MILES

0   200 400 600 800 KILOMETERS

FIGURE 6.13 Percentage of population aged 65 or older, ca. 1990. Both east/west and core/periphery patterns are evident. (Sources: diverse national censuses and statistical yearbooks; Korcelli/Potrykowska, 1988; *1993 World Population Data Sheet.* Undifferentiated sizable countries = BG, BY, CZ, H, RO, UKR.)

Communist takeover did education become available to the average Russian. In most of Europe, education spread to the masses because of ambitious government-supported education plans. European central governments direct the operation of schools, while in the United States local governments play a greater role. In France, for example, the government maintains control over the schools through the Ministry of Education. The state requires children to remain in school for a certain number of years.

The literacy rate offers a crude but still revealing measure of basic education (Figure 6.14). Over 95 percent of all Europeans above the age of 10 can read and write, and in the northwestern quadrant of the culture area, the proportion exceeds 99 percent. Only in Portugal, Malta, Cyprus, and portions of the Balkans does the level fall below 90 percent. The Mediterranean forms an educational fault line along Europe's southern boundary, beyond which literacy rates are far lower.

Other measures of education may prove even more revealing, as for example book readership. Northern Europe leads in the number of book titles published each year. Germany ranks first with 72,000 different titles printed annually, followed by the United Kingdom, France, Spain, and the Netherlands. The high position of Spain results in part from the demands of a huge, overseas Spanish-speaking population. On a per capita basis, Iceland, Denmark, Finland, and Switzerland lead, and in Iceland, one book title is published annually for each 164 people, the highest proportion in the world (Figure 6.14). The Icelandic, Danish, and Finnic achievements are made even more remarkable by the fact little or no foreign demand exists for books in the languages of those nations. Lowest levels of book production per capita occur in Ukraine, Romania, Belarus, and Albania with between 3400 and 6300 persons per book title, but even these countries compare favorably to bordering non-European states such as Tunisia, where the proportion is 27,000 persons per title.

Health

If Europeans are "wise," they are also usually healthy and wealthy. Access to high-quality affordable medical care remains the rule; doctor/patient ratios are low; the typical European consumes abundant, nutritional food; the traditional epidemic and endemic diseases have been banished; and life expectancy, with some notable exceptions, exceeds 70 years. These remarkable achievements in human health emanated from the core area of Europe and spread to the peripheries, a diffusion completed in fairly recent times. In Greece, representative of the European periphery, male life expectancy rose from 49 to 70 years in the half-century between 1930 and 1980. Only parts of Eastern Europe in which the collapse of Communism led to a rapidly deteriorating level of health care and nutrition after 1990 depart substantially from the prevalent high standards. In Russia, the modest reappearance by 1993 of diphtheria, cholera, and even bubonic plague testify to a partial breakdown of health and sanitation services. Male life expectancy in Russia fell to only 59 years in 1993, and death rates rose throughout most of the formerly Communist East.

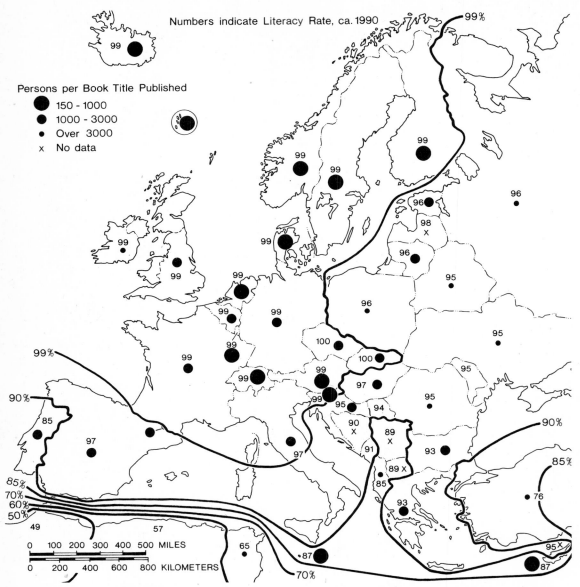

FIGURE 6.14 Literacy rate and persons per book title published, c. 1990. (Source: U.N. Statistical Yearbook.)

Due to the aged character of the European population, death rates do not rank low by world standards and are not very revealing of the welfare of the people. Rather, the most significant single indicator of health standards is the **infant mortality rate.** Indeed, this index, which shows the number of infants per thousand that die before reaching the age of 1 year, is widely regarded as the best single measure of the overall standard of living (Figure 6.15). Within Europe,

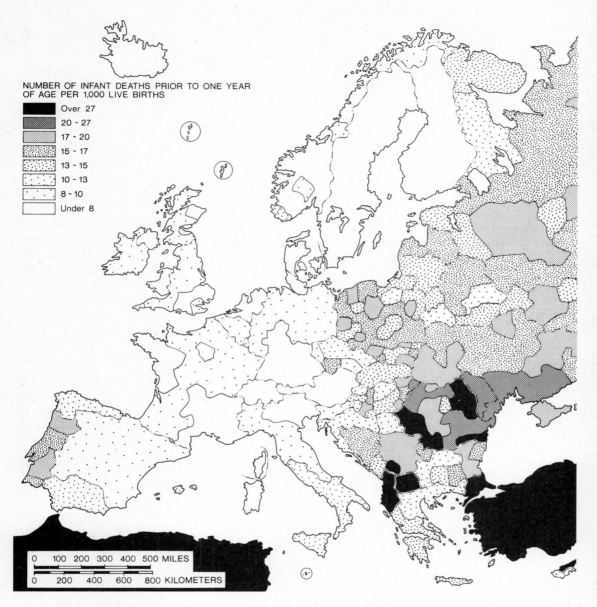

NUMBER OF INFANT DEATHS PRIOR TO ONE YEAR
OF AGE PER 1,000 LIVE BIRTHS

⬛	Over 27
	20 - 27
	17 - 20
	15 - 17
	13 - 15
	10 - 13
	8 - 10
⬜	Under 8

0   100 200 300 400 500 MILES

0   200   400   600   800 KILOMETERS

FIGURE 6.15 Infant mortality rate, or the number of deaths of children under 1 year
of age per 1000 live births, ca. 1990. Many experts feel that this rate provides the single
best index of the standard of living. Reputedly, rates have risen substantially in Eastern Europe since the most recent data were published, heightening the east/west contrast that already provides the most striking aspect of the map. Europe versus non-Europe is also abundantly evident. (Sources: In addition to the standard national statistical sources, I drew upon
a cartographic presentation for Eastern Europe prepared by Professor Kazimierz J.
Zaniewski of the University of Wisconsin at Oshkosh.)

a pronounced east/west contrast in the infant mortality rate exists. Moreover, recent substantial rises in infant mortality in much of Eastern Europe heightened the difference between the two sections of the culture area. In Russia the rate began gradually worsening in the 1980s, reputedly followed by an alarming increase from 17.1 in 1992 to 19.3 or 22.0 the following year, depending upon which estimates one believes. Romania, Macedonia, and Albania have the highest infant mortality rates in Europe. Bad as conditions have become in Eastern Europe, they remain good by world standards. In much of Africa and Asia, the infant mortality rate stands well above 100, and just across the Mediterranean and Aegean, one encounters rates such as 59 in Turkey, 61 in Algeria, and 68 in Libya. The world average is 70.

The major illnesses that still plague Europeans are those of the modern, industrial world: cancer, circulatory diseases, respiratory maladies, and, of course, AIDS. Environmental pollution can perhaps be blamed for many of these disorders. Respiratory diseases, for example, occur most frequently in the core countries of Europe, including the United Kingdom, Belgium, the Netherlands, Germany, Poland (which has the highest incidence in the entire world), and the Czech Republic, where atmospheric pollution is most severe. In other cases, diseases seem to occur selectively in certain ethnic groups. Stomach cancer rates, for example, are highest in northern Wales, a Celtic stronghold, and among the Dutch-speaking Belgians, suggesting a link to culturally based dietary preferences.

The AIDS epidemic reached Europe rather early, apparently diffusing from both Africa and North America. The disease took root initially in the southwest, especially in France and Spain, and the incidence remains highest there (Figure 6.16). No corner of Europe has escaped AIDS, with the possible exception of Albania, but the countries of Eastern Europe still report very low incidences. Some evidence suggests that the epidemic has peaked because the number of new cases declined every year since 1990. Still, over 90,000 new cases appeared in 1993. In Southern and Eastern Europe, AIDS occurs principally among heterosexuals or, in the tragic case of Romania, among children who received tainted blood transfusions.

Wealth

On the average, Europeans remain far wealthier than the greater part of humanity, but conditions vary substantially within the culture area. Personal income is a poor measure of wealth, due to the variability of benefits received from governments in various countries and greatly differing inflation rates. More revealing is the **gross domestic product** (GDP), a measure of all goods and services produced in a country or province within a given time span, particularly when calculated on a per capita basis (Figure 6.17). In a sizable part of western Europe, the annual GDP per capita exceeds $15,000.

In much of Eastern Europe, the GDP is alarmingly low and extremely volatile. Figures plummeted following the collapse of the Communist system. In

Ukraine, for example, a decline of 33 percent in the GDP occurred in the two years following 1991, while 1992 witnessed a 30 percent fall in Latvia, 20 percent in Estonia, 15 percent in Macedonia, and 27 percent in the remnant Yugoslavia. The Czech Republic, which suffered a 30 percent decline in GDP from 1989 to 1992, experienced no further decline in the following year, pointing to possible recovery, though neighboring Slovakia did not fare so well.

Other factors important in determining the relative affluence of a country include the inflation rate, unemployment rate, and availability of basic commodities. Chronically high rates of unemployment, in excess of 15 percent, plague many peripheral areas of Western Europe, including Italy's Mezzogiorno, most of Spain, eastern Germany, Ireland, and those parts of Great Britain lying north of the Severn-Wash Divide (Figure 6.17), though generous unemployment benefits ease the impact in some countries. In Eastern Europe, high unemployment rates are a post-Communist phenomenon, and benefits remain inadequate. Slovakia recently passed the 15 percent unemployed level, and for a time eastern Germany and parts of Poland endured a rate near 30 percent, as inefficient factories closed. Finland, hurt by the economic decline of Russia, had 20 percent of its work force unemployed by 1994.

Much of Eastern Europe experienced hyperinflation in the early 1990s, wiping out personal savings and reducing many people to the level of poverty. In 1993, inflation ran at over 40 percent *per month* in Ukraine and 25 percent in Russia. Yugoslavia experienced similar rates, due in no small part to the international trade blockade linked to the Balkan War. Slovakia, in its first year of independence, had an annual inflation rate of 20 percent. A sizable part of formerly Communist Europe suffered an annual inflation rate of over 100 percent in 1992 and/or 1993 (Figure 6.17).

Quality of Life

Health, wealth, and education all help shape the overall quality of life, as do certain other factors such as type of housing, availability of leisure time, and levels of political freedom, crime, and civil unrest. As indicated earlier, some experts believe that the infant mortality rate provides the best single indicator of quality of life since it reflects numerous causal factors such as medical care, nutrition, education and affluence (Figure 6.15).

More comprehensive indices can be obtained by combining a wider variety of social and economic factors. Two such composite measures appear on the accompanying map (Figure 6.18). All such measures remain selective and necessarily subjective, but they also likely convey a meaningful message or at least an index of Western materialistic success. Northwestern Europe enjoys the highest quality of life, and the Balkan Peninsula suffers the worst. Living standards fall dramatically from northwest to southeast, and sizable, less-advantaged parts of Europe do not differ greatly from surrounding non-European countries. Moreover, the gradient from high to low quality of life has steepened in recent years, in the post-Communist era.

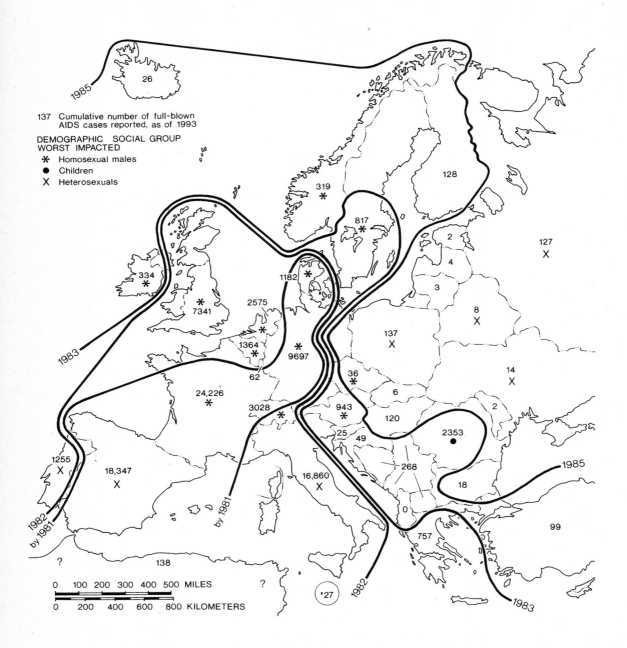

FIGURE 6.16 Diffusion and incidence of AIDS, to 1993. The disease spread from the southwestern part of Europe, where it first occurred in France. (Sources: Data provided by the World Health Organization; Gary W. Shannon et al., *The Geography of AIDS,* New York, USA: Guilford Press, 1991.)

FIGURE 6.17 Levels of wealth, middle 1990s. Numerous factors, such as gross domestic product (GDP) per capita, inflation rate, unemployment, the designation of "priority" assisted areas, personal income, results of economic reform in the former communist countries, the impact of warfare, and the effects of international economic sanctions were considered in compiling this admittedly subjective map. GDP is the value of all goods and services produced in a province or country in a year. Even in the "basket case" areas, many people (especially rural folk) were coping fairly well. The Severn-Wash Divide and the Mezzogiorno border are often mentioned as "limits of prosperity," but differences are always relative.

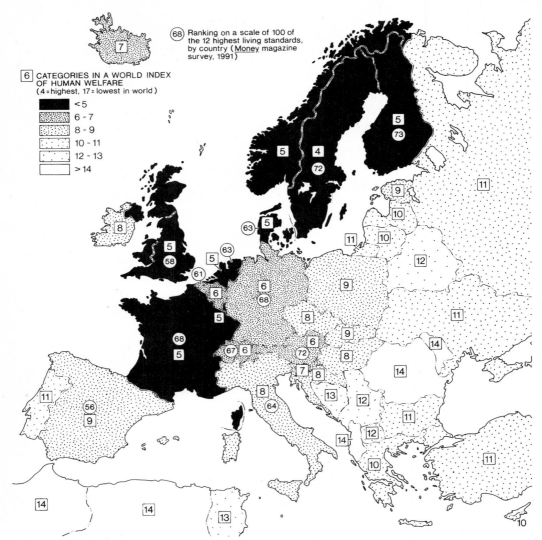

FIGURE 6.18 Quality of life and human welfare, ca. 1993. The shaded categories are based upon an index of human welfare, combining gross national product per capita, manufacturing value added per capita, primary industrial output per capita, arable land per capita, infant mortality rate, percentage of population rural, percentage obtaining higher education, access to mass media, government expenditures per capita, and access to political freedoms. The rankings of the 12 highest living standards are based upon 9 criteria: life expectancy, home ownership, unemployment rate, personal income, percentage college-educated, automobile ownership, murder rate, VCR ownership, and adequate leisure time. The figure for Germany excludes its eastern provinces. (Sources: Substantially updated from Robert J. Tata and Ronald R. Schultz, "World Variation in Human Welfare," *Annals of the Association of American Geographers,* 78, 1988, 586–588; Denise M. Topolnicki, "Why We Still Live Best," *Money,* Oct. 1991, 87–91.)

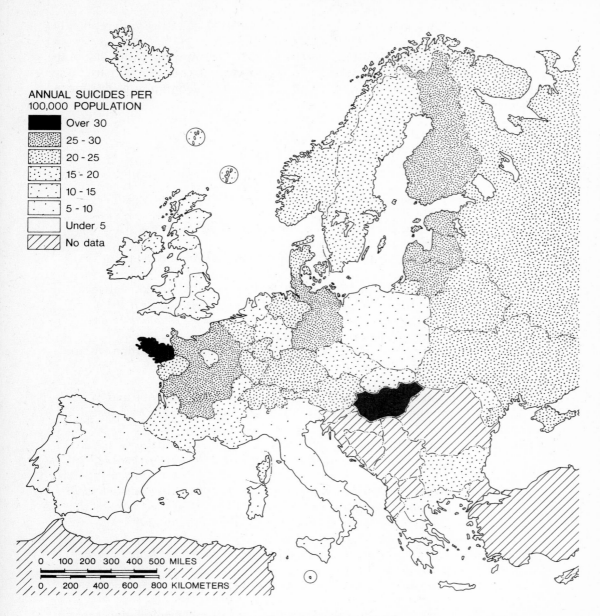

FIGURE 6.19 Suicide rate, about 1991. European rates are very high by world standards, particularly in the core region. Compare this map to Figure 3.16. Russia's rate reportedly leaped to 38 per 100,000 by 1993. (Sources: Various censuses and statistical yearbooks; U.N. Demographic Yearbook. The only countries for which internal differentiation is shown are D, E, F, GB, and GR.)

As an antidote to these Western, admittedly materialist-based measures, consider the suicide rate in Europe (Figure 6.19). A different pattern emerges, in which most peripheral areas have lower rates and some countries with reputedly high quality of life have disturbing incidences of suicide.

Europe, then, reveals vivid, ever-changing demographic contrasts, both internally and in comparison to bordering non-European countries. In part, these and other human patterns are rooted in the political geography of Europe, a topic dealt with in the next chapter.

Sources and Suggested Readings

Roberto Almagia. "The Repopulation of the Roman Campagna." *Geographical Review*. 19 (1929), 529–555.

Raoul Blanchard. "The Exchange of Populations Between Greece and Turkey." *Geographical Review*. 15 (1925), 449–456.

Toni Breuer. "Changing Patterns of the Population Distribution in Spain." *GeoJournal*. 13 (1986), 75–84.

Francis W. Carter, R. A. French, and J. Salt. "International Migration Between East and West in Europe." *Ethnic and Racial Studies*. 16 (1993), 467–491.

Ansley J. Coale and Susan C. Watkins (eds.). *The Decline of Fertility in Europe*. Princeton, USA: Princeton University Press, 1986.

John P. Cole and Igor V. Filatotchev. "Some Observations on Migration within and from the Former USSR in the 1990s." *Post-Soviet Geography*. 33 (1992), 432–453.

David A. Coleman. "Contrasting Age Structures of Western Europe and of Eastern Europe and the Former Soviet Union." *Population and Development Review*. 19 (1993), 523–555.

Paul A. Compton. "Religious Affiliation and Demographic Variability in Northern Ireland." *Transactions of the Institute of British Geographers*. 1 (1976), 433–445.

Robert E. Dickinson. *The Population Problem of Southern Italy: An Essay in Social Geography*. Syracuse, USA: Syracuse University Press, 1955.

Nicholas Eberstadt. "Demographic Shocks in Eastern Germany, 1989–93." *Europe-Asia Studies*. 46 (1994), 519–533.

Allan Findlay and Paul White (eds.). *West European Population Change*. London, GB: Croom Helm, 1986.

Alice Garnett. "Insolation, Topography, and Settlement in the Alps." *Geographical Review*. 25 (1935), 601–617.

Andryzey Gawryszewski and Alina Potrykowska. "Rural Depopulation Areas in Poland." *Geographia Polonica*. 54 (1988), 81–99.

James R. Gibson. "Interregional Migration in the USSR, 1981–1985 and 1971–1975." *Canadian Geographer*. 35 (1991), 143–156.

Josef Haliczer. "The Population of Europe, 1720, 1820, 1930." *Geography*. 19 (1934), 261–273.

Ray Hall and Philip Ogden. *Update: Europe's Population in the 1970s and 1980s*. Cambridge, GB: Cambridge University Press, 1985.

Kimberly A. Hamilton. *Migration and the New Europe.* Boulder, USA: Westview Press, 1994.

Carl Haub. "Population Changes in the Former Soviet Republics." *Population Bulletin.* 49:4 (1995).

Gerhard Heilig, Thomas Büttner, and Wolfgang Lutz. "Germany's Population: Turbulent Past, Uncertain Future." *Population Bulletin.* 45:4 (1990), 1–45.

E. Honekopp. *Migratory Movements from Countries of Central and Eastern Europe.* Strasbourg, F: Council of Europe, 1990.

Pieter Hooimeijer et al. (eds.). *Population Dynamics in Europe: Current Issues in Population Geography.* Utrecht, NL: Royal Netherlands Geographical Society, University of Utrecht (Netherlands Geographical Studies, No. 173), 1994.

G. Melvyn Howe (ed.). *Global Geocancerology: a World Geography of Human Cancers.* Edinburgh, GB: Churchill Livingstone, 1986, chapters 7 through 15.

George D. Hubbard. "The Geography of Residence in Norway Fiord Areas." *Annals of the Association of American Geographers.* 22 (1932), 109–118.

Brian W. Ilbery. "Core-Periphery Contrasts in European Social Well-Being." *Geography.* 69 (1984), 289–302.

James H. Johnson. "The Context of Migration: The Example of Ireland in the Nineteenth Century." *Transactions of the Institute of British Geographers.* 15 (1990), 259–276.

P. N. Jones and M. T. Wild. "Western Germany's Third Wave of Migrants: The Arrival of the Aussiedler." *Geoforum.* 23 (1992), 1–11.

Heather Joshi (ed.). *The Changing Population of Britain.* New York, USA: Basil Blackwell, 1989.

Dirk J. van de Kaa. "Europe's Second Demographic Transition." *Population Bulletin.* 42:1 (1987), 1–57.

Russell King (ed.). *Mass Migration in Europe: The Legacy and the Future.* London, GB: Belhaven Press, 1993.

Russell King (ed.). *The New Geography of European Migrations.* New York, USA: John Wiley & Sons, 1993.

Russell King and Alan Strachan. "Spatial Variations in Sicilian Migration." *Mediterranean Studies.* 2 (1980), 60–87.

Piotr Korcelli and Alina Potrykowska. "Redistribution of the Elderly Population in Poland." *Geographia Polonica.* 58 (1988), 121–138.

Leszek A. Kosiński. *The Population of Europe: A Geographical Perspective.* Harlow, GB: Longman, 1970.

Huey L. Kostanick. "Turkish Resettlement of Bulgarian Turks 1950–1953." *University of California Publications in Geography.* 8:2 (1957), 65–163.

C. M. Law and A. M. Warnes. "The Changing Geography of the Elderly in England and Wales." *Transactions of the Institute of British Geographers.* 1 (1976), 453–471.

Ron Lesthaeghe. "A Century of Demographic and Cultural Change in Western Europe." *Population and Development Review.* 9 (1983), 411–435.

Markku Löytönen. "The Spatial Diffusion of Human Immunodeficiency Virus Type 1 in Finland, 1982–1997." *Annals of the Association of American Geographers.* 81 (1991), 127–151.

James R. McDonald. "Labor Immigration in France, 1946–1965." *Annals of the Association of American Geographers.* 59 (1969), 116–134.

William R. Mead. "The Cold Farm in Finland, Resettlement of Finland's Displaced Farmers." *Geographical Review.* 41 (1951), 529–543.

Henning Mørch. "Two Types of Danish Rural Population Change Based on Natural Resources." *Geografisk Tidsskrift.* 88 (1988), 13–20.

Malcolm Murray. "The Geography of Death in England and Wales." *Annals of the Association of American Geographers.* 52 (1962), 130–149.

Hallstein Myklebost. "Migration of Elderly Norwegians." *Norsk Geografisk Tidsskrift.* 43 (1989), 191–213.

Daniel Noin and Robert Woods (eds.). *The Changing Population of Europe.* Oxford, GB: Blackwell, 1993.

Ann M. Oberhauser. "The International Mobility of Labor: North African Migrant Workers in France." *Professional Geographer.* 43 (1991), 431–445.

Philip E. Ogden and Paul E. White. *Migrants in Modern France.* London, GB: Unwin Hyman, 1989.

Alan C. Ogilvie. "Physiography and Settlements in Southern Macedonia." *Geographical Review.* 11 (1921), 172–197.

Charles J. Pattie and R. J. Johnston. "One Nation or Two? The Changing Geography of Unemployment in Great Britain, 1983–1988." *Professional Geographer.* 42 (1990), 288–298.

Frans W. A. van Poppel. "Regional Mortality Differences in Western Europe." *Social Science and Medicine.* 15D (1981), 341–352.

Norman J. G. Pounds and Charles C. Roome. "Population Density in Fifteenth Century France and the Low Countries." *Annals of the Association of American Geographers.* 61 (1971), 116–130.

Hubertus Preusser. "Entwicklung und räumliche Differenzierung der Bevölkerung Islands." *Geografiska Annaler.* 58B (1976), 116–144.

Peter R. Range and Joanna B. Pinneo. "Europe Faces an Immigrant Tide." *National Geographic.* 183:5 (1993), 94–125.

Allan Rodgers. "Migration and Industrial Development: The Southern Italian Experience." *Economic Geography.* 46 (1970), 111–135.

John Salt and Hugh Clout (eds.). *Migration in Post-War Europe: Geographical Essays.* London, GB: Oxford University Press, 1976.

Seppo Siirilä, Lauri Hautamäki, Jorma Kuitunen, and Timo Keski-Petäjä. "Regional Well-Being Variations in Finland." *Fennia.* 168 (1990), 179–200.

W. B. Stephens. *Education, Literacy and Society, 1830–70: The Geography of Diversity in Provincial England.* Manchester, GB: Manchester University Press, 1987.

Kirk H. Stone. "Finnish Fringe of Settlement Zones." *Tijdschrift voor Economische en Sociale Geografie.* 57 (1966), 222–232.

Kirk H. Stone. "Regional Abandoning of Rural Settlement in Northern Sweden." *Erdkunde.* 25 (1971), 36–51.

Kirk H. Stone. "Regionalizing Spain's Continuous and Discontinuous Settlement." *Geoforum.* 8 (1971), 9–14.

Kirk H. Stone. "Swedish Fringes of Settlement." *Annals of the Association of American Geographers.* 52 (1962), 373–393.

Sigurdur Thorarinsson. "Population Changes in Iceland." *Geographical Review.* 51 (1961), 519–533.

Pierre-Jean Thumerelle. "Migrations internationales et changement géopolitique en Europe." *Annales de Géographie.* 101 (1992), 289–318.

A. R. Toniolo. "Studies of Depopulation in the Mountains of Italy." *Geographical Review.* 27 (1937), 473–477.

Klaus Unger. "Greek Emigration to and Return from West Germany." *Ekistics.* 48 (1981), 369–374.

Abbott P. Usher. "The History of Population and Settlement in Eurasia." *Geographical Review.* 20 (1930), 110–132.

J. Velikonja. "Postwar Population Movements in Europe." *Annals of the Association of American Geographers.* 48 (1958), 458–481.

Kees Volkers. "Selective Migration in the Netherlands: The Case of the Northeast Polder." *Hommes et Terres du Nord.* (1991) 2/3, 181–188.

Jean-Paul Volle. *Bulgarie: les Systems de peuplement.* Montpelier, F: Maison de la Géographie, 1986.

James A. Walsh. "The Turn-Around of the Turn-Around in the Population of the Republic of Ireland." *Irish Geography.* 24 (1991), 117–125.

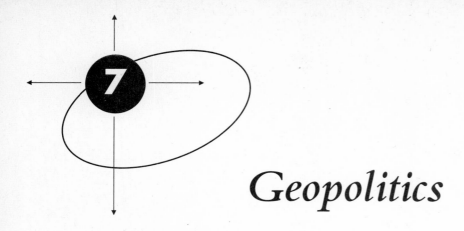

Geopolitics

Devotion to personal freedom and democracy appeared in Chapter 1 as among the cardinal traits that define Europe, adding a political dimension to the characterization of the culture area. As always, however, Europe defies such facile description. Democracy has deep roots in some countries, particularly in the West, while in others it forms merely a thin, fragile veneer over the face of a totalitarian heritage.

Fragmentation

In fact, a more compelling argument might be made for *fragmentation* as the defining political trait of Europe. Quite simply, the most distinctive aspect of European political geography, or *geopolitics*, is the splintering of the culture area into no fewer than 46 independent states (Figure 7.1). These countries, in turn, house as many or more autonomous regions and territories, some of which harbor separatist sentiments.

To gauge the magnitude of the fragmentation, consider that Europe to the Urals contains almost exactly the same amount of territory as the United States. Imagine the complexity that would exist if every state within the U.S. were independent and you will gain a useful political perspective of Europe. At the Russian border this fragmentation abruptly gives way to the largest independent state in the world, causing some to suggest that Europe ends at that boundary and providing us with another candidate in our unfinished quest to draw a line marking the eastern limit of the European culture area.

So severe is the political splintering of Europe that a number of *ministates* exist, so small as to be almost invisible on a map of the culture area. These include Andorra, Liechtenstein, Monaco, San Marino, and Vatican City. Most ministates have turned their size into advantage, offering services not always available in their larger neighbors, as for example the gambling casino in Monaco, the duty-free shops of Andorra, the postage stamp sales of San Marino, and the corporate headquarters lured to Liechtenstein by tax inducements. Of these,

FIGURE 7.1 The independent countries of Europe. Excluding Turkey, Europe now houses 46 independent states.

Andorra is surely the most spectacular. Much of the 41-km-long (25 mi.) trans-Andorran highway is now lined with duty-free shops selling an incredible diversity of consumer goods. Everything from diamonds to electronics, furs, and foods is available, seven days a week, and the purchasers flock in, often by the busload. The concentration of shops along the streets of the small capital city, Andorra la Vella, is truly astounding, and clerks quickly shoo along persons who dally too long in front of a shop window without making a purchase. Andorra is a commercial strip perhaps without equal in the world. In this way it has overcome its diminutive size.

Not only is Europe politically fragmented, but the level of internal division increased markedly during the twentieth century. In the year 1900, Europe exclusive of Turkey had 23 independent states; in 1930, 31; in 1985, 34; and by 1993, 46, double the total at the beginning of the century. The breakup of several great imperial states as a result of World War I, most notably the Austro-Hungarian and Ottoman Turkish empires, yielded many new countries. The collapse in

1991 of Europe's last surviving empire, the Soviet Union, coupled with the almost simultaneous disintegration of two smaller multiethnic states, Yugoslavia and Czechoslovakia, produced 13 more independent European states. Against this trend, the reunification of Germany offered a true anomaly.

Separatism

Nor has the fragmentation process necessarily run its course. Not every nation has yet become an independent state. Separatist movements of widely differing levels of intensity continue in Europe (Figure 7.2). Within Russia, for example, Chechenya, Tatarstan, and one Siberian republic have proclaimed their independence. With Russian assistance, Abkhazia, the westernmost province of Georgia,

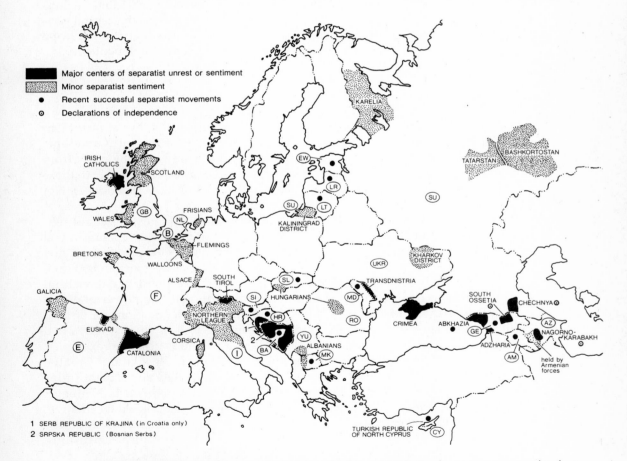

1 SERB REPUBLIC OF KRAJINA (in Croatia only)
2 SRPSKA REPUBLIC (Bosnian Serbs)

FIGURE 7.2 Separatist unrest in Europe, since 1980. Twelve new recognized independent states have appeared as a result of such movements, and several others, such as Turkish North Cyprus and Abkhazia, have achieved de facto independence. Most, but not all, separatism is ethnically based and occurs in peripheral regions within states.

won de facto statehood on the battlefield, and two other Georgian regions—Adzharia and South Ossetia—also seized virtual freedom. Serbs in both Croatia and Bosnia-Herzegovina carved out self-governing rebel republics, as did Slavs in the Transdnistria region of Moldova. Catalunya, northern Italy, and Scotland, among others, toy with the notion of independence. Since 1945 political conflict in Europe has shifted increasingly from the *inter*national to the *intra*national scene.

The proliferation of new states has occurred entirely in the eastern half of Europe. By contrast, Western Europe meanwhile moved significantly toward unification, within the framework of the European Union, as will be discussed later in this chapter. Even in the west, however, no sovereign nation has been extinguished, and separatism grips many provinces (Figure 7.2).

With the notable exception of the independence movement in Tatarstan, separatism occurs in *peripheral* areas of the countries involved. Such fringe regions often lag behind in economic development and suffer neglect by the central government. Most successful separatist movements in twentieth-century Europe have involved peoples who had, previously in history, enjoyed independence.

The Ethnic Mainspring

Separatism in Europe is not only usually peripheral in location but also *ethnic* in nature. That is, the groups seeking independence most often form an ethnic minority within a larger state. They differ linguistically and/or religiously from the country's majority. Compare the map of separatist unrest (Figure 7.2) to those showing language and religion (look back to Figures 1.6, 3.2, 3.18, and 4.1). Not all ethnic minorities pursue separatism, but many do.

If a country's population is relatively homogeneous linguistically and religiously, as in Denmark, Greece, Portugal, Germany, and Austria, separatism will not likely arise, but most European states house sizable, regionally concentrated ethnoreligious or ethnolinguistic minorities rooted in ancient homelands. Ethnicity is territorial by nature, and territoriality provides the very stuff of nationalism.

The present map of Europe bears abundant witness to the power of ethnic separatism. In spite of Europe's largely secularized nature, religion—or at least religious heritage—often provides the distinguishing trait of ethnic groups that seek and win independence. Ireland and Croatia provide successful examples, and religious heritage also motivated the Serb rebels in Bosnia and Croatia. Language even more commonly serves as the basis of ethnicity and separatism, as exemplified by the Catalans, South Tirol Germans, Frisians, Welsh, Flemings, Walloons, and Bretons. When language and religion *both* underlie ethnic identity, separatist tendencies can become even more potent. Examples include the secessions of Armenian Christians, Chechen and Abkhazi Caucasic Muslims, Lithuanian Baltic Catholics, and Turkic Muslim Tatars.

Not all, or even most, ethnic minorities pursue separatism in Europe. Switzerland, as we will see later, successfully joins four linguistic and two religious groups, none of which seeks to depart the Swiss Confederation. To spark separatism, ethnicity must be linked to some major grievance. If ethnic minority status means persecution, attempted ethnocide, forced assimilation, domination, lack of autonomy, or denial of access to the country's power structure, producing second-class citizenship, grievances usually develop. Europeans possess long memories, and even abuses that occurred generations ago are rarely forgotten. If, in addition, the peripheral location of the ethnic homeland causes it to be poorer economically than the country at large, then class struggle is added to ethnic grievance—a potent combination. Ethnicity then provides the vehicle for class struggle. Ireland provides a fine example. If, by contrast, the ethnic periphery becomes richer than the rest of the state, then the minority group chafes at the diversion of their wealth to poorer regions. Croats, Slovenians, and Catalans found themselves in this position.

As suggested earlier, it also matters whether an ethnic group enjoyed independence in some previous era, especially if that freedom was involuntarily relinquished. Memories of past statehood and greatness can be very powerful. Greeks, Poles, Lithuanians, Bulgarians, Irish, Czechs, Croats, Norwegians, Serbs, Albanians, Armenians, and Bosnians all harbored such memories and went on to achieve renewed independence, in some cases more than once. The former boundaries of their vanished empires sometimes lead newly independent states into foolish territorial conflicts in efforts to retrieve their golden age. The boundaries of medieval Serbia, for example, overlap so profoundly with those of modern Macedonia, Albania, Bosnia, Crna Gora, and even Greece, and memories of their former greatness remain so vivid among Serbs, that future Balkan peace might be endangered. Many Russians, too, look longingly toward the former frontiers of their recently collapsed empire.

Nonethnic Separatism

Not all secession movements in Europe have an ethnic basis. Other reasons can cause people to identify more closely with their province than with the central state, and the resultant regionalism or sectionalism often becomes sufficient to fuel separatist sentiment. Sometimes ethnic separatism within a state prompts other, nonethnic components of the population to seek a similar goal. In Spain, where Catalans, Basques, and Galicians won far-reaching autonomy, a mild separatist contagion spread to other provinces, where Castilian is spoken. By the middle 1980s, signs spray-painted on walls—a favored European way to express grievances—proclaimed that "Andalucía is a nation" or admonished people to vote "united Extremadura." Some Leónese object to being part of Castilla y León province and deface official signs with reference to the "pais leónes."

The Scottish separatist movement perhaps falls into the nonethnic category because the major bases of former Scottish identity—the Gaelic language and the clans—are moribund today. Yet a 1992 bumper sticker asked Scots to "rise up and be a nation again." Often, an *ethnic substrate* underlies seemingly nonethnic separatism. The people are no longer ethnic, but an echo of it survives to help form a special regional identity. Scotland, with its dimmed Celtic heritage, and

Andalucía, still bearing the impress of Arabic identity, both exemplify ethnic substrates.

Separatism can develop, however, in the complete absence of ethnicity or ethnic substrates. Geographers recognize that nationality can derive as much from region and place as from cultural affiliation. Attachment and loyalty to regions must be considered in studying nationalism, especially in Europe, where people typically live in areas inhabited by their ancestors for centuries or even millennia. Dramatic and mundane things happen in places over the centuries, lending them nationalistic meaning. We should not be surprised, for example, when the inhabitants of many German-speaking regions seek or desire no connections with Germany, as is true of the German-Swiss, or when many northern inhabitants of the Po-Veneto Plain seek to secede from Italy.

In this context, very large states exhibit more nonethnic regional tensions than small ones. The sheer size of Russia, even after the loss of its empire, perhaps encourages regional separatism, as does the existence of an exclave, separated from the main body of Russian territory, around Kaliningrad on the Baltic. In Italy, the Northern League advocates separatism in order to break free of the poverty-plagued, crime-ridden south. As a general rule, nonethnic separatist movements stand less chance of success, though the secession of Slovakia, based mainly in economic contrasts, provides an exception. The Slovaks, who differ only in dialect from the Czechs, nevertheless broke away, along a border that had long ago separated the empires of the Austrians and Hungarians. Their grievance lay partly in a tradition of regional poverty and neglect by the central government in Czech Praha, in spite of the fact that recent Czechoslovakian policy had addressed, with meaningful results, the issue of economic disparity. Too, Slovakia possessed many noncompetitive, inefficient manufacturing plants and stood to suffer greatly from Czech-led privatization following the demise of Communism. Again, European memories are long, and the we/they mindset becomes almost indelible.

Boundaries

The intricate political fragmentation of Europe into independent countries means that the culture area is crisscrossed by a web of international boundaries. All of these borders have an impact on landscapes and life, heightening the mosaiclike character of Europe.

Borders vary in diverse ways, including *age*. Some are very old, having existed in more or less their present location for 500 years or more, while others first found their place on the map of Europe within the last decade (Figure 7.3). The stablest, oldest boundaries lie mainly in Western Europe. International borders also vary greatly in *visibility*. All are marked in some way, but some contain barriers and cleared strips that can be clearly seen from the air. Oddly, even the peaceful, uncontested, and largely unmanned Sweden-Norway frontier, where

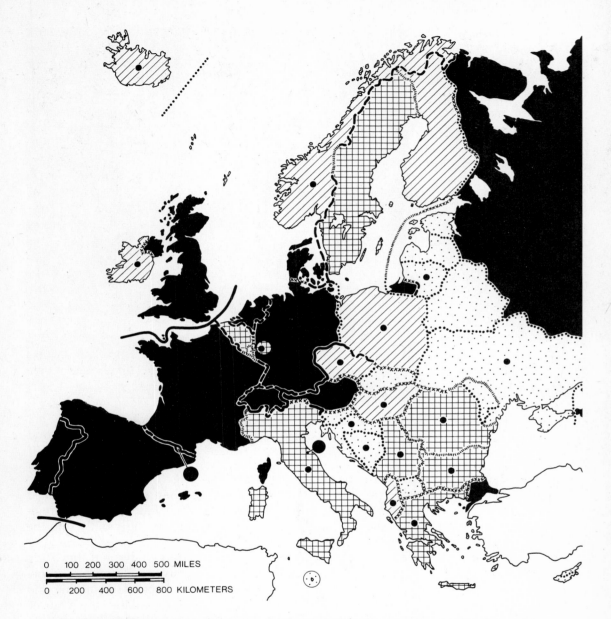

FIGURE 7.3 The age of states and boundaries. The greater political stability of Western Europe is reflected in the greater age of independent countries and borders there. Some states briefly lost their independence, such as Austria (1938–45) and Portugal, and some durable borders likewise disappeared for short intervals.

vehicles need not stop, is marked by a swath cut through the forest and by diverse official signs of varying age (Figure 7.4). The first acts of newly independent

Figure 7.4 Swedish-Norwegian border near Torsby, Sweden. The border is clearly marked by a strip cleared through the Finnskog, or "Finns' Forest." (Photo by the author, 1985.)

Estonia and Latvia included severing many connecting rural roads with trenchers, erecting street barriers within border towns, and establishing manned crossing points complete with booms (Figure 7.5). Their mutual border, previously a largely invisible line between Soviet republics, sprang vividly into the landscape.

All borders, to one degree or another, constrict traffic flow, but they vary greatly in ease of crossing. The least difficulty occurs within the European Union, where all border formalities will soon be discarded. By contrast, entering and leaving Russia by automobile can still be an adventure. Similarly, the motorist should expect lengthy delays of a day or more in crossing Poland's borders with Lithuania, Belarus, and Ukraine, due to the small number of crossing points, red tape, bribe-taking, and an enormous entrepreneurial traffic flow. Greece, which petulantly objects to both the name and flag of neighboring, newly independent Macedonia, blockades much commercial traffic at their mutual border. Perhaps the most difficult boundary to cross in Europe today is the one between Greek Cyprus and the Turkish Republic of North Cyprus, essentially a "green line" imposed through military force and manned by United Nations troops.

FIGURE 7.5 A new border in the making. No sooner had the Baltic republics of Estonia and Latvia regained independence than they began marking their borders. Here a rural farm-to-market road crossing the wholly peaceful Estonian/Latvian boundary has been severed by a trencher, disrupting the flow of transport in the interests of nationalism. (Photo by the author, 1992).

The policies and legislation of independent states often have a homogenizing effect within their borders, with the result that a steplike effect appears along international boundaries. An example is the Rhine River border between France and Germany. On the French side lies the province of Alsace, and on the German side, Baden. Both Alsace and Baden are, by tradition, German-speaking and predominantly Roman Catholic, and yet significant differences have developed between the two provinces. Prosperous Baden underwent rapid industrialization after 1945, absorbing numerous refugees from the former eastern German territories, while Alsace stagnated economically. In part, the economic malaise of Alsace was caused by repeated boundary changes when the province passed back and forth from German to French rule in 1871, 1918, 1940, and 1945, but the highly centralized government of France also bears part of the blame for the depressed condition of peripheries such as Alsace. Baden, as part of a much less centralized federal state, has fared better and wields more influence. Federal funds generously assisted resettled refugees in Baden, causing a boom in housing construction and renovation. Rural population density is now much lower on the Alsatian side, and the prosperity of Baden causes many French citizens to commute to jobs on the German side of the Rhine. The two provinces also differ in the configuration of rural village suburbanization, a process under way in both due to the growth of nearby cities such as Strasbourg and Freiburg. Partly as a result of differences in national planning legislation, the suburbs being added to villages in Baden tend to be compact, with apartment dwellings most common, while Alsatian villages sprawl loosely across the countryside due to the dominance of freestanding, single-family suburban houses.

This differentiating effect of borders extends to those that no longer exist. Even archaic borders, vanished more than a millennium ago, leave their trace. One of these can be detected in the German province of Hessen, through which, in ancient times, ran the northern border of the Roman Empire. The Roman system of law required that inheritances be divided among all heirs, in contrast to the tradition of the neighboring German tribes, which favored primogeniture. After the empire collapsed and the political border ceased to exist, the boundary separating the different inheritance systems persisted. As a result, the degree of fragmentation of rural land parcels even today clearly reveals the ancient Roman border (Figure 7.6). Not far south of Hessen, in northern Switzerland, runs another relic international border. In the 1500s, the present boundary between the cantons of Basel-Land and Aargau formed the Swiss-Austrian border. Today this line separates Catholic and Protestant districts. More subtly, the relict border could be detected in the cultural landscape at least as late as the 1800s in, of all things, the choice of roofing materials (Figure 7.7). Tiled roofs dominated Basel-Land, while thatching, an older folk type of roof, survived more abundantly in Aargau. How might such a contrast have developed? Swiss law, aimed at reducing fire danger, restricted the use of thatching, while Austrian law did not.

Types of States

To the complicated political mosaic of independent European states, even greater complexity is added by major differences among the various countries. For example, age varies greatly. Most Western European states are old, having maintained their independence for 500 years or more (Figure 7.3). Some others, especially in Eastern Europe, acquired statehood only in the 1990s, though in many cases these countries had enjoyed independence in earlier centuries and represent revivals of extinct states.

Most older states originated in small **core areas** and grew outward over the centuries into surrounding territory (Figure 7.8). Such core areas generally possessed some measure of natural defense against the encroachments of rival political entities, a fairly dense population, at least in comparison to surrounding regions, and a prosperous agricultural economy that produced a surplus capable of supporting a sizable military establishment. Perhaps most important of all, the core area required a government headed by ambitious leaders skilled in the military and diplomatic arts, bent on territorial aggrandizement. During the process of accretion, the core often retained its status as the single most important area in

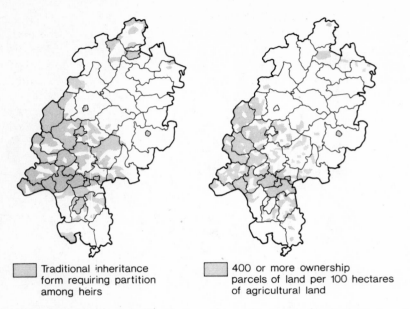

Traditional inheritance form requiring partition among heirs

400 or more ownership parcels of land per 100 hectares of agricultural land

FIGURE 7.6 Inheritance systems and land fragmentation in the German province of Hessen, 1955. In the southern and western parts of Hessen, the tradition, dating to Roman times, was to divide the farms among the various heirs. As a result, the farms there became ever smaller over the centuries, with excessive fragmentation of the holdings. Northern and eastern Hessen, by contrast, clung to the ancient Germanic custom of primogeniture, by which the farm passes intact to the eldest son. (Source: Adapted from Eckart Ehlers, "Land Consolidation and Farm Resettlement in the Federal Republic of Germany," in Robert C. Eidt, et al., eds., *Man, Culture, and Settlement*, New Delhi, IND: Kalyani, 1977, 124.)

the state, housing the capital city and the cultural and economic heart of the nation. The core area may be roughly centered in the national territory, or, if growth occurred mainly in one direction, it may be peripheral. Paris and the Île de France, the capital and core area of the French state, lie nearly in the middle of France, but Wessex, the nucleus of the United Kingdom, is eccentric. Spain also has a peripheral core, as do Italy, Russia, and Germany.

The typical core area contains the capital of the state, which is sometimes a "primate city," one that contains by far the largest population and greatest concentration of economic and cultural functions. Paris and Athínai are such core capitals enjoying national urban primacy. Not infrequently, however, the capital was removed from the original core, a relocation prompted by any one of several factors. In some instances, the political headquarters were relocated to the frontier of most active territorial expansion, in which case it is referred to as a *forward-thrust* capital. Sofiya (Sofia) succeeded earlier, more eastern capitals with Bulgarian expansion south and west at the expense of the Turks, while Lisboa and Madrid displaced northern capitals as the Portuguese and Spaniards pushed the Moors southward in Iberia. Peripheral St. Petersburg temporarily replaced

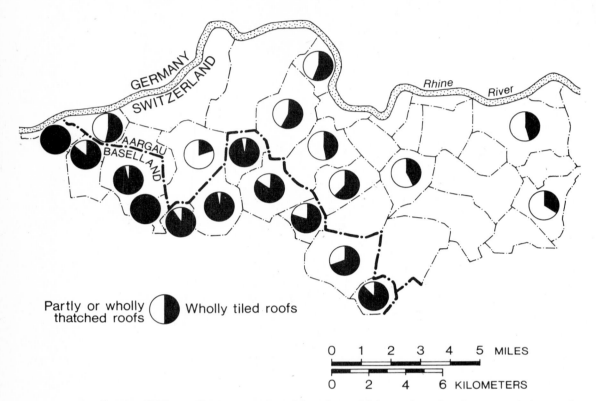

FIGURE 7.7 A relic international border within Switzerland, as revealed in roofing material, about 1800. In the 1500s, Aargau belonged to the Austrian Hapsburgs, while Basel-land formed part of Switzerland. The influence of the Swiss legal code, which banned thatch roofs, remained evident in the 1800s. (Source: Adapted from D. Opferkuch, *Der Einfluss einer Binnengrenze auf die Kulturlandschaft*, Basel, CH: Basler Beiträge zur Geographie, No. 21, 1977.)

Moskva as the Russian capital when the czars desired closer cultural contacts with Europe, and Oslo replaced Trondheim in Norway as a result of its greater proximity to Sweden and Denmark, which ruled and dominated Norway for many centuries.

Instability can result if states have no core areas or if multiple, competing cores are present. In the former category are Belgium, Belarus, and Albania, all born full-grown as children of power politics. Spain is plagued by the regionalism associated with two major northern medieval cores in Aragon-Catalunya (Catalonia) and Old Castilla, both now identified with linguistic groups. The competition is between Barcelona, successor to Aragon and Castilian Madrid. As the capital city, Madrid has never quite succeeded in dominating the state, in part because of the sparse population and low productivity of its surroundings.

FIGURE 7.8 Core areas and the evolution of European states. Most modern independent countries evolved gradually from core areas, though many in eastern Europe did not. Certain others possess ancient or medieval core areas that did not contribute directly to the birth of the modern state, but nevertheless belong to the collective national memory. (Source: Based in part upon Pounds/Ball, 1964, and McManis, 1967.)

Many older European states represent the remnants of former empires that once ruled much larger parts of the culture area. The United Kingdom, Russia,

Sweden, Denmark, Austria, and Turkey all fit this description. A great many other countries escaped colonial or imperial rule to become independent (Figure 7.9). Tensions typically exist between remnant empires and their former dependencies, especially in the Balkans and Eastern Europe.

We should also differentiate **nation-states** from multinational countries. In nation-states, the people share a common heritage, culture, and homeland. Patriotism and independence represent very potent reflections of the common culture and experience. The ideal nation-state possesses a homogeneous population, in which the large majority of the people—90 percent or more—have the same national identity. Many European countries fit this description, as for example, Germany, Poland, the Czech Republic, and Greece (Figure 7.9). Some other nation-states face instability because of sizable regional ethnic minorities who do not share the nationality that defines and dominates the state. Typically such minorities do not participate fully or at all in the political functioning of the state, and separatism can flourish in these situations. Most Eastern European nation-states face such problems, including the remnant Yugoslavia, Russia, Ukraine, and Bulgaria. Multinational states, an increasingly less common type in Europe since the collapse of the various empires, join peoples of different cultural background, and national identity does not rest upon a particular linguistic or religious group. Switzerland and Belgium, both astride the Germanic/Romance linguistic border, provide examples of multinational states. Bosnia-Herzegovina sought vainly to be such a country.

With the notable exceptions of Germany and Austria, culturally homogeneous nation-states are **unitary** in administrative structure, with power concentrated in the central government (Figure 7.9). Most European countries are unitary, perhaps in part because of their small size. In **federal** states, by contrast, the individual provinces retain considerable power or even autonomy. Federalism often results from a desire to accommodate otherwise restive minority groups, as in Spain, Russia, and the United Kingdom. Switzerland represents perhaps the purest example of a federal state, and that country did not even have a national capital until the midnineteenth century.

Finally, European countries differ greatly in the strength of that most admirable indigenous virtue, democracy. The tradition of freely elected governments remains strongest and oldest in *Western* Europe, while the East has only the shallowest and most fragile democratic experience. Germany, on the east/west interface, has fluctuated wildly between totalitarianism and federal democracy in the twentieth century.

Political Geography of France

With these considerations of boundaries, separatism, and types of independent state as background, we turn now to a political geographical analysis of selected European countries. *France* provides the first example.

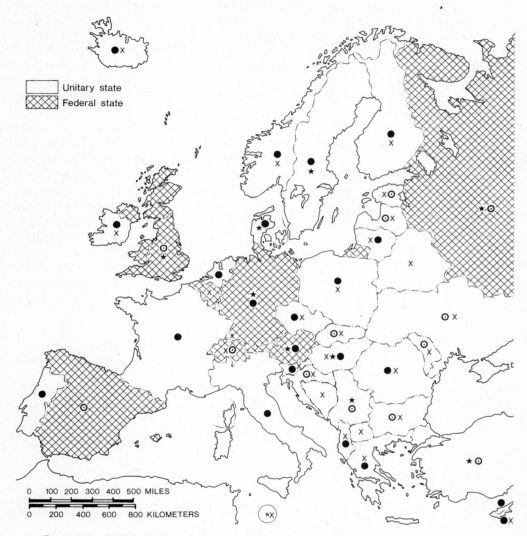

★ Remnant empire following loss of all or some restive dependent areas in Europe
X Escaped imperial rule to gain independence
● Nation-state with relatively homogenous population
⊙ Nation-state with sizable ethnic minorities

FIGURE 7.9 Types of independent states, based upon unitary versus federal governments, nation-state status, and imperial versus colonial origin. Some of these classifications are necessarily arbitrary or even debatable. Is Moldova, for example, a nation-state or merely a temporarily detached part of the Romanian nation-state? Did Belarus and Ukraine escape Russian imperial rule, or is their independence merely expedient and temporary?

An old and stable state, France in many ways offers a model for the development of a viable, successful independent country, possessing many political geographical strengths and few weaknesses. Though linked by language and religion to the Mediterranean, France owes both its origin and name to a Germanic tribe, the Franks, who built a large state in the power vacuum following the collapse of the Roman Empire. When this short-lived Frankish Empire fragmented in A.D. 843, the westernmost part—a loose federation known as the Kingdom of the West Franks—became the embryonic France.

After about A.D. 1000, the kings of France, based in Paris, began a program of conquest and annexation to convert the loose feudal federation, over which their rule was largely ceremonial, into a unitary state under royal domination. In this process, the so-called *Île de France*—the original, small domain of the kings—served as the core area of the evolving unitary state (Figure 7.10). The Île de France enjoyed splendid natural defensive advantage, sheltered behind cuesta escarpment walls. Initial expansion within the Paris Basin continued to benefit from these outward-facing cuesta rings (see Chapter 2) (Figure 7.10). Political geographers call such a naturally protected area a *folk fortress*, and even as late as World War I, France derived some protective advantage from the cuesta rings.

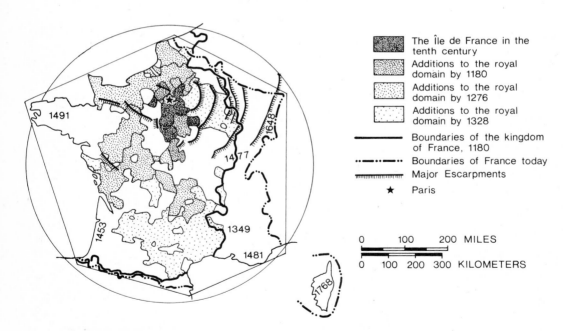

FIGURE 7.10 The growth of France. From an escarpment-shielded core area, the Île de France, the French kings steadily expanded their region of actual control, the domain, within the loose framework provided by the feudal kingdom. Later expansion provided a nearly ideal hexagonal shape for France, if Corsica is excluded. Peripheral annexations are indicated by dates on the map.

Their initial consolidation completed, the French kings undertook two additional, prolonged campaigns of expansion. The first led westward, where they sought control of the Atlantic shore, held by the Norman English and tribal Bretons. The Hundred Years' War, in the 1300s and 1400s, ousted the English and brought, among other rewards, French rule over the fertile Basin of Aquitaine, as well as Normandie. By 1500 the coast belonged exclusively to France, save the tiny Channel Islands, which remain British-ruled still today. The second great expansionary conflict led the French east, where they encroached upon a succession of German states, seizing the strategic Rhône-Saône corridor (see Figure 2.1) from Bourgogne and annexing the west bank of the German river Rhine. By 1650, France had reached roughly its present territorial limits, though German resistance to Gallic eastward expansion continued as late as 1945.

The resultant France was anything but a nation-state. As late as the 1790s, half the population spoke a language other than French. Following the Revolution, one of the first acts of the French Republic, in 1793, was to mandate elimination of regional languages and dialects, a policy continued by France until very recently, with considerable effect. Most minority tongues have subsequently become moribund. France's highly centralized unitary government thus created a nation-state out of ethnic diversity by crushing the minorities.

The most difficult geographical task of the French state has been to join the heavily Germanized north, from which the kings initially expanded, to a thoroughly Romanized, Mediterranean-oriented south (Figure 7.11). Fundamental contrasts still exist between those two large regions, but the culture and language of Occitania—the South—have largely succumbed to northern dominance.

The boundaries achieved by French expansion possess two major advantages. First, belts of mountains and hills parallel most of the borders, including the Pyrenees, Alps, Jura, Vosges, and Ardennes. These offer some defensive advantage. Second and equally important, the national territory enjoys a compact shape, shortening lines of communication and boundaries. Political geographers believe that the ideal state is hexagonal in shape—the most compact geometric figure that can be fit into a network—with a core area at the center. France more closely approximates that ideal configuration than any other state in the world, helping to explain its longevity and viability.

Germany: Federalism in the European Core

Just as France represents the legacy of the collapsed Frankish Empire in the west, *Germany* descends from the *east* Frankish Kingdom of A.D. 843. For the initial millennium of its existence, this German First *Reich*, unlike France, remained a loose federation of feudal states whose emperor had little authority outside his home statelet (Figure 7.12). Federalism, verging on virtual disunity, has been the normal German tendency, especially in the thousand years of the First Reich. Potential core areas, from which ambitious emperors might have forged a unitary state, certainly existed, such as the fertile *Börde* beyond the Ruhr River on the North European Plain, or the hill-ringed Upper Rhine Plain between

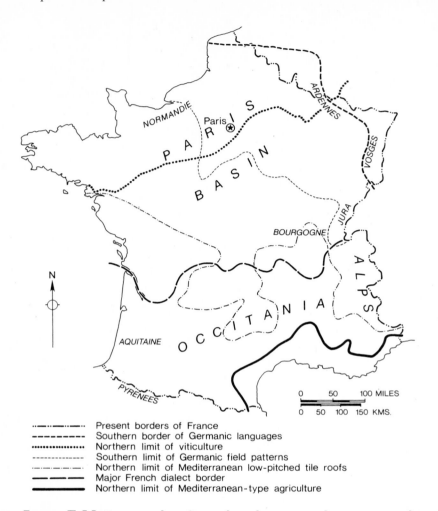

FIGURE 7.11 France, showing cultural contrasts between north and south.
The French state has been faced with the problem of fusing a Germanized north and a Latin south.

Frankfurt-am-Main and Basel (see Figure 2.1), but no such process developed. By the 1600s, the First Reich housed some 300 virtually independent states. German federalism came as a blessing for Europe because a powerful unitary state dominating the vital European core could have been a threat to the entire culture area, as the brief, atypical interval of totalitarian rule in Nazi Germany demonstrated all too vividly.

The loose-knit First Reich did succeed in expanding eastward, beyond the Elbe-Saale-Inn-Salzach line into the old Slavic tribal *marches* (buffer zone) of the Frankish Empire, following the path of German agricultural colonists and forest clearers spreading east on the North German Plain and along the Danube/Alps.

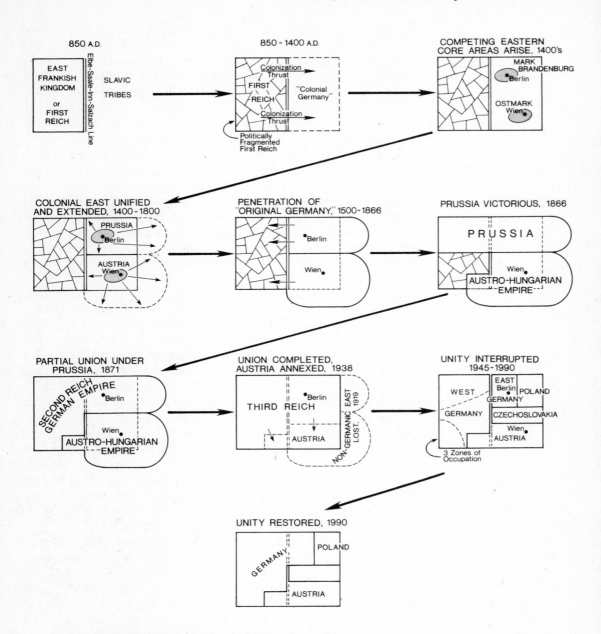

FIGURE 7.12 The evolving map of Germany, A.D. 850 to the present: a model. A federalized Germany has existed for more than a thousand years, but greater cohesion was added to the state through Prussian-led unification, emanating from its core area in Brandenburg. A brief episode of unitary rule in the Third Reich was followed by foreign occupation and then a restoration of federal rule.

In each of these two lobes of eastern expansion, a powerful state and ambitious royal family arose—*Prussia* (German *Preussen*) in the North European Plain, which grew from a core area in the *Mark* (March) Brandenburg under the rule of the Hohenzollerns, and *Austria*, which expanded from the Ostmark (Eastern March) around Wien under the Habsburgs. These two new states both functioned as part of the First Reich, even though some of the territories they annexed lay beyond its bounds. Once they consolidated their holdings in the colonial east, Prussia and Austria (by then called Österreich, or the "Eastern Empire") began competing with one another for control of the original western parts of the First Reich, each attempting to create a unitary German state under their rule. This contest lasted for centuries, but Prussia eventually emerged victorious in 1866. Five years later the Second Reich was born, a union of Prussia and western Germany. The Prussian capital, Berlin, was named the imperial capital and the Prussian kings became the German kaisers. Federalism persisted in the Second Reich, and member states such as Bayern and Sachsen retained their own monarchs and postal systems. Austria, the defeated rival, found itself excluded from the Second Reich (Figure 7.12).

Prussia's success seems remarkable. Its core area, the Mark Brandenburg, sandy-soiled, infertile, thinly populated, and lacking in natural defense, offered no advantages. The future imperial capital, Berlin, began improbably as a tiny Slavic fishing village on an island in the River Spree. In no small part, the Prussian success was a consequence of the Lutheran state's toleration of religious minorities, which attracted numerous French Huguenots, Mennonite Dutch, and Lutheran Salzburgers, who brought needed agricultural and industrial skills to the initially backward state. By 1800, fully one-third of the Prussian population was descended from immigrants who had come to seek freedom, to escape persecution in France, Austria, and other lands.

The Third Reich grew out of the Second, as the Nazis seized power and imposed the first dictatorship Germany had known. Unitary rule quickly replaced the traditional federalism, and not merely Germany but all of Europe felt the dire consequences. Nearly a half-century, marked by defeat and foreign military occupation, passed before the unified, federal Germany could be reestablished in 1990. Normalcy then returned to the European core.

The essential problem facing the German state through most of its existence is the cultural and economic dichotomy between northeast and southwest, between the original First Reich in the west and "colonial" Germany beyond the Elbe-Saale line in the east (Figure 7.13). The colonial east reveals a strong Slavic ethnic substrate, remained feudal longer, lay beyond the zone of influence of Latin civilization, and formed a Protestant stronghold, while the west/southwest displays Roman underpinnings and simultaneously has deeper German roots. The most recent manifestation of this split, coming in the wake of reunification, is the immense prosperity divide between western and eastern Germany. In an effort to mitigate this problem, the German government annually transfers about 100 billion dollars of assets annually into the troubled eastern provinces. In effect, the German state has struggled to bridge the cultural fault lines both between east/west and north/south in Europe, creating a political core in the

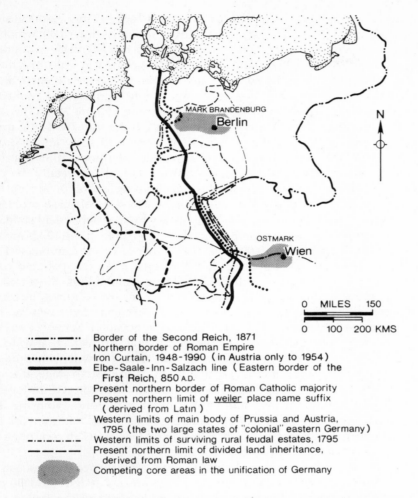

MILES   0   150
0   100   200 KMS

··—·—·—·· Border of the Second Reich, 1871
·—··—··—·· Northern border of Roman Empire
··············· Iron Curtain, 1948-1990 (in Austria only to 1954)
▬▬▬▬▬ Elbe-Saale-Inn-Salzach line (Eastern border of the
   First Reich, 850 A.D.
—··—··—··— Present northern border of Roman Catholic majority
▬▬ ▬▬ ▬▬ Present northern limit of <u>weiler</u> place name suffix
   (derived from Latin)
— — — — — Western limits of main body of Prussia and Austria,
   1795 (the two large states of "colonial" eastern Germany)
—··—··—··— Western limits of surviving rural feudal estates, 1795
▬ ▬ ▬ ▬ Present northern limit of divided land inheritance,
   derived from Roman law
   Competing core areas in the unification of Germany

**FIGURE 7.13 Selected cultural boundaries illustrating the split between east-
ern and western Germany.** The greatest challenge to the German state has been to tie
an older Roman-influenced Catholic south and west to a colonial, Slavicized, Protestant
north and east—in effect, to erect a state astride the east/west and north/south cultural fault
lines in Europe (see Chapter 13).

culture area where perhaps none was meant to exist. Federalism has provided
the mechanism for that bridging. Germany's path to statehood, then, led a very
different way from that of France, in spite of the similarity of origins.

Switzerland and Belgium

The most important language frontier in Western Europe separates Romance
speech in the south from the Germanic tongues of the north. Switzerland and

Belgium both straddle this cultural border and are in certain other respects similar, but only one of the two has achieved stability and relative internal harmony.

Switzerland, one of the most viable European states, has enjoyed considerable success in joining different linguistic and religious groups in a multinational country. About two-thirds of the Swiss speak German, 18 percent French, and a tenth Italian, in addition to a tiny Romansh minority. Religiously, the country is almost evenly divided between Catholics and Protestants (Figure 7.14). The Alps provide additional disruption, cutting directly through the state, dividing much of Switzerland into separate valleys, each with its own identity and sense of autonomy. Ideally, according to political geographers, the population distribution within a state should be denser in the central regions, especially the core area, and sparse in the border peripheries, but Switzerland's terrain pattern helped produce precisely the opposite arrangement. In spite of these problems, Switzerland recently celebrated its 700th anniversary as an independent state.

The origins of the Swiss state can be traced to a core area in the 1200s around the eastern shores of the Vierwaldstättersee (Lake of Four Forest Cantons or Lake Luzern) at the northern approach to St. Gotthard Pass, the principal land route between Italy and Central Europe in the Middle Ages. Feudal lords there banded together in 1291 for mutual defense and gradually over the centuries increased their autonomy within the loose-knit German First Reich, strengthened by their control of the strategic pass (Figure 7.14). The people of canton Schwyz assumed an early leadership role and gave their regional name, Schweizer-land, to the country at large. As time passed, neighboring cantons and towns were annexed by conquest, purchase, or voluntary association. In its formative stage, the state remained wholly German in speech, Catholic in faith, and centered on the lake that afforded easy communication among the member cantons. From the first, Switzerland formed a very loose federal state, or *confederation,* a framework that successfully accommodated subsequent linguistic/religious diversity as the country continued to grow from its tiny core area.

In the 1400s and 1500s, the confederation seized control over strategic Alpine passes and Rhine River crossings, annexing in the process Italian- and French-speaking districts. In more recent times, Switzerland has achieved prosperity and demonstrated an isolationist ability to avoid wars, accomplishments that greatly enhanced the value of Swiss citizenship and fostered nationalism.

Switzerland has faced its share of internal problems over the centuries, including at least five civil wars and, recently, ethnic tensions which led to the French-speaking part of a Canton Bern to break away and form Jura, a new Francophone canton. But all things considered, Switzerland must be regarded as an astounding success in an improbable setting.

Belgium also lies astride the Germanic-Romance linguistic border, joining the Dutch-speaking Flemings of Vlaanderen (Flanders) in the north with French of Wallonie in the south (Figure 7.15). It has an advantage in that its population is religiously uniform, adhering to Roman Catholicism. The Belgian state, with about the same territorial size and military strength of Switzerland, sought to duplicate the Swiss success in establishing neutralism and uniting diverse ethnic

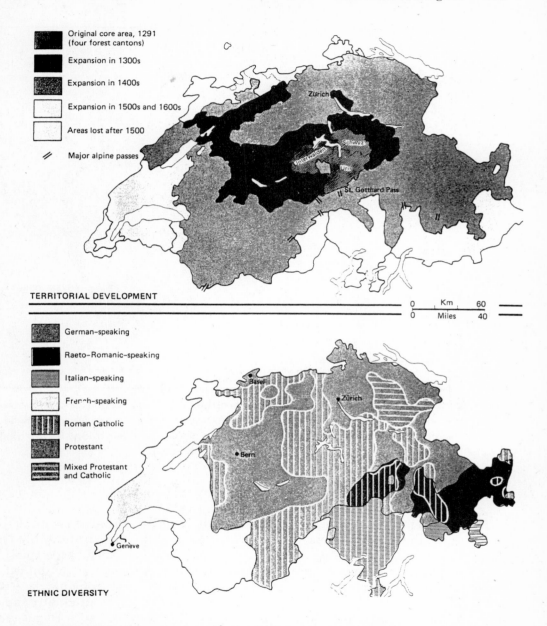

FIGURE 7.14 Switzerland: Territorial development and ethnic diversity. The Swiss state is a classic example of gradual expansion from a core area. It includes a mixture of Roman Catholics and Protestants and four linguistic groups. (Source: Based in part on Karl Schib, "Territoriale Entwicklung der Eidgenossenschaft . . . ," p. 21 in *Atlas der Schweiz . . .* , Wabern-Bern, CH: Verlag der eidgenossischen Landestopographie, 1965–1970.)

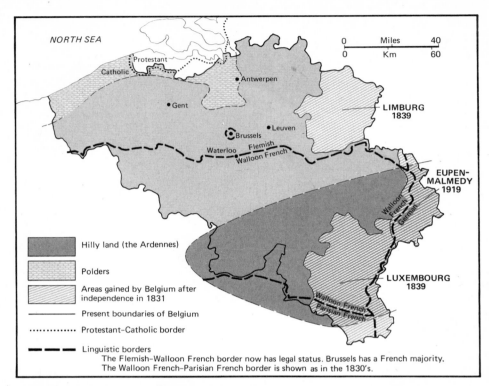

FIGURE 7.15 Belgium: Political-geographical factors. In addition to the problems caused by the Fleming-Walloon conflict, Belgium occupies the natural invasion route between Germany and France, which passes between the hilly Ardennes and the low-lying polderland. The Battle of Waterloo was fought on this route.

groups. The Belgians largely failed in this attempt, and their state became plagued by internal strife.

Belgium, a much newer state than Switzerland, dates only from 1830, when its Catholic population, with approval and encouragement from the Great Powers of Europe, broke away from the Protestant-dominated Netherlands. The crucial mistake came when the newly independent Belgium was constituted as a unitary state under Walloon French domination, in effect excluding the Dutch-speaking majority from the power structure. Only very gradually did the Flemings attain equal cultural rights, as in 1891 when the Dutch language first appeared alongside French on the country's postage stamps and currency or in 1898, when a regulation requiring that laws be published in Dutch first took effect. As a result, Flemings and Walloons developed a deep-seated mutual antagonism. Virtual partition came in 1963, with the drawing of an official language border within Belgium, north of which the Dutch tongue enjoyed preference (Figure 7.15).

   The Fleming-Walloon rivalry flared into violence in the 1960s with street fighting in the capital city, Brussels, which has a French majority but lies north of the linguistic border. Students at the traditionally French University of Leuven, in Flemish territory, rioted in successful support of demands that instruction be in the Dutch tongue and that French faculty be dismissed. Tension persists between the two groups, though in recent years violence has ceased. Reflecting this tension, the government has not enumerated linguistic groups since 1947.

Yugoslavia: A Balkan Tragedy

Belgium's problems astride a major cultural divide pale in comparison to the political geographical fate of Yugoslavia, the "land of the South Slavs." Formed following World War I when peacemakers unwisely appended various territories to previously independent Serbia, the new Yugoslavia straddled profound human fault lines. It joined shards of diverse former empires—Roman, Byzantine, Turkish, Austrian, and Hungarian—each of which had left indelible cultural residues. While largely Serbo-Croatian in speech, Yugoslavia inherited three major mutually antagonistic faiths—Catholicism, Orthodoxy, and Islam; two alphabets; diverse ancient legacies of hatred; and, physically, an awkward joining of the rugged, in places impassable Dinaric Range to the Hungarian Basin and Adriatic coast.

   Making matters worse, the Serbs dominated Yugoslavia from the first, regarding it in effect as their empire, a unitary Greater Serbia. Beograd, the Serb capital, became the national capital, and street signs there remained exclusively in the Cyrillic alphabet. No meaningful steps toward federalism came until far too late. Serbs saw themselves both as defenders of the Orthodox faith and of European civilization at large. Catholic Slovenes and Croats, as well as the Muslim Bosnians, though fellow South Slavs, thus became second-class Yugoslav citizens. Croats took advantage of the German occupation during World War II to commit various atrocities against the temporarily weakened Serbs.

   Also, major economic disparities developed among the various provinces of Yugoslavia, with Slovenia and Croatia becoming relatively prosperous while Macedonia and parts of Serbia fell behind. Add to this the fact that both Croatia and Bosnia-Herzegovina harbored memories of glorious medieval independence. The rise to power of an uncompromising Serbian nationalist leader in Yugoslavia sealed the doom of the state. In 1991 and 1992, four provinces seceded from Yugoslavia and achieved independence—Slovenia, Croatia, Macedonia, and Bosnia-Herzegovina. Only Crna Gora (Montenegro), itself formerly independent, chose to remain with Serbia in the remnant Yugoslavia (Figure 7.16).

   Because the provincial borders had not in most cases followed ethnic boundaries, many Serbs found themselves excluded against their will from the remnant Yugoslav state. The Krajina and Srpska republics in Croatia and Bosnia-Herzegovina represent the efforts of these Serbs to detach themselves through civil war from the secessionist states and, ultimately, to rejoin Yugoslavia. In the

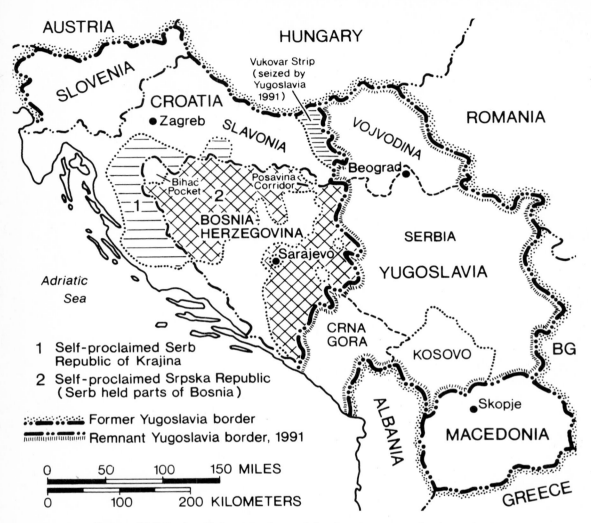

FIGURE 7.16 The disintegration of the former Yugoslavia and subsequent Serbian separatist movements in Croatia and Bosnia-Herzegovina. Note the awkward geographical shapes produced by the breakup of the country and the creation of the de-facto Krajina and Srpska republics. The Posavina Corridor, connecting the western part of the Srpska Republic and the adjacent Krajina to the larger remainder of Serb-ruled territory is particularly vulnerable, as are the routes linking the Slavonian part of Croatia to the coast. The situation shown is for May 1, 1995.

process, many culturally mixed districts experienced brutal "ethnic cleansing," in which non-Serb peoples were forcibly expelled.

Of the successor states to the former Yugoslavia, aside from the remnant, Serb-dominated country, the most viable would seem to be *Slovenia*, which stood aside from the subsequent troubles and, in any case, had only a tiny Serb minority. *Croatia*, plagued by an awkward shape and secessionist-minded Serbs in

Krajina, made matters worse by opting for a French-style unitary state that could not easily accommodate minority rights. Even some ethnic Croatian districts now grow restive. In Istra, the westernmost part of Croatia, many people feel a greater loyalty to province than to state. Istrians will tell the visitor that "we have an identity of our own" and "Zagreb seems far away." In response, the central government issues threats. *Macedonia* finds itself landlocked and blockaded by neighbor Greece, which petulantly regards the name "Macedonia" and the country's national flag as usurped Greek properties. In addition, Macedonia has sizable Albanian and other Muslim minorities and must cope both with Serbia's claim that Macedonians are actually Serbs and Bulgaria's belief that the Macedonians, instead, are more properly Bulgars! Least fortunate of all, *Bosnia-Herzegovina* has borne the brunt of Serb separatism, warfare, and ethnic cleansing before even having the chance to establish a viable multinational society. Bosnia's future remains bleak, in large part because it inherited the same cultural diversity that wrecked the former Yugoslavia and represents a microcosm of that failed state. Many issues and quarrels remain unresolved in the former Yugoslavia and stability in that region seems a distant hope at best. In the Balkans, European political fragmentation presently takes on its worst and most destructive aspects.

Russia: Nation-State or Empire?

In most respects, Russia presents a political anomaly in Europe. It is the only state to establish enduring unity over a sizable section of the culture area within the last millennium, causing Eastern Europe to assume a very different political character from the West. Even in its greatly diminished post-Soviet size, Russia remains by far the largest independent state in Europe and the entire world, retaining the aspect of empire long after the other great imperial states collapsed.

Early Russian attempts at state building, centered in Ukrainian Kyyiv, were destroyed by Asiatic invaders. Sheltered by extensive forests from the Asian hordes and favored by a radial pattern of navigable streams, Muscovy—the environs of Moskva—developed in the late Middle Ages as the new political focus of Russia (Figure 7.17). Growing from the Muscovy core area, the Russian state grew to dominate the East European Plain, a terrain unit that has ever since provided structure to the state. From a European perspective, Russia *is* the East European Plain, and the huge Siberian appendage beyond the Urals possesses little population or importance. To Russians, too, the "real" Russia lies in the great plain.

When the Soviet Union disintegrated in 1991, Russia faced a very difficult transition. An empire traditionally under despotic, unitary rule and far more like China than Germany, Russia evolved painfully and perhaps abortively toward nation-state status and federalism. In the Russia that emerged from the collapsed empire, about 82 percent of the people spoke Russian, and no single ethnic minority claimed as much as 4 percent of the population. Since 1991 the Russian proportion has increased as a result of international migration among the coun-

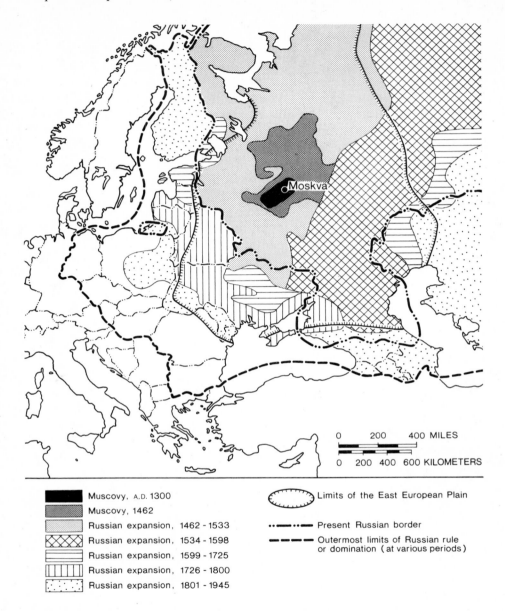

FIGURE 7.17 Territorial evolution of Russia in Europe. Russia grew from a core area, the Principality of Muscovy around Moskva, to encompass a huge empire which only collapsed in 1991. Its influence has at times extended deep into Europe and even more profoundly into Asia, but the East European Plain has always provided the spatial and physical focus of Russia.

tries of the former Soviet Union. Increasingly, Russian nationalists regard the country as a nation-state.

   Federalism, adopted in a series of changes in 1992/1993, seeks to accommodate the remaining ethnic minorities, some of which have secessionist goals. Various Turkic, Caucasic, and Muslim minorities seek, with greater or lesser fervor, to dismantle the nested doll "empire within the empire" (Figure 7.2). Chechenya, a "breakaway rogue state" on the borders of Georgia, declared an abortive independence in 1991, followed by Tatarstan in 1992 (see Figure 1.6). Some Russian nationalists, favoring a nation-state, agree that non-Russian minorities should be excluded.

   The position of Belarussians and Ukrainians toward a Russian nation-state remains confused. Russians regard both groups as ethnically Russian, and neither country actively sought independence, achieving that status almost accidentally and by default in 1991. Ukraine, and particularly Belarus, could quite conceivably become enmeshed in the new Russian nation-state. At the very least, Krym (Crimea), which has a sizable Russian majority, could be detached from Ukraine and join Russia (Figure 7.1). Also unclear is the fate of the Kaliningrad District, a Russian territorial exclave on the shores of the Baltic (Figure 7.2). Proposals to convert Kaliningrad, formerly a part of Germany, into a free-trade zone have so far remained largely unrealized.

   The political geographer tries to adopt the long-term view in assessing the evolution of independent states. From that perspective, we can predict that the Russia emerging from the present period of flux, whether nation-state or renewed empire, whether federal or unitary, will almost certainly perpetuate the ancient Slavic unification of the huge East European Plain and continue to present an anomaly in an otherwise politically fragmented culture area.

The European Union

Partly to present a more united front to Russia, some countries in politically fragmented Western Europe began moving in the 1950s toward a supranational federalism. This initiative began wholly in the economic sphere with agreements reducing coal and steel tariffs, and the greatest success so far has been in the realm of free trade. The multinational organization, formerly called the European Economic Community or the Common Market, began with six countries in the heart of Europe and has since expanded to 15 (Figure 7.18). In 1993 it assumed the name *European Union.*

   The Union has a parliament that meets in Strasbourg, and future plans envision a common currency, foreign policy, and security arrangements. Growing cross-border connectivity characterizes the Union, especially in investments, business mergers, labor mobility, and other economic-related matters. Clearly, the economic impetus is toward increased unity, a trend now under way for four decades, but Union progress politically and culturally has come far more slowly.

   Within the European Union, the power of the member independent states is being eroded or bypassed on two fronts. While the master plan of the Union

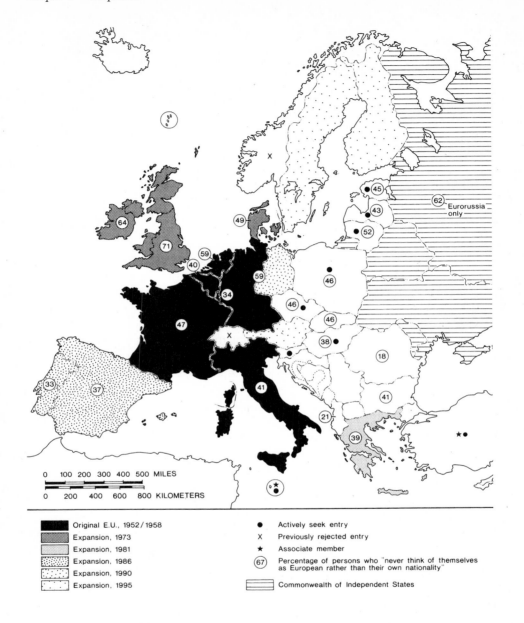

FIGURE 7.18 The European Union and Commonwealth of Independent States. From a six-country nucleus in the 1950s, the union has grown to include nearly all of Western Europe and seeks to impose federalism upon a part of the culture area long plagued by political fragmentation. Provincial and national allegiances are proving difficult to overcome. The C.I.S. is a shadow of the former Soviet Union. (Source: Opinion survey = *Eurobarometer/Gallup Poll, 1990/92.*)

envisioned decision making only at national and federation levels, many regions and provinces within the various countries now exert considerable power, linked to the issue of separatism discussed earlier. Spain, for example, has lost aspects of sovereignty both to the Union and to autonomous provinces such as Catalunya. Increasingly, one hears of a federalized "Europe of the regions" or "Europe of the fatherlands," implying a federal structure linking a mosaic of ethnic homelands in which the formerly independent states have been doubly demoted. The homelands would presumably offset the excess and sheer size of Union integration, allowing Europe's diverse regional cultures to survive and flourish. In any case, the cultural impetus within the Union runs counter to the economic thrust, favoring regionalism, separatism, and nationalism. A quite substantial proportion of Europeans, both within and outside the Union, never think of themselves as "Europeans" rather than, say, as Dutch, Scots, Spaniards, or Catalans (Figure 7.18).

Further complicating the Union's future is the fact that not all member countries are moving toward integration at the same rate. "Europe at two speeds" describes the rapid meshing under way in the central core countries as contrasted to peripheral laggards. Denmark, the United Kingdom, Greece, and Portugal, in particular, often seem out of step. The Danes recently demanded to be left out of any agreements concerning mutual security and defense. As a result, the E.U. seems to be fragmenting into inner and outer tiers, with only Germany, France, Belgium, the Netherlands, and Luxembourg on the fast track toward integration.

The eventual level of federalism and sacrifice of national sovereignties that will occur even in the inner tier remains unclear, particularly now that military confrontation with Russia has ended. A highly centralized and powerful Union government will not be created, but at the same time the member states will probably never regain their former level of sovereignty.

Meanwhile in the east, Russia has established the Commonwealth of Independent States (C.I.S.), an economic union of 12 of the former 15 republics of the Soviet Union. Only the three Baltic states—Estonia, Latvia, and Lithuania—rejected C.I.S. membership. A very different enterprise from the European Union, the C.I.S. has an even less certain future and will always be tainted by Russian domination and memories of Soviet imperialism.

Electoral Geography

As if the fragmentation into scores of independent states and autonomous regions were not complicated enough, additional political complexity is revealed by voting patterns. A free vote of the people on some controversial issue can be one of the purest expressions of culture. Free elections occur in every European country, and a vivid electoral mosaic exists, adding another revealing dimension of political and cultural geography.

In the accompanying map of voting behavior and ideology, a threefold classification has been employed—leftist, rightist, and centrist (Figure 7.19).

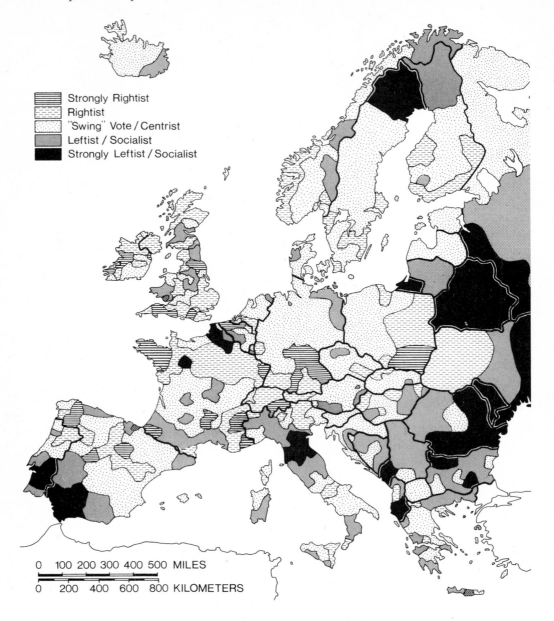

FIGURE 7.19 Electoral geography of Europe. As a general rule, the core of Europe is more rightist/conservative and the peripheries more leftist/socialist. (Sources: Vanlaer 1984 and 1991, 155; Sallnow et al. 1982; Martis et. al. 1992; Kostrubiec 1990; O'Loughlin and van der Wusten 1993; Gjuzelev, in *Südosteuropa*, 41, 1992, 620; *Post-Soviet Geography*, Oct. 1993, 484–485; John Sallnow, letter to T.G.J., May 7, 1992; Valen, 1964; Vandermotten and Vanlaer, in King, *Mass Migration*, 140; Johnston et. al. 1988; Passchier and van der Wusten 1990; and Sarramea 1985.)

Rightists, in this classification, include people who support the free enterprise system, oppose government intervention, and seek to reduce taxation in their lands. Leftists favor socialism and even Communism, while centrists work for compromise.

Viewed in this manner, Europe reveals a core/periphery configuration. As a general rule, rightist sentiment is strongest in the core region, especially south Germany (where Nazism arose) and adjacent parts of Alpine Europe. Northern Iberia, southern Great Britain, and the Polish/Ukrainian borderlands also form noteworthy rightist bastions. In prosperous Western Europe, rightist ideology has experienced a notable upswing recently, often tied to emotional issues such as the fate of resident foreign laborers from Third World countries.

Leftist sentiment remains strongest in the former Communist countries and in Northern Europe, where collectivism runs deep in the cultural tradition. Western Christianity tended to foster individualism, while the eastern church retained a more collectivist outlook, and the leftist tendencies of the Eastern European peripheries thus have roots far older than Communism. As a result, surveys concerning approval of a market economy regularly reveal steadily diminishing support as one progresses eastward across Europe. Leftist politics also prevail in declining manufacturing districts of the west, such as the British Midlands and northern France, and in troubled rural regions like southern Iberia. Again, much of the voting pattern can be understood as the reflection of a prosperous European core pitted against a problem-ridden periphery. In a recent survey, 20 percent of the electorate in the European Union claimed to be rightist, 28 percent leftist, and 34 percent centrist.

In some European regions, ethnic politics play a larger role than left/right/centrist ideologies. Groups such as the Hungarians in Slovakia, German-speaking Tirolers in Italy, and Turks in Bulgaria strongly support such parties. Separatist movements almost always find expression in ethnic political parties.

Political geography, then, whether reflected in the crazy-quilt of independent states or in the intricate mosaic of voting patterns, vividly reveals European internal diversity. The same spatial variety appears in the forms of livelihood pursued by Europeans, perhaps most notably in the ancient enterprise of agriculture, the subject of the following chapter.

Sources and Suggested Readings

Volker Albrecht. *Der Einfluss der deutsch-französischen Grenze auf die Gestaltung der Kulturlandschaft im südlichen Oberrheingebiet.* Freiburg, D: Geographisches Institut der Albert-Ludwigs-Universität, 1974.

Xavier Arbós. "Central versus Peripheral Nationalism in Building Democracy: The Case of Spain." *Canadian Review of Studies in Nationalism.* 14 (1987), 143–160.

Mark Blacksell. *Post-War Europe: A Political Geography.* Boulder, USA: Westview Press, 1977.

Frederick W. Boal and J. Neville H. Douglas (eds.). *Integration and Division: Geographical Perspectives on the Northern Ireland Problem.* London, GB: Academic Press, 1982.

Edmunds V. Bunkše. "God, Thine Earth is Burning: Nature Attitudes and the Latvian Drive for Independence." *GeoJournal.* 26 (1992), 203–209.

Andrew F. Burghardt. *Borderland: A Historical and Geographical Study of Burgenland, Austria.* Madison, USA: University of Wisconsin Press, 1962.

John P. Cole. "Republics of the Former USSR in the Context of a United Europe and the New World Order." *Soviet Geography.* 32 (1991), 587–603.

Daniele Conversi. "Language or Race?: The Choice of Core Values in the Development of Catalan and Basque Nationalisms." *Ethnic and Racial Studies.* 13 (1990), 50–71.

Vaughan Cornish. *The Great Capitals: An Historical Geography.* London, GB: Methuen, 1923.

Andrew H. Dawson. *A Geography of European Integration: A Common European Home.* New York, USA: John Wiley & Sons, 1993.

Christof Ellger. "Berlin: Legacies of Division and Problems of Unification." *Geographical Journal.* 158 (1992), 40–46.

W. A. Ettema. *Spanish Galicia: A Case Study in Peripheral Integration.* Utrecht, NL: Utrechtse Geografische Studie No. 18, 1980.

David Fitzpatrick. "The Geography of Irish Nationalism, 1910–1921." *Past and Present.* 78 (1978), 113–144.

H. J. Fleure. "Notes on the Evolution of Switzerland." *Geography.* 26 (1941), 169–177.

Wolfgang Framke, *Die deutsch-dänische Grenze in ihrem Einfluss auf die Differenzierung der Kulturlandschaft.* Bad Godesberg, D: Bundesforschungsanstalt für Landeskunde und Raumordnung, 1968.

Daniel A. Gómez-Ibáñez. *The Western Pyrenees: Differential Evolution of the French and Spanish Borderland.* Oxford, GB: Clarendon Press, 1975.

Chauncy D. Harris. "A Geographical Analysis of Non-Russian Minorities in Russia and Its Ethnic Homelands." *Post-Soviet Geography.* 34 (1993), 543–597.

Chauncy D. Harris. "New European Countries and Minorities." *Geographical Review.* 83 (1993), 301–320.

Chauncy D. Harris. "Unification of Germany in 1990." *Geographical Review.* 81 (1991), 170–182.

Marcus W. Heslinga. *The Irish Border as a Cultural Divide: A Contribution to the Study of Regionalism in the British Isles.* Assen, NL: van Gorcum, 1962.

David Hooson (ed.). *Geography and National Identity.* Oxford, GB: Blackwell, 1994, containing chapters on D, E, F, GB, PL, SLO, and UKR.

John R. G. Jenkins. *Jura Separatism in Switzerland.* Oxford, GB: Oxford University Press, 1987.

James H. Johnson. "The Political Distinctiveness of Northern Ireland." *Geographical Review.* 52 (1962), 78–91.

R. J. Johnston, C. J. Pattie, and J. G. Allsopp. *A Nation Dividing?: The Electoral Map of Great Britain, 1979–1987.* London, GB: Longman, 1988.

Vladimir Klenčič and Milan Bufon. "Cultural Elements of Integration and Transformation of Border Regions: The Case of Slovenia." *Political Geography*. 13 (1994), 73–83.

N. Kliot. "Mediterranean Potential for Ethnic Conflict: Some Generalizations." *Tijdschrift voor Economische en Sociale Geografie*. 80 (1989), 147–163.

Eleonore Kofman. "Differential Modernisation, Social Conflicts, and Ethno-Regionalism in Corsica." *Ethnic and Racial Studies*. 5 (1982), 300–312.

Benjamin Kostrubiec. "La carte électorale polonaise à visage découvert." *Hommes et Terres du Nord*. 1990:1, 25–29.

Walter Leimgruber. "Political Boundaries as a Factor in Regional Integration: Examples from Basle and Ticino." *Regio Basiliensis*. 22 (1981), 192–201.

Fermin Lentacker. *La frontière Franco-Belge: Étude géographique des effets d'une frontière internationale sur la vie de relations*. Lille, F: Morel & Corduant, 1974.

Thomas Lundén. "Proximity, Equality and Difference: The Evolution of the Norwegian-Swedish Boundary Landscape." *Regio Basiliensis*. 22 (1981), 128–139.

James M. Lutz. "Diffusion of Nationalist Voting in Scotland and Wales: Emulation, Contagion, and Retrenchment." *Political Geography Quarterly*. 9 (1990), 249–266.

Halford J. Mackinder. "The Geographical Pivot of History." *Geographical Journal*. 23 (1904), 421–437.

Douglas R. McManis. "The Core of Italy: The Case for Lombardy-Piedmont." *Professional Geographer*. 19 (1967), 251–257.

Kenneth C. Martis, Zoltan Kovacs, Dezso Kovacs, and Sandor Peter. "The Geography of the 1990 Hungarian Parliamentary Elections." *Political Geography*. 11 (1992), 283–305.

W. R. Mead. "Finland in a Changing Europe." *Geographical Journal*. 157 (1991), 307–315.

Julian V. Minghi. "The Franco-Italian Borderland: Sovereignty Changes and Contemporary Developments in the Alpes Maritimes." *Regio Basiliensis*. 22 (1981), 232–246.

John Mohan (ed.). *The Political Geography of Contemporary Britain*. London, GB: Macmillan, 1989.

A. S. Morris, "The Medieval Emergence of the Volga-Oka Region." *Annals of the Association of American Geographers*. 61 (1971). 697–710

Alexander B. Murphy. "Electoral Geography and the Ideology of Place: The Making of Regions in Belgian Electoral Politics," in *Developments in Electoral Geography*, ed. R. J. Johnston, F. M. Shelley, and P. J. Taylor. London, GB: Routledge, 1990, 227–241.

Alexander B. Murphy. *The Regional Dynamics of Language Differentiation in Belgium: A Study in Cultural-Political Geography*. Chicago, USA: University of Chicago Geography Research Paper No. 277, 1988.

John O'Loughlin and Herman van der Wusten (eds.). *The New Political Geography of Eastern Europe*. London, GB: Belhaven Press, 1993.

A. J. Parker. "Geography and the Irish Electoral System." *Irish Geography*. 19 (1986), 1–14.

Geoffrey Parker. *The Geopolitics of Domination: Territorial Supremacy in Europe and the Mediterranean from the Ottoman Empire to the Superpowers*. London, GB: Routledge, 1988.

N. P. Passchier and Herman van der Wusten. "The Electoral Geography of the Netherlands in the Era of Mass Politics, 1888–1986," in *Developments in Electoral Geography*, ed. R. J. Johnston, F. M. Shelley, and P. J. Taylor. London, GB: Routledge, 1990, 39–59.

Richard A. Patrick. *Political Geography and the Cyprus Conflict, 1963–1971*. Waterloo, Ontario, CDN: University of Waterloo Department of Geography Publication Series, No. 4, 1976.

J. Penrose. "Frisian Nationalism: A Response to Cultural and Political Hegemony." *Environment and Planning D: Society and Space*. 8 (1990), 427–448.

Thomas M. Poulsen. *Nations and States: A Geographical Background to World Affairs*. Englewood Cliffs, USA: Prentice Hall, 1995, chapters 2–7.

Norman J. G. Pounds. "France and 'Les Limites Naturelles' from the Seventeenth to the Twentieth Centuries." *Annals of the Association of American Geographers*. 44 (1954), 51–62.

Norman J. G. Pounds and Sue Simons Ball. "Core-Areas and the Development of the European States System." *Annals of the Association of American Geographers*. 54 (1964), 24–40.

Claude Raffestin. "Langues et pouvoir en Suisse." *L'Espace Géographique*. 2 (1985), 151–155.

Stein Rokkan and Derek W. Urwin. *The Politics of Territorial Identity: Studies in European Regionalism*. London, GB: Sage Publications, 1982.

Dean S. Rugg. "Communist Legacies in the Albanian Landscape." *Geographical Review*. 84 (1994), 59–73.

John Sallnow, Anna John, and Sarah K. Webber. *An Electoral Atlas of Europe, 1968–1981: A Political Geographic Compendium*. London, GB: Butterworth Scientific, 1982.

André-Louis Sanguin. *La Suisse: Essai de géographie politique*. Gap, F: Éditions Ophrys, 1983.

J. Sarramea. "Géographie électorale de la France." *L'Information Géographique*. 49:3 (1985), 95–108.

Peter Schöller. "Die Spannung zwischen Zentralismus, Föderalismus und Regionalismus als Grundzug der politisch-geographischen Entwicklung Deutschlands bis zur Gegenwart." *Erdkunde*. 41 (1987), 77–106.

Denis J. B. Shaw and Michael J. Bradshaw. "Problems of Ukrainian Independence." *Post-Soviet Geography*. 33 (1992), 10–20.

Fritz Spering. *Agrarlandschaft und Agrarformationen im deutsch-niederländischen Grenzgebiet*. Göttingen, D: Göttinger Geographische Abhandlungen, No. 76, 1981.

D. J. Spooner. "The Southern Problem, the Neapolitan Problem, and Italian Regional Policy." *Geographical Journal*. 150 (1984), 11–26.

Dan Stanislawski. *The Individuality of Portugal: A Study in Historical-Political Geography*. Austin, USA: University of Texas Press, 1959.

Peter Thomas. "Belgium's North-South Divide and the Walloon Regional Problem." *Geography*. 76 (1990), 36–50.

Henry Valen. "Regionale forskjeller i norsk politikk." *Forskningsnytt*. 10 (1964), 61–71.

Christian Vandermotten. "La résurgence des nationalismes en Europe centre-orientale et en Union Soviétique." *Revue Belge de Géographie*. 115 (1991), 87–101.

Jean Vanlaer. *200 millions de voix: une géographie des familles politiques européennes*. Brussels, B: Société Royale Belge de Géographie et Laboratoire de Géographie Humaine de l'Université Libre, 1984.

Jean Vanlaer. "Les premières élections libres en Europe de l'Est: systèmes de partis et clivages régionaux." *Revue Belge de Géographie*. 115 (1991), 140–157.

Dirk Verheyen. *The German Question: A Cultural, Historical, and Geopolitical Exploration*. Boulder, USA: Westview Press, 1991.

Trevor Wild and Philip N. Jones. "Rural Suburbanisation and Village Expansion in the Rhine Rift Valley: A Cross-Frontier Comparison." *Geografiska Annaler*. 70B (1988), 275–290.

Trevor Wild and Philip N. Jones. "Spatial Impacts of German Unification." *Geographical Journal*. 160 (1994), 1–16.

Allan M. Williams. *The European Community: The Contradiction of Integration*. Oxford, GB: Basil Blackwell, 1991.

Allan M. Williams. *Southern Europe Transformed: Political and Economic Change in Greece, Italy, Portugal and Spain*. London, GB: Harper & Row, 1984.

Colin H. Williams. "Ethnic Separatism in Western Europe." *Tijdschrift voor Economische en Sociale Geografie*. 71 (1980), 142–158.

Ronald Wixman. "Ethnic Nationalism in Eastern Europe." In *Eastern Europe: The Impact of Geographic Forces on a Strategic Region*. Washington, USA: Central Intelligence Agency, 1991, 36–47.

Peter Wörster. "From Germany's East Prussia to the Soviet Union's Kaliningrad Oblast: A Case of Sequent Occupance." *Soviet Geography*. 27 (1986), 233–347.

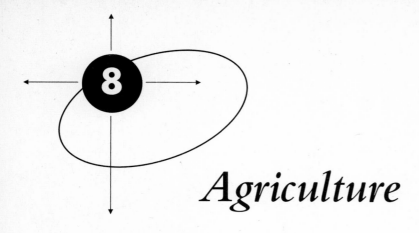

Agriculture

Europeans find numerous ways to obtain a living, but one of the oldest and most fundamental involves tilling the soil and tending herds—in short, agriculture. For most of European history, farming remained the dominant aspect of the economy, and even today about 85 percent of the land area of Western Europe remains classified as rural. True, the great majority of Europeans no longer farm, but the transition away from agriculture occurred relatively recently. To comprehend the remnant agrarian nature of Europe is essential to any broader understanding of the culture area at large. Indeed, agriculture played a role in the very creation of European culture.

Origin and Diffusion

In common with Christianity, the political state, and the Indo-European languages, agriculture did not originate in Europe. Instead, as earlier suggested, the domestication of plants and animals—the **neolithic** revolution—occurred in the Near East and entered Europe later, apparently borne by the proto–Indo-Europeans. For that reason, the maps of linguistic and agricultural diffusion largely match (Figures 4.2 and 8.1). Both language and agrarian technology advanced from southeast to northwest over a period of about four millennia. Agriculture first came to Greece and arrived last in the lands beyond the North and Baltic Seas. The only major unresolved diffusionary question is whether Afro-Asiatic-speaking peoples from North Africa introduced agriculture into Iberia by crossing the Strait of Gibraltar or whether Indo-Europeans achieved this diffusion by passing through the Pyrenees. Perhaps both occurred, as Figure 8.1 suggests.

The advent of agriculture seems to have occurred in two ways. In southeastern and Central Europe, agriculture made a sudden intrusion, producing a sharp break in the archaeological record and implying a displacement of hunters by farmers (Figure 8.1). This also forms the region of greatest Anatolian impact on blood chemistry in Europe (Figure 5.8), and no non-Indo-European linguistic

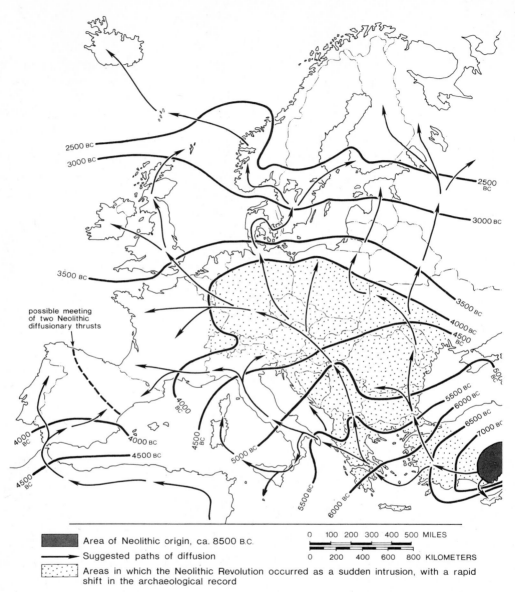

Area of Neolithic origin, ca. 8500 B.C.

Suggested paths of diffusion

Areas in which the Neolithic Revolution occurred as a sudden intrusion, with a rapid shift in the archaeological record

0   100 200 300 400 500 MILES

0   200   400   600   800 KILOMETERS

FIGURE 8.1 Neolithic origins and the diffusion of agriculture in Europe. Domesticated plants and animals reached Europe from the Near East. The map is based upon archaeological finds but nevertheless remains speculative and controversial in detail. Some archaeologists have proposed much earlier dates. (Sources: John Chapman and Johannes Müller, "Early Farmers in the Mediterranean Basin," *Antiquity,* 64 (1990), 128; Peter Breunig, [14]*C-Chronologie des vorderasiatischen, südost- und mitteleuropäischen Neolithikums,* Köln, D: Böhlau, 1987; Renfrew 1989 and Krantz 1988, both cited in Chapter 4; Sokal et al. 1991, cited in Chapter 5; Zohary/Hopf 1988, 210–211; and Dennell 1992, 78.)

remnants survived there. Elsewhere, the advent of farming occurred more gradually. Indigenous groups such as the Etruscans in Italy and Uralic speakers in the north often adopted agriculture rather than being displaced or absorbed. Transitional economies based both upon farming and hunting/gathering became typical, blurring the archaeological distinction between mesolithic and neolithic.

The earliest neolithic crop complex included wheat, barley, lentils, peas, and flax. Other crops came later, after the neolithic diffusion had reached Europe, but their origins almost invariably lay in the same Near Eastern zone. Most Old World garden vegetables, orchard trees, and the grapevine belong among these later introductions from the Near East by way of Anatolia.

Domestic herd animals also came from the Near East. Cattle, pigs, sheep, goats, donkeys, and horses all first entered Europe by way of Anatolia, as did poultry. So did the basic tools of agriculture, such as the hoe and plow, the technique of terracing, and irrigation technology. In the formation of early agriculture, then, Europe borrowed from higher civilizations to the east and south.

Spreading through Europe, agriculture, adjusting to different environments and cultures, fragmented into traditional regional types. The major ancient and traditional agrarian systems include: (1) *Mediterranean agriculture;* (2) *three-field farming;* (3) *hardscrabble herding/farming;* (4) *burnbeating;* and (5) *nomadic herding.*

Mediterranean Agriculture

The rural folk of Cyprus, Greece, the eastern Adriatic coast, peninsular Italy, the Languedoc Plain, and southern Iberia traditionally practiced a distinctive agrarian system appropriately referred to as **Mediterranean agriculture** (Figure 8.2). In essence, this system came unaltered from the neolithic hearth to the east. Agriculture had arisen in an eastern extension of the Mediterranean climate zone, and the southern European peninsulas offered a sufficiently similar setting that few adaptive changes were necessary.

By the time of classical Greco-Roman civilization, Mediterranean agriculture consisted of a trinity of distinct elements: a threefold system of *ager, hortus,* and *saltus* beautifully adapted to the unique climate and rugged terrain of Southern Europe. The Mediterranean climate, described in Chapter 2, has a long summer drought and mild, rainy winters. The *ager* (or field) involved the winter cultivation of small grains—wheat and barley. These thrived in the cool, wet season, without irrigation. Wheat and barley, sown with the arrival of the first autumnal rain showers, grew slowly through the winter months and reached maturity in the warm, sunny days of late spring. Harvesting occurred before the annual drought tightened its grip on the land (Figure 8.3). The great harvest festivals of Mediterranean folk accordingly came in the spring rather than fall. Typically, a two-field rotational system was employed in which farmers cultivated the land only every other year to prevent soil exhaustion. In many districts, the grain ager lay in the alluvial lowlands, often at the base of the slopes, while the farmers lived in strong-point villages on adjacent hilltops, a siting later reinforced by a desire to avoid the malaria of the lowlands. Wheat was generally the more raised

FIGURE 8.2 Ancient and traditional types of agriculture. The division between wheat and rye as the dominant bread grain is as of about A.D. 1900. Ancient and traditional systems gave way at widely different periods in the various parts of Europe.

important of the two grain crops, for Mediterranean peoples prefer light bread. Barley achieved greater importance in drier areas with poor soils, for it is hardier than wheat. In the middle 1900s wheat and barley still accounted for 40 percent of all tilled land in Italy and 50 percent in Greece. Many classical farmers also

FIGURE 8.3 Intertillage of wheat and olives in an alluvial valley in Greece.
Two typical Mediterranean crops share the same field on the island of Kriti. The wheat has only recently been reaped by hand and tied into bundles to be carried in for threshing. Intertillage is common in traditional Mediterranean agriculture. The month is May, the time of grain harvest before the drought of summer. Olives from these young trees will be ready for harvest in autumn. (Photo by the author, 1971.)

millet, a hardy grain that tolerates heat, drought, and poor soils. Millet, a warm season crop, is sown in the early spring and comes to harvest by July, still ahead of the worst part of the dry season.

Horticulture provided the second element of the Mediterranean agricultural trinity. This *hortus* included orchards and vineyards of drought-resistant perennials native to the Mediterranean region and able to withstand the summer dry season. The *grapevine* belongs in this category. From it Mediterranean farmers derived table grapes, raisins dried after the late summer harvest before the onset of rain, and wine, a beverage invented in the eastern Mediterranean lands. In the middle 1900s in Greece, about 40 percent of the harvest went to make wine, 25 percent for raisins, and 35 percent for table grapes. Southern Europeans are partial to wine, and in fact this alcoholic beverage has an ancient and enduring link to religion among them. About 1000 B.C., in the Greek lands, a cult devoted to the god Dionysus arose, in which wine and alcoholic intoxication served as aids to religious experience. The cult, not surprisingly, became very popular among the common folk and by the sixth century B.C. gained governmental approval.

Dionysus and wine spread to the western Mediterranean in part with Greek colonists, and the Romans subsequently accepted the cult, renaming the wine god Bacchus. After Christianization of the Roman Empire, wine retained its ancient Dionysian sacredness by finding a place in the eucharist as the symbolic blood of Christ. Vineyards grow both on terraced hillsides and on alluvial valley floors. The vine produces a crop of high value on a wide variety of surfaces and soils, including steep slopes, without irrigation.

The *olive* is a splendid, long-lived native tree, drought-resistant but not tolerant of a hard frost, long recognized as the single best indicator of the presence of Mediterranean climate and horticulture (Figures 8.2, 8.3). Some of these gnarled, twisted trees survive for a thousand years or more. The olive tree yields a crop only in alternate years, blossoming in the first year and bearing the next; harvesting is accomplished by hitting the branches with a pole. While Mediterranean peoples eat many olives, the principal value of the olive tree, both in ancient times and today, is as a source of fat and cooking oil. Butter has never been produced in Southern Europe, and olive oil provides a needed substitute. The image of butter-eating Germanic tribesmen was repulsive to the Roman writers who left behind descriptions of their northern neighbors. Italy, Spain, and Greece alone account for 75 percent of the world olive oil production. The olive tree thrives on slopes and hillsides as well as in valleys and does well in thin, rocky soils.

Other orchard trees of the classical Mediterranean included the *fig*, also drought-resistant, native to the area, and suited to hillsides; the *almond,* similarly endowed; the *chestnut,* used in many areas as food; and the *pomegranate,* a small tree that yields a tasty acidic flesh from the outer coating of its numerous seeds. While not actually part of the hortus, the *cork oak* also played an important role in some Mediterranean regions. Every seven to nine years, the outer bark of this wild tree can be stripped, using a pointed stick, producing a commercially valuable item of trade (Figure 8.4).

While hortus and ager typically occupied different areas within the village lands of the Mediterranean, *intertillage* also occurred. In this system, wheat and barley were sown among the widely spaced orchard trees, particularly when the olives or figs were young and still had not reached their maximum branch span (Figure 8.3).

The third element of traditional Mediterranean agriculture consisted of the *saltus,* or pasture. Village herders raised mainly small livestock, particularly sheep, goats, and swine. These animals are able to survive on the scanty forage offered by the rugged highland pastures and mountain oak forests of southern Europe. The goats and sheep moved with agility through the rocky landscape, and pigs thrived on the mast of live oak forests. Sheep, the most numerous livestock, provided wool, hides, and some meat, though the Mediterranean diet remained heavily vegetarian. Goats yielded mohair, milk, and hides, and to a certain extent they took the place of dairy cattle in Southern Europe (Figure 8.5). The cheeses produced in Mediterranean districts derived from goat's milk or more rarely from sheep's milk, as in Roquefort. Classical references to swine such as the Homeric episode concerning Circe suggest a widespread importance, but swine are now usually the least important of the three small livestock, in part

FIGURE 8.4 Cork newly stripped from the trunk of this oak tree in Extremadura, in southwestern Spain, near the pilgrimage town of Guadalupe. (Photo by the author, 1986.)

because the forests that provided their food steadily diminished. Today, swine remain common only in the remnant oak forests, such as those on the rainier slopes of mountains in southwestern Iberia, especially Extremadura, where air-cured pork remains a regional specialty. Even so, pigs provide another index for determining the southern boundary of Europe. By calculating the ratio of swine to population, we can reveal a sharp line separating Europeans from the Muslim and Jewish peoples to the south, based on the fact that Christians eat pork while both Islam and Judaism forbid its consumption (Figure 8.6).

The Mediterranean saltus remained largely divorced from the ager and hortus. No crop harvests went as feed or fodder for the herds, and animal manure was not collected as fertilizer for the fields or orchards. In fact, livestock often ranged very far from villages, under the constant care of migrant shepherds and swineherders. In the dry, hot summer, sheep and goats moved to high pastures in the mountains, where grass grew more abundantly, and during the winter they migrated down to marshy parts of the alluvial lowlands. The herders went with them, in a system called *transhumance,* and often months passed between the herders' visits to the home village. Well-established routes of transhumance, lined with rock fences, crisscrossed the countryside. When ranging near the village, herds sometimes grazed on the stubble of the harvested, fallow ager, but in general the raising of crops and livestock remained divorced.

The beast of burden of the traditional Mediterranean agriculture was the donkey, though some farmers did not own one, making do instead entirely with

FIGURE 8.5 A herd of goats and sheep being driven to pasture near the Guadiana River in far southeastern Portugal. These two types of livestock are the most common in
traditional Mediterranean agriculture. (Photo by the author, 1986.)

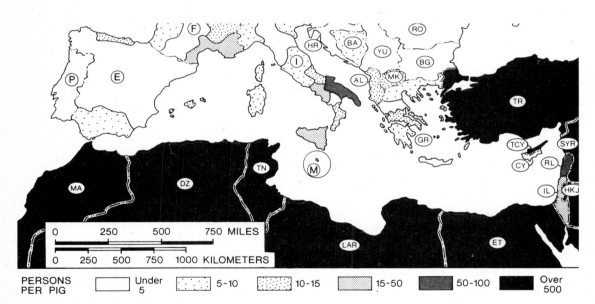

FIGURE 8.6 The population:swine ratio in the Mediterranean lands reveals a southern border for Europe. Pigs and pork are typical of almost all traditional European farming
systems and regional diets, but Islamic and Judaic law forbids the consumption of pork.
Some European Mediterranean lands became too deforested to permit large droves of pigs,
but they never disappeared altogether. (Sources: National statistical yearbooks.)

human labor. Even today, donkeys pulling the typical Mediterranean two-wheeled farm cart or being ridden to the fields can occasionally be seen on rural roads.

In traditional Mediterranean agriculture, the land belonged to the nobility in the form of large estates, or *latifundia*. Even as early as Homer's time, reference was made to peasant reapers who "drive their swaths through a rich man's field of wheat or barley." On these estates, some of which survive to the present day, tenants scratched out a living from tiny farms. A crude hand plow, called an *aratro*, broke the soil so that the seeds would germinate and the winter rains would not run off and erode the grain fields. The *aratro* merely scratched the surface and did not turn a furrow. A hoe, perhaps the main farming tool, was employed to weed the fields and vineyards to retard loss of moisture.

This, then, was the agriculture of classical times. All three of the basic enterprises were practiced on each farm, though one or another might have been emphasized. From the diverse unspecialized trinity of small grains, vine and tree crops, and small livestock, nearly all of life's necessities could be obtained, including woolen and leather clothing, bread, beverages, fruit, cheese, cooking oil, and even a cork for the leather wine container. Homer described this agriculture in the *Iliad*, where, for example, he mentioned a man who "had wheat-bearing fields and many orchards of trees apart, and many sheep."

Within the overarching unity of traditional Mediterranean agriculture, some regional diversity nevertheless appeared. Olives, for example, thrived best in Andalucía and Attiki, Sicilia was famous for wheat, and some of the best wines came from Toscana. In certain other regions, truly ancient farming techniques survived, even into the twentieth century. An example is the *dehesa* (or *montado*) system of southwestern Iberia (Figure 8.2), under which the ager was placed in the saltus. Dehesa farmers selected an area of open oak woods, the typical native vegetation of the ancient Mediterranean. They thinned out the foliage by removing some tree limbs to allow more sunlight to reach the ground, then plowed and sowed grain beneath the pruned forest. A crop could be obtained only about once in every five years in the dehesa system, and the fields had to be relocated every year, but the system proved sustainable and did not destroy the forest. Perhaps as a result, the greatest survival of native oak woodland in all the Mediterranean occurs in the dehesa region. Dehesa represents an archaic form of orchard intertillage. In fact, it may fairly accurately preserve the most ancient technique of grain farming, the type practiced at the dawn of agriculture in the Near East, 9000 years before Christ. It could also reflect an Afro-Asiatic, as opposed to an Indo-European, method, anciently diffused by way of North Africa. Rural Europe, even today, abounds in hints concerning ancient ways and diffusions.

Three-Field Farming

North of the Mediterranean, in the most favored lands beyond the mountains and centered in the Great and East European plains and the Hungarian Basin, a second traditional agricultural system once prevailed—**three-field farming** (Figure 8.2). In this system, found mainly among Germanic and Slavic peoples, grains were raised on a three-field rotation, in which the land was cropped two out of every three years. In this succession, any particular field was planted first to a summer crop, next to a winter grain, and then allowed to lie fallow for a year. At any given time, one-third of the land was at each stage in the cycle.

The grains differed somewhat within the area of three-field farming. In southern and western areas, including England, France, and northwestern Iberia, *wheat* was the principal and preferred bread grain. *Rye,* the second great bread grain, dominated the north, in Germany, Scandinavia, Poland, and Russia, where dark bread was and is preferred. Rye has greater resistance to cold and more tolerance for acidic, sandy soils than does wheat, allowing it to succeed better in northern and eastern regions. It provides not only bread but also whiskey and livestock feed. *Oats* share the hardiness of rye and grow, usually as a summer grain, throughout the three-field area, providing oatcakes, gruel, and—most important—the major livestock feed grain of the system. The fourth major grain, *barley,* provided beer, the northern substitute for wine, but was also raised primarily as a feed grain.

Oats and rye apparently joined the ancient Indo-European agrarian system as it spread north, into colder lands beyond the Vardar-Morava rift valley and Danube River (Figure 4.2). Earlier, these two grains had apparently grown only as weeds in the wheat and barley fields of early agriculturists in the south and east. Rye and oats may be the only crops domesticated within Europe.

Flax, one of the original Near Eastern crops, made the transition northward to find an important place in three-field farming as the major fiber crop. Linen garments are made from flax. Still today, the old three-field countries, led by Russia, produce over 80 percent of the world's flax.

Horticulture also survived the northward diffusion into colder lands, though a different array of fruit trees from those of the Mediterranean prevailed. In place of the olive, almond, fig, and pomegranate came the apple, pear, peach, cherry, and plum, all of Asian origin but also able to grow in the north. The grapevine eventually struggled northward, but reached its climatic limits roughly along the line of the Seine, Rhine, and Danube rivers. Even there, it thrived best on south-facing, sunny slopes, and the German word for vineyard, *Weinberg,* literally means "vine hill."

Another basic part of three-field farming, the cutting of hay from meadow-land, provided additional sustenance for livestock during the winter season. In our modern urban society, the meanings of "meadow" and "pasture" have become blurred, trending toward synonymity. Traditionally, livestock grazed the pasture but not the meadow, from which hay was to be cut. As the famous nursery rhyme admonishes, "sheep's in the meadow" was a state of affairs to be corrected. During much of the winter season, the livestock remained in stalls to consume hay and feed grains. At the opposite season, they grazed fallow fields, pastures, and remnant forests, which usually lay toward the periphery of village lands.

Livestock played a much greater role in three-field farming than in Mediterranean agriculture, supplying a larger part of the rural diet. Cattle, the dominant animals, provided meat, dairy products, manure for the fields, and, as oxen, power to pull the bulky plow characteristic of the Germanic and Slavic lands. In much of Central Europe, including Germany and Poland, swine were a more important source of meat than cattle, and pork is still a mainstay of the diet there. The unique value of swine is their ability to convert even the least savory garbage and waste into high-quality meat, and the mast of remnant oak and beech forests added to their diet. Few areas lacked flocks of sheep, but only in areas of poor quality, such as the Lüneburger Heath of northern Germany, did they serve as the most important livestock. Chickens, ducks, and geese were numerous on most farms.

Perhaps the key difference between three-field farming and Mediterranean agriculture was the close relationship in the former between crops and livestock. The Mediterranean farmer raised both plants and animals, but there was little or no tie between the two, and animal husbandry remained separate from tillage. In the three-field system, crops and livestock were inseparable, for the animals provided the manure used to maintain soil fertility and the power for plowing the fields. In turn, much of the produce of the cropland, particularly the barley and oats, went to feed the livestock, and meadow and pasture occupied extensive acreage.

In other respects, the traditional agricultural systems of Northern and Southern Europe were similar. A landed aristocracy dominated a tenant peasantry in both, and the individual farms were small and fragmented. Both three-field farming and Mediterranean agriculture were unspecialized, subsistence types of farming, designed to produce all of life's necessities.

Hardscrabble Herder-Farmers

Separating and surrounding the favored "fat lands" of the three-field farming and Mediterranean agriculture lay hardscrabble belts, afflicted with broken terrain, excessive cloudiness, and/or sterile soils (Figure 8.2). In these regions, open-range livestock herding constituted the dominant traditional activity, with crop farming minor and secondary in importance. From ancient times, stable village-dwelling farmers of the Mediterranean and Germano-Slavic lands both vilified and romanticized the herders of the peripheries—Celts, Vikings, Basques, Berbers, Vlakhs, and others.

In common with Mediterranean shepherds, the herder-farmer hardscrabble folk relied heavily upon transhumance, shifting their herds seasonally. While these shifts usually occurred between highlands in the summer and lowlands in the winter, other patterns also developed. For example, in Las Marismas, the great marsh at the mouth of the Guadalquivir River in Spain, longhorn cattle entered the core of the wetlands in the dry summer and then retreated to the peripheries of the marsh as the floods of winter turned the area into a huge lake.

In Somersetshire, England, an expanse of low wetlands also provided the summer pastures, and in fact the word Somerset means "summer pastures."

Cattle were the favored animals of the herder-farmers, as in Las Marismas, the Rhône Delta, Celtic fringes, Alps, Massif Central, and Kjölen Range. A milking culture-complex characterized most of these areas, and bovine dairying provided an important component of the diet. Alpine areas, even before the beginning of the Christian Era, exported cheese, and by about A.D. 1100 a distinctive high-mountain system of dairy cattle herding developed among the Walser people there, involving transhumance, hay cutting, winter stall-feeding, milk products, and sheep raising. Sheep dominated most of the other hill and mountain areas and were the favored animal of the Vlakhs, Basques, and Dinaric folk. In response to the demands of late medieval and Renaissance woolen textile industries, as well as the mechanized woolen mills of the Industrial Revolution, many highland herding areas shifted from cattle to sheep.

The role of crops in this traditional system, while secondary, was still significant. In most areas, an *infield-outfield* system was practiced, involving a small, continuously cropped area close to the farmstead, the "infield," surrounded by a much more extensive "outfield." Only a small part of the outfield was planted at any given time, and a lengthy fallow period of a decade or more was needed to restore fertility after several crops. During the fallow period, the outfield served as pasture. Rye, oats, and barley grew as the principal grains, and the hardscrabble farmers regularly consumed oats—a livestock feed elsewhere in Europe—either as gruel or oatcakes. Wheat did not thrive in these hard lands.

In the British Isles the infield lay enclosed by a rock fence called the *inner dyke*, allowing the most prized livestock to be penned there after the harvest and fed through the winter. Their manure refertilized the infield, permitting it to be planted every year. The outfield, too, was ringed by a fence, the *acrewall*, and the less-valuable animals foraged there in the cold season. Beyond and above the acrewall lay the permanent cattle pasture, used during the crop season when all livestock were banished from both infield and outfield. Still higher stood the *moor wall*, separating the good-quality cattle pastures from the poorer sheep-grazing lands of the heath and moor.

Not all herder-farmers employed the infield-outfield system, and many local differences in land use patterns existed. In western Jylland, for example, the *field-grass* system prevailed, involving a rotation of four years of cropping followed by four years of pastured grass-fallow. In non-British areas, the pastures generally had no fences, allowing an open-range system to prevail.

Burnbeaters of the North

In the subarctic expanse of taiga and sterile podsols, certain Finnic peoples of the forests practiced another traditional farming system called **burnbeating** or **shifting cultivation** (Figure 8.2). They cut down trees in small clearings, allowed the dead vegetation to dry, burned it, and then sowed rye and barley in the fertile ashes amongst the stumps (Figure 8.7). After a year or two, burnbeaters abandoned the clearing and made another. One important variant of this system, called *huuhta,* possessed the unique advantage of rendering the infertile, acidic soils of the virgin *taiga* highly productive for one crop year. Farmers practicing *huuhta* cut or girdled trees in the early spring of the first year and allowed the wood to dry until midsummer of the third year and then set fire to the clearing (Figure 8.7). They then planted rye, which came to harvest in the fourth summer, after which the field was abandoned. A second method of shifting cultivation, called *kaski,* occurred in areas covered with birch and other deciduous trees, a second-growth forest that appeared after 20 or 30 years in the old *huuhta* fields. In *kaski,* the woodland was felled in summer at maximum leaf and burned early in the following summer, followed by rye and barley planting. Either system offered the spectacular sight of flaming tree trunks being rolled over the ground by soot-blackened men and women to ignite the leaf mold. Finnish burnbeaters also kept cattle herds in the woods, and they relied as much on hunting and fishing as upon agriculture for livelihood. So successful was their system that the Swedish crown introduced Finnish burnbeaters into interior Scandinavia as colonists after about 1575. In the long run, however, population pressures made shifting cultivation untenable in northern Europe, and it has not been practiced since about 1920.

FIGURE 8.7 Finnish farmers in the interior of their country practicing a traditional form of shifting cultivation that required the repeated clearing and burning of woodland. The fields were used only for one or two years before being abandoned. (Photo by the author, 1985, at the Kuopion Museo in Kuopio, SF.)

The Finnic burnbeating system represented a partial acceptance of agriculture by non-Indo-Europeans. Before the coming of agriculture, the Uralic peoples lived solely by hunting, fishing, and gathering in the forests. All of these traditional activities survived in burnbeating to the extent that a total crop failure did not bring starvation or even severe deprivation.

Nomadic Herding

In the outermost peripheries of Europe, crops failed to gain acceptance, in part due to climatic extremes of cold, infertility, or aridity and also as a result of Asian invasions. Only the herd animals, not the crops of the ancient Near East agricultural hearth, reached the Asiatic nomadic peoples. They wandered from place to place, seeking fresh pastures for their animals and had no fixed residence. The steppe corridor of the southeast and the Hungarian Puszta received wave after wave of such nomadic herders, who raised horses, sheep, goats, and cattle. Among them were the Magyars, Avars, Bulgars, Tatars, and many others, driving their flocks and herds westward in a competition for land, pitting Europe against Asia. Europe eventually won this contest but only with difficulty and amid cultural compromise.

A unique group of nomadic herders, the Sami, inhabited Sapmi (Lapland) in the far north. None of the Near Eastern herd animals could survive in the arctic tundra, but the Sami observed their linguistic cousins, the Finns, herding cattle. Following that example, they or some neighboring tundra people domesticated the reindeer, which became the sole basis of their herding system (Figure 8.8). The Sami had no other animals and no crops at all. Like the Finns, they also engaged in hunting and fishing, but Sami herders acquired many of the necessities of life from the reindeer: meat for food, skins for housing and clothing, and bone for tools and instruments. They spent the summer herding stock on the tundras of the hilly interior and northern Scandinavian coastal fringe, including some islands off the coast of Norway. In wintertime, the reindeer migrated into the protective coniferous forests adjacent to the tundra, which afforded shelter from the bitterly cold winds of the open tundra. Autumn and spring were spent en route to and from the summer pastures on the tundra. The Sami had no awareness of international boundaries and moved freely through what is today Norwegian, Swedish, Finnish, and Russian territory.

Little survives today of traditional agricultural systems. Here and there, in remote hill areas of rural Europe one can occasionally glimpse archaic elements of the older, largely vanished ways, but for the most part pervasive change meets the eye. These changes occurred in the types of crops raised, land tenure, levels of commercialization and specialization, intensity of land use, and the proportion of the population working in agriculture.

FIGURE 8.8 Norwegian Sami engaged in the traditional nomadic reindeer herding. This large reindeer herd is in Finnmark, Norway's northernmost and easternmost province. Tent housing is employed during the migrations, and the principal vehicle is the sled, several of which are shown. These two herders also have skis to facilitate movement. (Photo courtesy Norwegian National Travel Office.)

New Crop Introductions

Two enormously significant diffusions brought exotic crops to Europe during the past two millennia, radically altering agriculture. The first wave came from the Arabic Muslim lands across the Mediterranean, bearing the *citrus fruits*, which had apparently been unknown to the classical Greeks, though the mythological eleventh labor of Hercules had been to obtain the "golden apple" from the Garden of the Hesperides, a possible reference to the orange. Apparently the ancient Greeks knew of citrus but had no firsthand experience with it. Hercules' quest supposedly took him into the warm lands to the south, where the orange in fact grew in the irrigated gardens of Arabia. Hercules failed to get the job done properly, but the Arabs brought citrus into Europe when they conquered Iberia and parts of Italy in the Middle Ages. The Arab word *naranj*, accepted into Spanish as *naranja*, later entered English corrupted as *orange*. Citrus quickly

FIGURE 8.9 An orange grove with irrigation system at Carcagente, in the coastal plain near Valencia, eastern Spain. Three basic modifications of classical Mediterranean agriculture are visible in the picture, including the introduction of citrus, an accomplishment of the Arabs, and the specialized production for market, largely the result of European urbanization in the last century and a half. The coastal plain around Valencia now resembles one huge citrus orchard, a monoculture fundamentally different from the traditional diversified subsistence farming of the Mediterranean. (Photo courtesy Spanish National Tourist Office.)

became a basic part of Mediterranean horticulture, though these fruits lacked drought resistance and required extensive development of irrigation (Figure 8.9). The Arabs also added apricots, carobs, and sugar cane to the Mediterranean hortus, as well as sorghum, cotton, and rice to the ager.

The second revolutionary introduction of crops came from the American Indian as a result of the Age of Discovery. Two distinct diffusions occurred. The first involved the intertilled Mesoamerican food complex of *maize* (corn), *chili peppers, squash, beans,* and *pumpkins,* to which was appended the *turkey* and perhaps the *tomato.* Improbably, this food complex did not reach Europe directly, by way of the Spaniards in Mexico. Indeed, Iberians largely rejected these foods and still do. Instead the complex of Mexican domesticates accompanied the

Portuguese around Africa to India and from there to Turkey, gaining acceptance at every stop. All spread into Balkan Europe with the Turkish conquests and adoption of the Mesoamerican complex remains greatest there, even to the present day. Taste the paprika in Hungarian food, observe the expansive tomato fields of Bulgaria, watch stick-wielding Peloponnesian women drive flocks of turkeys through the streets, see the festival corn decorations of the South Slavs, consider that *mamaliga* (cornmeal mush) serves as a main Romanian food staple, and you will grasp the extent to which Balkan agriculture has been reshaped in a Mesoamerican image.

Andean Indians of highland South America provided the other major New World crop, the so-called Irish *potato*. It spread to Europe by an altogether different route. Arriving in Spain from Peru in 1565, the potato quickly reached Spanish-ruled Belgium. Within two centuries it gained acceptance throughout most of the three-field farming region and the herder-farmer hardscrabble periphery, completely revolutionizing both. The potato provided four times as much carbohydrate per hectare as wheat and became the principal food crop of most peoples living north of the Alps and Pyrenees. It yielded large amounts of food from small fields, even in a cloudy, cool climate. Temporarily, at least, the potato ended famines wherever it gained acceptance. Hunger returned again only when the potato itself became blighted in the 1840s.

Specialization and Commercialization

Even more radical changes in European agriculture occurred after about 1850 as a result of the urbanization and industrialization of the culture area. Farmers stopped producing at a subsistence level, no longer content merely to provide their own needs and have a small surplus left over to sell. Instead, the large urban markets prompted them to focus on production of commodities for sale.

Subsistence breeds diversity, while market orientation usually leads to **specialization**. No longer would the Mediterranean farmer pursue a threefold system; no longer would three-field agriculture retain its multiplicity of crops and livestock. Small aspects of the traditional diversified systems would become the only agricultural pursuit. Specialization remains an ongoing process in Europe, increasing decade by decade. As a result, the map of agricultural types in Europe has been almost totally redrawn, with focus on individual cash products replacing the older, many-faceted systems (Figure 8.10). In Mediterranean Europe, specialization was usually achieved by elevating the hortus to the only agricultural pursuit. Ager and saltus shrank and disappeared, crowded out by the expansion of orchards, vineyards, and vegetable fields or else abandoned. The result was a modern, specialized type of agriculture called **market gardening** or truck farming (Figure 8.10).

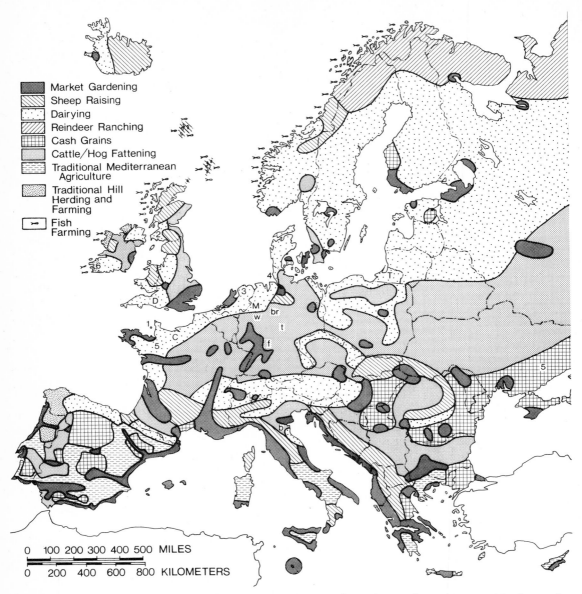

Market Gardening
Sheep Raising
Dairying
Reindeer Ranching
Cash Grains
Cattle/Hog Fattening
Traditional Mediterranean Agriculture
Traditional Hill Herding and Farming
Fish Farming

0   100 200 300 400 500 MILES

0   200   400   600   800 KILOMETERS

FIGURE 8.10 Specialized types of agriculture in modern Europe. Numbers refer to source regions of selected dairy breeds: **1** = Guernsey and Jersey, **2** = Ayrshire, **3** = Friesian, **4** = Holstein, **5** = Maine-Anjou, **6** = Kerry. Capital letters refer to the place of origin of selected generic cheeses: C = Camembert, D = Cheddar, G = Gruyère, M = Muenster, T = Tilsit. Lower-case letters refer to the origin of selected generic meat products: b = bologna, br = braunschweiger, f = frankfurter, w = westphalian ham. (Sources: Kostrowicki 1984 and numerous regional studies cited in the chapter bibliography.)

Market Gardening

Actually, Mediterranean specialization centered not merely upon the hortus, but also upon specific elements within it. A farmer might choose to produce olives or oranges, wine grapes or garden vegetables. Entire districts focused upon a single orchard or vineyard product. The Languedoc Plain, for example, became one huge "sea of vines" stretching as far as the eye can see; the irrigated *huertas* of eastern coastal Spain developed specialized citrus cultivation and gave the name to the Valencia orange (Figure 8.9); while Andalucía, the Adriatic coast of Italy, and the Riviera achieved fame for their olives. Northern Sicilia and the area around Napoli also became noted for citrus, and the valley of the Douro River in Portugal expanded production of the famous *port* wines. One of the most remarkable agricultural sights in the Mediterranean lands is the view from adjacent mountain heights of the olive-clad expanse of the once-sacred Plain of Krissa, near Delfi in Greece. This plain, now one solid olive orchard to the almost complete exclusion of other trees or crops, gives the appearance from above of a gray-green embayment of the adjacent Gulf of Kórinthos (Corinth). Nearby, Homer's "wheat-bearing Argos" became one immense citrus orchard.

The older, diversified Mediterranean system has not completely disappeared. Rougher, interior districts, poorly endowed with irrigation water or sufficient flat land, retain relics of the older system. Fine examples of traditional Mediterranean agriculture can be seen in such districts as the southern flank of the Pyrenees in Spain; the upper Algarve around Sao Brás de Alportel in far southern Portugal; and in the mountains of Kriti in insular Greece. In effect, two quite different agricultural types developed in Southern Europe, one preserving the traditional system and the other evolving into market gardening. Alongside methods dating to the time of Homer, we find modern scientific agriculture. Here we can view two worlds—one reminiscent of the neolithic and classical past, which survives in small holdings where people live their lives traditionally, and one inhabited by the specialized, cash-crop farmers serving the world markets (Figure 8.9). In places, the juxtaposition of traditional Mediterranean farming and modern agribusiness is quite startling. For example, the district called Las Alpujarras, south of Granada in the Spanish Bética Range, displays an almost unaltered ancient agrarian system. Tiny fields and orchards, laboriously won from mountainside and flood plain, yield a variety of Mediterranean crops, while sheep and goats graze high above. Machines are few, with the necessary labor provided by people and donkeys. Little in the way of agricultural produce reaches market from Las Alpujarras. Homer would find the district a familiar place. Journey a very short distance southward toward the Mediterranean shore, over the ridge known as the Sierra de Gádor, and you enter the altogether different agricultural world of the flat Campo de Dalías. Most of these plains are covered with huge sheets of white plastic, beneath which grow irrigated winter vegetables in one of the most impressive market-gardening enterprises anywhere in the world. The boomtowns of the Campo de Dalías offer agribusiness sales and service outlets for plastic sheeting, pipe, insecticides, and pump systems. Perhaps nowhere else in the world do such contrasting types of agriculture coexist in such a small area.

Market gardening also emerged north of the Alps, mainly in small pockets of the old three-field region. Each sizable city there acquired a surrounding "halo" of truck farms producing fruit and vegetables for the nearby urban market (Figure 8.10). Other local districts of northern market gardening appeared in climatically favored places, where one or another crop thrived particularly well. For example, Bretagne in France today specializes in apples and cider; nearby Picardie produces potatoes; Holland is a center for flowers and bulbs; Bulgaria is known for tomatoes; and cherries thrive on the shores of the Bodensee in southern Germany.

The most impressive and lucrative northern example of market gardening is found in the wine-producing vineyards of the Bordeaux region, Champagne, Bourgogne (Burgundy), the middle Rhine Valley, Austria's Weinviertel (wine region) north of Wien (itself named for wine in Roman times), and certain other favored *adret* (see Chapter 2) districts. Traceable to monastic settlements of the fourth century founded to produce sacramental wine, northern viticulture expanded rapidly in the last century and a half to supply growing urban and export markets.

Dairying

Milk cows enjoyed importance in several traditional agricultural systems, especially in the three-field system and highland herding-farming of Scandinavia, the Alps, Celtic fringe, Massif Central, and Pyrenees. When specialization and commercialization came, many such districts elevated bovine **dairying** to their only major activity. Cropland was converted to pasture and meadow, herd size increased on each farm, and an elaborate network of milk processing plants, creameries, cheese factories, and milk transport systems developed. As a result, the great European *dairy belt* took shape around the shores of the North and Baltic seas, including much of the British Isles, coastal France, the Low Country, northern Germany, and the Scandinavian lands. An outlier lies to the south, in the Alps of Switzerland and Austria (Figure 8.10). The dairy belt occupies the cloudiest, coolest part of northwestern Europe, a land better suited to pasture and the raising of hay than to field crops such as wheat. Similarly, the rugged mountain terrain of the Alps is more easily adapted to the raising of grasses, and hay can be mown on the steep slopes where crop tillage would be difficult. Extensive areas of mountain pasture, the *almen*, lie too high to be farmed but serve well a livestock-based economy.

The trend toward specialized dairying can be traced to the Middle Ages in some parts of northern Europe. In England, the counties of Essex and adjacent East Suffolk, on the North Sea coast northeast of London, became known for dairying in the late Middle Ages. In the 1600s, the shires of Hertford and Buckingham north of the British capital adopted the same agricultural specialty, as did certain districts in the English Midlands. Generally the more peripheral dairy areas produced cheese, which was less perishable. Also in the 1600s, the French provinces of Normandie on the English Channel and Brie near Paris became famous as dairy areas, as did parts of the Low Country. In the nineteenth century, commercial dairying spread to its present limits, displacing grain farming in countries such as Denmark. Dairying now enjoys overwhelming importance in the belt devoted to it. In Finland, for example, milk production accounts for 38 percent of the total agricultural income of the country, while meadow, pasture, and silage crops cover a third of the arable land.

The dairy belt enjoys an importance extending far beyond the confines of Europe. Developments in dairying in the European culture area shaped subsequent similar economies in overseas colonial settlement zones, including Anglo-America, New Zealand, and Australia. For example, every major breed of dairy cattle in the world today derives from the European dairy belt, and the breeds bear names indicative of their origin. The Jersey and Guernsey commemorate the names of two of the Channel Islands, which lie between France and England; the Ayrshire breed reminds us of a Scottish county; the Holstein-Friesian comes from Friesland in the Netherlands and the north German province of Holstein; the Brown Swiss was originally bred in the canton of Schwyz in central Switzerland; the Maine-Anjou breed honors two old provinces of western France; and the Kerry breed reveals its Irish county of origin (Figure 8.10). Similarly, the famous cheeses of the world often have the names of towns and cities in the European dairy belt, including Edam (Netherlands), Münster (northern Germany), Camembert (Normandie), Gruyères (French-speaking Switzerland), Cheddar (English Somerset), and many others.

Pronounced regional contrasts exist within the European dairy belt, both in type of produce and intensity of farming. Denmark, which specializes in butter production and contributes a substantial percentage of all butter entering international trade, exemplifies highly developed dairying. The Danish farmers banded into local cooperatives, mainly for purposes of marketing but also for the construction of creameries. Land and livestock remain privately owned. Each package of butter bears a stamp with the code number of the cooperative and the individual farmer so that customer complaints concerning quality can be directed to the farmer responsible and fines levied. This system produces the highest-quality butter found anywhere, supplemented by fine pork and bacon from swine fattened on skim milk, a by-product of the butter-making process. In the Netherlands, attention is focused on milk and high-quality cheeses. Another advanced dairy country, the United Kingdom, has farmers specializing in fluid milk.

In hilly and mountainous areas, where commercial dairying succeeded subsistence herding and farming, many aspects of the older system survive, in particular transhumance. Dairying in Switzerland, Austria, and Norway still utilizes high mountain pasture (Alpine *almen,* Norwegian *seter*) in the summer season. Herdsmen living in small huts milk the animals to be collected and taken down to market. In the meantime, fellow workers at the farmsteads in the valleys raise feed crops and cut hay for the winter, when the dairy cattle come back down-slope to barns during the cold season.

Cattle/Hog Fattening

Another element of traditional three-field farming that survived into the modern age of commercialization and specialization is the breeding and fattening of cattle and hogs. Germanic and Slavic Europeans retain their preference for beef and pork. Most of the protein in their diet comes from these sources. As a result, an elongated belt of commercial cattle/hog-fattening farms now stretches from the Paris Basin through Germany, Poland, and Ukraine into Russia (Figure 8.10). Feeder specialization began at least as early as the 1600s in parts of England, particularly in East Anglia northeast of London and Leicestershire in the Midlands. Similar developments occurred about the same time in parts of Germany and the Netherlands, but most such developments awaited the growth of urban markets in the 1800s.

Raising of livestock feed replaced production for human consumption, and a pronounced regional contrast developed in the choice of crops. South of a rather sharp line across the neck of the Balkan Peninsula, the Alps, and on through central France, maize is the principal feed crop used to fatten livestock, as in the American corn belt, but north of the line small grains and root crops dominate, including barley, oats, potatoes, and sugar beets. In Germany, 70 percent or more of the potato harvest goes for livestock feed.

Just as the European dairy belt gave names to many important breeds and dairy products, so the livestock-feeder area influenced the names of meats and sausages. For example, Thüringer, Braunschweiger, and Westphalian ham (actually beef) all derive from the names of provinces in the cattle/hog-fattening areas, while Frankfurter, Wiener, and Bologna bear the names of cities there.

Sheep Raising

A great portion of the hardscrabble regions originally devoted to herding with secondary crop farming is now engaged in specialized **sheep raising.** The Celtic fringes of the British Isles, Massif Central, Dinaric Range, Carpathians, and Iceland all contain important sheep-raising districts today (Figure 8.10).

The market that prompted this specialization lay in the woolen textile districts, especially in Great Britain (see Chapter 11). In the 1700s and 1800s, landlords in the British highlands converted the far greater part of their estates to sheep pasture. Raising sheep required only a small resident population of herders. Most of the tenant farmers pursuing the traditional agricultural system became superfluous and found themselves cruelly evicted from the land in a long series of "clearances," their houses pulled down stone by stone and their stored food destroyed to make sure they could not return. Many perished. Others fled to Australia or North America, leaving behind hilly homelands devoted almost solely to sheep raising. Cattle largely disappeared from these areas, as did crops. The visitor to the British sheep-raising districts today should be aware of the enormous human suffering and death caused by the advent of specialized agriculture.

Sheep are raised for both wool and meat, and most European pastures support very large flocks by world standards. In the Shetland Islands of Scotland, for example, 1.6 sheep can be kept on each hectare (.65 head per acre). Europeans consume far more mutton and lamb than do Americans, giving an added market impetus to raising sheep.

Cash Grain Farming

In some regions, the grain ager prevailed in the age of specialization and commercialization (Figure 8.10). *Wheat* became the most common cash grain and today dominates the former nomadic herding region in the steppes of Ukraine and Russia, forming Europe's greatest wheat belt. Large wheat farms also appear in parts of the Castilian plateau, served by migratory harvesting crews using giant American-made combines. Tall grain elevators now compete visually with Castilian church spires in local market towns, and much of the landscape has taken on the appearance of Kansas or Saskatchewan. Irrigated cash *rice* farms now occupy former wetlands in coastal Portugal, Las Marismas in Spain, and the Po-Veneto Plain. In beer-drinking areas, north of the wine lands, *malting barley* is widely raised as a cash grain, and commercial *rye* farming occurs through much of northern and eastern Europe.

Reindeer Ranching

Not even Sapmi, in the remotest northern fringes of Europe, has been immune to the far-reaching changes in the agricultural economy. Traditional nomadic herding by the Sami has been destroyed. Beginning in 1852, certain borders closed to their international migration, forcing the Sami to accept citizenship in one or another country and disrupting many routes of seasonal movement. An agreement allowed some Swedish Sami to use summer tundra pastures in Norway in exchange for the use of Swedish forests for winter refuge by Norwegian Sami, but border crossings are generally rare. Another significant change involved range fencing, separating the herds of adjacent groups and ending the traditional open-range system. One such fence parallels most of the Norwegian-Finnish border, and others have been built within the various nations. Sweden designated a Sapmi (*Lappmark*) border within its territory, north of which the Sami have precedence in rural land use. Even so, the Sami lost large areas that once belonged to them, particularly in Finland, where dairy farmers pushed far to the north. Commercial lumbering, utilizing large machines and clear-cutting techniques, damaged woodlands that once supported large herds. In the words of one Swedish Sami, "the cutting method of the Forest Board . . . is damaging the ground and spoiling the reindeer grazing." Some herds starved recently because of clear-cutting.

Those who remain herders have adopted new, different methods. Snowmobiles replaced skis in reindeer herding, and the stock receive less frequent attention nowadays, owing to the fencing of ranges and the reduction of predators. As a result, the reindeer have become semiferal. Herders now belong to cooperatives, which operate much like collective farms. Norway established a Reindeer Office within its Ministry of Agriculture, and the Sami herders of that country belong to the National Association of Reindeer-Herders. The Reindeer Office requires reports of the number of livestock each year, supervises migrations, and demands that each owner mark his or her deer and register the mark. Sanitary slaughter sheds and meat-freezing plants have been built, and commercial marketing of reindeer meat advanced.

Most Sami abandoned herding altogether, accepting employment in fishing, mining, and other industries. Only about 4000 still engage in reindeer raising. In the Swedish province of Västerbotten, for example, about 100 herder families remain in business, owning an average of 500 reindeer each. Even they gave up tent housing for more permanent, though often rather wretched, shacks. A visitor to Sapmi is strongly reminded of American Indian reservations. Nomadism has all but disappeared, replaced by a transhumance in which the people remain sedentary for five to six months during the year. The end product is better described as livestock ranching than nomadic herding. Europe and Asia met in these northlands, and Europe won.

Fish Farming

Some modern types of agriculture do not derive from traditional types. One example is hothouse market gardening near Reykjavik in Iceland, where all sorts of warmth-loving crops such as bananas grow beneath glass. **Fish farming** provides another example. In the past two decades or so, northern Scotland, parts of Ireland, and the Faeroe Islands have become fish-farming centers, an enterprise that grew out of the traditional importance of fishing (Figures 8.10, 8.11). Fish farming focuses mainly upon salmon, raised in anchored cages moored in the saltwater inlets, bays, and channels of peripheral northwestern Europe. In the same region, trout grow to maturity in freshwater ponds, often providing a second income on sheep farms. These valued fish find a ready market in the urban areas of Western Europe and now offer significant competition for the fishing industry.

Agricultural change in Europe extended far beyond new crop introductions and the rise of specialized, market-oriented types. Radical changes occurred and are still happening in land tenure.

Land-Tenure Changes

Traditionally, almost all of rural Europe belonged to a landed aristocracy. The peasantry labored as tenants, required to pay a share of their produce as rent. Only the Finnish burnbeaters and nomadic herders escaped this pervasive bondage. In a few regions, large landed estates survive to the present day, as in southern Iberia, parts of southern Italy, and some British Highland areas.

FIGURE 8.11 A salmon fish farm in Sundini, the saltwater sound between the two main Faeroe islands, Eysturoy and Streymoy. The fish are confined to the circular enclosures, and food for them is being strewn from the boat. (Photo by the author, 1994.)

Elsewhere, agrarian *land reform* took place. In most of Western Europe, a steady move toward peasant landownership occurred between about 1650 and 1850 with a gradual elimination of the landed aristocracy. This transition occurred in various ways, but the sequence of events in the Po Valley of northern Italy is illustrative. Landlords there by law had to pay outgoing peasant tenants for any improvements made during their terms as renters, and failure to do so forced the owner to renew the lease at no increase in rent. These improvements included clearing of woodland, marsh drainage, or even irrigation development, for which the landlords were hard pressed to pay, and typically they allowed the lease to be renewed. The rent thus remained constant while inflation lowered its relative cost, until eventually the peasant could buy the land. In Greece, the successful rebellion against Turkish rule had the side effect of destroying the landed aristocracy, composed primarily of Turks. Typical of present conditions is the Greek island of Kriti, where 96 percent of the farmers now own their land.

In Eastern Europe the landed aristocracy persisted, and few farmers gained possession of the fields they worked. Many aspects of medieval bondage survived into the 1900s in Slavic Europe and eastern Germany. A more drastic and violent solution came there—liquidation of the landed aristocracy under

Communist dictatorships. Typically, the Communists won early peasant support by promising the farmers landownership. In 1946, for example, such a campaign occurred in Soviet-occupied East Germany under the slogan *"Junker Land in Bauern Hand"* ("Aristocrats' lands in farmers' hands"). After a brief period of peasant ownership, the state confiscated the land and established *collective* and *state farms.* Collectives involved farmers operating as a unit, more or less in business for themselves as a group, paying rent to the state and splitting profits. In the less-common state-farm system, the farmers labored as salaried state employees for a fixed wage on huge superfarms, turning all produce over to the government. Collective and state farms became dominant in most Communist countries.

Since the collapse of Communism, land tenure has once again undergone fundamental changes in Eastern Europe. Every formerly Communist country is presently experiencing privatization of the agricultural sector, with differing results and rates of progress (Figure 8.12). In most of the countries of the former Soviet Union, relatively little privatization at the level of the individual farmer has occurred because collectivization happened so long ago that rural folk know nothing of private enterprise. Many collectives made the transition directly to agribusiness when the Communist-era farm directors seized ownership and became capitalistic entrepreneurs. Even so, some 270,000 privately owned farms had been created in Russia by January 1994 (Figure 8.12).

Restitution of land to former owners early became the policy in the post-Communist Czech Republic, Slovakia, Hungary, Bulgaria, and Romania. Hungary boasts many new privately owned farms, but they tend to be undercapitalized, backward, and poor. Romania and Bulgaria seem to have achieved a more orderly transition, fostering cooperative "associations" that join the advantages of collectivization to the incentives of restored private property. Bulgaria allowed each collective to oversee its own dissolution, dividing fixed assets and land as fairly as possible. In Romania, a 1991 law mandated privatization of agricultural lands, with restitution to former owners given priority. Families landless prior to the advent of Communism received farms only as available. By the end of 1991, nearly half of all parcels had passed into private hands, though the mean size of each such farm in Romania was only about 6 ha (15 acres). In Estonia, where the first privately owned farms appeared in 1987, the number of such enterprises rose to 9000 by 1993. Averaging only about 25 ha (63 acres) in size, many of these will likely fail. Most lack any legal recognition.

In some countries, agrarian chaos followed the demise of Communism. Albania announced land privatization, but the peasant response was to loot and destroy the complex of buildings belonging to the collectives. In Lithuania, farmers quickly slaughtered the collective livestock herds, causing the number of swine to drop by nearly half and cattle by a quarter in a single year, from 1991 to 1992. The former East Germany experienced perhaps the worst disruptions. Most rural laborers simply left the land, causing the farm population to plummet from 850,000 in 1989 to 250,000 at the end of 1991. Some 600,000 ha (1.5 million acres) of land became fallow during that same period. Few of those departing found jobs, and some later returned. The path to privatization in East Germany has been hindered by the government's decision to allow the pre-Communist

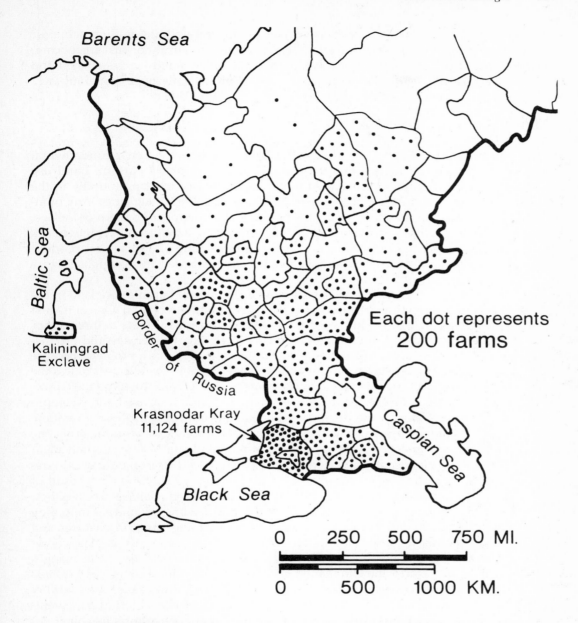

FIGURE 8.12 Distribution of private farms in European Russia, midsummer 1992. The greatest progress had been made in southern Russia, in the districts north of the Caucasus Mountains. In all of Russia, some 133,000 such "peasant" farms existed, averaging about 42 ha (104 acres) in size and occupying 5% of the country's arable land. By 1994 the total increased to 270,000. (Source: adapted from Judith Pallot, in *Post-Soviet Geography*, March 1993, 215–216.)

landowners and their descendants to put forward claims to regain their property, even if the dispossessed belonged to the hated, abusive Junker aristocracy and no longer resided in the area. German courts clogged with 2.4 million actual or potential land claims in the former East. Even so, privatization was largely completed in eastern Germany by 1992, with over 16,000 family farms created and over four-fifths of the land organized into new private-enterprise cooperatives.

Development of Core and Periphery

The commercialization of European agriculture led to another fundamental change—the emergence of a pronounced core/periphery pattern. Land use intensified throughout Europe in the modern age but most profoundly in the central regions closest to the industrial complexes and growing cities. Any number of statistical measures reveal the agrarian core/periphery pattern of Europe, including grain productivity per hectare, percentage of land cultivated, livestock density, amount of fertilizer applied per hectare, value of agricultural produce per capita, and the distribution of economically distressed rural regions (Figure 8.13).

Increased intensity of land use in the European core began in England in the 1700s and is sometimes referred to as the Agricultural Revolution. One of its first victims was the traditional three-field system. Fallowing one year in three disappeared from the three-field rotation, greatly increasing the acreage and production of feed crops. Fallowing had always been something of a problem, because the field quickly became choked with grass and weeds in the idle year unless the farmers continually cultivated it. In many areas, turnip crops replaced the fallow, with repeated hoeing employed to keep the weeds out. Improved, more complicated crop rotations were developed, such as the Norfolk four-course rotation, which included turnips. Improved pastures and meadows resulted from the spread of new varieties of clover, and the increased planting of turnips and sugar beets added significantly to the amount of livestock feed. The amount of pastureland declined, and many old grazing areas became cropland. The net result of the changes was a marked increase in the amount of feed available for livestock, and the numbers of animals rose accordingly. Stall-feeding became all-important, for many stock were kept penned rather than roaming about in pastures and forests. Increased confinement of animals also allowed a more complete collection of manure, which in turn aided the elimination of fallowing. The changes occurred in a spiral: the elimination of fallowing → an increase in yield of feed crops → more livestock per farm → more manure per farm → increased fertility of fields → increased yields of feed crops, and so on. Chemical fertilizers, invented by the Germans, assisted the upward spiral, as did agricultural machinery of various kinds. Later, in the twentieth century, pesticides further enhanced productivity, at least in the short run. Increased attention to selective breeding produced better-quality livestock and hybrid seeds.

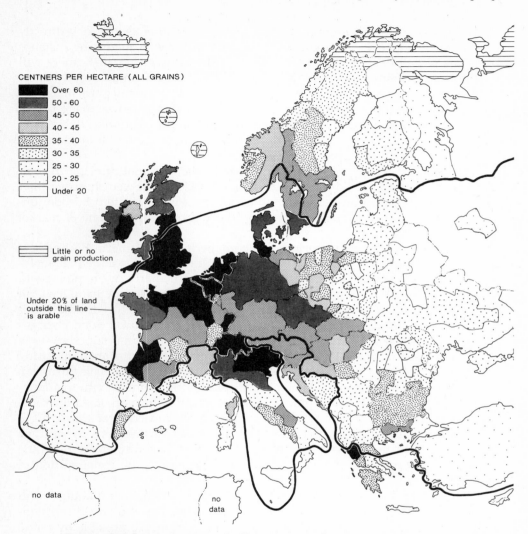

FIGURE 8.13 Production of all grains per hectare. A classic core/periphery pattern is revealed, a recurring geographical configuration in Europe. Anomalies include the cultivation of irrigated rice in some small Mediterranean districts and maize in the Balkans, which yields far more per unit of land than the European small grains. The principle of land rent is evident in this pattern. (Sources: National statistical yearbooks and censuses.)

In all of these changes, peripheral parts of Europe lagged behind the core. The reason lay largely in the geographical principle of *land rent*, originally revealed in the work of J. H. von Thünen. Land rent, the return for the use of land in excess of the minimum expenditure required to operate a farm, is directly proportional to land value, and both of these decrease with increasing distance from market, all other factors being equal. If we assume that all farmers will maximize land rent and possess the knowledge to do so, then an orderly set of concentric zones of land use ought to surround a market. For any particular crop, the intensity of production decreases with increasing distance from market since more and more capital or time must be expended on transportation rather than on production. The most intensive forms of agriculture, then, will lie closest to the market, producing a core/periphery pattern.

Figure 8.13 reveals the geographical impact of the land-rent principle in commercialized agricultural Europe. As early as the 1920s, the Swedish geographer Olaf Jonasson demonstrated that the industrial belt of northwestern Europe constituted one huge urban area or supercity, flanked by an inner zone of market gardening and dairying.

The land-rent concept of agricultural core/periphery zoning in Europe as a whole was further developed by the geographer J. R. Peet, who added an analysis of changes that have occurred through time, particularly in the nineteenth century. Growth of urban population, with resultant changes in demand for farm products, had an effect on agriculture in the surrounding zones, as did the development of new and cheaper means of transporting produce. Such changes occurred in nineteenth-century northwestern Europe, where a supercity took shape composed of myriad industrial centers lying in the belt of manufacturing on the coalfields of Britain, the Low Country, and Germany. The European supercity can be termed the "Thünen World City." A huge increase in total population accompanied its development, greatly enlarging the market. At the same time, transportation of farm produce became easier and cheaper through the building of canals, railroads, and oceangoing steamers. Furthermore, the average income of the urban population of the Thünen World City rose markedly in the 1800s, magnifying the purchasing power and increasing the consumption of foods.

The increased demand for a given farm product intensified its output and led to an expansion of its zone of production. The increased demand for high-quality foods such as fruit, dairy products, and meat, made possible by rising incomes in the Thünen World City, led to more intensive market gardening, dairying, and livestock fattening in areas traditionally devoted to those specialties and a displacement of less intensive forms of agriculture as the zones of dairying, livestock feeding, and truck farming expanded. The decline of commercial wheat farming in the 1800s in countries such as Denmark, where dairying now dominates, fits neatly into this perspective. Land rent provides a connection between industrialization/urbanization as a cause and the spread of commercial agriculture through Europe in the 1800s. Furthermore, land-rent concepts help explain the distribution of dairying, livestock fattening, and commercial food-grain farming evident in present-day Europe (Figure 8.11). The land-rent principle, however, assumes that people behave rationally. Often they do not. Communism, for example, imposed irrational, ideological inefficiencies that long retarded development in the eastern half of Europe, with consequences evident in Figure 8.13.

On a more local scale, cultural differences play a similarly disruptive role. These anomalies warn us against the facile generalizations of economic determinism. A series of studies of agriculture along the German/French language border prove revealing in this context. In the Jura region of Switzerland, the German/French linguistic boundary marks an agricultural divide of sorts. Swiss geographer Kurt Wasmer-Ramer found French-speaking farmers more willing to accept innovations and to invest capital in their operations than the nearby German-Swiss. Moreover, the German-speakers placed more emphasis on crops as opposed to pasture and remained truer to traditional agricultural methods, including ecologically sound techniques. The causes for these contrasts remain unclear, but they obviously lie in the respective cultures. Not far to the north, in eastern France, the same language border again reveals itself in the agricultural geography. In Lorraine province, many agricultural features virtually duplicate the language pattern (Figure 8.14). On the German-speaking side of the line, farms remain smaller and more fragmented, causing farmers to seek second jobs to support their families. Dairy cattle and swine are more important among the German-speaking farmers. The rural population density is greater on the German side, and farmers use more machinery. Those who would understand Europe must never lose sight of the internal diversity and causal influence of its cultures.

Rural Depopulation

Another profound agricultural change in Europe during the past two centuries has been the flight of people from the land. Today only a small minority of Europeans still work in agriculture, constituting in some districts less than 3 percent of the labor force (Figure 8.15). The decline of farm population has been absolute as well as proportional, and flight to the cities continues today.

In large part, economic causes explain the emigration of rural people. Europe's small farms simply could not effectively compete on the world market when the commercialization of agriculture occurred. At the same time, the growing cities offered abundant jobs at salaries allowing a higher standard of living. One of the criteria defining economically depressed regions in Europe today is a higher-than-average proportion of the workforce in agriculture. Those who remain in farming often take second jobs to augment their income.

Increasingly, people left in the countryside are elderly. In many districts, especially in the Mediterranean countries, the median age of farmers now exceeds 55 years. Aging of the agricultural population guarantees that the numbers engaged in farming will continue to dwindle.

A map showing the proportion of the labor force working in agriculture reveals several basic geographical patterns that should by now be familiar to you. A core/periphery configuration appears, in which the lands bordering the North Sea rank lowest in percentage employed in farming (Figure 8.15). The eye also detects north/south and east/west contrasts.

Emigration from the countryside caused both a decline in the number of farms and an increase in their size. In western Germany, for example, 80 percent

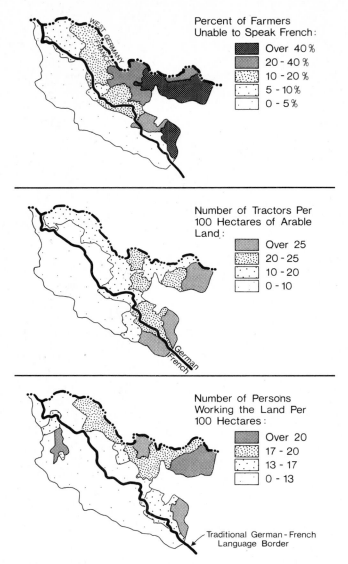

FIGURE 8.14 Agricultural contrasts along the German-French language border in Lorraine province, eastern France, about 1970. (Source: After Cabouret.)

of all farms contained less than 10 ha (25 acres) of land in 1950, but the proportion dropped to 59 percent by 1977 and has continued to decline. The number of farms in Finland fell by half between 1960 and 1990, and a third of all French vineyards disappeared in that same period. In every country, the agricultural contribution to the national economy has declined and continues to do so. Some

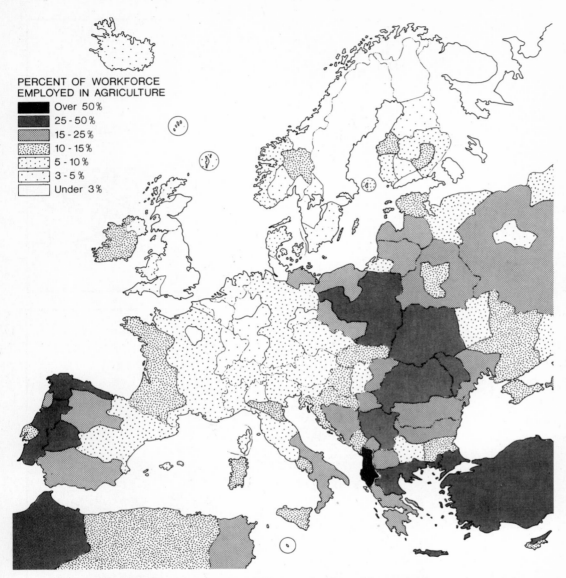

FIGURE 8.15 Percentage of workforce employed in agriculture. The pattern is complicated, revealing north/south, east/west, and core/periphery elements. Percentages have recently dropped in many formerly Communist countries, and these changes are not well reflected on the map, due to unavailability of statistics. (Sources: National statistical yearbooks and censuses.)

countries, most notably Norway, provide subsidies designed to keep people working the land, with results readily visible when one crosses the Norwegian/Swedish border, but the trend nevertheless continues.

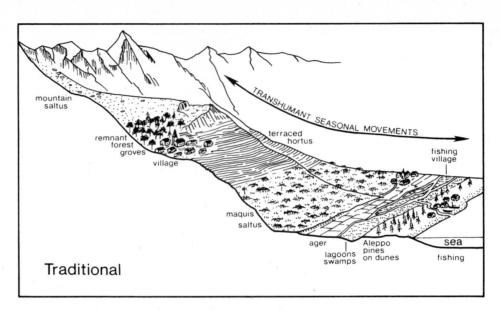

Traditional

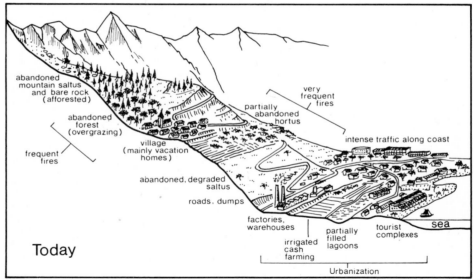

Today

FIGURE 8.16 Change comes to a rural Mediterranean slope. Many of the modern changes in European agriculture discussed in the text are summarized in this sketch. (Source: Adapted with major modifications from Grenon and Batisse, cited in Chapter 2 bibliography, Fig. 1.3.)

Rural depopulation produced not merely larger farms, but also large-scale land abandonment. In particular, farmland of marginal quality has gone out of production. In eastern Germany's sandy Brandenburg province, for example, almost one-fifth of the farmland was abandoned at the collapse of the Communist collectives in 1991–1992. One Brandenburg collective, in a conversion loaded with irony and symbolism, became a golf course for affluent West Berliners.

Indeed, recreational land use of one type or another, including tourism, has taken over much of Europe's abandoned farmland, a trend likely to continue (Figure 8.16). Many Europeans own second homes in the countryside, often converted farmhouses purchased cheaply from departing agriculturists. Also helping to fill the rural void are large-scale afforestation projects, especially in the Mediterranean and Celtic fringe, as mentioned in Chapter 2.

In spite of its decline, agriculture remains linked to a vivid, distinctive rural landscape in Europe. The following chapter deals with this agricultural landscape.

Sources and Suggested Readings

Swanzie Agnew. "The Vine in Bas Languedoc." *Geographical Review*. 36 (1946), 67–79.

Robert Aitken. "Routes of Transhumance on the Spanish Meseta." *Geographical Journal*. 106 (1945), 59–69.

Jean Andrews. "Diffusion of Mesoamerican Food Complex to Southeastern Europe." *Geographical Review*. 83 (1993), 194–204.

Graeme Barker. *Prehistoric Farming in Europe*. Cambridge, GB: Cambridge University Press, 1985.

Richard Belding. "A Test of the von Thünen Locational Model of Agricultural Land Use with Accountancy Data from the European Economic Community." *Transactions of the Institute of British Geographers*. 6 (1981), 176–187.

Jean Boyazoglu and Jean-Claude Flamant. "Mediterranean Systems of Animal Production." In John G. Galaty and Douglas L. Johnson, (eds.). *The World of Pastoralism*. London, GB: Belhaven Press, 1990, 353–393.

Karl W. Butzer, Juan F. Mateu, Elisabeth K. Butzer, and Pavel Kraus. "Irrigation Agrosystems in Eastern Spain: Roman or Islamic Origins?" *Annals of the Association of American Geographers*. 75 (1985), 479–509.

Michel Cabouret. "Aperçus Nouveaux sur l'Agriculture de la Lorraine du Nordest: Les Répercussions de la Division Linguistique du Département de la Moselle." *Mosella*. 5 (Oct.–Dec., 1975), 51–58.

Jean Chiffre. "Les agriculteurs âgés dans la Communauté Européenne." Revue *Géographique de l'Est*. 29 (1989), 23–47.

M. C. Cleary. "Contemporary Transhumance in Languedoc." *Geografiska Annaler*. 69B (1987), 107–114.

Hugh Clout. "The Recomposition of Rural Europe." *Annales de Géographie*. 100 (1991), 714–729.

James R. Coull. "Fish Farming in the Highlands and Islands: Boom Industry of the 1980s." *Scottish Geographical Magazine.* 104 (1988), 4–13.

William K. Crowley. "Changes in the French Winescape." *Geographical Review.* 83 (1993), 252–268.

William A. Dando. "Wheat in Romania." *Annals of the Association of American Geographers.* 64 (1974), 241–257.

Robin W. Dennell. "The Origins of Crop Agriculture in Europe." In *The Origins of Agriculture: An International Perspective,* ed. C. Wesley Cowan and Patty J. Watson. Washington, USA: Smithsonian Institution Press, 1992, 71–100.

D. M. Epstein and A. Valmari. "Reindeer Herding and Ecology in Finnish Lapland." *GeoJournal.* 8 (1984), 159–169.

E. Estyn Evans. "The Ecology of Peasant Life in Western Europe." In *Man's Role in Changing the Face of the Earth,* ed. William L. Thomas, Jr. Chicago, USA: University of Chicago Press, 1956, 217–239.

Virginia K. Fry. "Reindeer Ranching in Northern Russia." *Professional Geographer.* 23 (1971), 146–151.

J. H. Galloway. "The Mediterranean Sugar Industry." *Geographical Review.* 67 (1977), 177–194.

Isabelle Geneau de Lamarlière. "Le Marché Commun agricole: essai de bilan géographique." *Revue Géographique de l'Est.* 29 (1989), 97–116.

Douglas W. Gilchrist-Shirlaw. *Agricultural Geography of Great Britain.* Oxford, GB: Pergamon Press, 2nd ed., 1971.

Desmond A. Gillmor. *Agriculture in the Republic of Ireland.* Budapest, H: Akadémiai Kiadó, 1977.

Matti Häkkilä. "Some Regional Trends in Finnish Farming with Special Reference to Agricultural Policy." *Fennia.* 169 (1991), 39–56.

William A. Hance. "Crofting in the Outer Hebrides." *Economic Geography.* 28 (1952), 37–50.

Reijo K. Helle. "Reindeer Husbandry in Finland." *Geographical Journal.* 145 (1979), 254–264.

Burkhard Hofmeister. "Four Types of Agriculture with Predominant Olive Growing in Southern Spain: A Case Study." *Geoforum,* 8 (1971), 15–30.

W. B. Johnston and I. Crkvencic. "Examples of Changing Peasant Agriculture in Croatia." *Economic Geography.* 33 (1957), 50–71.

Olaf Jonasson. "The Agricultural Regions of Europe." *Economic Geography.* 1 (1925), 277–314; 2 (1926), 19–48.

A. H. Kampp. *An Agricultural Geography of Denmark.* Budapest, H: Akadémiai Kiadó, 1975.

Russell King and Laurence Took. "Land Tenure and Rural Social Change: The Italian Case." *Erdkunde.* 37 (1983), 186–198.

Jerzy Kostrowicki. "The Types of Agriculture Map of Europe." 9 sheets, scale 1:2,500,000. Warsaw, PL: Institute of Geography and Spatial Organization, Polish Academy of Sciences, 1984.

Paul E. Lydolph. "The Russian Sukhovey." *Annals of the Association of American Geographers.* 54 (1964), 291–309.

Teodoro Marañón. "Agro-Sylvo-Pastoral Systems in the Iberian Peninsula: Dehesas and Montados." *Rangelands.* 10:6 (1988), 255–258.

Ian M. Matley. "Transhumance in Bosnia and Herzegovina." *Geographical Review.* 58 (1968), 231–261.

Alan Mayhew. "Structural Reform and the Future of West German Agriculture." *Geographical Review.* 60 (1970), 54–68.

Sigvard Montelius. "The Burning of Forest Land for the Cultivation of Crops: Svedjebruk in Central Sweden." *Geografiska Annaler.* 35 (1953), 41–54.

E. Müller. "Die Herdenwanderungen im Mittelmeergebiet." *Petermanns Geographische Mitteilungen.* 84 (1938), 364–370.

T. G. Nefedova. "Natural and Socio-Economic Factors of Regional Development of Agriculture of the USSR European Territory." *Revue Belge de Géographie.* 115 (1991), 219–233.

Robert M. Netting. *Balancing on an Alp: Ecological Change and Continuity in a Swiss Mountain Community.* Cambridge, GB: Cambridge University Press, 1981.

Mark Overton. "Diffusion of Agricultural Innovations in Early Modern England, 1580–1740." *Transactions of the Institute of British Geographers.* 10 (1985), 205–221.

James J. Parsons. "The Acorn-Hog Economy of the Oak Woodlands of Southwestern Spain." *Geographical Review.* 52 (1962), 211–235.

J. Richard Peet. "Influences of the British Market on Agriculture and Related Economic Development in Europe." *Transactions of the Institute of British Geographers.* 56 (1972), 1–20.

Gottfried Pfeifer. "The Quality of Peasant Living in Central Europe." In *Man's Role in Changing the Face of the Earth,* ed. William L. Thomas, Jr. Chicago, USA: University of Chicago Press, 1956, 240–277.

Anette Reenberg. "Agricultural Land-Use in Denmark in the 1980s." *Geografisk Tidsskrift.* 88 (1988), 8–13.

Richard Rose and Yevgeniy Tikhomirov. "Who Grows Food in Russia and Eastern Europe?" *Post-Soviet Geography.* 34 (1993), 111–126.

Klaus Rother. "Agrarian Development and Conflicts of Land Utilization in the Coastal Plain of Calabria (South Italy)." *GeoJournal.* 13 (1986), 27–35.

Siegfried Schacht. "Portuguese Agrarian Reform and Its Effects on Rural Property and Agricultural Enterprise Conditions." *Erdkkunde.* 42 (1988), 203–213.

Karl H. Schröder. "Das bäuerliche Anwesen in Mitteleuropa. *Geographische Zeitschrift.* 62 (1974), 241–271.

Ellen Churchill Semple. "Ancient Mediterranean Agriculture." *Agricultural History.* 2 (1928), 61–98, 129–156.

Ellen C. Semple. "The Influence of Geographic Conditions upon Ancient Mediterranean Stock Raising." *Annals of the Association of American Geographers.* 12 (1922), 3–38.

Arvo M. Soininen. "Burn-beating as the Technical Basis of Colonisation in Finland in the 16th and 17th Centuries." *Scandinavian Economic History Review.* 7 (1959), 150–166.

Dan Stanislawski. "Dionysius Westward: Early Religion and the Economic Geography of Wine." *Geographical Review.* 65 (1975), 427–444.

Dan Stanislawski. *Landscapes of Bacchus: The Vine in Portugal.* Austin, USA: University of Texas Press, 1970.

K. F. Stroyev. "Agriculture in the Non-Chernozem Zone of the RSFSR." *Soviet Geography: Review and Translation.* 16 (1975), 186–196.

J. R. Tarrant. "Some Spatial Variations in Irish Agriculture." *Tijdschrift voor Economische en Sociale Geografie.* 60 (1969), 228–237.

Evelio Teijon Laso. "Los modos de vida en la dehesa salmantina." *Estudios Geográficos.* 9 (1948), 421–441.

Karl Troll. "Die Landbauzonen Europas in ihrer Beziehung zur natürlichen Vegetation." *Geographische Zeitschrift.* 31 (1925), 265–280.

Samuel van Valkenburg. "An Evaluation of the Standard of Land Use in Western Europe." *Economic Geography.* 36 (1960), 283–295.

Tim Unwin. "Structural Change in Estonian Agriculture: From Command Economy to Privatisation." *Geography.* 79 (1994), 246–261.

Kurt Wasmer-Ramer. *Studien über die Agrarlandschaft beidseits der deutsch-französischen Sprachgrenze im Nordschweizer Jura.* Basel, CH: Basler Beiträge zur Geographie, No. 30, Geographisches Institut der Universität Basel, 1984.

Daniel Zohary and Maria Hopf. *Domestication of Plants in the Old World: The Origin and Spread of Cultivated Plants in West Asia, Europe, and the Nile Valley.* New York, USA: Oxford University Press, 1988.

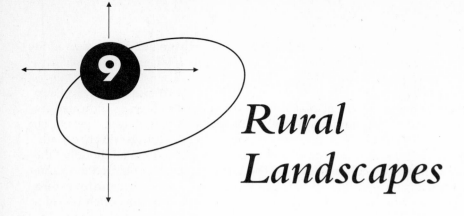

Rural Landscapes

While agriculture engages a very small part of the European population, the area devoted to tilling and herding constitutes the far larger part of Europe's land surface. The resultant *agricultural landscape* becomes, therefore, a highly visible aspect of the culture area. This rural landscape, a vivid imprint of diverse peoples and farming systems, varies strikingly from one part of Europe to another. To a quite remarkable degree, the rural landscape of Europe remains traditional, reflecting distinctive folk cultures many centuries old. Europeans, by and large, treasure their diverse traditional landscapes and strive to keep archaic villages, houses, fences, and hedges functional in an age of modernized agriculture. The result is a rural landscape of charm and appeal, sufficiently attractive to prompt tourism. The geographer studies three major aspects of the rural landscape: (1) the *settlement pattern,* or distribution of farmsteads; (2) the *field pattern,* or the form resulting from the division of the land for productive use; and (3) *house and farmstead types.*

Settlement Patterns

Europe displays a variety of rural settlement patterns. Farm dwellings can be (1) clustered in villages, (2) dispersed through the countryside, or (3) semiclustered, forming a pattern intermediate between these extremes. Most European farmers live in clustered **villages**, leaving the surrounding arable land bare of structures. The people journey daily out to their fields. A church, perhaps a few shops, a school, and other local service functions normally appear in such places.

Numerous causes, primarily historic rather than modern, encouraged nucleation of the rural population. One was the need for defense prompted by the insecurity of the European countryside, where bands of outlaws and raiders once held sway. Farmers could better defend themselves against such dangers by grouping together. Villages often grew larger during periods of insecurity and war, only to shrink when peace and security returned. European farm villages frequently occupy the most easily defended sites in their vicinity, producing so-called *strong-point* settlements. The greatest era of village building occurred in medieval times, especially between about A.D. 500 and 1000, an era of insecurity following the collapse of the Roman Empire.

Family and clan ties proved even more important as a cohesive force. Kinship gave rise to the desire to live in close proximity to one another, as indicated by many place names. The common Western European suffixes *-ingen, -inge, -ing, -ange,* and the like, as in Trossingen (Germany), Challerange (France), and Kolding (Denmark), all derive from the Germanic tongue and mean literally "the people of," suggesting a cohesive group. The prefix typically contained the name of the family or clan leader, so that Sigmaringen, a town in southwestern Germany, means "the people of Siegmar." Such social ties in turn often reveal a peasant communalism, in which cropland, pastures, and forests belonged to the village at large rather than to private individuals. Cropland was allotted so that each villager had equal acreage, distance to travel to reach it, and soil fertility. The land used by any farmer lay fragmented in a number of separate parcels, lying in different directions and at varying distances from the village, including a cross section of soil types. In addition, these parcels were periodically redistributed so that a farmer in any given year might till different land than in the previous year.

Scarcity of water, especially in areas of permeable rock such as limestone, where moisture quickly percolates into the ground, encouraged clusters of farmsteads where water was available. Such *wet-point* settlements can be centered on deep wells, communally dug and maintained, or at widely scattered springs. The region of Picardie in France and the south Wiltshire Downs of southern England are both underlain by permeable rock and typified by clustered villages. Conversely, the superabundance of water in marshy areas and zones subject to flood can stimulate clustering on available *dry-points* of higher elevation. In the Low Country, tightly compact settlements developed on artificial mounds, as was described in Chapter 2 (Figure 2.21).

Of the factors causing clustering into villages, the historic presence of clan communalism and its perpetuation under the manorial system of the feudal era should be judged the most important. People bound together by such ties normally created clustered settlements. The gradual disappearance of communal organization, which accompanied the decline of feudalism, left behind the farm village as an economically inefficient relic of a bygone age. Similarly, the day when a village provided farmers any significant measure of defense in times of warfare and raiding is long past, but its legacy remains.

Village Types

The farm villages of Europe vary greatly in outward appearances from one region to another, and geographers distinguish a number of major types (Figure 9.1). One of the most common types, the *irregular clustered village,* occurs in parts of western Germany, northern France, lowland Britain, and much of southern Europe (Figure 9.1). As its name implies, the irregular clustered village presents a

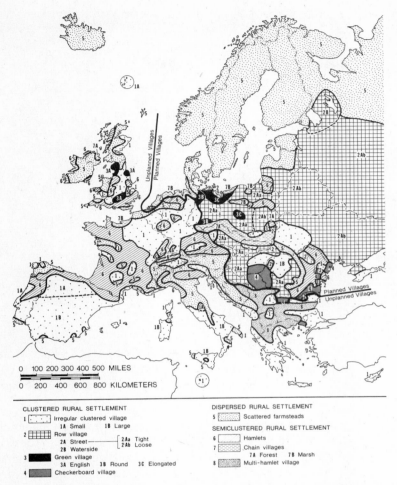

FIGURE 9.1 Forms of rural settlement. (Sources: In part after Houston; Uhlig; Stamp; Smith; Cvijić; Meitzen, 1895; Stone; Radig; Schröder; Gradmann; Beuermann; Roberts; and Thorpe, 1961.)

haphazard appearance devoid of planning, with winding streets and randomly bunched farmsteads (Figure 9.2). Usually somewhere toward the center of the cluster stands the village church, surrounded by the farmhouses, barns, and vegetable gardens of the villagers. The minimum number of farmsteads required to form a village is about 20, but size varies greatly, usually ranging from perhaps 400 to 1000 population in the Germanic lands to 10,000 or more in the hilltop agricultural settlements, or *agrotowns,* of southern Italy, and even as many as 20,000 or 30,000 inhabitants in the large agrarian settlements of the eastern Hungarian Basin. The latter, called *kertes varos,* represent a Magyar response to the military danger presented by the Turks. The large Italian hilltop villages reflect post-Roman insecurity. Similarly, the sizable irregular clustered villages of southern Iberia survive as testimony to the bitter fighting between Christians and

Figure 9.2 A large irregular clustered farm village of the type found in southern Iberia. This village, or "agrotown," lies in the hills of southern Portugal. (Photo by the author, 1986.)

Muslims that ended five centuries ago. By contrast, much smaller villages characterize the plateau of Old Castilla to the north (Figure 9.1). The key to the origin of irregular clustered villages lies in the obvious lack of planning. In all probability, they began as a loose grouping of only a few farmsteads of related families, forming a clan hamlet. Over the centuries the population grew and new farmsteads were added, enlarging the settlement and making it more compact.

By contrast, in much of Eastern Europe, beyond the ancient German-Slav border of circa A.D. 800, most village types exhibit a high degree of planning. East of this old line following the Elbe-Saale-Inn-Salzach rivers, in the traditional Slavic domain, the settlements appear regular in shape and layout. The most typical of these planned forms, the *row village,* appears in several subtypes. Most numerous are *street* villages (type 2A in Figure 9.1). Instead of the disorderly maze of streets found in the irregular clustered village, we find only one straight street with all of the farmsteads lined up along it. Houses face the street and gardens lie out behind (Figures 9.3, 9.4). Street villages vary greatly in size, from small forms usually found on side roads or on dead-end lanes to large, long settlements on main highways inhabited by hundreds of people. The western street villages tend to be tightly clustered, with farmstead structures abutting one another along a narrow road (type 2Aa). To the east, in the more purely Slavic areas on the East European Plain, individual farmsteads lie further apart and the

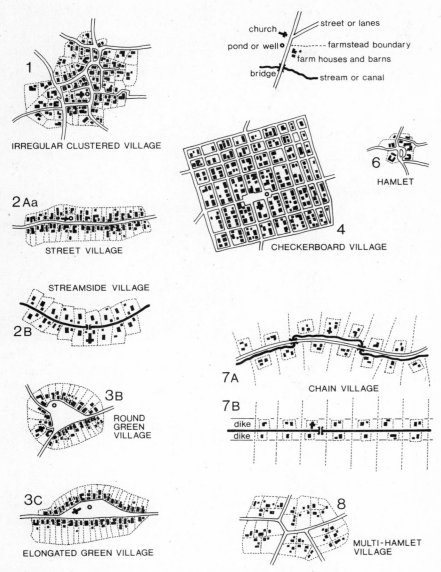

FIGURE 9.3 Selected types of rural settlement in Europe. For the distribution of each type, see Figure 9.1. (Sources: In part after Martiny, Meitzen, Wilhelmy, and Schlüter.)

street is much wider (type 2Ab), giving the Russian villages a much more open appearance. Most likely, the street row village has a Slavic origin. Even in eastern Germany, many street villages, particularly the smaller ones, bear Slavic names, including the suffixes *-ow, -in, -itz,* and *-zig.* To cross the Elbe River from western Germany, with its chaotic irregular clustered villages, into Mecklenburg in eastern Germany is to enter a different rural landscape and subculture. Suddenly the

FIGURE 9.4 A typical tightly clustered eastern German street village, Breunsdorf, south of Leipzig in Sachsen. Note the single central street, along which the farm buildings are tightly clustered, and the kitchen gardens and orchards on the periphery of the village behind the buildings. (Photo from Creutzburg.)

villages bear names like Wendisch Rambow, street villages lend visual order, and more than a few broad Slavic faces appear among the dolichocephalic Saxons. One has entered Eastern Europe.

The *waterside row village,* a second subtype, appears among the Finnic and Russian peoples of the Karelian Republic, in the north (Figure 9.1). Instead of a street, a stream or lake shore provides the focus of the settlement; boats traditionally served as the dominant means of transportation. Farmsteads line both banks of the stream or one stretch of lake shore, spaced somewhat apart in the manner of a Russian street village (Figure 9.3). Saunas and gardens stand in front of the houses, and an occasional footbridge spans the stream.

Another type of clustered rural settlement displaying planning is the *green village,* distinguished by an open commons or green, in the center of the village. The green village appears widely through various parts of the Great European Plain, from lowland Britain to Poland (Figure 9.1). Traditionally, the green served as a festival ground, a marketplace, and a protected enclosure for livestock. The shape of the green and with it the configuration of the entire settlement varies greatly, including ovals, rectangles, and triangles, giving rise to several subtypes of green villages.

One green village subtype is the *round village.* In these, the core of the village is formed by a circular or triangular green, around which individual farmsteads

FIGURE 9.5 Buberow, a round green village, (type 3B) in eastern Germany, near Gransee, north of Berlin. Farmsteads of the courtyard type surround the central open place, which is occupied by the church. Gardens stretch out behind the farmsteads. Only one road leads into the village, an indication of an original defensive function. The -ow suffix on the place name indicates a Slavic origin of the village. (Photo from Creutzburg.)

group (Figures 9.3, 9.5). Round villages are limited mainly to the lower Elbe River and the east bank of the Saale River, in Germany (Figure 9.1). Formerly they were also found in Denmark. Round villages are sometimes of Slavic origin, for they frequently bear names indicative of that ethnic group, such as Buberow and Wutzow. Round villages, admirably suited for defense, occur mainly along the ancient German-Slav border. The central green could serve the same function as the courtyard of a castle or the interior of a circle of covered wagons. Often, a dead-end street entered the village, leaving only one opening. On the green, the village well and pond provided water, with room left over to gather the livestock for protection. The *elongated green village* (type 3C), sometimes also called a street-green village, occurs in small parts of the North European Plain. Sharing characteristics of both round villages and street row villages, they probably developed as enlargements of round villages. The *English green village,* in effect an irregular clustered village with an open commons at the center, displays much less geometric order and planning than other green villages. Green villages possibly represent a modern survival of one of the most ancient settlement forms in Europe. Archaeologists have discovered green villages as old as Iron Age times, and some evidence suggests they might be of even greater antiquity. Part of the difficulty in tracing their former distribution is that green villages easily evolved into irregular clustered villages if, as often happened, later generations of farmers built houses and barns on the green.

Still another planned settlement form of Eastern Europe, the *checkerboard village* appears mainly in the middle and lower valley of the Danube River in parts of Hungary, Yugoslavia, Romania, and Bulgaria (Figure 9.1). A similar type appears in some areas bordering the northern shore of the Aegean Sea in Greece. In contrast to the village types mentioned above, these have a relatively recent origin. The government of the Austro-Hungarian Empire founded many checkerboard villages beginning about 1750, particularly in the Banat district of Yugoslavia and southern Hungary, as part of a project to repopulate areas ravaged by warfare. The Greeks also established some in districts ethnically cleansed of Turks in the 1920s. More recently, in the Communist era, large planned collective agrotowns in Russia took this form. All streets meet at right angles, forming a gridiron pattern (Figure 9.3).

Dispersed Settlement

While most European farmers live in villages, *isolated farmsteads* dominate some districts. Each rural family lives at a distance from its neighbors, as in America. The factors encouraging dispersed settlement are precisely the opposite of those favoring village development, including (1) an absence of the need for defense, prompted by peace and security; (2) colonization by individual pioneer families rather than by groups bound together by the ties of blood relationship; (3) agricultural private enterprise rather than communalism; (4) unit-block farms rather than fragmented holdings; (5) a rural economy dominated by livestock raising; (6) hilly or mountainous terrain; and (7) readily available water. In addition, dispersed settlement can result from deliberate governmental action designed to break up villages, piece together fragmented holdings, and produce a more efficient agriculture. Isolated farmsteads dominate Scandinavia, highland Britain, the Alps and certain other mountain districts, and various smaller regions scattered around Europe, such as Vlaanderen and the lower Loire valley of France (Figure 9.1).

Dispersed farmsteads fall into two categories: those of great antiquity that represent a traditional form and those that appeared in recent times as a result of governmental action or economic change. Some derive from ancient Roman times. The security offered by the Roman Empire encouraged dispersed rural settlement in areas as diverse as Lazio (Latium) near the capital city, where scattered farmsteads accounted for 43 percent of the total in classical times; Roman Britain; and southern France. Some Mediterranean areas had dispersed settlement as a preclassical tradition, as suggested by some passages in Homer's *Odyssey*. Also rather old are many of the scattered farmsteads of northwestern Germany and the adjacent Netherlands, where individual farmers excluded from property rights in the clustered settlements through the practice of undivided inheritance went out into the surrounding bogs and marshes and reclaimed land, upon which they built their homes and began farming in *kamp* settlements. Iceland's dispersed farmsteads date to the original Viking settlement over a millennium ago, and each stead has its own name, displayed on a road placard.

More commonly, however, dispersed farmsteads date from relatively recent times. In certain Scandinavian countries, governmental decrees issued in the late 1700s and early 1800s led to the dispersal of the large majority of the rural population (Figure 9.6). In one small district of southern Germany adjacent to the Bodensee (Lake Constance) and the foot of the Alps, local feudal rulers began dispersing the farmers in the 1500s. The conversion from arable land to sheep pasture in much of the British Isles, associated with a cruel and drastic population expulsion from rural areas and a replacement of fragmented holdings by unit-block farms, caused scattered farmsteads to replace many villages and hamlets, beginning in the 1400s. Landlords in Latvia and Estonia dispersed peasants under their control as early as the 1600s to achieve greater efficiency of production. More recently, the Italian government in the 1920s and 1930s began a program of creating scattered farmsteads in the southern part of that country.

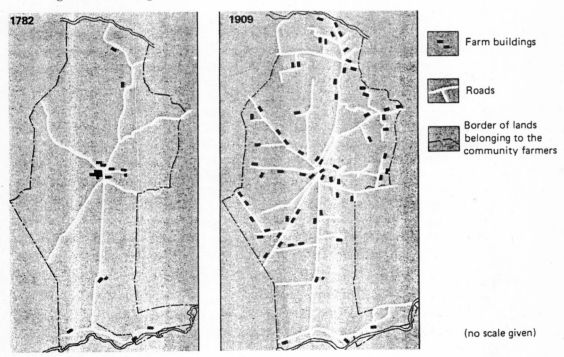

(no scale given)

FIGURE 9.6 The Danish farm community of Solbjerg before and after partial dispersal of settlement. In 1782, the farmers nearly all lived in a clustered village, but by the early twentieth century, the majority had relocated in scattered farmsteads, leaving behind a partially deserted village. (Source: After M. Vahl, "Types of Rural Settlement in Denmark," *Comptes Rendus du Congrès International de Géographie, Paris 1931,* Paris, F: Armand Colin, 1934, 3, 174–175.)

Dispersed settlement is superior to the village pattern in an economic sense. The key factor involves the time required to travel from farmstead to fields in the village system. A study in the Netherlands, for example, revealed that farmers made less intensive use of land that lay farthest from their villages. At the same time, the village offers many social contacts, while the life on isolated farmsteads often seems lonely, especially to people with a village heritage. The Italian government noted with concern the high rate of mental depression among farmers resettled out of villages into the countryside. Many Europeans prefer the village way of life and the companionship it provides. The French geographer, Paul Vidal de la Blache, expressed this European feeling quite well in his description of the isolated farmstead landscape of the west of France, declaring that "the impression gained from such a landscape is one of isolation, and the stranger finds himself ill at ease" in a countryside that "seems inhospitable, even hostile." The current trend in most parts of Europe is toward gradual elimination of the farm village and its replacement by scattered farmsteads, though land-use zoning regulations often make dispersal impossible.

Semiclustered Settlement

A number of rural settlement forms in Europe do not fit well into either the clustered or dispersed categories, sharing some characteristics of both. These are best referred to as **semiclustered**, for they are intermediate between the two extremes.

The most common semiclustered type is the *hamlet* (Figure 9.3), consisting of 20 or fewer farmsteads. As in farm villages, the hamlet farmsteads lie in settlement nuclei, separate from the cropland, but the hamlet differs in its smaller size (Figure 9.7). Too, hamlets normally lack the church, tavern, school, and other central place functions associated with villages. Hamlets, widespread in Europe, occur particularly in southern France, parts of Germany, and certain areas in Iberia and northern Italy (Figure 9.1). Many districts now characterized by dispersed farmsteads once had hamlets, as for example the Celtic *clachans* of the British and Irish highlands. Often, hamlets appear mixed in among dispersed farmsteads, as in Galicia in northwestern Spain (Figure 9.8). Hamlets have complex and diverse origins. In south Germany, as well as adjacent parts of Switzerland and France, the hamlets may be a heritage of Roman rule, as is suggested by the frequency of occurrence of the place-name suffix *-weiler*, which derives from the Latin word *villare*, meaning "farmstead." Original isolated farmsteads probably developed into hamlet clusters through the Roman-law practice of divided inheritance by which each child receives some land. Among numerous examples of the *-weiler* suffix on hamlet place names in Romanized Danubian Germany are Habertsweiler in the province of Bayern (Bavaria) and Martinsweiler in Baden-Württemberg. The word *weiler* came to mean "hamlet" in the German language. The French geographer Albert Demangeon suggested the same origin for hamlets in the southern part of his country. Failure of the hamlets to grow still more and become villages probably reflects the low potential productivity of the hilly areas where they occur. The population presumably increased until inferior lands such as the Massif Central of France could support

FIGURE 9.7 A hamlet settlement (Type 6) on the shore of the Olafsfjörd, on Iceland's Arctic shore. It consists of a loose clustering of less than 10 farmsteads, and its inhabitants engage in both farming and fishing. Most rural Icelanders live in isolated farmsteads, and hamlets are unusual there. (Photo by the author, 1994.)

no more. Hamlets, then, are "stunted" villages whose growth was hindered by environmental factors. Other scholars argue instead that hamlets represent the oldest settlement form, dating from the earliest sedentary colonization of clan and extended-family groups rather than derivatives of initially dispersed farmsteads. In this view, hamlets had much their present form when initially established.

The *multi-hamlet villages* of Balkan Europe present another semiclustered form. Individual communities consist of three or four separate hamlet clusters, segregated on the basis of blood relationship, religion, and/or language. The collection of hamlets bears a single name, and the people all have a sense of belonging to one community, but their individual clusters lie somewhat apart (Figure 9.3). The total population of the hamlets in a given settlement often achieves village proportions, but the compactness of the village form is absent. The great ethnic diversity of the Balkans encouraged segregation within settlements. The multi-hamlet villages of southeastern Europe are variously called *ibar, machali,* or *starivlah* settlements in the languages of that area.

Another widespread semiclustered type in Europe is the *chain village.* The individual farmsteads lie along a single road or waterway, similar to the row villages described earlier. However, the chain village differs in that the farmsteads are spaced farther apart and all of the land belonging to each farmer is contained

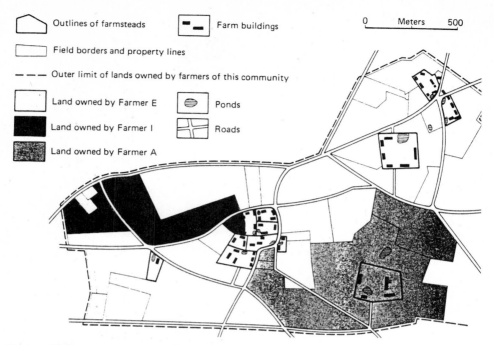

FIGURE 9.8 An example of partial dispersal of settlement in an area where land reform has occurred. A hamlet in France composed of eight farmsteads coexists with five dispersed farmsteads. Such mixture of settlement types is becoming increasingly common in Europe. (Source: After Albert Demangeon, *La France,* Vol. 6 of *Géographie Universelle,* Paris, F: Armand Colin, 1946.)

in a long-lot, extending out behind the farmstead (Figure 9.3). In row villages, only the gardens lie adjacent to the houses, and the fields are some distance away, composed of numerous scattered parcels of land. By contrast, farmers in the chain village live on their farm, which forms the elongated unit block. In this respect, the chain settlements resemble scattered farmsteads. However, the narrowness of the long-lots and the concentration of houses at the front of the farms create a certain degree of clustering not typical of dispersed farmsteads. Moreover, the residents of such settlements generally have the feeling of belonging to a village, with resultant social contacts. Chain villages vary from a half-dozen member farms up to a hundred or more, and the width and depth of the lots also vary.

Distinct subtypes exist. Most common is the *forest chain village,* occurring in a broken belt through the Hercynian hill lands of Central Europe and on eastward into the Carpathians. The settlement focus is a road following a valley. Long-lot farms extend back on either side, as far as the adjacent ridges. Generally, the steeper hinter portions of these farms remain forested. The configuration of the entire settlement is shaped by the windings of the valley, and perfectly straight

FIGURE 9.9 "Ladder" farms, so-named because the division of the long-lot farms into separate fields and pastures on the hill slope resembles a ladder, line the Antrim Glens in Northern Ireland. The farmsteads at the base of the hill, along the shore, form a chain village. A similar settlement type occurs in the Faeroe Islands. (Photo by the author, 1992.)

property lines rarely occur (Figure 9.3). The *ladder farms* of parts of Ireland, which are of fairly recent origin, belong to this chain village subtype (Figure 9.9).

A second variety, the *marsh chain village,* appears in poorly drained lands of the Great European Plain, including the Low Country polders (Figure 9.1). A drainage canal flanked on either side by broad, artificial dikes provides the focus for the settlement. Farmsteads line the dikes, and each farm stretches out as a long-lot into the lower-lying land behind. Marsh chain villages usually have a much more regular, rigid geometry than the forest subtype, often with arrow-straight canals and property lines (Figure 9.3). The marsh subtype appeared earliest, about A.D. 900 in the Netherlands, during an initial period of dike building there. The first marsh chain village in Germany appeared about 1100 on wasteland along the lower Weser River near Bremen.

Marsh chain villages later spread both east and west, reaching the Polish river marshes in the 1500s and 1600s and the lower Seine River of France. Dutch migrants played an instrumental role in the dispersal. The type proved well suited to a dike landscape and practicality explains its popularity. The forest chain village probably arose independently, linked to one of the patterns of Germanic forest clearance (see Chapter 2), but it could have evolved from the marsh type, which originated earlier.

Also in the category of semiclustered settlement, *partially deserted villages* occur widely in Scandinavia and lowland Great Britain, where government-led reforms have caused many or most of the farmers to relocate in isolated farmsteads, leaving behind a village that contains only a fraction of its former population. In Denmark, the large majority of the rural population now lives dispersed. Vestiges of villages remain, although the surviving farmsteads are more loosely clustered owing to the removal of many in the dispersal process (Figure 9.6).

The different types of settlement pattern often influence other facets of rural culture. For example, the isolation resulting from dispersed settlement tends to favor the survival of minority languages, while clustering in villages promotes assimilation. Some European languages perhaps owe their survival in part to a pattern of scattered farmsteads in the areas (compare Figures 4.1 and 9.1). In France the Dutch language has long been identified with a zone of dispersed settlement in the north, and the same is true of Welsh in the United Kingdom. The remarkable survival of Basque may be the result in part of the pattern of scattered farmsteads in the Pyrenean borderlands. Similarly, Spanish inroads in the area of Galician speech in northwestern Iberia were perhaps blunted by the dispersal of the population there. Village settlement, on the other hand, may have facilitated German assimilation of the Slavic farm population of the North German Plain east of the Elbe-Saale line during the Middle Ages. Large numbers of German settlers moved into the Slavic villages in that period of Teutonic colonization, and the Slavs were absorbed into German culture.

Field Patterns

Field patterns provide a second basic aspect of the European rural landscape. Many European farmers today do not have unit-block farms in the American or Australian style but instead fragmented holdings in which the land they own and work is scattered in many separate parcels in varying directions and at different distances from their farmsteads in the villages. Only the garden lies in the village or hamlet adjacent to the buildings. The farmers reach cropland, pasture, and meadow by traveling out of the village. This odd pattern does not derive from factors operating today, for the fragmented holding represents a cultural relic, just as does the farm village.

The origin of fragmented holdings goes back to the practice of *open fields*. Communalism remained very strong under this ancient system, which has now almost vanished. An entire village community worked together in the fields, observing set dates for plowing, planting, and harvesting. The choice of crops, made by the village elders, generally followed one or another of the rotations described in the previous chapter. Farmland lay divided into a number of large units. One particular unit might be planted to wheat in a certain year, while another remained fallow and a third had oats or barley. Each farmer worked one or more small parcels within each of these large units, following the dictates of the village elders as to when to work and what to plant. Individual parcels remained unfenced, leading to the term "open fields." Land was periodically redistributed so that an equality was achieved among the various farmers. Each had some good soil and some poor, some distant plots and some close at hand.

Two major field patterns were associated with the fragmented holdings of the open-field system. In Slavic and Germanic areas, the individual scattered parcels took the odd shape of ribbonlike strips, very elongated and narrow (Figure 9.10). This accommodated the large, unwieldy moldboard plow, invented by the Slavs and later accepted in most lands north of the Alps. The plow proved difficult to turn around because of its size and bulk, prompting the farmers to use long strip fields requiring less turning. A very different field pattern prevailed in Mediterranean Europe. The individual plots were irregular in shape or

Buildings

132

Gardens, vineyards, and orchards

0   400   800
m

FIGURE 9.10 Fragmented landholdings in French Lorraine. Small strip fields surrounded the irregular clustered village of Seichamp, near Nancy in northeastern France, before land reform. The 132 separate strips belonging to one sample farm are shaded. Compare to Figure 9.13. (Source: Same as Figure 9.8.)

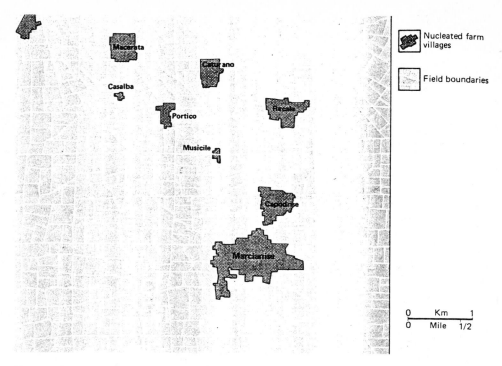

FIGURE 9.11 Field patterns exhibiting Roman influence, in the Campania just north of Napoli, Italy. Fields in the areas dominated by use of the small Roman plow take on rectangular rather than strip shape. In this instance, the rectangularity has been made even more pronounced by the survival of the Roman rectangular survey system. This map shows the field pattern as it was in the nineteenth century. (Source: After Meitzen, 1895.)

roughly rectangular. In some limited areas, a checkerboard was imposed on field patterns by the Roman grid land-survey system (Figure 9.11). The small plow used in the grain fields of Mediterranean areas was, in contrast to the northern type, small and easy to handle. Further, much of the productive cropland of southern Europe lay in orchards and vineyards, where the hoe rather than the plow provided the principal agricultural tool. Consequently, narrow strip fields offered no advantage.

As long as peasant communalism persisted, the awkward system of open fields and fragmented holdings possessed some degree of efficiency. Time weakened the bonds of clan membership and group cohesiveness, however, and private enterprise gradually supplanted communalism. Periodic redistribution of the land ceased, and farmers acquired permanent ownership of their scattered parcels. No longer were all plots in a given open field planted to the same crop, for farmers could now raise whatever they pleased. In this manner present-day farms evolved, consisting of a farmstead and garden in the village and several tens or hundreds of scattered tiny fields in the outlying vicinity (Figure 9.10).

Land Consolidation

Fragmented holdings are extremely inefficient. For example, in a community near Zamora, in the Spanish province of León, one farmer owned 394 separate parcels of land, averaging only 0.07 ha (0.17 acre) each, while in the village of Seichamp in French Lorraine, the 325 ha (800 acres) belonging to the resident farmers once lay divided into 1451 separate parcels, a little more than 0.22 ha (half an acre) per plot. Such tiny fields and the time required to travel to them obviously placed European farmers at a competitive disadvantage. In recognition of this problem, most governments took steps to bring about **land consolidation,** in which the property lines were redrawn to reduce or eliminate the fragmentation of holdings.

Land consolidation began as early as the 1200s in England as part of the movement known as *enclosure,* which reached its peak between 1450 and 1750. Landlords abolished the fragmented holdings and replaced the open fields with unit-block farms enclosed with hedges, often as a result of their desire to convert from crop production to sheep raising. By about 1525, almost half of the 8500 parishes in England had undergone enclosure. The British government joined with landlords to complete consolidation in the 1700s, and today very few fragmented holdings remain in the United Kingdom. The visually dominant aspect of the rural British landscape today consists of hedges and rows of trees along property lines and field borders. In Scandinavia, where land fragmentation was less severe, consolidation occurred under government direction the 1700s and 1800s. The Danish government issued a decree in 1781 demanding an end to open fields and consolidation of parcels, a process largely completed by 1835.

Eastern Europe experienced an altogether different process in the elimination of fragmented holdings. Under Communism in the middle 1900s, large fields suited to collective agriculture replaced fragmented private farms almost overnight, radically altering the rural landscape. Afterward, the airline traveler could easily tell which part of Europe—west or east—lay below (Figure 9.12). Today, a pattern of smaller, unit block farms replaces the giant fields wrought by socialism in many areas. Other communities in a variety of formerly Communist countries have chosen to retain a collectivized agriculture and with it the large fields.

In Britain, Scandinavia, and most of Eastern Europe, then, land fragmentation no longer exists at a significant level. Elsewhere, progress has come more slowly. Certain countries still struggle to complete the consolidation process, and some fragmentation persists in many areas. In western Germany, only half the agricultural land had been consolidated by the middle 1970s, and often the redrawing of property lines failed to abolish fragmentation entirely. Imperfect consolidation also plagued many French efforts (Figure 9.13). In Spain, land consolidation began only in 1952, but since then almost 600,000 unit-block farms have been created and the national average is today only eight parcels per farm. The typical farm in Greece today consists of four to six parcels.

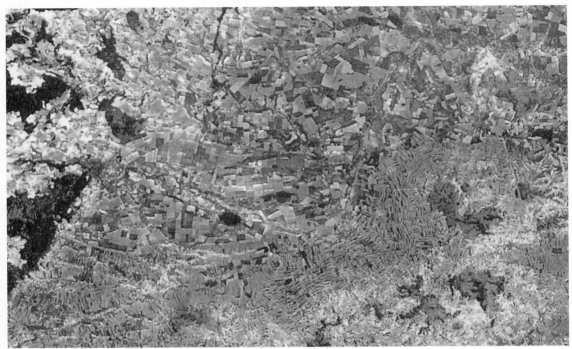

FIGURE 9.12 A satellite image of the border area of Austria and the Czech Republic clearly reveals the contrast between Austria's small, fragmented farms and the large collective enterprises of the formerly Communist east. You should be able to spot the border rather easily. (Source: United States Landsat imagery.)

Farmstead Types

In the complicated rural cultural landscape that meets the traveler's eye in Europe, no single element reveals more geographical variation than traditional **farmstead types.** Almost every small district offers its own distinctive folk architecture and building methods. Perhaps the most basic contrast involves the choice of building material (Figure 9.14).

Traditionally, European rural folk employed many different building materials in erecting structures, none more ancient than the use of earth. Sun-dried *adobe bricks* appear as a building material in some alluvial plains of Mediterranean Europe, in particular Greece and Spain. Another method, *clay-walling* or "cob" construction, consists of earth mixed with straw or some other binder and put up wet, in rounds, between wooden forms, or else damp, in which case no forms were needed. Each round was allowed to dry and harden before adding the next layer. Clay-walling appears in diverse areas from the Celtic peripheries of the west to Estonia. In the grasslands of Eastern Europe, especially Ukraine, houses made of sod bricks are still common today, while in

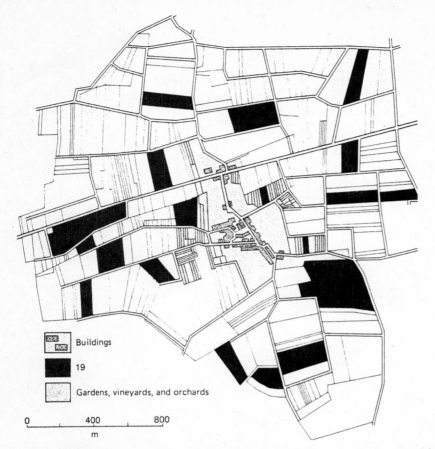

Buildings

19

Gardens, vineyards, and orchards

0   400   800
        m

FIGURE 9.13 Seichamp after land reform. This is the same village and farmland as in Figure 9.10 but after land reform took place, greatly reducing the number of parcels. The sample farm, shown shaded, remained approximately the same size but was reduced from 132 to 19 parcels. (Source: Same as Figure 9.8.)

Iceland, walls traditionally consisted of turf and clods of earth on which grass grew. Only the front side of the house was boarded with driftwood.

Stone construction dominates most of southern Europe, extending up the Atlantic front into portions of the British Isles. For the most part, this zone is mountainous or hilly, with bare rock exposed in many places. Stone is readily available except in the larger river deltas and plains, with easily worked limestone widely distributed. Stone construction lends distinctiveness to the cultural landscape of Southern Europe, for nearly all human-made features consist of this material, including houses, churches, terraces, bridges, fences, windmill towers, and even the ruins of ancient civilizations (Figure 9.15). Stone construction provides, as Vidal de la Blache suggested, "a guarantee of whatever permanence is consistent with human undertakings," though Mediterranean peoples have long plundered the ruins of older structures to acquire stone for new buildings. The

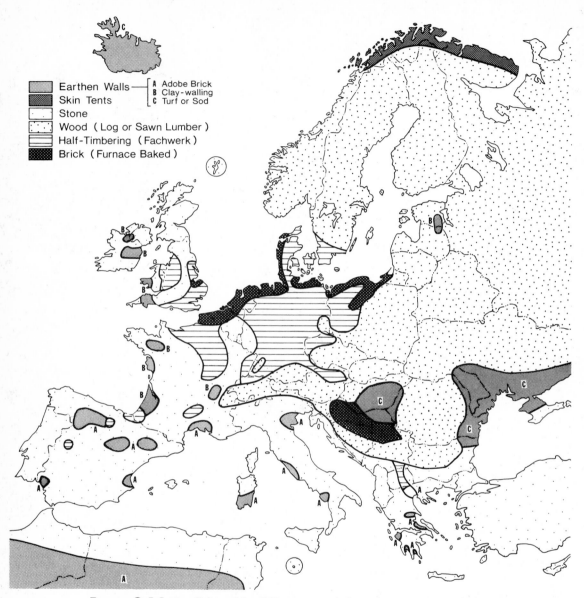

FIGURE 9.14 Traditional building materials. (Sources: In part after Paul Vidal de la Blache, *Principles of Human Geography*, New York, USA: Henry Holt, 1926; Houston; Boyd; Jessen; Batsford; and Milojević.)

belt of stone construction corresponds very closely to the regions of most complete deforestation. Only when the forests vanished did stone become the dominant material.

FIGURE 9.15 A village in the southern European zone, where stone construction is dominant. These unique domed houses, called *trulli,* are typical only of a portion of the southern Italian province of Puglia. Note that the walls, roofs, fences, and streets are all built of stone. (Photo ENIT, courtesy Italian State Tourist Office.)

Wooden construction long prevailed in the northern and eastern parts of Europe, including the Scandinavian countries and the huge Slavic realm, as well as hilly and mountainous areas in Central Europe. These form regions of greatest forest survival, and as a general rule, wood remains the dominant building material wherever timber is plentiful. *Notched-log* construction remains the most common type of building in wood, surviving in great abundance even in modern Europe (Figure 9.16). New log houses are still being built in parts of Russia and Sapim. This ancient method of construction apparently arose about 1800 B.C., probably among proto-Celtic peoples, somewhere in southern Germany or Switzerland. Its diffusion northward came slowly, for the Vikings in their great age of expansion still did not know the notched log technique, using *stave* construction instead, in which vertical boards set in grooves formed the walls. Norway still has some surviving stave churches. The present-day use of notched log construction extends even into the cities and towns of the north and east. A few specimens of log construction still stand in cities such as Oslo, Trondheim, Bergen, Riga, and Moskva. The town of Tampere in Finland remained 84 percent of wooden construction as recently as 1900. The chief disadvantage of wood buildings is their susceptibility to fire, particularly when packed together in towns or farm villages. Fire destroyed settlements in Switzerland even in the present century, and cities such as Bergen and Moskva were, on occasion, wiped out.

FIGURE 9.16 Notched-log Barn in the Swiss canton of Graubünden, not far from the region where such construction first appeared some 4000 years ago. (Photo by the author, 1978.)

Along a narrow strip of coastal marshes and river deltas on the North and Baltic sea shore of the Low Country, Germany, Poland, and northern France, kiln-fired *brick* construction predominates. This area had no forests owing to flooding, and the depth of alluvial deposits often made stone inaccessible. Bricks provide a practical alternative, and their reddish hue, derived from the native clays, produces a distinctive cultural landscape (Figure 9.17). The impression of colors carried away by the visitor to this coastal land is of bright green pastures, herds of black and white Holstein-Friesian cattle, and red-brick buildings.

Most of the remainder of Europe, primarily Germany, Denmark, southern Sweden, northern France, and parts of lowland England, forms a zone of traditional *half-timbering* (Figure 9.18). A framework of heavy oaken beams, typically with angular supports, provides the weight-bearing skeleton of the building, and the interstices are filled in with a woven wattle of twigs and small branches mixed with clay (Figures 9.14, 9.18). In more recent times, brick has often replaced wattling. Generally the interstices are plastered over and whitewashed, and the beams are stained or painted a darker color, producing a striking and distinctive appearance. While half-timbering has become identified with Germany so closely as to be part of the stereotyped image foreigners have of that

FIGURE 9.17 A cultural landscape In brick —the Danish town of Ribe in the North Sea coastal margin. The brick is almost universally red. (Photo by the author, 1981.)

country, it appears commonly in the non-German districts mentioned, and some parts of Germany have none. Half-timbering rarely occurs south of the Danube or west of the Rhine in the areas once ruled by the Romans. Probably Germanic in origin, it presumably reached England and France with the Saxon and Frankish invaders.

Half-timbering also appears linked to zones of deciduous woodland and moderate deforestation, where enough oak timber remained for the substantial framework but not for the complete walls. Half-timbering may also be viewed as an intermediate type between the timber construction to the north and the southern earthen-building zone. Half-timbering also occurs in parts of the Balkans, the Basque lands, Spain, and in Cévennes, a district in southern France.

In recent times, particularly within the past half-century, traditional building materials have been abandoned in most parts of Europe, replaced by modern materials, such as cinder blocks. Half-timbering, for example, is rarely used now, even in Germany. However, the traditional, older, well-constructed houses remain very much a part of the cultural landscape, and their durability guarantees a presence for many years to come.

FIGURE 9.18 Hessian half-timbering, or *Fachwerk,* adds a distinctive appearance to the cultural landscape in this farm village on the Lahn River in Germany. (Photo by the author, 1991.)

Folk Architecture

The style of architecture is visually as noticeable as the materials used, and even more important in the classification of house and farmstead types (Figure 9.19). Within the great diversity of folk architecture in Europe, we can distinguish two broad categories: the *unit farmstead,* in which both human and animal quarters, as well as storage facilities, are housed under a single roof; and the *multiple-structure farmstead,* involving a number of separate buildings.

The unit house has two subtypes. In a belt stretching across the North German Plain into the Low Country and Flanders, the *single-story* unit farmstead prevails, in which the people and livestock occupy different parts of the same floor. Included in this group, among others, is the *Saxon* type, characterized by living quarters and stalls at opposite ends of an elongated structure separated by the hearth, by half-timbering with brick filler, and by a thatched roof (Figure 9.20). These single-story unit farmsteads of the Great European Plain represent ancient Low German types that survived to the present day. Single-story unit farmsteads also

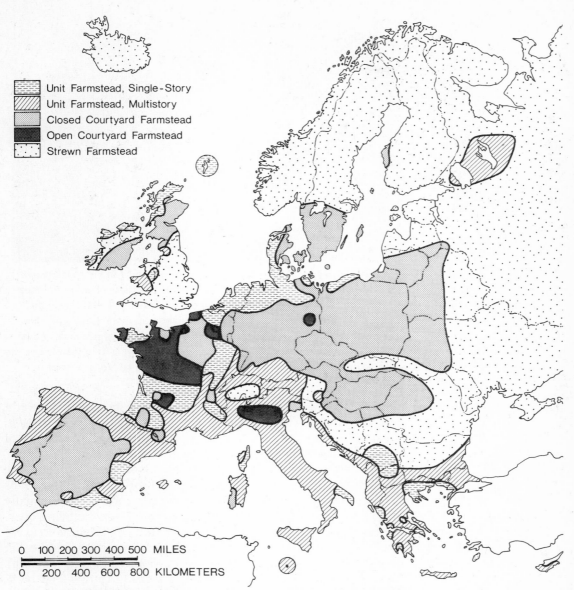

FIGURE 9.19 Traditional rural house and farmstead types. (Sources: After Demangeon; Milojević; Houston; Wagstaff, 1965; Giese; Meirion-Jones; P. Smith; Schröder;
Gailey; and A. Haberlandt, map of house types in Central Europe, in Georg Buschan, ed.,
Illustrierte Völkerkunde, Vol. 2, Part 2, Stuttgart, D: Strecker und Schröder, 1926, following
p. 176.)

occur in the Celtic fringes, where they are referred to as the British *longhouse.*
Included are the former "blackhouses" of the Scottish Isles, where people and

Figure 9.20 Two Saxon-type single-story unit farmsteads in the round green village of Mammoisel, central Germany. The livestock are housed toward the front of these half-timbered structures, while the people live toward the rear. The larger window in the side of the house on the right marks the beginning of the human quarters. Originally, the roofs of these houses were probably thatched, but in recent times various substitutes have been used, such as the corrugated metal on the right house. The view is from the central, circular village green, around which the Saxon houses are arranged like the spokes of a wheel. (Photo by the author, 1971.)

animals shared a small single-room structure. Iceland shares the longhouse tradition, but the absence of sizable roof timbers there forced the Viking settlers to erect an oddly shaped "sawtooth" roof with multiple gables, employing three or four short ridgepoles instead of one long one.

Much more common is the unit farmstead of *multiple-story* construction, the dominant type in southern Europe and many mountain or hill districts such as the Alps and Schwarzwald (Figure 9.21). Here the people and livestock usually occupy different stories, normally with the stalls at ground level, the living quarters immediately above, and perhaps an attic for hay storage. Cellars for cheese making are typical of the Alpine area, and in vineyard districts, a wine cellar may be directly under the residence. Elsewhere, as in southern Bayern (Bavaria), these farmsteads often consist of a multistory house attached to a two-level barn. The Schwarzwald house of southwestern Germany, the Swiss chalet of the Alps, the Catalan *masia* house of northeastern Spain, and various Pyrenean farmsteads provide examples of the multi-story unit type in the southern half of Europe. Far to the northeast, in the boreal reaches of the East European Plain, the *North Russian* house offers another, often spectacular example of the multi-story unit farmstead, a type also found among the eastern Karelians (Figure 9.22).

The remainder of rural Europe has multistructure farmsteads of several types. The *courtyard farmstead,* in which the house, barn, and other buildings cluster tightly around three or four sides of a central, closed farmyard, occurs in a

FIGURE 9.21 A multi-story unit farmstead of the Bernese type, found in central Switzerland. The two floors with windows are the human quarters, the livestock are housed on the ground level, and the attic is used for storage of hay. Such farmsteads, in various local forms, are typical of many of the southern German-speaking peoples of Europe. (Photo courtesy Swiss National Tourist Office.)

broad, wedge-shaped area of central Europe, extending from an apex in northern France eastward into Lithuania, Belarus, and the Balkans (Figures 9.5, 9.19). The best-known example of this type is the *Frankish* farmstead, which corresponds fairly well in distribution to the Middle German dialect and the ancient zone of influence of the expansive Frankish tribe. In most instances, buildings flank three sides of the Frankish courtyard, with a fence and gate completing the enclosure. The courtyard farmstead was perhaps designed to provide defense on the family level. Farther south, in Iberia, courtyard farmsteads of Moorish origin dominate much of Spain, perhaps reflecting the centuries of religious warfare there (Figure 9.23). Similarly, courtyard farmsteads prevail in the old Christian-Turk conflict zone in the northern Balkans. Parts of southern Scandinavia and the Po-Veneto

FIGURE 9.22 The North Russian house, typical of the northern part of the East European Plain especially Karelia. This notched-log example is from the Novgorod area. A two-story house occupies the front portion, while barn and stables are attached at the rear. (Photo by the author, 1992.)

Plain also have courtyard farmsteads, as is true of the British Isles (Figure 8.12). In some parts of Europe, particularly western France, the arrangement of structures around the courtyard is looser, with open spaces between creating a distinctive subtype (Figure 9.19).

Other multistructure farmsteads consist instead of a loose assemblage of buildings scattered about the area near the house. Geographers designate this type as the *strewn farmstead,* most numerous in the north and east (Figure 9.19). It appears commonly in the zone of wooden construction in Northern and Eastern Europe, where the spacing of buildings provides a practical solution to the danger of fire (Figure 9.24). Also, the strewn farmstead appears to be related to dispersed farmsteads and unit-block farms, where crowding of buildings is unnecessary, unlike the clustered villages farther south and west, which have limited space. Even in the strewn farmstead, house and barn are often attached, especially in cold climates. The typical Russian strewn farmstead of the northern East European Plain consists of a one-story housebarn and a scattering of outbuildings such as a sauna, storage sheds, pigsty, hayshed, draw well, and granary.

Preserving the Landscape

The cultural landscape of rural Europe reflects the antiquity of the culture area. As August Meitzen said, "we walk to a certain degree in every village among the ruins of antiquity." The forces that produced field patterns, house types, and

FIGURE 9.23 A courtyard farmstead amid the fields and olive groves of Spanish Andalucía near the town of Jódar. In this example, courtyard farmsteads reveal Moorish influence, and similar ones can be seen across the Strait of Gibraltar in Morocco. (Photo by the author, 1986.)

farm villages often lie so remote in time as to be unknown to present scholars. Slowly, however, the traditional forms, often ill suited to the demands of the modern age, disappear. The European countryside becomes gradually "Americanized," with scattered farmsteads, unit-block holdings, and contemporary building materials, and new architectural styles replacing the traditional forms. Alarming signs of deterioration appear, owing to land abandonment—ruined stone farmhouses in Ireland, derelict vineyards in the German Rhine gorge, shrunken villages in Spain. Rural suburbanization, in which growing cities and towns spill out into the nearby villages, enlarging and transforming them, provides as much of a threat to the traditional landscape as rural depopulation.

Europeans in many countries have responded to the endangerment of their rural landscapes with effective, subsidized preservation programs. In the Netherlands, for example, some 43,000 features of the cultural landscape were listed and protected by the middle 1980s, including 5300 farm buildings and 1000 mills. Even wayside shrines receive attention. In various countries, rigorously enforced building codes restrict the demolition of traditional structures and regulate their renovation into homes for the future. Today, beneath the facade of a seventeenth-century farmhouse often lies a suburban dwelling equipped with central heating, jacuzzi, and all the modern appliances. New houses often must be designed to blend architecturally with the local folk style. Many urban Europeans now own second homes in rural areas, often in foreign countries, and

FIGURE 9.24 A strewn farmstead on the plains of southwestern Iceland, typical of the better agricultural areas of that country. (Photo by the author, 1994.)

they have greatly assisted the conservation and preservation movement. Abundant government funds provide assistance. In short, Europeans have inventoried their rural landscapes, passed protective legislation, and implemented subsidized preservationist measures. At the same time, rural land-use planning regulations have saved open space and retained the agricultural character of many districts. The result of all these efforts at management of the countryside has been the rescue of many traditional landscapes. Much was lost, especially in Romania, but enough survives to perpetuate the rich mosaic of rural landscapes. America has not been so progressive or fortunate.

Still, the typical European pursues an urban life. They may venerate the countryside and even view it as the "real" part of their nation, but in fact they are city folks. Urbanism is one of the basic "European" traits, and we now turn our attention to the cities of the culture area.

Sources and Suggested Readings

Frederick H. A. Aalen. "Vernacular Architecture of the British Isles." *Yearbook of the Association of Pacific Coast Geographers.* 35 (1973), 27–48.

Frederick H. A. Aalen. "Vernacular Buildings in Cephalonia, Ionian Islands, Greece." *Journal of Cultural Geography.* 4:2 (1984), 56–72.

Swanzie Agnew. "Rural Settlement in the Coastal Plain of Bas Languedoc." *Geography.* 31 (1946), 67–77.

Alan R. H. Baker and Robin A. Butlin (eds.). *Studies of Field Systems in the British Isles.* Cambridge, GB: University Press, 1973.

Michael Barke. "The Growth and Changing Pattern of Second Homes in Spain." *Scottish Geographical Magazine.* 107 (1991), 12–21.

Harry Batsford. "Types and Materials of Houses in England." *Geography.* 12 (1923–1924), 42–50.

Maurice W. Beresford. "The Lost Villages of Medieval England." *Geographical Journal.* 117 (1951), 129–149.

Arnold Beuermann. "Typen ländlicher Siedlungen in Griechenland." *Petermanns Geographische Mitteilungen.* 100 (1956), 278–285.

Louise A. Boyd. *Polish Countrysides: Photographs and Narrative.* New York, USA: American Geographical Society, 1937.

Nikolaus Creutzburg. *Kultur im Spiegel der Landschaft: das Bild der Erde in seiner Gestaltung durch den Menschen.* Leipzig, D: Bibliographisches Institut, 1930.

Jovan Cvijić. *La Péninsule Balkanique: Géographie humaine.* Paris, F; Armand Colin, 1918.

H. Clifford Darby. "The Changing English Landscape." *Geographical Journal.* 117 (1951), 377–398.

Albert Demangeon. "L'habitation rurale en France: essai de classification des principaux types." *Annales de Géographie.* 29 (1920), 352–375.

Albert Demangeon. "Types de villages en France." *Annales de Géographie.* 48 (1939), 1–21.

Robert E. Dickinson. "Dispersed Settlement in Southern Italy." *Erdkunde.* 10 (1956), 282–297.

Robert E. Dickinson. "Rural Settlement in the German Lands." *Annals of the Association of American Geographers.* 39 (1949), 239–263.

Frans Dussart. "Geographie der ländlichen Siedlungsformen in Belgien und Luxemburg." *Geographische Rundschau.* 9 (1957), 12–18.

H. Fairhurst. "Types of Settlement in Spain." *Scottish Geographical Magazine.* 51 (1935), 283–296.

Alan Gailey. *Rural Houses of the North of Ireland.* Edinburgh, GB: Donald, 1984.

Max Geschwend. "Bäuerliche Haus- und Hofformen" and "Bäuerlicher Hausbau." Plates 36, 36a, and 37 in *Atlas der Schweiz.* Wabern-Bern, CH: Verlag der eidgenossischen Landestopographie, 1965–1970.

Wilhelm Giese. "Los tipos de casa de la Península Ibérica." *Revista de Dialectologia y Tradiciones Populares.* 7 (1951), 563–601.

Desmond A. Gillmor. "An Investigation of Villages in the Republic of Ireland." *Irish Geography.* 21 (1988), 57–68.

Desmond A. Gillmor, (ed.). *The Irish Countryside: Landscape, Wildlife, History, People.* Dublin, IRL: Wolfhound Press, 1989.

Robert Gradmann. "Die ländlichen Siedlungsformen Württembergs." *Petermanns Geographische Mitteilungen.* 56 (1910), part 1, 183–186, 246–249.

William A. Hance. "Crofting Settlements and Housing in the Outer Hebrides." *Annals of the Association of American Geographers.* 41 (1951), 75–87.

S. Helmfrid (ed.). Vadstena Symposium: "Morphogenesis of the Agrarian Cultural Landscape." *Geografiska Annaler.* 43: 1–2 (1961), 1–328.

George W. Hoffman. "Transformation of Rural Settlement in Bulgaria." *Geographical Review.* 54 (1964), 45–64.

W. G. Hoskins. *The Making of the English Landscape.* London, GB: Hodder & Stoughton, 1957.

James M. Houston. *A Social Geography of Europe.* London, GB: Duckworth, 1953, chaps. 4–6.

Dimitri Jaranoff. "Die Siedlungstypen in der östlichen und zentralen Balkanhalbinsel." *Zeitschrift der Gesellschaft für Erdkunde zu Berlin*, 1934, 183–191.

Otto Jessen. "Höhlenwohnungen in den Mittelmeerländern." *Petermanns Geographische Mitteilungen.* 76 (1930), 128–133, 180–184.

James H. Johnson. "Studies of Irish Rural Settlement." *Geographical Review.* 48 (1958), 554–566.

Murray E. Keeler and Dimitrios G. Skuras. "Land Fragmentation and Consolidation Policies in Greek Agriculture." *Geography.* 76 (1990), 73–76.

Russell L. King. *Land Reform: The Italian Experience.* London, GB: Butterworths, 1973.

Russell L. King and Alan Strachan. "Sicilian Agro-Towns." *Erdkunde.* 32 (1978), 110–123.

Lester E. Klimm. "The Relation Between Field Patterns and Jointing in the Aran Islands." *Geographical Review.* 25 (1935), 618–624.

Audrey M. Lambert. *The Making of the Dutch Landscape: An Historical Geography of the Netherlands.* London, GB: Seminar Press, 2nd ed., 1985.

Marguerite A. Lefèvre. *L'habitat rural en Belgique*, Liège, B: H. Vaillant-Carmanne, 1926.

Martti Linkola. "On the History of the Rural Landscape of Finland." *Ethnologia Scandinavica.* (1987), 110–127.

Carl-Christoph Liss. "Entwicklung und Stand der Flurbereinigung in Spanien." *Erdkunde.* 39 (1985), 99–115.

David Lowenthal and Hugh C. Prince. "The English Landscape." *Geographical Review.* 54 (1964), 309–346.

Rudolf Martiny. "Die Grundrissgestaltung der deutschen Siedlungen." *Petermanns Mitteilungen Ergänzungsheft, No. 197.* Gotha, D: Justus Perthes, 1928.

Alan Mayhew. *Rural Settlement and Farming in Germany.* New York, USA: Barnes and Noble, 1973.

Gwyn I. Meirion-Jones. *The Vernacular Architecture of Brittany: An Essay in Historical Geography.* Edinburgh, GB: Donald, 1982.

August Meitzen. *Das deutsche Haus.* Berlin, D: Dietrich Reimer, 1882.

August Meitzen. *Siedelung und Agrarwesen der Westgermanen und Ostgermanen, der Kelten, Römer, Finnen und Slawen.* 3 vols. and atlas. Berlin, D: Wilhelm Hertz, 1895.

R. N. Millman. *The Making of the Scottish Landscape*. London, GB: Batsford, 1975.

Borivoje Milojevic. "Types of Villages and Village-Houses in Yugoslavia." *Professional Geographer*. 5:6 (1953), 13–17.

Wilhelm Müller-Wille. "Haus- und Gehöftformen in Mitteleuropa." *Geographische Zeitschrift*. 42 (1936), 121–138.

Lancelot O'Brien. "Rural Housing in Ireland: A Description and Classification for the 1980s." *Irish Geography*. 22 (1989), 1–12.

Erich Otremba. "Die deutsche Agrarlandschaft." *Geographische Zeitschrift Beiheft*. 3 (1961).

J. Pallot. "Open Fields and Individual Farms: Land Reform in Pre-Revolutionary Russia." *Tijdschrift voor Economische en Sociale Geografie*. 75 (1984), 46–60.

Werner Radig. *Die Siedlungstypen in Deutschland*. Berlin, D: Henschel, 1955.

Brian K. Roberts. *The Making of the English Village*. Harlow, GB: Longman, 1987.

Brian K. Roberts. *Rural Settlement in Britain*. London, GB: Hutchinson, 1979.

H. J. Savory. "Settlement in the Glamočko Polje." *Geographical Journal*. 124 (1958), 41–55.

Karl H. Schröder and Gabriele Schwarz. *Die ländlichen Siedlungsformen in Mitteleuropa*. Bad Godesberg, D: Bundesforschungsanstalt für Landeskunde und Raumordnung, 1969.

D. J. Shaw. "The Problem of Land Fragmentation in the Mediterranean Area: A Case Study." *Geographical Review*. 53 (1963), 40–51.

Peter Smith. *Houses of the Welsh Countryside: A Study in Historical Geography*. London, GB: Her Majesty's Stationery Office, 2nd ed., 1988.

"Special Issue—Landscape History." *Geografiska Annaler*. 70B (1988), 1–237.

L. Dudley Stamp. "The Common Lands and Village Greens of England and Wales." *Geographical Journal*. 130 (1964), 457–469.

Kirk H. Stone. "Regionalization of Spanish Units of Settlement." *Tijdschrift voor Economische en Sociale Geografie*. 61 (1970), 232–241.

Dorothy-Sylvester. *The Rural Landscape of the Welsh Borderland: A Study in Historical Geography*. London, GB: Macmillan, 1969.

Harry Thorpe. "The Green Village as a Distinctive Form of Settlement on the North European Plain." *Bulletin de la Société Belge d'Études Géographiques*. 30 (1961), 93–134.

Harry Thorpe. "The Influence of Inclosure on the Form and Pattern of Rural Settlement in Denmark." *Transactions and Papers of the Institute of British Geographers*. 17 (1952), 111–129.

David Turnock. "The Planning of Rural Settlement in Romania." *Geographical Journal*. 157 (1991), 251–264.

Harald Uhlig. "Old Hamlets with Infield and Outfield Systems in Western and Central Europe." *Geografiska Annaler*. 43 (1961), 285–312.

Ingolf Vogeler. "The Rundling: A Slav Village Type?" *The Geographical Survey* (Blue Earth Geographical Society, Mankato, USA). 3 (1974), 73–98.

John M. Wagstaff. *The Development of Rural Settlements: A Study of the Helos Plain in Southern Greece*. Avebury, GB: Avebury Publishing Co., 1982.

John M. Wagstaff. "The Study of Greek Rural Settlements." *Erdkunde*. 23 (1969), 306–317.

John M. Wagstaff. "Traditional Houses in Modern Greece." *Geography*. 50 (1965), 58–64.

Michael T. Wild and P. N. Jones. "Rural Suburbanization and Village Expansion in the Rhine Rift Valley: A Cross-Frontier Comparison." *Geografiska Annaler*. 70B (1988), 275–290.

Herbert Wilhelmy. *Hochbulgarien, I: Die ländlichen Siedlungen und die bäuerliche Wirtschaft*. Kiel, D: Geographisches Institut der Universität, 1935.

Herbert Wilhelmy. "Völkische und koloniale Siedlungsformen der Slawen." *Geographische Zeitschrift*. 42 (1936), 81–97.

Eugen Wirth. "Die Murgia dei Trulli (Apulien)." *Die Erde*. 93 (1962), 249–278.

Brian J. Woodruffe. "Conservation and the Rural Landscape." In David Pinder, (ed.). *Western Europe: Challenge and Change*. London, GB: Belhaven Press, 1990, 258–276.

E. M. Yates. "The Evolution of the English Village." *Geographical Journal*. 148 (1982), 182–206.

Bruce S. Young. "Agricultural Landscapes of the Maltese Islands." *Journal of Geography*. 63 (1964), 23–32.

Bogdan Zaborski. "Sur le forme des villages en Pologne et leur repartition." *Boletin de la Société de Géographie de Québec*. 22 (1928), 65–76.

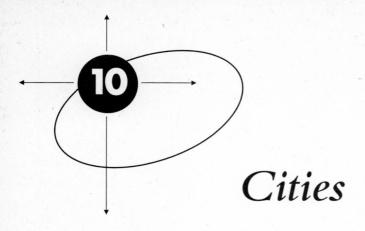

Cities

Much that we regard as "European" has its roots in the city. The innovations, changes, and great ideas used in Chapter 1 to epitomize Europe sprang, with few exceptions, from the urban population of Europe. In some provinces and countries, more than four-fifths of the population live in cities and towns, and the proportion in Belgium has reached 97 percent (Figure 10.1). A city may be defined as a relatively large, permanent settlement containing a dense cluster of socially heterogeneous people engaged in specialized, primarily nonagricultural types of work.

Origin and Diffusion

Though the city epitomizes European civilization and represents an ancient, vital institution there, its origins lie elsewhere. In fact, the diffusion of urbanism followed the same northwestward path from the Near East that brought the Indo-European languages, Christianity, agriculture, and the political state to Europe (Figure 10.2). Many of these innovations were interrelated in that agriculture greatly increased food production per capita, freeing a portion of the population to engage in urban activities, such as trade, crafts, the military, and political administration. These occupations all became centered in cities and in fact provided the very reason for urban existence. Trade represented the most important single function, and the term *mercantile city* best describes European urban centers prior to the great Industrial Revolution of the 1700s and 1800s.

Cities thrive in peace, law, and order, conditions best produced when organized political states replaced tribal governments. In turn, cities serve as centers of administration. Rulers found cities convenient bases from which to rule. Symbiotically, then, cities housed the very governments that fostered them. Some early cities probably arose as religious sites, centered on temples, and the priestly class also formed an influential part of urban population from the very first. Scholars, artists, and philosophers early joined the merchants, artisans, rulers, soldiers, and clerics as urbanites, making the city a center of learning and creativity.

FIGURE 10.1 Urban population as a percent of total population and distribution of large metropolitan areas. Countries differ somewhat in their definition of *urban* and *metropolitan area,* but the figures are roughly comparable. *Urban* is defined as settlements of 10,000 or more population. The core of Europe is more highly urbanized, in general, than the peripheries.

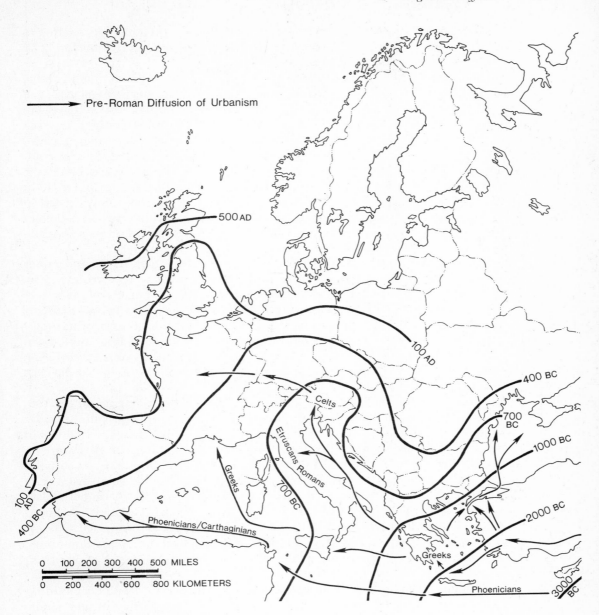

FIGURE 10.2 Diffusion of the city. The source and paths of diffusion show striking similarities to the diffusionary routes of the Indo-European languages, agriculture, the political state, and Christianity. Just as was probably true in the spread of agriculture and languages, Iberia received its first urban impulse from Afro-Asiatic peoples by way of North Africa. (Source: Based in part upon Pounds, 1969, with major modifications.)

Human heterogeneity and crowding energized the urban population, leading to new ideas and inventions. Not the least of these was democracy, the noblest of all European ideas and born of its cities.

The first Europeans to receive urbanism from the Near East and Anatolia, about 2000 B.C., were the Greeks. Within seven centuries, small city-states, each ruling a small tributary rural territory, dotted the Peloponnisos and Aegean shores, forming the basis of the Greek *heroic* age, which ended soon after the sack of Troy, about 1200 B.C.. After a brief dark age, the Greeks began their greatest era of city-founding some three centuries later, culminating in the Hellenic golden age. Greek colonists carried urbanism as far afield as the Black Sea coasts, southern Italy, and the south of France. Siracusa on Sicilia and Marseille in Languedoc represent their work. By about 500 B.C., some 600 cities existed in peninsular Greece and the Aegean. The Phoenicians, a Mediterranean people of the Near East, also founded some cities as trading colonies in Europe, especially in southern Iberia.

Most of these early Mediterranean cities remained small in size and rather unimpressive in appearance. Unlike farm villages, they were surrounded by walls and often boasted a temple, a palace, a theater, and a marketplace. Rarely did they exceed 5000 in population, though Athínai may have had as many as 300,000 residents in the peak of its classical glory and Kórinthos (Corinth) perhaps 90,000. Only the larger acquired importance beyond their local areas. Even at the apex of classical urban development, as little as one-quarter of the Greek population lived in cities. As in the heroic age, the city-state dominated the classical Hellenic world.

The idea of urbanism spread quickly in Europe. Beginning about 800 B.C., Celts established a number of small cities in the Alpine peripheries, most notably at Hallstatt in Austria, and the Etruscans of Italy became active city builders in the same period. Romans, destined to become the greatest of all European cityfounders, were influenced by both Greeks and Etruscans. They eventually replaced the concept of the city-state and their troublesome small wars with empire and the *pax Romana*. At the dawn of Roman greatness, the imperial core districts of Latium (modern Lazio) and Etruria (modern Toscana) contained some 42 cities; by midpoint in the empire's life span under Augustus, 430 new cities existed in Italy alone (Figure 10.3). In its classical grandeur, Roma may have boasted a population of a half-million, packed into an area of barely 23 sq km (9 sq. mi.).

Romans speeded the diffusion of urban life through Europe by founding new cities in France, Germany, Britain, interior Iberia, and the Danube lands. Some new towns grew around military barracks or camps, an origin suggested by the British town suffixes *-caster* and *-chester,* as in Lancaster or Winchester, derived from the Latin word *castra,* or "army camp." Three areas stood out as centers of urban development under Roman rule—central Italy, Greece, and Andalucía in Spain (Figure 10.3). Most of these cities remained small by modern standards. In France the Roman towns ranged from about 600 to 35,000 in population, while in the British periphery of the empire the size varied from 500 or less up to the 17,000 inhabitants of London.

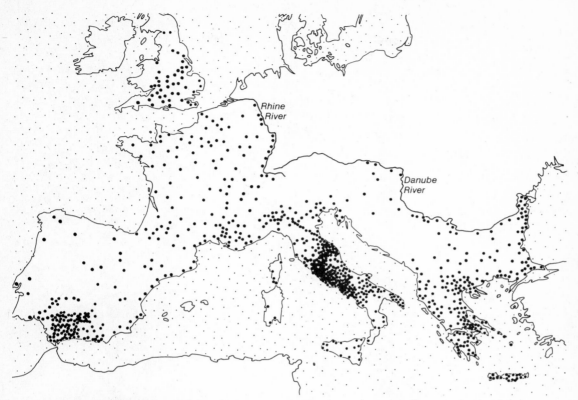

FIGURE 10.3 Cities of the Roman Empire by the third centuries A.D. Note the clusterings in central Italy, southern Spain, and Greece. (Source: After Pounds, 1969.)

The heritage of Roman urbanization is considerable. Many sites have been continuously occupied since Roman times, as, for example, the city of Trier in Germany, and other sites were reoccupied after a period of abandonment. Even names are often corruptions of the original Latin form, as for example Köln (Cologne, Latin Colonia Agrippinensis) and London (Londinium). One of the most interesting names, Zaragoza, began as the Roman Caesarea Augusta and was corrupted by the Arabic Moorish conquerors to Zarakusta and again by the Christian liberators of Spain to its present form.

Following another dark age after the fall of the Roman Empire, during which urban population shrank and some towns became totally abandoned, Europe entered its last great age of city founding in the Middle Ages, taking advantage of the security provided by the feudal system. Germanic peoples established most of the new cities during this era. Europe's urban focus shifted to new regions, allowing the Po-Veneto Plain and the Low Country/Rhinelands to replace the earlier southern concentrations (Figure 10.4).

Most Germanic towns grew from fortified *preurban cores,* sites dominated by the stronghold of a feudal lord. The A.D. 800s and 900s had been a major period

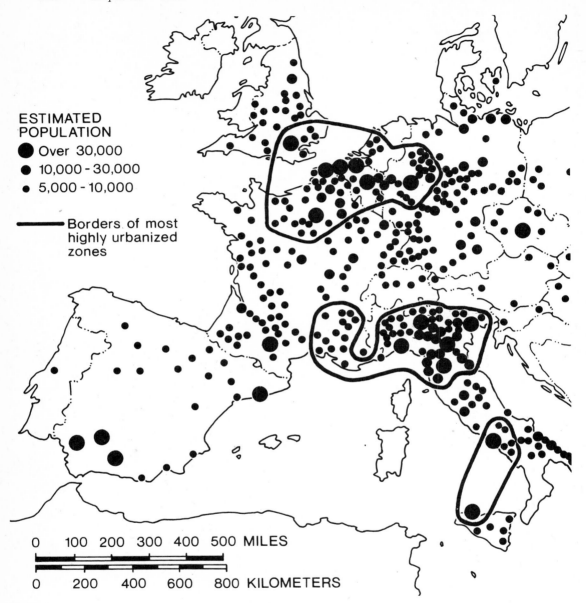

FIGURE 10.4 Distribution of important cities, About A.D. 1500 Northern Italy and the Low Country had become the new urban centers in Europe. Thousands of smaller towns do not appear on the map. (Sources: After de Vries, 160; and Herman J. G. Pounds, *Hearth and Home,* Bloomington, USA: Indiana University Press, 1989, 260.)

of castle construction by feudal landowners as they sought to secure the surrounding countryside. The catalysts in changing most preurban cores to towns were itinerant traders, who initially made use of secure marketplaces adjacent to strongholds along transport routes. In time, the desire for safe winter quarters led the traders to establish permanent residence at the preurban cores, creating merchant colonies. Artisans were attracted by the presence of merchants, and the town population grew steadily. In an early stage of development, a "town" often consisted of several distinct nuclei: the feudal fortress; one or more marketplaces; scattered, fortified houses of merchants; a church; and some farmhouses. The German city of Braunschweig, for example, originated in 1269 through the union of five distinct nuclei, each of which had its own name. In an earlier era, Roma had arisen in a very similar manner as the union of adjacent hilltop villages.

The three essential attributes of the feudally derived medieval Germanic city included the charter, the town wall, and the marketplace. The charter, a governmental decree from an emperor or lesser ruler granting political autonomy to the town, freed its populace from the manorial restrictions of the rural areas. The city became self-governing and responsible for its own defense. Charters were typically requested by colonies of well-to-do merchants, who found that manorial restrictions hindered the mobility and exercise of personal initiative so vital in trading activities. Many cities date their founding from the granting of a charter, though most existed prior to that time. City-states similar to those of classical Greece, legitimized by charter, appeared throughout most of Central and Western Europe.

Self-government demanded self-defense, and the castles and fortified houses gave way to city walls (Figure 10.5). All important parts of the city lay inside the wall, including the mercantile and manufacturing establishments, the fortress, the church, and the homes of the majority of the population. Urban expansion often required the construction of new, more inclusive walls, and some larger cities eventually needed three or four rebuildings. In the period before gunpowder came into widespread use, city walls adequately repelled invaders.

The marketplace, often supplemented by a bourse, or trading hall, served as the focus of economic activity in the town, for the mercantile function remained dominant throughout the medieval period. Larger places held annual trade fairs, some of which began in the days of itinerant traders before permanent settlement had transformed the preurban cores into towns. Some of the more famous of these fairs survive to the present day, as at Leipzig, Frankfurt-am-Main, Milano, and Lyon. In size, the towns of the Middle Ages closely resembled their classical ancestors. Few exceeded 100,000 in population. Gent, the famous textile center of Vlaanderen, had only 56,000 inhabitants in the mid–1300s. Paris, the largest European city, and Napoli were the only two with more than 100,000 by the year 1400.

After about 1500 the founding of new cities declined markedly, except in the far north. City-states gave way to larger, more powerful kingdoms. Tiny San Marino represents one of the very few surviving European city-states, clinging to its independence in the Appennini Mountains. Urbanization continued to affect a small part of the European population. In 1600 only 4 million of the 85 million Europeans lived in towns of 15,000 population or more, about 5 percent of the

FIGURE 10.5 Avila, on the Castilian Meseta of interior Spain. The city retains its splendid ring of medieval walls. (Photo by the author, 1986.)

total. The Netherlands and Italy, the most highly urbanized countries, could claim only about 12 or 13 percent of their populations as urban, while only 2 percent of the Germans, French, and English lived in large towns at that time.

The Industrial City

European cities changed rapidly after about 1800 as a result of the Industrial Revolution. Manufacturing became the dominant function of many urban centers, putting an end to the age of mercantile cities. The hallmark of the industrial phase was the great increase in city size, prompted by the gravitation of the majority of the European population to urban, industrial areas. England and Wales urbanized more than half their population by the 1850s. A half-century later, more than three-quarters of the English and Welsh lived in cities, and Germany had become the second nation to have over half of its population urban. Many other countries, especially in northwestern Europe, reached this level by 1930, and the trend continues to spread toward the peripheries of the culture area (Figure 10.1).

The Industrial Revolution produced the first European cities to have more than a million inhabitants. London passed the million mark in the first decade of the nineteenth century and exceeded 2 million by 1850. Paris claimed more than a million by the middle of the 1800s, and by the turn of the century, Berlin, Wien, St. Petersburg, and Moskva had reached this level. By 1994, some 68 metropolitan areas west of the Urals and south to the borders of Christendom claimed more than a million inhabitants. Scores more have populations of between 500,000 and 1,000,000. A core/periphery pattern appears in the geographical distribution of these large cities (Figure 10.1).

Counterurbanization

In the late twentieth century, particularly after about 1965, a new trend called *counterurbanization* began to influence Europe. Counterurbanization is the deglomeration or decentralization of population, as sizable numbers of people leave cities and move to semirural fringes or even to fully rural peripheries. Larger cities stagnate or decline in population due to net migratory losses, while villages and smaller urban places grow. Improved transportation and communications networks permit fairly long-range commuting, and many jobs can be performed at home. As a rule, the movement away from cities is limited to the more affluent segment of the population, and it often occurs in stages, beginning with the acquisition of a second home for vacation purposes. An author, data processor, or designer comes to realize that his or her job can be performed just as well in locations remote from the urban office. The products of their work can be shipped, mailed, or electronically transmitted to the city.

The aging of the European population, with 15 percent or more of all persons now over 65 years old in many regions, also contributes to counterurbanization because affluent retired people often relocate to rural areas. The sudden, rapid decline of such traditional manufacturing industries as textiles and steel also caused many overspecialized cities to lose population. Equally important, waves of foreign immigrant guest workers began arriving in the cities, causing many natives to flee. In addition, large numbers of Europeans embraced *antiurbanism*, a perception based in urban problems, crowding, and stress, as well as the attractive counterimage of the countryside as a place of harmony, civility, and sociability.

The United Kingdom, the first country to urbanize massively, also became the first to feel the effects of counterurbanization in the 1960s. Western Germany experienced an almost simultaneous onset of the phenomenon, followed by the Low Countries, France, and Denmark. The period 1975–1982 in France saw the rural population grow more rapidly than the urban for the first time in well over a century. France's Atlantic coastal, Mediterranean, and Alpine provinces gained population most rapidly. Peripheral parts of Europe have yet to experience any profound counterurbanization. Not all counterurban growth occurs in areas far removed from the large cities. Many people who move seek out villages and small towns fairly near major urban centers. The term *periurban* is used increasingly to describe such a pattern; it amounts to a type of suburbanization.

Counterurbanization slowed in most countries in the 1980s, leading some urban geographers to label it as a temporary and inconsequential shift. France experienced a resurgence of growth in the largest metropolitan areas by 1990, and only the decaying heavily industrial cities exhibit long-term population loss-es. Germany, too, saw a slowing down of counterurbanization in the late 1980s, following 15 years during which the trend intensified.

Most Western European countries now invest heavily in urban redevelop-ment, making the cities more attractive places to live. These improvements, cou-pled with the ancient, traditional prestige of urban living in European culture, have apparently blunted any further large-scale counterurbanization, at least in the West. Eastern Europe may experience the trend next, as manufacturing industries collapse and people flee to rural areas, where food is more readily available. In the Karelian Republic, a part of northwestern Russia, the percentage of the population living in urban areas reputedly dropped from 82 percent in 1989 to 65 percent by 1991.

Urban Site

Geographers study diverse spatial and ecological aspects of urbanization. Perhaps none is more fundamental than an analysis of the specific physical loca-tion, or **site.** Decisions that determined the sites of most European cities rested heavily upon the need for defense and access to trade routes. An easily defended site was particularly important to feudal lords who built strongholds during the insecure period after the Roman Empire fell. Romans themselves rarely chose protected sites for their army camps and other settlements, because their military force enjoyed superiority to that of neighboring tribes. Roman camps typically possessed *offensive* advantage, along roads and navigable streams rather than on high points. Still, episodes of piracy in the classical and preclassical Mediterranean influenced the defensive siting of Athínai and Roma, both of which lie a short distance inland from the coast.

Many types of defensive sites exist. The *river-meander site,* with the city locat-ed inside a loop where the stream turns back upon itself, leaves only a narrow neck of land unprotected by the waters. Besançon on the river Doubs in far east-ern France provides an example of a meander site. *Incised* meanders proved par-ticularly popular because the river loop became permanent by cutting down to form a steep-sided valley. The city of Bern, capital of Switzerland, on the Aare River, offers a splendid example of an incised river meander site (Figure 10.6), as does Toledo in Spain.

Similar to the meander site but even more advantageous, the *river-island site* combined a natural moat with an easier river crossing, the latter an advantage for the merchant trade. Paris began as a town on the Île de la Cité, or "island of the city," in the middle of the Seine River, as did Wroclaw on the Odra (Oder) in Poland, Limerick in Ireland, and others. Stockholm, the capital of Sweden, occu-pies a *lake-island site,* originating on a dozen or so small islands in the area where Lake Mälaren joins the Baltic Sea. Perhaps even more satisfactory, the *offshore-island site,* combined defense with a port facility. The classic example, Venèzia, rests on wooden pilings driven into an offshore sandbar, which separated a coastal lagoon from the open Adriatic Sea. The same category includes the famous town and abbey of Mont-Saint-Michel, situated on a rock off the coast of

FIGURE 10.6 Bern, the capital city of Switzerland, an example of a river-meander urban site. The original settlement, now the core of the city, lay inside the loop of the incised meander of the Aare River. Such a location provided natural defense on three sides. As the city expanded in modern times, it came to include the opposite bank of the river. (Photo courtesy Swiss National Tourist Office.)

Normandie in France (Figure 10.7). At high tide, the rock and town become insular, while at low tide, tidal flats formerly made access difficult. A causeway changed this situation in modern times. Danger from the direction of the sea often prompted *sheltered-harbor sites,* where narrow entrances could be easily defended. Oslo, at the head of a fjord in Norway, and the Portuguese capital of Lisboa both occupy sheltered harbors.

High points offered obvious defensive advantages. Many towns lie at the foot of a fortified high point (Figure 10.8). Such cities often derived their names from the stronghold, as is indicated by many place names ending or beginning in *-burg, -bourg, -borg, castelo-, -grad,* and *-linna,* all of which mean "fortress" or "castle" in various European languages. Scottish Edinburgh ("Edwin's fort"), dominated by the impressive Castle Rock, provides a good example, as do Salzburg in Austria and Castelo Branco in Portugal. Other cities sited adjacent to fortified high points include Praha, Vaduz in Liechtenstein, Sion in Switzerland, and Budapest.

Closely akin are those towns and cities that, in their formative stage at least, lay entirely on high ground, often adjacent to the stronghold. Examples include Beograd (Belgrade, "white fortress"), on a high bluff overlooking the confluence of the Danube and the Sava; Segovia and Zamora in Spain; Laôn in France; Shaftesbury, a Saxon hill town in England; and Castelo de Vide in Portugal.

FIGURE 10.7 The town and abbey of Mont-Saint-Michel, France, an example of the offshore-island urban site. At low tide, as in this picture, the town is connected to the nearby Normandie mainland by an expanse of sand, but at high tide it is an island. In modern times, a causeway was built to the mainland. Such a site offered obvious defensive advantages. (Photo courtesy French Government Tourist Office.)

Often such hill towns in Romance-language lands bear the place name prefix *Mont-* or *Monte-*, as in Monte Corno, Italy.

Merchants, largely responsible for the development of cities from preurban cores, generally selected stronghold sites that lay on *trade routes.* Numerous types of sites possessed advantages for the merchants. In the early medieval period, before bridges became common, *river-ford sites,* where the stream was shallow and its bed firm, offered good sites. Some cities bear names that indicate the former importance of fords, including the German and English suffixes *-furt* and *-ford.* Frankfurt ("Franks' ford") in Germany lies at an easy crossing of the Main River, where the ancient trade route from the Upper Rhine Plain passes northward toward the Great European Plain. Upstream on the Main from Frankfurt we find the towns of Ochsenfurt ("ford for oxen"), Schweinfurt ("swine-ford"), Hassfurt ("Hessians' ford"), Trennfurt, and Lengfurt. The English cities of Oxford on the Thames, Hertford on the Lea, and Bedford on the Ouse again suggest the former importance of river shallows in urban siting. The Latin word for "ford," *trajectus,* also survives in corrupted form in the town names Utrecht (*trajectus ad Rhenum,* or "ford on the Rhine") and Maastricht (*trajectus ad Mosam,* "ford on the Maas") in the Netherlands.

FIGURE 10.8 The city of Salzburg in Austria, an example of the high-point urban site. Salzburg developed at the foot of the fortified high point, or acropolis. The beautifully preserved fortress, or burg, still dominates the skyline of the city. Merchants who were responsible for creating the original urban nucleus chose to locate adjacent to the fortress for reasons of security. (Photo courtesy Austrian National Tourist Office.)

A similar function was served by *bridge-point sites,* where streams narrowed down and possessed firm banks and beds. Town names including *pont, bridge, brück,* and the like indicate that the site was originally chosen for bridge construction. The Romans, great bridge builders, founded many towns that derive both their site and name from the Roman structure, as for example Les-Ponts-de-Cé ("bridges of Caesar") on the Loire River in France, and Paunton (from the Latin *Adpontem* or "at the bridge") in Lincolnshire, England. Historic London Bridge, of which several have existed through history, originally stood at a point on the Thames just upstream from the marsh-flanked estuary, at a site where the banks were firm and the stream narrow. It served as an important river crossing on the Roman route from the Strait of Dover to the interior of England. Examples of other bridge-point cities named for their function include Cambridge ("bridge on the Cam River") and Brigham ("bridge settlement") in England, Pontoise ("bridge on the Oise River") near Paris, Bersenbrück ("broken bridge") in northwestern Germany, Bruchsal ("bridge over the Salzbach") in the German province of Baden, Innsbruck ("bridge on the Inn River") in Austria, and Puente-la-Reina ("queen's bridge") in Spain.

Many city sites north of the Alps are riverine because navigable streams have long served as trade routes. *Confluence sites,* where two rivers meet, are common. The German city of Koblenz, at the juncture of the Rhine and the Mosel, actually derived its name from the Latin word for confluence, while Passau in the German province of Bayern may be the only city where three rivers—the Danube, Inn, and Ilz—meet at precisely the same point. The rise of Paris was facilitated by the convergence of the Marne, Oise, and Seine rivers in the general vicinity of the city, and Lyon profited from its position at the confluence of Rhône and Saône. *Head-of-navigation sites* serve as transshipment points, such as Basel on the upper reaches of the navigable sector of the Rhine River in Switzerland. In countries such as Finland, where an intricate network of lakes and rivers provided the major trade routes, fortifications built at strategic narrows sometimes provided urban nuclei, as at Savonlinna ("castle in Savo province") and Hämeenlinna ("castle in Häme province") (Figure 10.9).

Crossroad sites occur throughout Europe. One of the more famous is Wien, the Austrian capital, located where an east-west route connecting the Hungarian Plain with southern Germany along the Danube Valley met the ancient north-south route, which skirted the eastern foot of the Alps and passed through the Moravian Gate to Poland and the Baltic. Hannover in Germany stands at the juncture of an old route that runs along the southern edge of the North German

FIGURE 10.9 The castle that gives a name to the Finnish city of Savonlinna.
It was founded by the Swedes to command the narrows between Lakes Pihlajavesi and Haukivesi. Even today Russian and Finnish ships pass beside the fortress as they ply a major trade route. (Photo by the author, 1985.)

Plain and the road that follows the course of the Leine River through the Hercynian hills south of the city.

Seaport sites occur in two basic types. Those at or near the juncture of navigable rivers or estuaries and the coast include such cities as London, Hamburg, Bordeaux, and Gdańsk. In Southern Europe, however, the seasonality of precipitation and short length of many streams rendered rivers less useful for transportation. Great ports usually developed at the juncture of highways and the coast rather than at the marshy, shallow river mouths. Cádiz lies some 30 km (20 mi.) south of the mouth of the Guadalquivir, and Marseille is well to the east of the Rhône delta marshes in southern France. Other Mediterranean rivers such as the Po and Tevere (Tiber) also have no major ports at their mouths, in part because of silting.

Mercantile activity was by far the most significant of the economic functions served by the preindustrial city. However, other economic factors were occasionally determinant in siting, in particular mining and the operation of health resorts. Extraction of iron ore, copper, salt, silver, and other minerals or metals often gave rise to mining towns. In Germany and Austria, place names including *Salz* or *hall* ("salt"), *Eisen* ("iron"), *Gold,* and *Kupfer* ("copper"), as in Salzburg (Austria) and Kupferberg (Germany), indicate the present or former importance of mining. The German city of Halle still has a saline spring in its very center, where the settlement began in Celtic times. *Spa sites* include towns that developed around mineral or hot springs, long sought by Europeans for relief from any number of ailments. Spa towns often date to Roman times. These places typically bear names indicative of their function, including elements such as *bains, Bad(en),* or *bagni,* all of which mean "bath." Examples are Bad Pyrmont and Wiesbaden in Germany, Bagnoli ("bath") near Napoli in Italy, and Luxeuil-les-Bains in eastern France. The English city of Bath, known to the Romans as Aquae Sulis, has an ancient resort tradition.

Cityscapes

Europe's urban places reveal a distinctive morphology, or "cityscape," differing markedly from cities in North America and other overseas areas colonized by European emigrants. The urban *street pattern* represents one easily observable element of the cityscape.

In most European cities, the street pattern exhibits irregularity and a lack of planning. Streets meet at odd angles and seem to run every which way. Blocks take on the shape of parallelograms or triangles, and the visitor easily becomes disoriented. Automobile traffic moves with great difficulty, for thoroughfare avenues are rare (Figure 10.10). This haphazard street pattern resembles an irregular clustered farm village grown to a much larger size, and many European cities originally evolved from such unplanned farming settlements. The streets often follow the irregular outline of preexisting field patterns, as when the English city of Leeds in Yorkshire expanded to accommodate the growth of the Industrial Revolution. In parts of southern Europe, particularly Iberia, Arabic

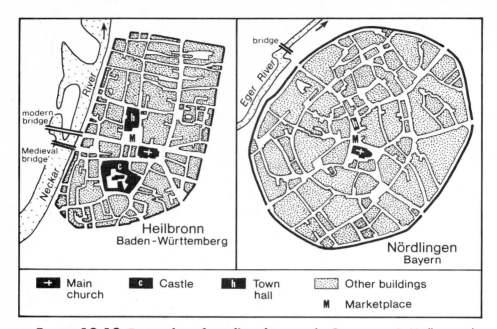

FIGURE 10.10 Examples of medieval towns in Germany. In Heilbronn, the castle-fortress (Deutschherrenhof) was the successor to an ancient Frankish fortress. The church, town hall, and marketplace shared the center of the city with the fortress. Heilbronn was heavily damaged in World War II. Nördlingen, where the old outer wall is still intact, has the maze of the streets typical of medieval towns. An earlier wall that was outgrown is clearly traced by the circular street. The overall street pattern is of the type referred to as *radial-concentric*. (Source: After Erwin A. Gutkind, *International History of City Development*, New York, USA: Free Press, 1964–1969.)

influence in street pattern produced a twisted maze with numerous dead ends, as in the old quarters of Toledo, Lisboa, and Sevilla.

Further complicating the irregularity of street pattern is the common practice of giving several different names to an avenue or street along its short, sinuous course. Often the name changes at almost every intersection. Over a length of only six blocks in München, for example, one reasonably straight street bears the names Maxburgstrasse, Löwengrube, Schäfflstrasse, Schrammerstrasse, and Hofgraben. Additional confusion comes from an unsystematic and unpredictable numbering of the houses and buildings.

Europeans have in general resisted recent attempts to modify the crazy-quilt pattern of streets and render it more suitable for motorized traffic flow. Wartime destruction leveled as much as 80 percent of the buildings in some German cities, providing an opportunity to revise street patterns in the central portions. Urban planners in western Germany wanted to lay out broader and straighter streets, ample parking space, and freeways, but their advice generally fell on deaf ears. Few western German cities acquired thoroughfares in the process of rebuilding. In contrast, the Dutch and British reconstruction of Rotterdam and Coventry pro-

FIGURE 10.11 The Champs Élysées, Paris, looking toward the Arch of Triumph. Such broad, straight avenues are rare in European cities. Most, including the Champs Élysées, were imposed on the earlier irregular street patterns of national capitals by royal decree in the eighteenth or nineteenth centuries. Many older buildings had to be torn down to permit such a revision. (Photo courtesy French Government Tourist Office.)

duced cities better adapted to the needs of the automobile. Even earlier, in the 1700s and 1800s, authorities in some larger cities created grand, straight ceremonial avenues or boulevards (Figure 10.11). Thousands of Parisians, for example, lost their homes through royal decree to make way for the Champs Elysées. These impressive avenues provide a marked contrast to the remainder of the street pattern.

The traffic problems created by the irregularity of street patterns become more critical because of the narrowness of thoroughfares and the scarcity of parking space. In the German city of Bremen, 84 percent of the total street mileage is less than 7 m (23 ft.) wide, a minimum width for handling heavy two-way traffic. Even so, Bremen is better off than the German cities of Lübeck, with 91 percent less than 7 m, and Oldenburg, in which only *1 percent* of all street mileage measures wider than that. Averages for 141 German cities indicate that 77 percent of the total urban street mileage remains too narrow for safe and efficient two-way traffic of any considerable volume. In consequence, most central-city streets carry only one-way traffic. Sizable districts have been designated as pedestrian zones, with automobiles banished. Pedestrians in the central section of a typical European city no longer feel intimidated by traffic or repelled by the visual blight of "machine space." Things seem drawn on a human scale and aesthetically pleasing.

In marked contrast to such an irregular street pattern are European cities laid out on a grid or checkerboard pattern. Some of these are quite ancient, for the Greeks, Etruscans, and Romans sometimes used the grid pattern, particularly in colonial towns. The Roman plan featured two axial thoroughfares that met in the center of the town at the market, flanked by lesser avenues that completed the grid. One can still see traces of the ancient pattern today in cities such as Pavia and Napoli in Italy, Köln in Germany, Zaragoza in Spain, and Chester in England (Figure 10.12). In later times the gridiron plan experienced a revival and served as the model for new towns founded by the Germans in east-central Europe, by the French kings in southern France, by the Swedish Empire in northern Europe, and by Renaissance town builders in northern Italy. Some of these newer planned cities display a striking plan (Figure 10.13). Often, however, the gridiron layout remains confined to the original part of the town, and suburbs added later reveal the more typically chaotic European street pattern (Figure 10. 14). Irregularities also often developed later in the original grid of Roman-founded towns, as at Pavia (Figure 10.12).

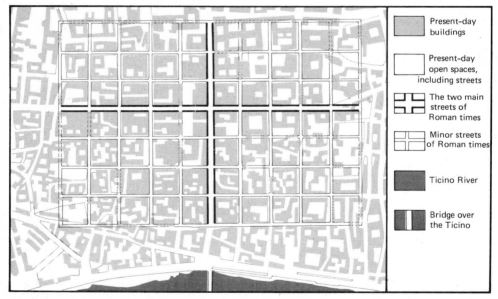

FIGURE 10.12 Survival of the Roman grid pattern in Pavia, Italy. To walk in the central section of modern Pavia (Roman Ticinum) is to be guided in the footsteps of the ancient Romans. The degree of survival of the Roman checkerboard pattern is quite remarkable, for most of the original streets are still in use after 20 centuries. The two main intersecting streets of Roman times have even maintained their dominance. Note how much less regular the streets are outside the old Roman core. Pavia is on the Ticino River south of Milano. (Source: After Erwin A. Gutkind, *International History of City Development*, New York, USA: Free Press, 1964–1969.)

The legend of the figure reads:

- Present-day buildings
- Present-day open spaces, including streets
- The two main streets of Roman times
- Minor streets of Roman times
- Ticino River
- Bridge over the Ticino

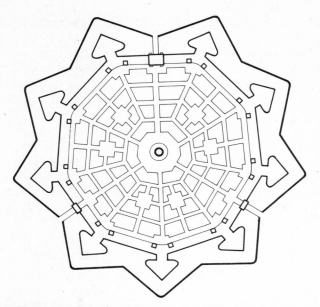

FIGURE 10.13 Central part of Palmanova, Italy, in the far eastern Po-Veneto Plain. Founded in 1593 during the Renaissance era, Palmanova displays a highly planned street pattern, as did most of the cities established after the end of the Middle Ages.

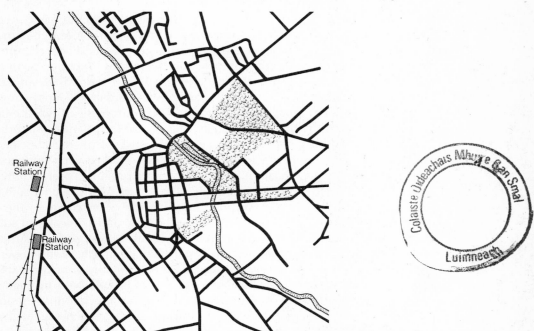

FIGURE 10.14 The city of Koszalin (formerly German Köslin) in Poland near the Baltic Sea. The original gridiron core of this German colonial city remains intact, though the later expansion reveals a less regular pattern.

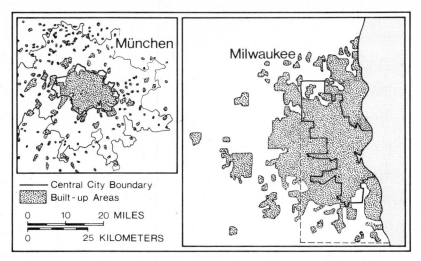

FIGURE 10.15 München, Germany, and Milwaukee, Wisconsin, metropolitan areas drawn to the same scale. The two urban areas each have about 1.5 million inhabitants, but notice how much more compact the built-up area of München is. (Source: After Lutz Holzner, in *Research Profile*, Milwaukee, USA: University of Wisconsin-Milwaukee, Graduate School, 9:2 (1986), 18.)

Another morphological measure of the European city is the *degree of compactness.* In comparison to North American and Australian urban centers, Europeans cities of comparable population cover much less geographical area (Figure 10.15). A foreign visitor often gains the impression that European cities seem smaller than they actually are in terms of population. In 1960, for example, single-family detached homes accounted for only 16 percent of all urban residences in western Germany. Since then, detached housing has risen dramatically in the cities of Western Europe, but without completely sacrificing compactness. Suburban lots tend to be considerably smaller than in Canada or the United States, and front yards are generally absent. Eastern European cities retain a very low percentage of single-family homes. Throughout Europe, many urbanites prefer to live close to the center of town, where the old city core serves as a place to gather after work, to stroll, and to dine. Apartment housing allows proximity to the central city, and most urban cores suffer little blight, decay, and crime. Even suburban housing, in countries as diverse as Iceland, Spain, the Czech Republic, and Latvia, often takes the form of high-rise apartment complexes. On the periphery of most European cities lie tiny garden allotments for the apartment dwellers, serving in effect as their "backyards." In smaller towns, both in Eastern and Western Europe, privately owned, detached housing appears much more commonly than in the cities (Figure 10.16). In European cities the medieval custom of combining residence and place of work survives to a surprising degree. Bakers, butchers, or restaurant owners often live above their shops. Most city dwellers reside at least within walking or cycling range of their place of employment, though commuting is now common in Western Europe.

FIGURE 10.16 Single-family detached private housing in the small Swedish mill town and service center of Torsby, in Värmland province. Surrounded by a well-kept, fenced lawn and garden, this home is typical of smaller urban centers in Europe. (Photo by the author, 1985.)

The *skyline* or visual profile of the European city also presents a distinctive appearance. North Americans, accustomed to a skyline dominated by huge high-rise buildings, or skyscrapers, at the center of the city, with progressively lower structures toward the suburbs, find the European city inverted. The urban skyline of Europe features a central skyline still dominated by church spires, the venerable hilltop fortress, or some special landmark such as the Eiffel Tower (Figure 10.8). The central cities of Europe typically contain historic buildings of considerable age, erected before modern structural technology permitted great height. Edifices of more than five or six stories remain uncommon.

Even when catastrophes destroy the old urban cores, Europeans generally rebuild them as before. World War II, for example, altered few skylines. A comparison of photographs of prewar and postwar München—80 percent of which was destroyed by bombing—reveals a striking similarity. As in the reestablishment of the old, pre-automobile street patterns, Europeans simply revived the vanished cities of prewar times. Perhaps the most remarkable re-creation took place in the former German Baltic port city of Danzig, present Gdańsk, Polish since 1945. The German population of the severely damaged city was expelled,

but the Poles then proceeded to spend huge sums of money to produce a duplicate of the old German Hanseatic city. Their attention to detail in reconstruction
was simply astounding. The end product is a museum town from another age,
but Poland solidified, with time, effort, and money, a valid claim to a city that
Germans and Russians destroyed.

Beyond the central city, with its low skyline profile, lie rings of taller buildings, including huge apartment blocks. High-rise commercial skyscrapers have
appeared in some urban peripheries, presenting precisely the opposite arrangement than one finds in an American city. Taller buildings form a doughnut-
shaped rim in the European city, surrounding the low-profile center (Figure
10.17).

Urban Zones

The preceding section on urban morphology implies a distinctive zonation within European cities. Age, continued growth, governmental policy, and city planning produced a compartmentalization unique to European urbanism.

FIGURE 10.17 Paris, looking westward from the Eiffel Tower. An American
would mistake this as a view toward the center of the city, whereas in reality the modern
high-rise buildings stand in Paris' outer ring. (Photo by the author, 1978).

As suggested earlier, the center of the European city consists of the *preindustrial core*, the mercantile city of past times, including all districts that formerly lay within the ramparts and walls. Remnants of these walls often survive, marking the outer limits of the core. The famous Porta Nigra ("Black Gate") in the German city of Trier is a Roman survival, while the Holstentor ("Holstein Gate") at Lübeck survives as a remnant of medieval walls. In some instances, the entire circuit of city walls remains to enclose the old core. Lugo in Spanish Galicia retains its Roman walls and Ávila, in the Castilian heartland of Spain, boasts a medieval ring of walls and gates that ranks among Europe's finest (Figure 10.5). Óbidos in Portugal, Carcassonne in France, Dinkelsbühl in Germany, and Ródos in Greece offer other examples of surviving or rebuilt town walls. More often, the walls no longer exist, their place taken by a ring street and a string of parks. Riga in Latvia and Frankfurt-am-Main fit this description, as do many other places.

Within the old preindustrial core, a number of venerable buildings and squares survive, including an impressive cathedral, bearing witness to the extraordinary importance and vitality of Christianity in the Middle Ages. Even as early as the era of classical Greece, municipal pride in public buildings and religious edifices was one of the principal traits that distinguished townsfolk from residents of farm villages, and citizens bore the large expense involved in cathedral construction with little complaint. Many of these churches, such as Notre Dame on the Île de la Cité in Paris, San Marco in Venèzia, the Köln Cathedral, St. Stephans in Wien, the magnificent cathedral at Chartres, southwest of Paris, and Santa María in Burgos, Spain, rank among the great architectural treasures of the world.

If the city served as the residence of a royal family, the urban core usually includes a palace or fortress. Examples include the Louvre in Paris, the Hofburg in Wien, Edinburgh Castle, and the Palazzo Ducale in Venèzia. In some cities, the royal residence in the medieval core was identical with the feudal stronghold on high ground, which had originally attracted urban settlement. In many instances, royalty abandoned these residences in the central city to build splendid new palaces in the suburbs. Versailles supplanted the Louvre in Paris and set the standard for other European royalty. The Hapsburgs of Austria built Schönbrunn Palace on the outer fringe of Wien and the Wittelsbachs of Bayern in southern Germany ordered the construction of the beautiful Nymphenburg Palace on the western outskirts of München.

The urban core area centers on the old marketplace, which often lies in front of the cathedral (Figure 10.18). These public squares are often very impressive, ringed with arcades, as at the Plaza Mayor in Salamanca, Spain, and decorated with plantings or fountains, as at the Prato della Valle in Padova, Italy. Most cities have several such fine squares, each with a distinctive character and function. Near or on one of these squares stands the town hall, housing the city government.

In an economic sense, the urban core serves a great number of purposes, retaining the multifunctional character of medieval times. It houses a variety of small retail stores, cafés, restaurants, multifamily residences, and workshoplike factories of craftsmen workers. The distinction between residential, industrial, and commercial zones is rather weak, with a great deal of areal interweaving.

FIGURE 10.18 The arcaded town square is the pride of Novy Jičín, in Morava province, Czech Republic. Commanding the strategic Moravian Gate trade route, Novy Jičín, founded by Germans as Neutitschein, retains much of its preindustrial core. (Photo by the author, 1982.)

Gild houses of the medieval crafts still stand in many preindustrial urban cores, as does the bourse, a trading hall for merchants. Institutional functions also remain common in the central city, including governmental agencies and museums. Indeed, some well-preserved urban central areas have become virtual outdoor museums, bypassed by economic activity and increasingly depopulated, though this trend seems to be reversing. Some central-city dwellers complain they cannot be expected to live in an unchanging, romanticized setting of past times. The crumbling architectural heritage of the past is expensive to maintain and difficult to adjust to the modern age. Venèzia, where a substantial part of the city forms a historic district, provides an extreme example. Plagued by flooding, decay, and pollution, Venèzia is already somewhat of a ghost town during the winter. Its population has declined from 137,000 in 1961 to only 88,700 today. *Façadism* has provided another increasingly popular solution. Outwardly, buildings look much as they did 500 years ago, preserving the historic appearance of the preindustrial city, but inwardly a thoroughly modern remodeling has occurred. As a result, these buildings are rarely what they seem to be.

Though some European central cities remain choked by automobile traffic, perhaps most notoriously Roma, most others have taken major steps to restrict motorist access. Pedestrian zones have proliferated since about 1970, parking space has been drastically reduced, bicycle routes provided, and mass transit upgraded. Zürich recently eliminated 10,000 central-city parking spaces, and voters in Amsterdam in 1992 approved a plan to eliminate most automobile traffic in the entire old quarter of the city. In Freiburg, Germany, a leader in the pedestrian zone movement, the use of cars for intracity trips dropped from 60 percent in 1975 to 46 percent by 1993. In nearby Heidelberg, nearly a quarter of all non-pedestrian traffic now moves by bicycle.

Surrounding the preindustrial core in the European city lies the *inner ring*. It began as a slum outside the city walls—in French the *faubourg,* or "false city." In time slum hovels gave way to more substantial buildings as the city grew, and some fine neighborhoods developed. In function, the inner ring remains predominantly residential, as opposed to the retail/institutional focus of the city center. This zone is sometimes called the "preindustrial suburb." The inner ring frequently contains the railroad stations, which ring the periphery of the old medieval core. The tight clustering of venerated old structures made it impossible for railroad lines to penetrate the interior. Such large cities as Paris and London have a circle of rail terminals, and the stations typically bear the name of the major city that lies on their rail route: In Paris one finds the Gare de Lyon, the "station of Lyon," at the terminus of the rail line leading out to that city in the Rhône-Saône Valley, the Gare St. Lazare, the Gare d'Orléans, and so on. In many instances, one suburban railroad station serves as the main one, where trains for all destinations may be taken, but sometimes the traveler must choose correctly among five or more stations to find the right train.

The Industrial Revolution added a *middle ring* to the European city, mainly in the 1800s. A dingy halo of factories and huge workers' apartment blocks or row houses, the middle ring, often called the "industrial suburbs," became by far the largest part of the typical European city, dwarfing the older core and inner ring.

It housed the burgeoning population that made Europe dominantly urbanized, as commoners finally became urbanites. A controlled-access perimeter highway now often marks the outer limits of the middle ring.

Since about 1950, many European cities, especially in the west, have added an *outer ring* or "postindustrial suburb." It consists of a loose assemblage of low-density residences dominated by detached single-family houses, modern factories devoted to high-tech industry, and firms specializing in data gathering and processing. Some planned satellite towns also appear in the outer ring, as do the garden plots of the inner-city population. In spite of the low density of building, the outer ring often contains American-inspired glass-and-steel high-rise commercial structures (Figure 10.17). Access to the city center by mass transit is normally available. Typically, the outer ring developed in segments and usually remains incomplete. In London, for example, (where the outer ring lies beyond a zoned, largely open "green belt") a high-class residential fringe began taking shape in the western periphery by the 1950s and has since spread clockwise around to the northeast. In East Anglia, where much of London's outer belt growth is now centered, the urbanized area increased by 14 percent between 1969 and 1988.

Human Patterns

At best, a study of urban site, morphology, and zones reveal the mere skeleton of the European city. We must now flesh out the urban image by considering vivid human patterns, the mosaic of neighborhoods. The European city is decidedly heterogeneous culturally, racially, and socially. That has been true since the time of ancient Greece, when the first European urbanites segregated themselves along tribal lines.

Religion long acted as one of the most powerful forces segregating people within the towns of Europe. In Roman cities, evidence strongly suggests that Christians occupied certain neighborhoods early in the diffusion of their faith. The term *ghetto*, to designate a Jewish neighborhood, derives from medieval Venèzia, and most European towns of the Middle Ages had separate Jewish districts, reminders of which are still seen in names such as the German *Judengasse* ("Street of the Jews") or Sevilla's *Calle Judaría* ("Street of the Jewish Quarter"). Even today, residential segregation along religious lines can be seen in Belfast and Londonderry, Northern Ireland, where one finds Roman Catholic and Protestant neighborhoods (Figure 3.14). Nor is such segregation confined to cities where religious strife is common. Jews in the United Kingdom have formed suburban concentrations in some cities.

Linguistic differences also traditionally separated people within European cities, a practice most common in areas of speech diversity. Brno, in the Czech province of Morava, had a medieval residential pattern in which Germans lived in the northern part of the city and Czechs in the south. Towns such as Armagh and Downpatrick in Northern Ireland developed distinct quarters in the seventeenth century, as is indicated by the survival of English Street, Irish Street, and

Scotch Street. In medieval Caernarvon, Wales, the portion of the town enclosed by walls housed the English, while Welsh clustered in the faubourg just outside the walls.

The huge immigration of foreigners to European cities since about 1950 greatly increased cultural diversity and potential for ethnic and racial neighborhoods. Some 15 million foreigners lived in northwestern Europe by 1980, nearly all concentrated in cities. Frankfurt-am-Main had a population over 20 percent foreign by then. Most of these immigrants found homes in the decaying residences of the preindustrial core and inner ring, often occupying apartments abandoned by natives who moved to the periphery.

Oddly, few ethnic neighborhoods and ghettoes developed from this influx. True, when viewed on a citywide perspective, European urban centers do reveal an ethnic patterning. In Paris, for example, foreigners cluster in the northeastern quadrant, including parts of both the inner and middle rings (Figure 10.19). Nürnberg in Germany displays a similar pattern (Figure 10.20). However, a closer look at almost any Western European city shows that foreign ethnic segregation normally occurs at the level of individual apartment houses, rarely at the scale of city blocks, and never at a district level. In Brussels, for example, no area the size of a census tract has a majority consisting of a single foreign group (Figure 10.21). Tiny, multiple concentrations of individual foreign ethnic groups remains the rule (see Figure 5.9). If standard statistical measures of segregation are applied, equally surprising results appear, such as the fact that Greeks have a higher index of residential clustering than do Turks in German cities.

Clearly, forces other than ethnicity underlie most human patterning in Europe's cities. Socioeconomic class appears to be far more important in determining where people live. Traditionally, the most expensive and prestigious residences lay nearest the city center, and, as earlier suggested, the early peripheral faubourgs began as slums. In other words, the European city displayed a geographical pattern precisely the reverse of what would seem normal to Americans.

Within the better sections of the preindustrial city, segregation often occurred along occupational lines. Surviving street names again provide clues. In München, for example, we find the Ledererstrasse ("Street of the Leather-Workers"), Färbergraben ("Street of the Cloth-Dyers"), Sattlerstrasse ("Street of the Saddlers"), and others. Such names referred to the artisans' places of work and usually also their residences. In medieval Lübeck, merchants lived to the west of a main north-south street, while artisans resided to the east. Ordinary laborers lived outside the town walls.

Residential neighborhoods in European cities today remain rooted in class. The clustering of foreign laborers in certain districts speaks of their socioeconomic status rather than their ethnic background, and that explains their near-chaotic mixing. After World War II, a more Americanlike pattern began to emerge, in which prestigious neighborhoods developed in the outer ring. For example, in present-day Liverpool, England, persons engaged in the professions, business owners, and administrators live in residential areas farthest from the city center, while unskilled and semiskilled laborers reside in and near the preindustrial core.

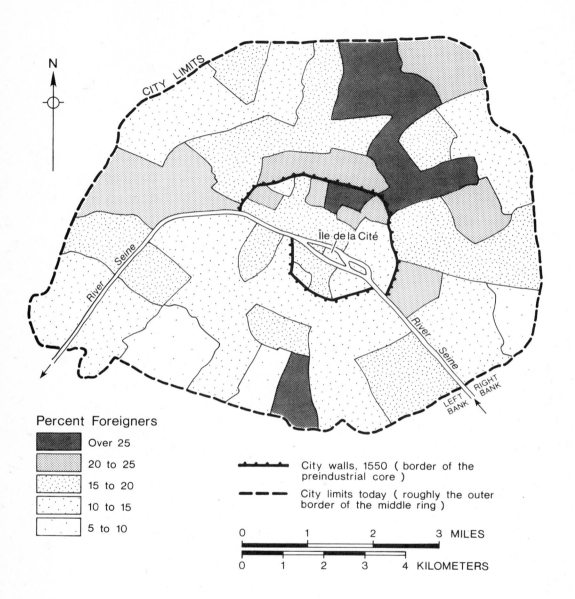

FIGURE 10.19 The resident foreign population within the city limits of Paris in the 1980s, by city district and shown as a percentage of total population. At this map scale, European cities such as Paris seem to have ethnic neighborhoods, but the appearance is misleading. The city limits of Paris include only the preindustrial core plus the inner and middle rings. The Île de la Cité is the original nucleus of Paris and the walls of 1500 mark the limits of the preindustrial core. (Source: Modified from Paul White, in Glebe/O'Loughlin, 1987, 193.).

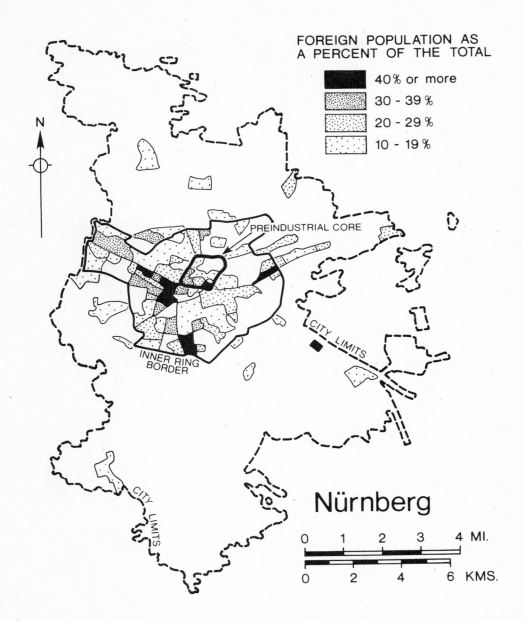

FOREIGN POPULATION AS
A PERCENT OF THE TOTAL

- 40% or more
- 30 - 39 %
- 20 - 29 %
- 10 - 19 %

N

PREINDUSTRIAL CORE

CITY LIMITS

INNER RING
BORDER

CITY LIMITS

Nürnberg

0   1   2   3   4 MI.

0   2   4   6 KMS.

**FIGURE 10.20 Nürnberg, Germany: foreigners as a percentage of popula-
tion** by districts in the 1980s. Turks formed the largest foreign element. Note the distribution as it relates to the urban zones of preindustrial core (*Altstadt*), inner ring, and middle
ring. Most foreigners in western European cities live in the inner ring. Overall, Nürnberg is
11% foreign. Compare this to Figure 10.19. (Source: Modified from Jones, 1983, 124.)

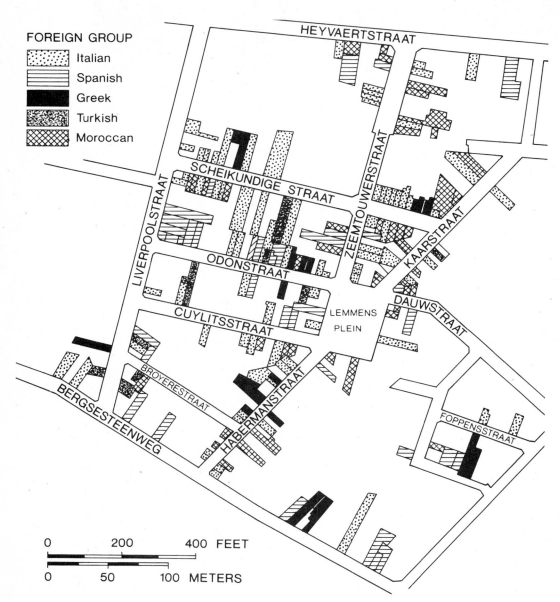

FIGURE 10.21 Distribution of selected foreign groups in a part of the Rosée neighborhood, Brussels, by apartment house, in the middle 1970s. Unshaded units were either nonresidential or inhabited by other groups, including Belgians. Note that the foreign groups lived mixed on every street, rather than in ethnic neighborhoods. This pattern remains typical of cities in northwestern Europe. (Source: Adapted from Christian Kesteloot, in Glebe/O'Loughlin, 1987, 228.)

As earlier suggested, the "Americanization" of European cities seems to be ending. *Gentrification*—the upgrading of older, decaying central-city and inner-ring residential areas for occupancy by upper-income people—is far more common in Europe than in the United States. Rather than continuing to explode spatially into surrounding rural areas while the inner city goes to ruin, Europe's city dwellers appear to be turning inward and "recycling" older neighborhoods.

Gentrification acts to displace the lower classes. Conflicts inevitably result. Perhaps the group most adversely affected consists of urban squatters—homeless people who illegally take up residence in derelict, empty buildings. Called *kraakers* in the Netherlands and *squats* in Britain, this preponderantly young, anti-establishment group began seizing abandoned central-city buildings in the 1960s. Amsterdam, London, Hamburg, West Berlin, and København became the major scenes of urban squatting. The movement peaked in the 1980s and has since largely succumbed to police pressure and gentrification. Some squatters relocated to formerly Communist cities after 1990, especially East Berlin and Praha.

Types of Cities

Preceding sections of this chapter perhaps led you to believe that a European type of city exists, and to a certain degree that is true. Some features occur widely, such as the presence of a preindustrial core and the prestige attached to the old town market square. Still, each European city possesses its own distinct character and personality. Many aspects of European urbanism vary regionally, and we can discern different types of cities. The classification presented here consists of five regional types: British, Mediterranean, Central European, Nordic, and post-Socialist cities (Figure 10.22).

The **British city,** more than others in Europe, resembles the urban centers of the United States, though differences also exist. A high rate of owner-occupied housing and detached or semidetached, single-family residences, as well as flight to the suburbs of the outer ring characterize both British and American cities. Inner urban decay and blight, coupled with poverty, diminishing services, and crime, afflict all the major British conurbations. Britons devote less attention to the preservation of inner-city historic structures than do most Europeans. Some experts now speak of urban "decline" and "crisis" in Britain. Journalist and former Londoner Peter Kellner said the "downward spiral of decay" caused him to leave the city, and he and others lament the pollution, filth, eroding tax base, decaying infrastructure, rat infestations, "squats," and widespread vagrancy. As a result, counterurbanization has worked more vigorously in Britain than the rest of Europe. Greater London's population, excluding the outer ring, dropped from over 8 million in the 1950s to 6.5 million at the most recent census. Counterurbanization also feeds upon the British perception that the "real" England lies in the countryside and that the city is an anomaly and aberration. Suburban expansion causes the British city to be less compact than normal for Europe and produces a steep population-density gradient from core to periphery. Americans find all these British urban conditions familiar, but continental

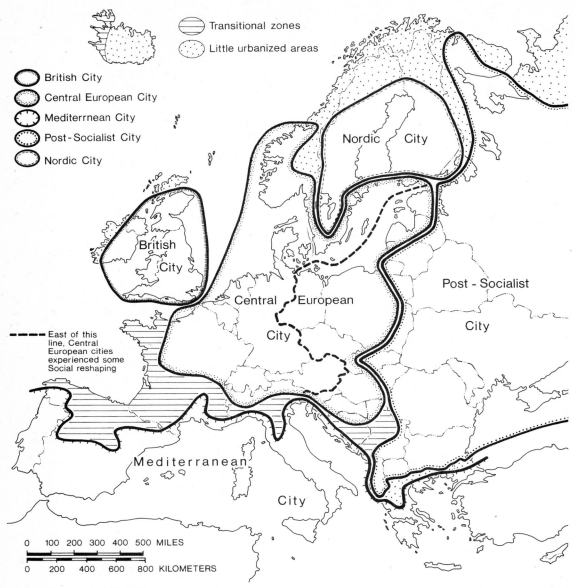

FIGURE 10.22 Distribution of European city types. Considerable overlapping of types occurs but is not shown, as for example where Socialist influences partially reshaped many Central European cities in the Communist era. (Sources: Based in part upon Leontidou 1990, 4; Hamilton 1978; French/Hamilton 1979; Karger/Werner 1982; and Lawless/Raban 1986.)

Europeans regard them as odd and generally undesirable. Clearly, the British city represents a distinctive urban type within Europe.

At the same time, the British city has experienced far more inner-area gentrification than its American counterpart, and the government has become quite active in the effort to stem decay. In Belfast, for example, the proportion of "unfit" housing declined from 25 to 8 percent between 1978 and 1992, largely as a result of public expenditures on urban regeneration. The walled inner city of Londonderry (or Derry, as Irish separatists prefer), has recently undergone refurbishing. The once-blighted East End district of Glasgow became transformed in the 1980s, and many similar projects are presently under way. In urban regeneration, the British city occupies an intermediate position between those of the United States and western Europe.

The **Central European city,** sometimes called the *Germanic* type, characterizes the core of the culture area (Figure 10.22). In origin, the Central European city reflects mainly the period of urban genesis led by the Germans during the feudal Middle Ages. The early attainment of city-state status, which allowed a quasidemocratic form of government to take root in the Germanic cities while the countryside remained under feudal despotism, fostered a profound sense of urban superiority and a strong antirural bias. One is either a burgher or a *bauer* (farmer). City governments, visually represented by the town hall, or *Rathaus,* retain considerable importance. Some cities even preserve a vestige of their former independent city-state rule, as for example Hamburg and Bremen, which enjoy provincial status within Germany, and Luxembourg, which remains in effect a free city-state. Central European citizens attach great importance to the preindustrial core, the root of urban self-government and democracy, and as a result central-city decay has never approached the British levels (Figure 10.23). The preindustrial core, wreathed by parks and remnant walls, remains a prestigious place to live, and historic preservation and renewal projects, including abundant façadism, typify the Central European city. The central public square retains great importance. Counterurbanism, blunted by the appeal and snobbery of the city and the antirural bias, proved weaker than in Britain and suburbanization is now apparently diminishing. In housing density, the Central European city falls between the extremes of the British urban area, dominated by single-family residences, and the cities of Southern and Eastern Europe, where apartment housing prevails. Urban planning and land-use zoning enjoy popular support and have greatly contributed to the renewal, aesthetic appeal, and liveability of Germanic cities. The pedestrian zone movement began here and still enjoys its greatest acceptance in Central Europe.

In some areas the problems associated with British cities have taken root in Central Europe, but they are aggressively combatted. Economically depressed industrial cities in Germany's Ruhr and the coalfields of the Belgian-French border region offer examples of blight and decay, as do many cities in the east that long remained under Communist rule. Even these can now expect a renewal, or re-Germanization. Dresden, Schwerin, and many other blighted eastern cities are being transformed in the 1990s.

In the **Mediterranean city,** a greater spontaneity of growth and development occurred, with minimal attention to urban planning or zoning. The Germanic

FIGURE 10.23 The preindustrial core of the small Hessian city of Weilburg, on the Lahn River in Germany. A typical Central European city, Weilburg perches on an incised meander of the river and the urban core retains its royal palace, cathedral, and town hall. Many people still reside in the central city, though new suburbs appear in the distance. Little evidence of urban decay can be found in such places. (Photo by the author, 1991.)

rural/urban dichotomy is absent in Mediterranean civilization and the transition from the city to the countryside appears more gradually. Since classical times, many farmers and rural laborers have resided in Mediterranean cities, prompting many such places to be labelled *agrotowns*. Less compartmentalization and social segregation occur, though both are now increasing. Small workshops are scattered through the city, and mixed land-use reflects the lack of zoning. Owners more typically live above their place of business than in the British or Central European cities, and most other people live close to their place of work. A patchwork of economic activity and a mixing of the middle class and workers characterizes much of the city. Inhabitants tend to view the city rather than the home as the principal venue for life, and as a result more people are to be seen in the streets, plazas, and shops. A central business district in the British/Germanic sense does not exist, and small shops appear even in the finer residential neighborhoods. To the Germanic eye, the Mediterranean city seems disorderly, but the people of the south see their cities instead as places of "light, heat, and spontaneity," a welcome contrast to the "cold, disciplined" cities beyond the Alps.

Mediterranean cities represent the most compact type in Europe, with very high residential densities and virtually no development of an outer ring. High-status residential areas lie instead in the inner ring, adjacent to the preindustrial core and linked to it by a fine boulevard (Figure 10.24). While the old walled part of the town retains great prestige and swarms with life, it is often largely given over to institutional functions, especially schools, museums, churches, and convents. A failure to restrict automobile access to the center creates a nightmare of traffic congestion, noise, and air pollution in the preindustrial core, and the pedestrian zone concept remains in its infancy here.

The periphery of the Mediterranean city is the most stigmatized section, in contrast to the British model. Industries are concentrated there, as are poor people living in spartan high-rise apartment blocks or illegal squatter slums of self-built huts reminiscent of Third World countries.

Geographers have distinguished different subtypes of Mediterranean cities, and some feel the larger category is too inclusive to be very useful. One expert argues for the existence of the "South Italian city," while another presents a case for the "Spanish city." All such proposals have merit and remind us again of the great internal diversity of the European culture area (Figure 10.24).

The **post-Socialist city** represents a legacy of Communism and dominates Eastern Europe, particularly those countries weakly urbanized prior to the Communist era. In the Soviet Union in 1926, for example, only 18 percent of the population lived in cities, but by 1989 the proportion there had reached 66 percent. In such countries, Socialist doctrine shaped urban development in diverse ways, and the legacy will persist long into the future. Under Communism, the government controlled urban development, including the demand for and supply of housing. Land, in effect, had no monetary value.

The ideal Socialist city would have abolished socioeconomic residential segregation; guaranteed availability of public services such as child care; provided abundant public-green space; offered equal, if rudimentary, access to all consumer goods; and created self-sufficient, small neighborhoods where residents lived, worked, and shopped. In many respects, Eastern European cities reflect these Socialist goals, particularly in Russia, Ukraine, Belarus, and the Balkans. The post-Socialist city resembles a collection of separate towns jammed together and bound by mass transit. Population densities remain remarkably high in comparison to cities in most of the remainder of Europe, and the normal gradient toward lesser densities on the urban periphery is retarded and in some cities even reversed, with an outer rim of higher concentration of people. All of Moskva has a population density comparable to that of *central* London. A far less marked spatial difference of function occurs within the city than in the West, including a much more even spread of industries throughout the urban area, a phenomenon associated with the absence of cash values for land. Social, economic, and ethnic segregation by districts or sectors is diminished. Ghettoes do not exist. Workers in a particular industry might be segregated in response to a desire to minimize the journey to work. Public mass transportation prevails and the automobile remains a less important means of moving about the city than in Western countries. Russian subways are among the best in the world. Even those workers who inhabit the characteristic belt of prefabricated high-rise apartments, grouped in neighborhoods of 2000 to 5000 people, enjoy easy access to the city center. In comparison to the West, a higher proportion of the urban workforce finds employment in manufacturing, construction, and transportation, with

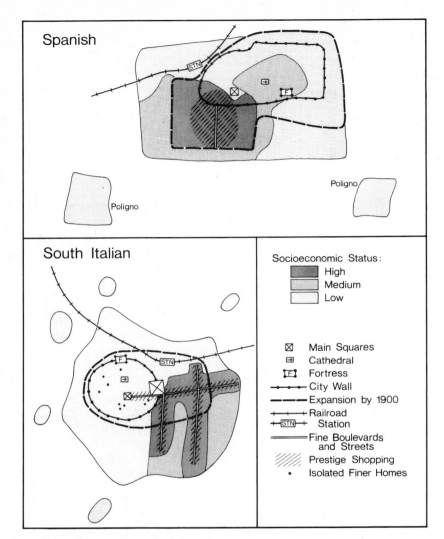

FIGURE 10.24 Models of the typical Spanish and southern Italian city both are examples of the Mediterranean city type, but they are sufficiently distinctive to be considered regional subtypes. The outlying clusters, called *polignos* in Spain, are recent laborer apartment blocks or squatter settlements. In the southern Italian type, the core has a maze of dead-end streets and remains largely residential, while in the Spanish type, most of the core is now institutional and has connecting streets. (Sources: After Ford 1985, 268; Sabelberg 1986.)

lower percentages in trade, administration, and services. The confused Westerner still hunts long and hard for a gasoline station, café, or shop.

Post-Socialist cities remain dominantly industrial centers devoted to manufacturing, reflecting one of the principal goals of Communism—to convert rural peasant societies into proletariat-based industrial powers. One side effect was to produce very high levels of environmental pollution in almost every Eastern European city. The rapid collapse of the manufacturing sector in the post-Socialist era brought economic crisis to nearly all urban centers.

Sinister forces also helped shape the Socialist city and will long leave a visible legacy in post-Socialist times. Authorities sought to convey the power of the state and the insignificance of the individual person. Governmental buildings of overwhelming size, reflecting a monumentality in architecture, provide one example. Oversized public squares, in which mass political rallies could be held appear gargantuan, cold, and empty at other times. Worst of all, the cult of personality associated with some Communist dictatorships, most notoriously in Romania and Albania, allowed megalomaniacal leaders massively to reshape cities, often destroying much of the beauty from earlier eras. The pre-Communist city disappeared from central Bucureşti, and the imprint of a personality cult will long linger there.

At the same time, infrastructure decayed alarmingly in Socialist cities. Shoddily constructed new buildings and inadequately maintained older ones caused the socialist city to appear drab and to suffer from rotting of the urban fabric. The post-Socialist city inherited all of these deficiencies, and the cost of correcting them lies beyond the means of the successor states.

Still, privatization will undoubtedly alter the post-Socialist cities of Eastern Europe, though initial progress has in places been unexpectedly slow. A July 1991 decree provided for privatization of apartments in Russian cities. In Moskva, the Russian capital, some 25 percent of all housing had been privatized by 1993 as had nearly 5000 businesses, mainly those engaged in consumer services such as retailing. The post-Socialist city should be regarded as a type in transition, one that will remain distinctive but whose future configuration is uncertain.

A special case is provided by those cities, most of the Central European type, which experienced a half-century or so of Communist rule, cities such as Warszawa, Budapest, and Leipzig. These cities bore the strong earlier imprint of capitalism and Central European urban culture, reflecting a long tradition and were fully developed cities at the time of the Communist takeover. Utopian Socialist ideals never completely or even largely transformed them, for the old capitalist legacy placed constraints, just as Socialism does, on the post-Socialist city. Communism did retard low density suburbanization, but socioeconomic segregation survived. In Warszawa, for example, an early Communist-directed residential mixing of social groups in the central city following World War II steadily gave way during the following 40 years to a reemergence of class-based neighborhoods. The traditional Central European veneration of living in and near the preindustrial core also survived, partly and ironically in response to the Communist-directed reconstruction of the bomb-damaged core to its prewar appearance. Budapest, too, became an odd amalgamation of Central European and Socialist urbanism (Figure 10.25). Berlin, long divided into Socialist and capitalist halves, though the entire preindustrial core lay in the Communist-ruled part, presents a unique situation today after German reunification. Rapid change, even metamorphosis, grips the former East Berlin. But, then, change has always been the hallmark of European culture.

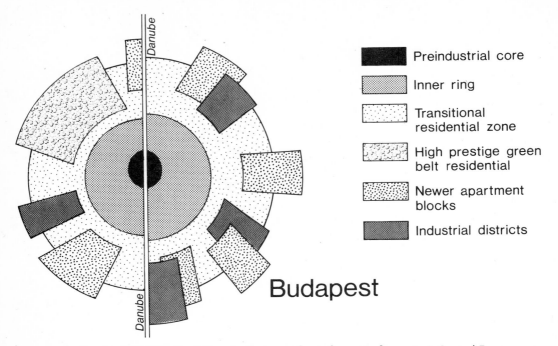

FIGURE 10.25 A stylized scheme of modern Budapest. A Central European type of city in heritage, Budapest reflects that tradition in its preindustrial core and inner ring. A Socialist city from the late 1940s until 1990, Budapest accordingly has peripheral apartment blocks located adjacent to industrial complexes. The high-prestige green belt represents an anomaly for a Socialist city and reflects the significant inroads made by capitalism in Hungary beginning in the late 1960s. (Source: Adapted from Enyedi/Szirmai, 1992, 99.)

A minor type, the **Nordic city**, occurs mainly in Sweden and Finland. More recent in origin and usually founded under Swedish rule, these cities generally date from the 1600s and 1700s, the era of the Swedish Empire. A grid pattern of streets invariably characterizes the core of the Nordic city, though often that pattern breaks down in the suburbs (Figure 10.26). A waterside site was unfailingly chosen for the Nordic city, whether marine, riverine, or lakeside. Of the various European urban types, the Nordic city is the least compact, with broad avenues, abundant freestanding single-family residences, and spacious open areas. In fact, some Nordic cities consist of several different clusters separated by green space or even farmland, heightening the dispersed urban character (Figure 10.27). Trees grow more abundantly along the urban streets, revealing the strong northern love of forests. The Nordic city is modest in size, usually having less than 100,000 inhabitants, and the local industries typically consist of small firms manufacturing high-quality, even luxury products. In spite of their size, Nordic cities offer an impressive array of amenities, from museums, sport complexes, and hospitals to symphony orchestras and bicycle paths. Surely these rank among the most appealing and liveable cities in the world.

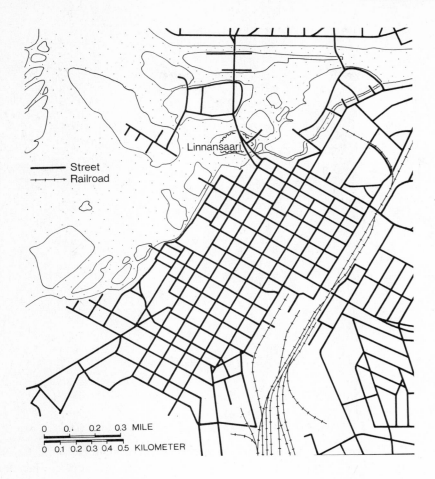

FIGURE 10.26 Oulu, a Nordic city of Finland. Clearly preserved in its central section are the gridiron plan and public squares laid out by its Swedish founders. The city dates from 1605 and was originally protected by the island fortress on Linnansaari.

The Urban Network

Site, morphology, and internal cultural/economic patterning, while essential geographical attributes of cities, do not complete the spatial analysis of urbanism. The distribution of cities must also be considered, especially their location relative to each other in an **urban network**.

    In spite of the fact that Europe forms the most highly urbanized culture area in the world, *megalopolis* development remains uncommon there. A megalopolis constitutes a supercity that forms when adjacent urban areas grow until they coalesce. The region between Boston and Washington, D.C., in the United States is a megalopolis. In Europe, because of better land-use planning and greenbelt preservation, megalopolis formation remained less common. Among the few examples are *Randstad Holland* (Figure 10.28), with a collective population of

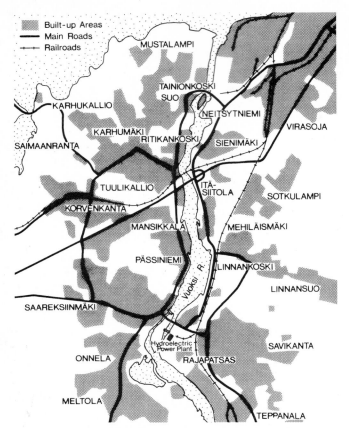

Figure 10.27 Imatra, a Finnish city consisting of scattered clusters. The clusters are loosely focused on the hydroelectric plant at the famous Imatra rapids, where the waters of the Finnish Lake Plateau escape through the Salpausselkä moraine wall. Imatra is a small city of 34,000 population.

close to 6 million; the *Ruhr-Rhein* in western Germany, containing three metropolitan areas of over 1 million population and an additional three with more than 500,000; the *Donbas* of eastern Ukraine; and *Lancs-Yorks* in the old industrial heart of England in the triangle formed by Sheffield, Leeds, and Liverpool. Even these megalopolises retain more open space than would be expected, due to rigorous zoning policies. The Randstad Holland, for example, remains doughnut-shaped, due to a largely successful plan to keep the center, called the "Green Heart," open (Figure 10.28). By and large, European megalopolises owe their existence to concentrations of manufacturing industry.

Some geographers join the Randstad to the Ruhr-Rhein and intervening cities such as Brussels and Antwerpen to form one massive multinational megalopolis along the axis of the lower Rhine. Others point to a banana-shaped urban core of Europe, reaching from Liverpool and Leeds through London and the Rhenish lands on to Milano and Torino in the Po-Veneto Plain. These more inclu-

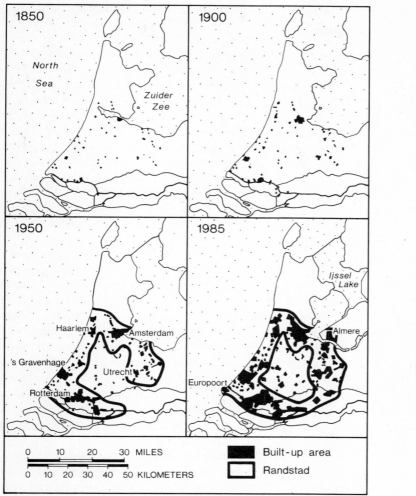

FIGURE 10.28 Development of Randstad Holland, a megalopolis in the Netherlands. Land-use planning and zoning are being employed to keep the central area, or
"doughnut hole," open, but suburban development is encroaching. Note the use of some reclaimed Zuider Zee polderland for expansion of the Randstad. (Sources: After *Randstad
Holland,* published by Information and Documentation Centre for the Geography of the
Netherlands, Utrecht and 's Gravenhage, NL, 1980, 14; van Wessep et al., 1993;
Wrathall and Carrick, 258; and Ottens.)

sive groupings overextend the concept of megalopolis, though they are useful in
restressing the core/periphery pattern of urbanization in Europe.

    If traditional heavy-industry manufacturing, in the absence of land-use plan-
ning, tended to generate megalopolises, the *service* functions of cities work to
produce an orderly network of regularly spaced urban places. These services,
forming a *tertiary* sector of the economy (see Chapter 12), include a variety of

governmental, educational, medical, retail, and related activities. The German geographer Walter Christaller proposed **central place theory** to explain the spatial networks of cities generated by service functions. He defined a central place as any settlement that served as the center of its rural hinterland and the economic mediator between its surroundings and the outside world. Crucial to the theory is the fact that different goods and services vary (1) in range, the maximum distance or radius from the supply center at which the goods and services can reach the consumers, and (2) in the size of population required to make provision of services economically feasible. For example, it requires a larger number of people to support a hospital, university, or department store than to support a gasoline station, post office, or grocery store. Similarly, consumers will travel a greater distance to consult a heart specialist, record a land title, or purchase an automobile than they will to buy a loaf of bread, mail a letter, or fill their automobile with gasoline. People spend as little time and effort as possible in making use of the services of central places, but they must travel farther to use services that require a large market.

The range variance of different central goods and services produces a hierarchy of central places in terms of the size of population and the number of goods and services available. At the top of the hierarchy stand regional metropolises, which offer all services associated with central places and have very large tributary hinterlands. These are often national capitals, or at least the political centers of sizable regions. At the opposite extreme the small market village or hamlet may contain nothing more than a post office, café, or service station. Between the two extremes we find central places of various degrees of importance. Ascending the hierarchy, one finds that each higher order of central place provides all of the goods and services available at centers next lower in the hierarchy *plus* some not provided by them. Central places of a lower order greatly outnumber the few at the higher levels of the hierarchy. One regional metropolis may contain hundreds of smaller central places in its tributary area.

Based upon this hierarchy, Christaller proposed the *market principle*, resting on the assumption that any region will be supplied with goods and services from the minimum number of functioning central places, all other factors being equal. Ideally, the market area of a central place would be circular, drawn on the radius of the range of central goods, but adjacent centers of the same hierarchical rank necessitate the paring of the circle to a hexagon, the geometric figure closest to the shape of a circle that permits a complete network of market areas without the overlapping or underlapping produced by circles (Figure 10.29). The pattern of interlocking hexagons is the ideal distribution of tertiary towns and cities. Any variations from that pattern must be explained in terms of other, disruptive locational factors.

Christaller applied central-place theory to the distribution of tertiary settlements in south Germany and concluded that the market principle described with "astonishing exactness" the actual location of central places (Figure 10.30). However, south Germany, has an urban network based to a remarkable degree in the Middle Ages. Towns such as Nördlingen, Dinkelsbühl, and Rothenburg-ob-der-Tauber remain so perfectly preserved from medieval times as to serve as tourist attractions, in addition to being central places. Miraculously spared by

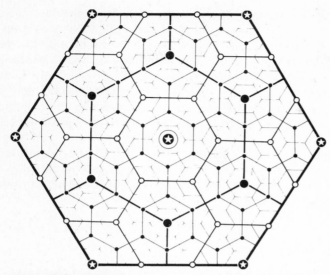

FIGURE 10.29 Distribution model of central places according to the market principle. (Source: After Christaller.)

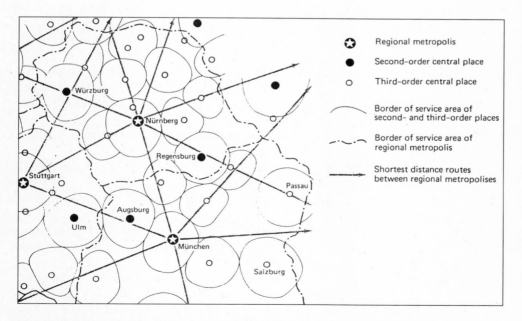

FIGURE 10.30 Distribution of major central places in the province of Bayern, Germany. Even with a multitude of distorting forces at work, the distribution of the three highest orders of central places in south Germany bears a clear relationship to Christaller's model. The wreath of second- and third-order central places around München and Nürnberg is quite suggestive of the ideal market-principle pattern. (Source: After Christaller.)

war, they stand within their walls as museum pieces. Their spacing more nearly reflects the range of central goods typical of the fifteenth century or even earlier feudal times than the modern era. The ability of a medieval peasant to walk from his home to town and back in a single day apparently provided a more important criterion in the spacing of south German central places than the mobility offered later by railroads and motor vehicles. Christaller's mode, then, may be applicable only for the *central European* or even south German city. He underestimated the cultural variety of Europe and the remarkable persistence of the archaic.

The zenith of European urbanization came with industrialization. Cities grew to unprecedented size under this stimulus and became reshaped in diverse ways, as did much of the remainder of European culture. The following two chapters deal with industrial Europe.

Sources and Suggested Readings

Hermann Achenback. "Venedig-Lübeck-Amsterdam: Drei historische Seestädte im Wandel der Zeiten." *Die Erde.* 113 (1982), 205–220.

John Agnew and Calogero Muscarà. *Rome.* London, GB: Belhaven Press, 1993.

O. Basovsky and B. Divinsky. "The Development of Modern Urbanisation in Slovakia and Its Present Problems." *Revue Belge de Géographie.* 115 (1991), 265–277.

James H. Bater. "Privatization in Moscow." *Geographical Review.* 84 (1994), 201–215.

Jacqueline Beaujeu-Garnier. "Urbanization in France since World War II." In *World Patterns of Modern Urban Change,* ed. Michael P. Conzen. Chicago, USA: University of Chicago, Department of Geography, Research Paper No. 217–218, 1986, 47–62.

Leonardo Benevolo. *The European City.* Trans. Carl Ipsen. Oxford, GB: Blackwell, 1993

William H. Berentsen. "Settlement Structure and Urban Development in the GDR, 1950–1985." *Urban Geography.* 8 (1987), 405–419.

Erdmann D. Beynon. "Budapest: An Ecological Study." *Geographical Review.* 33 (1943), 256–275.

Alison Bowes, Jacqui McCluskey, and Duncan Sim. "The Changing Nature of Glasgow's Ethnic-Minority Community." *Scottish Geographical Magazine.* 106 (1990), 99–107.

Joachim Burdack. "Jüngere Tendenzen der Bevölkerungsentwicklung im Städtesystem Frankreichs." *Erdkunde.* 47 (1993), 52–60.

David Burtenshaw, M. Bateman, and G. J. Ashworth. *The City in West Europe.* New York, USA: Wiley, 1981.

Francis W. Carter. *Dubrovnik (Ragusa): A Classic City-State.* London, GB: Seminar Press, 1972.

Harold Carter and C. Roy Lewis. *An Urban Geography of England and Wales in the Nineteenth Century.* London, GB: Edward Arnold, 1991.

A. G. Champion. *Counterurbanisation: The Changing Pace and Nature of Population Deconcentration.* London, GB: Edward Arnold, 1989.

Gordon Cherry. *Birmingham: A Study in Geography, History and Planning.* Chichester, GB: John Wiley, 1994.

Walter Christaller. *The Central Places of Southern Germany.* Trans. Carlisle W. Baskin. Englewood Cliffs, USA: Prentice-Hall, 1966.

David Clark. *Urban Decline: The British Experience.* London, GB: Routledge, 1989.

John R. Clark. *Turkish Cologne: The Mental Maps of Migrant Workers in a German City.* Michigan Geographical Publication No. 19. Ann Arbor, USA: University of Michigan, Department of Geography, 1977.

Paul Claval. "Reflections on the Cultural Geography of the European City." In *The City in Cultural Context,* ed. John A. Agnew, John Mercer, and David E. Sopher. Boston, USA: Allen and Unwin, 1984, 31–49.

Phil Cooke. *The Changing Face of Urban Britain.* Winchester, USA: Unwin Hyman, 1989.

Vaughan Cornish. *The Great Capitals: An Historical Geography.* London, GB: Methuen, 1923.

D. F. W. Cross. *Counterurbanisation in England and Wales.* Aldershot, GB: Avebury, Gower, 1990.

Darrick R. Danta. "Ceausescu's Bucharest." *Geographical Review.* 83 (1993), 170–183.

Darrick R. Danta. "Hungarian Urbanization and Socialist Ideology." *Urban Geography.* 8 (1987), 391–404.

G. Dematteis. "Counter-Urbanization in Italy." In *Progress in Settlement Geography,* ed. L. S. Bourne et al. Milano, I: Franco Angeli, 1986, 161–193.

Richard Dennis. *English Industrial Cities of the Nineteenth Century: A Social Geography.* Cambridge, GB: Cambridge University Press, 1986.

Robert E. Dickinson. "The Morphology of the Medieval German Town." *Geographical Review.* 35 (1945), 74–97.

Mick Dunford and Grigoris Kafkalas (eds.). *Cities and Regions in the New Europe: The Global-Local Interplay and Spatial Development Strategies.* New York, USA: Wiley, 1992.

Marijean H. Eichel. "Ottoman Urbanism in the Balkans: A Tentative View." *East Lakes Geographer.* 10 (1975), 45–54.

Christof Ellger. "Berlin: Legacies of Division and Problems of Unification." *Geographical Journal.* 158 (1992), 40–46.

György Enyedi and Viktória Szirmai. *Budapest: A Central European Capital.* London, GB: Belhaven Press, 1992.

A. J. Fielding. "Counterurbanisation in Western Europe." *Progress in Planning.* 17:1 (1982), 1–52.

Larry R. Ford. "Continuity and Change in Historic Cities: Bath, Chester, and Norwich." *Geographical Review.* 68 (1978), 253–273.

Larry R. Ford. "Urban Morphology and Preservation in Spain." *Geographical Review.* 75 (1985), 265–299.

D. J. Fox. "Odessa." *Scottish Geographical Magazine.* 79 (1963), 5–22.

R. A. French. "The Changing Russian Urban Landscape." *Geography.* 68 (1983), 236–244.

R. A. French and F. E. Ian Hamilton (eds.). *The Socialist City: Spatial Structure and Urban Policy.* New York, USA: Wiley, 1979.

Lucien Gallois. "The Origin and Growth of Paris." *Geographical Review.* 13 (1923), 345–367.

Jorge Gaspar and Allan M. Williams. *Lisbon.* London, GB: Belhaven Press, 1994.

Günther Glebe and John O'Loughlin (eds.). *Foreign Minorities in Continental European Cities.* Stuttgart, D: Franz Steiner, 1987.

Peter Hall. *London 2001.* Winchester, USA: Unwin Hyman. 1990.

F. E. Ian Hamilton. "The East European and Soviet City." *Geographical Magazine.* 50 (1978), 511–515.

Keith Hoggart and David R. Green. (eds.) *London: A New Metropolitan Geography.* London, GB: Edward Arnold, 1991.

Lutz Holzner. "Containing the Metropolis and Saving Downtown: The Case of Munich." *Urbanism Past & Present.* 5:2 (1980), 12–20.

Lutz Holzner. "The Role of History and Tradition in the Urban Geography of West Germany." *Annals of the Association of American Geographers.* 60 (1970), 315–339.

James M. Houston. *A Social Geography of Europe.* London, GB: Duckworth, 1953, chaps. 7–9.

Ioan Ianos. "Comparative Analysis of Urban and Industrial Hierarchies of Romanian Towns in 1990." *GeoJournal.* 29 (1993), 49–56.

Sven Illeris. "Counter-Urbanization Revisited: The New Map of Population Distribution in Central and North-Western Europe." *Norsk Geografisk Tidsskrift.* 44 (1990), 39–52.

A. C. M. Jansen. *Cannabis in Amsterdam: A Geography of Hashish and Marihuana.* Muiderberg, NL: Dick Coutinho, 1991.

Rein B. Jobse. "The Restructuring of Dutch Cities." *Tijdschrift voor Economische en Sociale Geografie.* 78 (1987), 305–311.

Emrys Jones. *A Social Geography of Belfast.* London, GB: Oxford University Press, 1960.

P. N. Jones. "Ethnic Population Succession in a West German City, 1974–80: The Case of Nuremberg." *Geography.* 68 (1983), 121–132.

Adolf Karger and Frank Werner. "Die sozialistische Stadt." *Geographische Rundschau.* 34 (1982), 519–528.

Gerry Kearns and Charles W. J. Withers (eds.) *Urbanising Britain.* Cambridge, GB: Cambridge University Press, 1991.

Thomas Kontuly and Roland Vogelsang. "Explanations for the Intensification of Counterurbanization in the Federal Republic of Germany." *Professional Geographer.* 40 (1988), 42–54.

W. deLannoy. "Residential Segregation of Foreigners in Brussels." *Bulletin, Société Belge d'Études Géographiques.* 44 (1975), 215–238.

Paul Lawless and Colin Raban (eds.). *The Contemporary British City.* London, GB: Harper & Row, 1986.

Lila Leontidou. *The Mediterranean City in Transition: Social Change and Urban Development.* Cambridge, GB: Cambridge University Press, 1990.

Elisabeth Lichtenberger. *Vienna: Bridge Between Cultures*, trans. Dietlinde Mühlgassner and Craig Reisser. London, GB: Belhaven Press, 1993.

Andrew MacLaran. *Dublin: The Shaping of a Capital.* London, GB: Belhaven Press, 1993.

Thomas Maloutas. "Social Segregation in Athens." *Antipode.* 25 (1993), 223–239.

Ger Mik. "Residential Segregation in Rotterdam: Background and Policy." *Tijdschrift voor Economische en Sociale Geografie,* 74 (1983), 74–86.

Richard L. Morrill. "The Development of Spatial Distributions of Towns in Sweden: An Historical-Predictive Approach." *Annals of the Association of American Geographers.* 53 (1963), 1–14.

Rhoads Murphey. "The City as a Center of Change: Western Europe and China." *Annals of the Association of American Geographers.* 44 (1954), 349–362.

Alexander B. Murphy (ed.). *Brussels.* London, GB: Belhaven Press, 1993.

Allen G. Noble and Frank J. Costa. "The Growth of Metro Systems in Madrid, Rome, and Athens." *Cities.* 7 (1990), 224–229.

Daniel Noin and Paul White. *Paris.* London, GB: Belhaven Press, 1993.

E. F. Nozeman. "Dutch New Towns: Triumph or Disaster?" *Tijdschrift voor Economische en Sociale Geografie.* 81 (1990), 149–155.

Philip E. Ogden. "Counterurbanisation in France." *Geography.* 70 (1985), 24–35.

Henk F. L. Ottens. "Spatial Development in the Green Heart of the Randstad: Policies versus Theoretical and Empirical Evidence." *Tijdschrift voor Economische en Sociale Geografie.* 70 (1979), 130–143.

Michael Pacione. "Neighbourhood Communities in the Modern City: Some Evidence from Glasgow." *Scottish Geographical Magazine.* 99 (1983), 169–181.

John B. Parr. "Frequency Distributions of Central Places in Southern Germany: A Further Analysis." *Economic Geography.* 56 (1980), 141–154.

C. G. Pooley. "The Residential Segregation of Migrant Communities in Mid-Victorian Liver-pool" *Transactions of the Institute of British Geographers.* 2 (1977), 364–382.

Norman J. G. Pounds. "The Urbanization of the Classical World." *Annals of the Association of American Geographers.* 59 (1969), 135–157.

Grazyna Prawelska-Skrzypek. "Social Differentiation in Old Central City Neighbourhoods in Poland." *Area.* 20 (1988), 221–232.

Edward T. Price. "Viterbo: Landscape of an Italian City." *Annals of the Association of American Geographers.* 54 (1964), 242–275.

Joanna Regulska and Adam Kowalewski. *Warsaw.* London, GB: Belhaven Press, 1993.

Per Ronnås. *Urbanization in Romania: A Geography of Social and Economic Change Since Independence.* Stockholm, S: Economic Research Institute, Stockholm School of Economics, 1984.

Elmar Sabelberg. "The South-Italian City—a Cultural-Genetic Type of City." *GeoJournal.* 13 (1986), 59–66.

M. B. Stedman. "The Townscape of Birmingham." *Institute of British Geographers, Transactions and Papers.* 25 (1958), 225–238.

Colin Thomas. "Moscow's Mobile Millions." *Geography.* 73 (1988), 216–225.

David Thomas. "London's Green Belt: The Evolution of an Idea." *Geographical Journal.* 129 (1963), 14–24.

James E. Vance, Jr. *The Continuing City: Urban Morphology in Western Civilization.* Baltimore, USA: Johns Hopkins University Press, 1990.

Jan deVries. *European Urbanization, 1500–1800.* Cambridge, USA: Harvard University Press, 1984.

David Ward. "The Pre-Urban Cadaster and the Urban Pattern of Leeds." *Annals of the Association of American Geographers.* 52 (1962), 150–166.

Jan van Wessep, Frans M. Dieleman, and Rein B. Jobse. *Randstad Holland.* London, GB: Belhaven Press, 1993.

Paul D. White. *The West European City: A Social Geography.* London, GB: Longman, 1984.

J. W. R. Whitehand. "The Changing Urban Landscape: The Case of London's High-Class Residential Fringe." *Geographical Journal.* 154 (1988), 351–366.

W. William-Olsson. "Stockholm: Its Structure and Development." *Geographical Review.* 30 (1940), 420–438.

Allan M. Williams. "Bairros Clandestinos: Illegal Housing in Portugal." *Geografisch Tijdschrift.* 15 (1981), 24–34.

J. E. Wrathall and R. J. Carrick. "Almere—New City in the Ijsselmeerpolders." *Geography.* 68 (1983), 257–260.

Kazimierz Zaniewski. "Change in the Inner City: The Case of Warsaw, Poland." *Geographical Perspectives.* 57 (1986), 19–31.

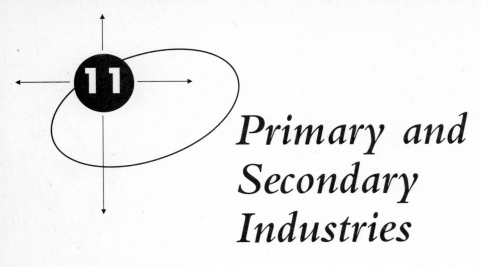

Primary and Secondary Industries

Europeans are an urban people because, preponderantly, they find employment in industrial pursuits. The geographer distinguishes three types of industrial livelihood: primary, secondary, and service. The present chapter deals with the first two types. **Primary** industries are those involved in extracting resources from the earth and seas. Mining, fishing, and lumbering (see Chapter 2) provide three principal examples of primary industry. **Secondary** industry is the processing stage, commonly called *manufacturing,* in which the materials collected by primary industries are converted into finished products. Ore is converted to steel, fibers made into cloth, steel and textiles become clothing, automobiles, machines, and the like. The number and proportion of the European work force employed in primary and secondary industries have declined markedly since about 1960 but still remain large (Figure 11.1).

Historical Geography

European culture has been closely intertwined with primary and secondary industries since the time of the Bronze and Iron Ages, the origins of which lie in prehistory in the same Near Eastern culture hearth that gave Europe agriculture, Christianity, Indo-European speech, the city, and the political state. Over the centuries, many geographical changes occurred in primary and secondary industries within Europe, and centers of political power and cultural flowering shifted spatially with the rise and fall of industrial activity. Ultimately, Europe placed its highly distinctive mark upon industry in a great wave of innovations that form the basis of modern European civilization.

Initially, primary and secondary industries were centered in Mediterranean Europe, particularly in Greece. By the golden age of Greece, the cities of Athínai and Kórinthos led in manufacturing, boasting cloth makers, dyers, leather workers, potters, weapon makers, jewelers, metalworkers, stonemasons, and shipwrights to keep the great Greek merchant fleets and navies afloat. The Hellenic leadership in artisanry passed temporarily to the Romans, only to return to the

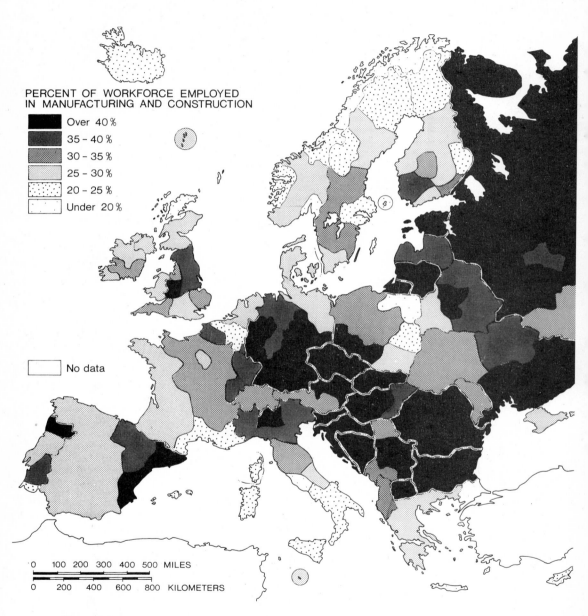

PERCENT OF WORKFORCE EMPLOYED
IN MANUFACTURING AND CONSTRUCTION

- Over 40%
- 35 – 40%
- 30 – 35%
- 25 – 30%
- 20 – 25%
- Under 20%

No data

0   100 200 300 400 500 MILES

0   200   400   600   800 KILOMETERS

FIGURE 11.1 Percentage of labor force employed in manufacturing, mining, and construction—the principal primary and secondary industries. Manufacturing tends to be most important in the core of Europe and in the formerly Communist east.

Byzantine Greeks. Constantinople (modern Istanbul) was in time rivaled by Moorish Spain, where Toledo developed a reputation for high-quality steel and Córdoba produced fine leather goods. The single most significant development of the Middle Ages, however, involved the rise of northern Italy to industrial leadership. Above all, the growth of Italian industry resulted from the dominant position achieved by its merchants, who ranged from China to England.

Cities such as Genova, Milano, Firenze, and Venèzia acquired widespread fame for their silks and other textiles, cloth dying, brassware, weaponry, glass, and shipbuilding. At its peak, Venèzia housed 16,000 shipwrights, who turned out an average of one galleon per day, using prefabricated parts in an early-day assembly-line production. By 1307, artisans of the city of Firenze fabricated 100,000 pieces of cloth per year, and Milano became the chief European center of weaponry manufacture. A system of free craftsmen facilitated the northern Italian achievement, a major departure from the classical tradition of slave artisans.

The industrial-commercial leadership next shifted north to Belgium, Switzerland, and southern Germany in particular, where Italian skills were in some instances transplanted. Other Italians founded the silk industry of Lyon, in the Rhône-Saône Corridor of France. An even more important industrial district of the north lay in Vlaanderen, where the first major developments occurred in the 1100s. Vlaanderen, like northern Italy, acquired its industrial importance partly as a result of a favorable trade location. A fortunate concentration of river, highway, and marine trade routes allowed the province to achieve the same dominance in northern Europe that the Italian towns had in the Mediterranean. Cloth making was first centered at Ypres, Gent, Brugge, and Douai, which drew on the wool of England and Spain as primary raw material. In the 1400s, linen joined wool as a major product of the Flemish towns and attained an importance that persisted into the nineteenth century.

Carried by emigrant artisans, the influence of Vlaanderen was instrumental in the industrial development of the Netherlands beginning in the 1400s. Flemish tradesmen skilled in woolen-textile manufacture also migrated to England, particularly Yorkshire, as early as the 1300s. The Netherlands rose to industrial dominance in the seventeenth century, while northern Germany outstripped the southern Teutonic lands.

The gradual northward shift of industrial activity and corresponding decline in southern Europe meant that manufacturing became increasingly identified with Germanic, Protestant areas and less with Roman Catholic, Romance-language countries. Some writers have even suggested that certain social characteristics of Protestantism, including approval of change and veneration of work, proved more conducive to industrial development. Persecution and expulsion of Huguenot merchants and artisans by the Catholic-backed French government and similar pressure on Protestant Flemings by the Spanish rulers contributed materially to the industrial rise of the Netherlands, northern Germany, and England. The most important European manufacturing lay in Protestant, Germanic lands by the 1700s.

Traditional Manufacturing Systems

Traditional European manufacturing was carried on in two different systems: *gild* and *cottage* industry, the former based in towns and cities, the latter largely rural. The gild was a professional organization of free artisans skilled in a particular craft. The skills involved passed from generation to generation through an apprenticeship system. A boy served as apprentice, for example, to a cooper, potter, mason, iron worker, glassblower, silversmith, sculptor, or master weaver and worked for years as a helper. At the end of apprenticeship, the young man demonstrated his skill before an examining board composed of members of a particular gild. Approval allowed the apprentice to be a member of the gild and begin practicing the trade on his own. In larger cities, each major gild had a house on the main municipal square, and some of these survive today in well-preserved towns such as Gent, Brugge, and Antwerpen in Belgium.

Many relics of the gild system remain today, and craft shops are still surprisingly numerous, even in the more advanced countries such as Germany. In that nation scores of registered crafts still exist, represented by thousands of local gilds, including tailors, bakers, knifesmiths, sausage makers, and others. The same high standards for membership typical of medieval times survive to the present day.

A much more common traditional system of manufacturing, *cottage industry*, remained confined to European farm villages, generally practiced as a sideline to agriculture. A village might have a cobbler, weaver, miller, and blacksmith, who spent part of their time farming and the remainder, during slack periods in the fields, working at the household trade. The abundance of people today with surnames such as Smith, Miller, Potter, Weaver, Weber, and the like suggest the former abundance of village crafts. Little formality surrounded the passing on of skills, and sons most commonly learned from fathers and daughters from mothers simply by observing the work being done. Cottage trades survive today in some parts of Europe, particularly if they attract buyers from beyond the village community. In certain areas of Scotland, for example, women still weave the famous Harris tweed on looms in their individual cottages.

The Industrial Revolution

In Britain during the 1600s, some skilled craftsmen began moving to rural areas to escape the confining, formal character of the urban gilds, which acted to keep membership and production low, while the quality of goods and prices remained high. By fleeing to villages and small towns, they acquired the freedom to increase output and cheapen products, thereby enlarging the market. Simultaneously, some workers engaged in cottage industry began increasing their output and selling wares in a larger territory, abandoning farming altogether. Among such protoindustrial villagers—fugitive gildsmen and, particularly, cottagers—in a small corner of England, a series of revolutionary manufacturing innovations occurred in the 1700s, forever changing England, Europe, and the entire world.

Both primary and secondary industry, both gild and cottage manufacturing systems, were fundamentally altered by this **Industrial Revolution**. Collectively, the associated inventions represent the most rapid and pervasive technological change in the history of the human race. Two fundamental modifications accompanied the revolution. First, machines replaced human hands in extracting primary resources and in fashioning products. The word *manufacturing* ("made by hand") became technically obsolete. No longer would the weaver sit at the hand loom and painstakingly produce each piece of cloth; instead, huge mechanical looms were invented to do the job faster and more economically. In many industries the machine made possible the use of interchangeable parts and the assembly line. A second change involved the rise of inanimate power, as humans harnessed water, steam, and eventually electricity, petroleum, and the atom. The new technology did not appear overnight but in bits and pieces over many decades and centuries. Nearly all of the interconnected developments of the formative stage of the Industrial Revolution, from about 1730 to 1850, occurred in back-country Great Britain. That is, the Industrial Revolution arose in a peripheral part of Europe, in a small and previously insignificant kingdom. Innovations often occur in such peripheries, where orthodox thinking and behavior are weaker. Europe offers numerous examples (Figure 1.8).

The *textile* industry first felt the effect of the Industrial Revolution. Beginning in the 1730s, major advances led to mechanical spinning and weaving devices driven by waterpower and operated by semiskilled labor. These technological breakthroughs occurred in village and small town areas, where cottagers and the antigild mood had long favored quantity of goods over quality and low price over high. The lower price of goods expanded the market available for manufactured cloth. The textile revolution did not occur in London, Bristol, or Edinburgh—the great gild cities of Britain—but instead in the small towns and villages of dominantly rural areas such as *Lancashire, Yorkshire,* and the *Midlands* (Figure 11.2). New mechanized factories soon appeared wherever waterfalls and rapids could power the machine looms, particularly on the eastern and western sides of the Pennines, where some traditional textile making had long been centered. In Yorkshire, on the eastern flank, a woolen textile center since late medieval times, the same streams that had long provided the soft water for cleaning wool now turned the waterwheels that drove the new machine looms. Lancashire, on the western Pennine flank, applied the power loom to cotton textile manufacture. To a lesser extent, the Midlands and, somewhat later, the *Scottish Lowlands* shared the water-powered textile boom. By 1830, Britain produced 70 percent of the world's cotton textiles.

Waterpower dominated the early textile phase of the Industrial Revolution, but not for long. James Watt and others perfected the steam engine in the 1760s, and the first steam-powered cotton textile mill went into operation shortly thereafter. General acceptance followed in the 1790s. The steam engine required fuel, but Great Britain, an almost totally deforested land, had an inadequate supply of wood. The island fortunately possessed an even better fuel—coal. The *mining of*

FIGURE 11.2 The concentrations of primary industry and traditional heavy manufacturing, about 1960. Major manufacturing districts = 1. Lancashire, 2. Yorkshire-Humberside, 3. English Midlands, 4. Scottish Lowlands, 5. South Wales, 6. Newcastle-Tyneside-Tees, 7. Greater London, 8. Sambre-Meuse-Lys, 9. Ruhr, 10. Upper Ślask, 11. Bohemian Basin, 12. Saxon Triangle, 13. Saar-Lorraine, 14. Lower Sachsen, 15. Randstad Holland, 16. Upper Rhine Plain, 17. Greater Hamburg, 18. Paris-Lower Seine, 19. Upper Po Plain, 20. Swedish Central Lowland, 21. Bergslagen, 22. Swiss Plateau-Jura, 23. Rhône-Alps, 24. Greater Moskva, 25. Greater St. Petersburg, 26. Donets Basin-Lower Don, 27. Kryvyy Rih-Dnipro Bend, 28. Ploëşti, and 29. Kiruna-Gällivare. Key for the fishing areas: C = cod, F = flounder, H = herring, M = mackerel, O = oysters, S = sardines, Sp = sponges, St = sturgeon, and T = tuna.

coal represented the second major industry to be affected by the Industrial Revolution. In Lancashire, a key district in the rise of the Industrial Revolution, increases in coal production began as early as the 1690s, with major growth between 1720 and 1740. The growth of a glassmaking industry at Liverpool prompted some of the increase in production, but domestic household use probably accounted for the major market prior to the spread of the steam engine.

Coal had one problem. It was bulky and difficult to transport any great distance, especially at the turn of the nineteenth century, before the railroad, internal-combustion engine, and bulk-carrying ships had been developed. Consequently, the industries that relied upon coal as fuel were drawn to the coalfields, just as the earlier factories had been attracted to waterfalls and rapids. The Midlands, Lancashire, and Yorkshire, as well as the Scottish Lowlands, possessed noteworthy coal deposits, allowing a smooth transition from water to thermal power with a minimum of factory relocation. In addition, substantial reserves of coal occurred along the coastal fringe of southern Wales and in the region of Newcastle on the North Sea coast near the Scottish border (Figure 11.2).

A distinctive trait of the Industrial Revolution had become evident: areal concentration of industries. True, certain towns and districts had been known for a particular product under traditional manufacturing systems, but many such industries lay dispersed through a large number of small towns over fairly large regions. In contrast, mechanized production focused on a small number of cities and districts, which attracted very large populations. Gravitation to the coalfields accelerated the areal focalization of industry, causing great increases in population in favored districts and substantial emigration elsewhere.

Metallurgical industries, including the making of *iron and steel*, also felt the effects of the Industrial Revolution. Throughout most of history, the smelting of iron remained a primitive process, and few who practiced it had any valid understanding of what happened chemically. Iron ore was simply heated over a charcoal fire, and the charcoal's carbon combined with the ore's oxygen to free the iron. Some carbon also combined with the iron to provide hardness, for pure iron is rather malleable and easily cut. Too much carbon resulted in brittle cast iron; a proper amount resulted in steel. Different varieties of steel could be produced by accidental or purposeful addition of various *ferroalloys*, metals such as nickel or chrome. Before the mid–1700s much superstition, ritual, and ceremony were associated with steel making as the keepers of the forges sought to make good steel. Those towns that became famous for high-quality steel, such as Toledo or Solingen, more often than not owed their reputation to particular local ores that spontaneously produced fine steel when smelted. Iron processing had changed little in thousands of years, and the industry in Europe was thoroughly dispersed geographically, with small forges located wherever iron was found. The industry, more rural than urban, was often found in thinly populated hill districts. Charcoal remained dominant in the smelting process.

The Industrial Revolution brought major changes to the iron and steel industry. The pivotal early developments occurred in Coalbrookdale, a town and valley in the Midlands (Figure 11.2). There, in 1709, *coke* was first substituted for charcoal in smelting, a process that caused steelmaking to become cheaper and permitted the use of lower-grade ores. By 1790, Coalbrookdale produced almost 50 percent of Britain's iron. Coke, nearly pure carbon, burns at a higher temperature than charcoal and is derived by heating high-grade coal to draw off the gaseous constituents. In timber-poor Britain, the use of coke became important in the early 1700s and increased rapidly after midcentury. By 1788, some 70 percent of all blast furnaces in England and Scotland relied on coke instead of charcoal, and by 1806 the proportion had reached 97 percent. Acceptance of coke drastically changed the areal distribution of steelmaking. The industry abandoned countless scattered small forges and, out of necessity, relocated in the coal districts, where coke could be obtained most cheaply. Iron and steel thus contributed to the accelerating nucleation of industries in small coalfield districts.

Other technological changes reshaped British steelmaking. The traditional hammer and anvil gave way to the rolling mill as the final processing stage, blast furnaces supplanted small ovens, and metallurgical science arose to replace superstition and ritual. Through such innovation and change, the steelmakers of Britain achieved world leadership in the nineteenth century.

Steelmaking initially remained concentrated in the Midlands because coal and iron ore both occurred there. Birmingham became as synonymous with steel as Toledo had been in a different age and culture. The Midlands meant to steel what Lancashire and Yorkshire did to textiles. In other developing British manufacturing areas where both ore and coal occurred, additional concentrations of steel mills soon developed, as in the *Newcastle-Tyneside-Tees* district, where the legendary coal of Newcastle supplemented iron ore from the nearby Cleveland Hills; in *South Wales;* and in the western part of the Scottish Lowlands (Figure 11.2).

Another industry forever changed by the Industrial Revolution was the ancient and honored craft of *shipbuilding.* Traditionally, ships had been small, wooden, and powered by wind or oars. The Industrial Revolution created demands for larger, faster ships to transport bulky raw materials and finished products and provided the technology needed to produce such vessels. Iron barges first appeared in the late 1700s, and experimental steam navigation began about the same time. Steam-powered steel ships arose in the 1830s, and wooden sailing vessels disappeared a generation later.

The major shipbuilding centers in Britain arose where coalfields and steel mills bordered tidewater. One such location was the Tyneside, but the major center developed on the *Clydeside* near Glasgow in the Scottish Lowlands. By the 1890s, British shipyards produced 80 percent of the world's seagoing tonnage, and Britannia ruled the waves.

Textiles, coal mining, steelmaking, and shipbuilding formed the core of the Industrial Revolution, but other industries were also involved. The shift to machinery gave rise to an entire new engineering industry specializing in the manufacture of machines and machine tools. Both the raw material of this industry—steel—and its market—other manufacturing industries—lay in the coalfields, and as a result the machine makers located there too. As machines became more numerous and complex, the industry that supplied them grew steadily.

Another basically new industry arose, devoted to the large-scale manufacture and processing of various *chemicals,* including dyes, paints, fertilizers, drugs, explosives, soap, and, eventually, products such as synthetic fibers. Many such items could be salvaged from by-products of the coking process, and, partly for this reason, many chemical factories developed in the coalfields. Other industries besides shipbuilding and machine making used finished steel as a raw material, and these often located near steel mills: manufacturers of cutlery, surgical instruments, locks, locomotives, automobiles, and weaponry. Similarly, textile-using industries, such as the making of clothing, found it advantageous to be situated near the textile factories.

The snowballing accumulation of a great variety of industries in the coalfield districts of Britain caused hundreds of thousands of people to migrate there seeking factory employment. In short order, the British population massed in a small number of clusters. These concentrations in turn attracted still other manufacturers, primarily those that needed to be close to the consumers of their products, such as bakers, brewers, meatpackers, and other food processors.

The importance of coal as a locational factor in the formative stages of the British Industrial Revolution was so great that all but one of the major industrial districts developed on the coalfields. London provided the only exception (Figure 11.2). Remote from coal deposits, it had no significant natural resources other than a navigable river; yet London developed into the largest single industrial center in the United Kingdom. Its advantages were several. First, London had already accumulated a large population before the Industrial Revolution, reaching 700,000 in the late 1600s and accounting for one out of every ten Britishers. This population offered both market and labor supply when industrialization came. Second, London served as the center for commerce and trade of the country, handling in its harbor three-quarters of the nation's overseas trade by 1700. As a result, a concentration of banks, insurance firms, and shipping brokerage houses developed, which in turn stimulated the process of growth. Industries that depended on foreign areas either as suppliers of raw materials or as consumers of finished products found advantage by locating in London. Third, the large, well-to-do merchant class of the city controlled a huge amount of capital, needed for investment in industrial activities. Consequently, London thrived in the Industrial Revolution. Its diverse industries eventually ranged from clothing and food processing to oil refining, various engineering and electronic industries, printing, and automobile and aircraft manufacture.

On a far more modest scale, coastal *Northern Ireland* followed Greater London's example and industrialized in the absence of coal (Figure 11.2). Linen textiles and shipbuilding became the principal industries of cities such as Belfast and Londonderry.

Diffusion to the Mainland

On mainland Europe, numerous industrial districts rose in the nineteenth century. With some notable exceptions, the spread remained confined to Germanic areas, especially northern Germany. Through good fortune, the Germanic people found parts of their land much better supplied with coal than did the French, Iberians, and Italians.

As in Britain, manufacturing on the European mainland tended to localize in small coalfield districts. The first mainland area to feel the effects of the British innovations, the *Sambre-Meuse-Lys,* straddled the Belgian-French border (Figure 11.2). Long before the Industrial Revolution, textile manufacture was well established, especially in the basin of the Lys River. Even before 1800, British textile technology began to be adopted. Traditional metalworking industries had long lined the region's rivers, and in the Middle Ages, copper, brass, and iron came from towns such as Dinant, Namur, and Huy. Around Namur in the mid-1500s, 120 forges and furnaces supported the activities of 7000 charcoal burners in the surrounding forests. A district of adjacent Brabant became known as the "forest of the charcoal makers."

Coal in the Sambre-Meuse area occurs on the Great European Plain at the foot of the belt of hills and low mountains, in this case the Ardennes. Some use was made of the coal as early as the 1500s, but major mining activities awaited the nineteenth century. The first major use of coke on the European mainland occurred in the Sambre-Meuse area. A coke-fired blast furnace operated at Liège by 1823, and within two decades 45 of 120 furnaces used coke. Expansion of coke production outstripped any other mainland industrial district. Sambre-Meuse craftsmen served as leaders in adopting British techniques, remaining ahead of better-endowed districts in Germany until the mid-1860s. Textile production became centered in Lille, France, known for cottons, linens, and woolens; in Verviers, Belgium, where woolens dominated; and the southern Netherlands. The Sambre-Meuse-Lys district departed from the nineteenth-century European industrial norm in being only partially Germanic, although it included a northern projection into Dutch and German territory.

One mainland manufacturing district, the *Ruhr* in Germany, eventually surpassed all the others in importance and even eclipsed the British parent districts (Figure 11.2). Situated at the juncture of the Great European Plain and the hilly regions to the south called the Sauerland and Siegerland, it lies largely in one of the many fertile loessial *Börde* that appear along the southern edge of the plains (Figure 11.3). Underlying the *Börde,* huge deposits of high-grade coal, reached to the surface near the southern fringe of hills.

Development of the Ruhr district lagged considerably behind English or even Belgian efforts. Small amounts of coal had been chipped away from the surface outcroppings at least as early as the thirteenth century A.D., mainly to provide heat for local houses. In medieval times, a significant iron and steel industry under the gild system developed at the town of Solingen and elsewhere in the hilly Sauerland and Siegerland, based on local deposits of iron ore and the survival of large, charcoal-producing forests. Linen textiles made from locally grown flax by both gildsmen and cottagers were similarly well established in the area by the late Middle Ages. As late as 1800 the steelmakers continued to function in the traditional way, as did the textile weavers. Little or no suggestion of the Industrial Revolution sweeping Britain was visible in the Ruhr, though steam pumps installed in 1801 combatted water seepage in some of the small coal mines. The towns remained small, confined within medieval walls and function-

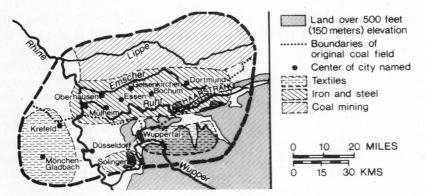

FIGURE 11.3 The Ruhr industrial district, about 1960. The southern part of the coalfield had been largely mined out, and mining migrated steadily northward. Steel mills remained concentrated between the Ruhr and Emscher rivers, while textiles were manufactured at Wuppertal and in the cities west of the Rhine.

ing primarily as agricultural trade centers. A visitor from the thirteenth or fourteenth centuries would have felt quite at home in the Ruhr at the beginning of the 1800s. Even the next half-century brought few changes, and a traveler in 1847 described the Ruhr as "poetically rural." Coal mining was still carried on in hundreds of small rural mines, employing in total only some 13,000 men. Urban growth had not been rapid, and gilds still dominated the manufacture of steel at Solingen. Nevertheless, the first mark of the Industrial Revolution had been placed on this pastoral setting. Mechanized, steam-powered textile mills arose by 1850 in Krefeld and the twin cities of Mönchen-Gladbach, west of the Rhine. The textile gilds and cottage weavers rapidly gave way to the new technology. As in Britain, the textile industry led the way.

In the last half of the nineteenth century, the Ruhr underwent almost complete change, emerging by the end of the 1800s as the most important European industrial center. Annual coal production increased by 33 times in the last half of the century. The mines grew from small rural enterprises scratching at the surface of the earth to become sizable urban establishments employing hundreds of thousands of workers and utilizing sophisticated mining machinery. The manufacture of iron and steel shifted primarily to the coalfield, and large plants using coke supplanted the charcoal-burning gilds of Solingen. The small, local iron-ore deposits proved inadequate to supply the demand, and the Ruhr reached out to Sweden, Spain, and Lorraine for additional ore, exporting in exchange large amounts of coking coal. The Rhine River forfeited much of its romantic character, steeped in German mythology, to become the major transport route linking the Ruhr to the rest of the world. Barges bearing coal and ore came to dominate the riverine scene at the foot of the Lorelei Cliffs, as progress shoved aside poetry. Industrial names such as Krupp and Thyssen joined Schiller and Goethe in the German pantheon.

The population of the Ruhr exploded, as towns became sprawling industrial cities. A line of urban centers developed from Dortmund in the east through Bochum, Essen, and Oberhausen to Duisburg on the Rhine in the west. Essen, which had a population of only 4000 within its medieval town walls in 1800 and still only 10,000 at midcentury, became a city of 200,000 by 1900. The local agricultural population proved inadequate as a labor supply, and workers immigrated from other parts of Germany, as well as from Belgium, the Netherlands, Italy, and the Slavic lands of the east. A melting pot of peoples assembled, giving the Ruhr a distinctly different ethnic character from the rest of Germany. A gray pall of smoke settled over the district, blackening buildings and human lungs and blotting out the sun. With the smoke came a prosperous, powerful Germany, which assumed its place among the leading nations of the world.

Near the headwaters of the Wisla and Odra rivers in southern Poland, where the North European Plain joins the hills and mountains of Central Europe in another of the loessial embayments, lies the *Upper Ślask* (Silesia) industrial district (Figure 11.2). Though German in origin and development, today it lies in Poland. A tradition of iron smelting, well established here by the 1700s, relied on abundant local forests for charcoal and on small amounts of iron ore found in the region. The large coal deposits remained very nearly untouched. Upper Ślask lay on a remote frontier, the outermost tip of Prussian, and later German, territory, in an area far removed from markets and sparsely populated. The upper Odra River offered fewer possibilities for transport than did the mighty Rhine, and the sea lay far away. Furthermore, the coal deposits were smaller than those of the Ruhr. In spite of these shortcomings, Upper Slask underwent industrialization in the nineteenth century, in large part because the Prussian government desired it. Financial encouragements, including subsidies, went to the wealthy landlords who owned most of the area, and they responded with investments in industry. Because coking coal was less abundant than in the Ruhr and the quantity of timber very great, the use of charcoal persisted much longer in Upper Ślask, even into the 1860s. Local iron ores were soon exhausted, and imports from Austria via the Moravian Gate rail route became necessary. After major improvements to the Odra waterway in 1895, allowing easier access to the Baltic Sea, Sweden became the dominant supplier of ore. The district never rivaled the Ruhr, but it did produce about 10 percent of Germany's iron by 1900. Before World War I, almost the entire district lay in Germany, with only a small part across the border in Austria-Hungary; after the war, half of the region was awarded to the new Polish state on the basis of a plebiscite. In 1945 the Poles seized the remainder, expelling most resident Germans. Poland, industrially backward, in this way acquired an important manufacturing base.

Another of the coalfield industrial districts developed largely by the Germans, the *Saar-Lorraine,* straddles the present border between Germany and France, also including parts of southern Luxembourg (Figure 11.2). The German Saar contains the greater part of the coal, while French Lorraine is one of the traditional centers of iron-ore mining in Europe. Here, too, industrialization occurred rather late, lagging considerably behind the British districts. Coke, first used in 1838, only gradually replaced charcoal. Major steel plants with blast furnaces appeared only in the 1850s. In fact, the major development of the district did not occur until after Germany annexed Lorraine in 1871. The principal hindrance to expansion was that most of the Saarland coal could not be coked, necessitating the import of Ruhr coals. The industrial value of the Saar-Lorraine areas prompted numerous boundary changes. Germany twice seized and lost part of the iron-ore deposits, and France twice unsuccessfully sought to detach Saarland from Germany. The peripheral border location of the Saar-Lorraine district long presented a problem, not unlike that faced by Upper Śląsk.

Another area of industrialization in nineteenth-century Europe lay in the northern part of the province of Čechy (Bohemia), until 1918 a part of German-ruled Austria but today the core of the Czech Republic (Figure 11.2). Under encouragement from the Austro-Hungarian government, a well-rounded industrial area had developed by the 1870s, though this *Bohemian Basin* district faced the same problems of remoteness and poor water-transport facilities that plagued nearby Upper Śląsk. The coal deposits were also much smaller than in the more important industrial regions of Germany, Belgium, and Britain. Iron and steel manufacture, based on coal deposits northwest of Praha and ore from the nearby Krušné Hory (Ore Mountains) on the north, became centered in the cities of Kladno and Plzeň, contributing to the world-famous Skoda armaments works. Other diverse industries of this district include cotton and linen textiles, especially around Liberec; heavy machinery and clothing manufacture at Praha; world-famous ceramics and glassware from Karlovy Vary; and food processing, including brewing at Plzeň, which gave its name to the well-known Pilsner beers.

Another German industrial region of importance arising in the nineteenth century lay in the *Saxon Triangle,* with apexes at the cities of Plauen, Halle, and Dresden, an area traditionally part of the Kingdom of Sachsen (Saxony) (Figure 11.2). The local coalfield included only small, scattered deposits of a lower quality. Privileges and subsidies offered by the Saxon government, coupled with the presence of iron ore in the mountains to the south, stimulated industrial growth here as early as the 1600s. Immigrant artisans, mainly French Huguenot refugees and Dutch, greatly aided the establishment of porcelain, textile, and armament manufacture. Textiles clustered at Plauen and Chemnitz, where original use of waterpower gave way to coal as a fuel. Halle and Bitterfeld produced chemicals, based in part on potash deposits. The tradition of fine porcelain manufacture became established in the Dresden area; and printing and publishing in Leipzig.

The last coalfield industrial complexes to be developed lay far to the east, in Slavic Ukraine and Russia. Major coal deposits in the *Donets Basin,* or "Donbass," combined with the huge iron ore deposits of nearby *Kryvyy Rih* (formerly called Krivoy Rog), permitted development of one of Europe's most important centers of heavy industry. Most of this development occurred under early Soviet Communist rule in the 1920s and 1930s, and by the time of World War II, Germans regarded the complex as a major military objective. Lesser coal deposits of lower quality contributed to the rise of *Greater Moskva* as a manufacturing center (Figure 11.2). Communist planning always greatly favored development of heavy industry.

Spreading Beyond the Coalfields

In most areas not gifted with coal deposits, the nineteenth century witnessed slow industrial growth, or even decline in the face of competition from the coal areas. Some urban centers with sizable populations in the pre-Industrial Revolution period imitated the success of London in attracting industries on the basis of a large, ready-made labor force and market. In this category were such districts as Paris, Hamburg, Wien, and Randstad Holland. *Paris* developed two basic industries: high-quality luxury items such as fashion clothing, cosmetics, and jewelry, distributed in small workshop factories around the city; and engineering industries, dominated in the present century by automobile manufacture and concentrated in the suburb towns. Most of remaining France lagged behind industrially, not only because coal was absent, but also because of the slow French population growth rate, which affected both labor supply and market; a transport system so highly centered in Paris that outlying districts had difficult access to raw materials and market; and a lack of governmental encouragement of non-Parisian industrialization in the 1800s. The Rotterdam-Europoort section of the *Randstad Holland* industrial district has in recent decades developed a large oil-refining and petrochemical industry (Figure 11.2).

Another major district that developed in the nineteenth century lay in the *Upper Rhine Plain* of southwestern Germany and French Alsace, including cities such as Mannheim and Frankfurt-am-Main (Figure 11.2). This area lay on an ancient routeway between the Mediterranean coast and the North European Plain, and many cities had a heritage of gild industries. In the 1800s, new industries moved here, especially those producing textiles and chemicals. Ludwigshafen, a city founded in the nineteenth century on the Rhine River adjacent to Mannheim, became the site of the famous Farben chemical works, and the Frankfurt suburb of Höchst developed a similar industry. In the twentieth century, the Upper Rhine and nearby Neckar Valley acquired important automobile factories, including the Daimler-Benz works at Stuttgart and the Opel plant at Rüsselsheim near Frankfurt. Alsace early developed textile mills at waterpower sites along the foot of the Vosges.

Hydropower, converted into electricity, helped revive the former industrial greatness of northern Italy, particularly in the area between Milano and Torino in the upper reaches of the *Po Plain* (Figure 11.2). Milano became the first European city to have electric lights, in 1883. The government provided added subsidies and incentives to industrialization, and a sizable work force of cheap labor was assembled from among the peasantry of the adjacent Alpine fringe and southern Italy. The diverse industries eventually included iron and steel, based on imported raw materials; automobile manufacture, including the Fiat plant at Torino; and textiles. The district is served by the port of Genova, across the Appennini Mountains on the Mediterranean coast, a city that acquired sizable iron and steel mills and shipbuilding yards of its own. Once-proud Venèzia profited relatively little from the rise of the Po Valley industries, for the Adriatic Sea remained a backwater, leading away from the major markets and suppliers of raw materials.

The industrial portion of Switzerland, lying to the north of the Alps on the *Swiss Plateau* and in the hilly Jura, developed industries adapted to a scarcity of raw materials (Figure 11.2). The Swiss relied on highly skilled labor to produce quality goods with a high value added in the manufacturing process. Hydroelectric power brought a major expansion of industry in the twentieth century. Watchmaking, concentrated in numerous small towns and cities of the Jura, is a typical Swiss industry, retaining a pre-Industrial Revolution areal dispersal and veneration for craftsmen. St. Gallen in the east became the major textile center, producing such items as luxury silks, laces, and ribbons, while Basel in northwestern Switzerland evolved into an important chemical center at the head of barge navigation on the Rhine. Other industries specialized in the production of various kinds of machinery or food processing, including milk-chocolate candies.

Several small areas in northern Spain also felt the effects of the Industrial Revolution, particularly the Barcelona area on the Mediterranean shore and the Bay of Biscay coast around Bilbao and San Sebastián (Figure 11.2). In the latter area, major iron-ore deposits and minor coalfields supported a local steel industry, which in turn provided raw material for shipbuilders. Barcelona, whose rising industrial capacity presented a Catalonian challenge to the primacy of inland Madrid, became the scene of diverse manufacturing, including textiles.

Despite very early industrial beginnings, Sweden had become a poor country by the late 1800s. Though endowed with fine iron ore and copper deposits, which had been mined in the *Bergslagen* area since the Middle Ages, Sweden lacked coal deposits and could not share in the early Industrial Revolution (Figure 11.2). Its steelmakers, known for the high quality of their product, continued to use charcoal. Adoption of hydroelectric power finally permitted the modernization of Swedish industry around 1900, eventually creating an economic well-being unsurpassed in the world. Hydropower fueled electric furnaces employed in steelmaking, and while Sweden's output of steel never rivaled Germany or Britain, the quality was unsurpassed, including various steel alloys. When the Bergslagen ores played out, Sweden developed new iron ore mines in the far north, around Kiruna and Gällivare (Figure 11.2). A variety of local engineering industries rely on this steel, including manufacturers of machines, automobiles, ball bearings, electrical equipment, aircraft engines, bicycles, diesel motors, armaments, and ships of exceptionally high quality. Steel production remained concentrated in the Bergslagen area, but the engineering industries scattered widely in the nearby *Swedish Central Lowland,* a belt between Stockholm and Göteborg, including such enterprises as the Volvo automobile industry and household-appliance factories (Figure 11.2).

Finland, also late to industrialize, relied upon its abundant water power and forests to develop a manufacturing complex in the southwest and far-flung primary industry in the woodlands. On that precarious base, the Finns, too, achieved an enviable standard of living. Wood products remain a specialty in Finland.

The period 1900–1960 witnessed other efforts to industrialize the European peripheries. Ties to raw material sites weakened with improved transportation. Ports became favored new places for steel making because ore and coal could be shipped by sea. As a result, coastal steel mills developed at seaports such as Valencia in eastern Spain and Piombino, Genova, Taranto, and Napoli in Italy.

Deindustrialization

In the year 1900, all of the European industrial districts combined accounted for about 90 percent of the world's manufacturing output, an overwhelming dominance. The power and prosperity of the Germanic industrial core reached unprecedented heights, and European colonial empires ruled the far greater part of the Eastern Hemisphere. In spite of two highly destructive world wars, Europe remained the industrial heartland of the world in the 1960s, though not as dominant. Few if any experts viewing the industrial geography of Europe in 1960 anticipated the radical changes that lay immediately ahead.

Put simply, the most important mass-production industries, both primary and secondary, went into severe and irreversible decline, prompting use of terms such as *deindustrialization, industrial crisis,* and *industrial fallibility.* Once-prosperous industrial districts became, within no more than two decades, "derelict," "pauperized," and eligible for economic assistance. The blue-collar labor force in a single generation deteriorated into "a dispirited people who reflected a growing passivity to their plight," to use words of geographer Shane Davies. Entire working-class communities became devastated and dependent upon unemployment relief.

The statistical evidence of deindustrialization is both convincing and sobering. In the United Kingdom, birthplace of the Industrial Revolution, the labor force employed in manufacturing plummeted from 9,119,000 in 1966 to 5,172,000 by 1987 (Figure 11.4). In the Midlands district, where the modern coal and steel industry was born, manufacturing employment fell by 55 percent during that two-decade span. In Wales, "its spirit and wealth now broken," employment in mining dropped from an all-time high of 250,000 to only 24,000 by 1982. All of Britain could claim only 22 coal mines, with 12,000 employees by 1994. Even in London, the manufacturing work force declined by 40 percent in the brief period between 1975 and 1982.

Western European mainland industrial districts fared little better. The peak year of coal production in the Saar-Lorraine was 1957, and 20 years later it had been labeled a "problem region," as had the Ruhr and Sambre-Meuse-Lys. In western Germany, the work force employed in coal mining dwindled from 600,000 in 1955 to 95,000 by 1995. The Ligurian coast around Genova in Italy and the Bay of Biscay coast of northern Spain also joined the list of severely stricken industrial regions (Figure 11.4).

The crisis began in the primary sector, in particular coal mining. A steadily decreasing demand for coal, principally the result of a shift to alternative energy sources, especially petroleum, brought depression to mining. Also contributing to the decline of the mining sector was the depletion of minerals such as iron ore. Saar-Lorraine ore peaked in output in 1960, and even in Sweden, Europe's leading iron ore producer, the reserve is now small and yield falls. As a result, Western European steel production has declined from its peak year in 1974.

Textile manufacture also suffered. Britain's position began to slip even in the nineteenth and early twentieth centuries, as its share of world cotton textile pro-

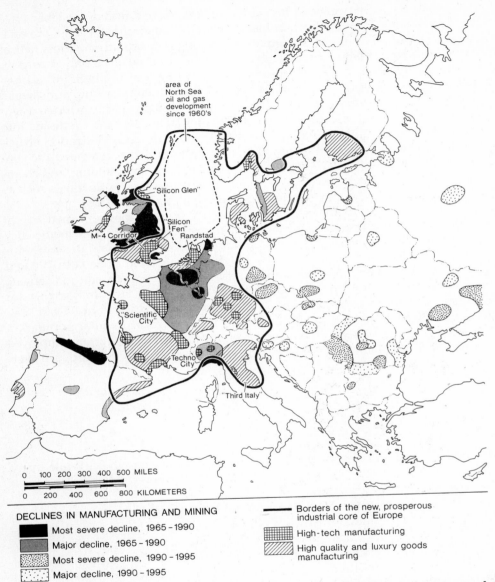

Figure 11.4 Zones of deindustrialization and of new manufacturing growth. Decline and growth remain largely separate geographically. The emerging new core of primary and secondary industries, based on high-tech, crafts, and, to a lesser extent, petroleum, is more confined areally than its predecessor and excludes virtually all of the formerly Communist east.

duction dropped from 56 percent in 1870 to 38 percent in 1915. An extreme example of decline is provided by the linen industry of Northern Ireland. Between 1950 and 1970, the labor force and number of factories in the Belfast area fell by half, a critical decline in the local economy, since a fifth of the labor force had been employed in the linen industry. Shipbuilding declined even more catastrophically. As recently as 1948, the United Kingdom produced almost half of the world tonnage launched, but by 1980 its share had fallen to only 4 percent. The 1960s witnessed the most rapid decline. The plight of shipbuilding is illustrated by the Clydeside district in the Scottish Lowlands. Local shipyards began their rise to world importance in the 1830s, only to find prosperity arrested a century later. Foreign competition, particularly from Japan, sent the Clydeside into severe depression after the middle 1950s. In short, deindustrialization struck hardest at the traditional mass-production enterprises that had formed the core of the Industrial Revolution—textiles, steel, coal mining, shipbuilding, and chemicals—and at the districts overspecialized in these pursuits. Textile towns such as Troyes in France and mining centers like South Wales suffered most.

In Eastern Europe, traditional mass-production industries remained free of competition in the absence of a market economy before 1990. Their inefficiency did not lead to decline as long as the Communist system of central planning survived and subsidized them. As a result, deindustrialization came both late and very abruptly to the east, largely running its course in a half-decade and causing massive economic problems and social dislocations (Figure 11.4). In Romania, for example, the labor force declined by 7 percent in just two years, from 1989 to 1991. The East German industrial city of Plauen lost a third of its total population between 1990 and 1994. Still today, however, the proportion of workers employed in manufacturing in the eastern countries remains higher than the European average (Figure 11.1).

Industrial Rejuvenation

Deindustrialization never became pervasive in Europe as a whole. While many major industries and districts declined into crisis, others retained stability or achieved impressive growth.

In the primary sector, the collapse of coal mining and decline of iron ore production occurred simultaneously with the rise of the great North Sea oil and natural gas field, a submarine deposit shared by the United Kingdom, Norway, Denmark, Germany, and the Netherlands (Figure 11.4). The northern forests of Sweden, Finland, and Russia, a renewable primary resource, continued to yield their sizable harvests. Far northern Europe still provides about 20 percent of the world's sawn lumber exports and 25 percent of the wood pulp and paper.

Much more important than these primary industries to European rejuvenation has been the shift to the manufacture of high-quality goods requiring a skilled labor force, ongoing innovation, and/or sophisticated technology. Western Europeans have successfully moved from emphasis on mass-produced goods requiring large factories and minimally skilled labor to a focus on labor-intensive operations producing items of high value. They have, in short, chosen to depend upon the cardinal virtues of European culture—education, individualism, and innovation.

The most glamorous of these new enterprises can be grouped under the much-used term *high-tech*. Properly speaking, these include industries manufacturing high-technology products such as electronic and microelectronic devices, data processing equipment, robotics, telecommunications apparatus, and the like. To these should be added firms which make preponderant *use* of such sophisticated products in the manufacturing process, such as pharmaceutical firms and pesticide makers. Central to the entire high-tech enterprise is the computer. All such manufacturers invest heavily in research and development, in order to foster the innovations that drive the volatile high-tech industry, though these innovations more often than not spawn new companies. Research and development activity constitutes a *service industry* and as such will be considered in Chaper 12. While much is made of high-tech manufacturing and several European countries have tied their industrial future to such activity, these firms employ far fewer people than the old, collapsed ones. Their rise has done little to address the problems associated with deindustrialization, and high-tech manufacturing will not likely achieve the century-long stability and prosperity of the older system.

Perhaps more promising for Europe's future is the manufacture of high-quality expensive luxury goods, mainly for export. These factories operate as *labor-* and *design-* (rather than technology-) intensive craft industries and represent, in fact, a revival of gildlike manufacturing. Indeed, the apprenticeship system has survived from gild times, under government protection in countries such as Germany. The highly skilled workforce enjoys high wages, job security, and the satisfaction of laboring in "a positive culture of work." Creativity, skill, and craftman pride are all essential components. Factories tend to be small and the workplace pleasant. Typical products include ceramics, pottery, decorative glassware, fine clothing, jewelry, quality leather goods such as shoes, well-crafted wood products, and luxury automobiles. Such manufacturing survived in Europe even during the heyday of heavy industry, especially in non-coalfield districts such as the Swiss Plateau-Jura, but a major expansion has occurred since 1970. High quality craft industries have one great potential weakness—their dependence upon a high level of prosperity among consumers, many of whom reside outside Europe. Any major worldwide depression would undermine such industries. Western Europe's continued prosperity and high standard of living are always at risk.

Geographically, deindustrialization and rejuvenation occurred in quite distinct European regions, with relatively little overlap (Figure 11.4). The districts characterized by high-tech and craft industries tend to lie outside the economically depressed, deindustrialized areas, in regions that had little heavy industry in earlier times. Geographer Allen Scott calls these "new industrial spaces." Southern England, southern Germany, and southern France have eclipsed the northern parts of those countries as the centers of manufacturing, while the eastern part of the Po-Veneto Plain has surpassed the older Milano-Torino focus.

High-tech industry, which tends to be drawn to universities, major airports, suburbs, small towns, and medium-sized cities, developed in places such as the "M–4 Corridor," a crescent-shaped area west of London; "Silicon Glen" in the Lothians near Edinburgh; "Scientific City," southwest of Paris; Mediterranean France; and the suburbs of München, Augsburg, Nürnberg, and several other south German cities. In some cases, the older, declining industrial centers have sought to claim a share of high-tech industry, as at Torino in Italy, where "Tecnocity" has been developed, but these efforts remain the exception rather than the rule.

The regions devoted to craft-style manufacturing include, most notably, the "Third Italy," which by 1981 claimed 37 percent of all manufacturing employment in that country; the provinces of Bayern and Baden-Württemberg in South Germany, where conservative state governments fostered such development; the south of France; southern England; central Denmark; most of south-central Sweden; and southwestern Finland (Figure 11.4).

As a result, the present industrial geography of Western Europe contains an odd patchwork of decayed, distressed deindustrialized districts alongside booming centers of high-tech and craft manufacturing. Most distressed of all is Eastern Europe, where deindustrialization has not been accompanied by any noteworthy rise of new enterprises devoted to sophisticated technology, skilled crafts, or new discoveries of primary resources. The east/west industrial contrast has become vivid and alarming, given the social and political connotations. Decades of suppressed individualism and ideologically based education deprive Eastern Europe of precisely the sort of people needed to develop such industries.

Core and Periphery

Both the old and new industrial order in Europe feature a core/periphery pattern (Figures 11.2, 11.3). Under the geographical configuration that prevailed before deindustrialization, manufacturing districts lay mainly in the European core, with few exceptions, even though the Industrial Revolution began in a peripheral area. In that pattern, the European periphery housed mainly primary industries that supplied raw materials for the manufacturing core. These included forest products from the north; fishing in the peripheral oceans and seas; mining, as at Kiruna and Kryvyy Rih; and the extraction of petroleum and natural gas at places such as Ploëşti in the Valachian Plain and in the hinter reaches of the East European Plain (Figure 11.2).

In the seas that flank Europe on the south, west, and north, a great variety of commercially valuable fish is found. These are exploited in part by peoples of the less-industrialized periphery of Europe, particularly Norwegians, Icelanders, Færoese, Portuguese, Greeks, Dalmatian Croats, and Basques. Norway, with one of the smallest populations in Europe, accounts for 2.5 percent of the total world catch of fish each year. Fishing occupies a very sizable segment of the labor force in Iceland and the Færoe Islands. The great fisher folk have generally occupied lands poorly suited for agriculture; in Norway, for example, only 3 percent of the national territory is arable.

The types of fisheries vary from one peripheral sea to another in Europe. Mediterranean fishermen go after tuna, sardines—which are named for the Italian island of Sardegna—and sponges, found particularly in the Aegean. The Black and Caspian seas yield sturgeon, from which caviar is obtained, while the North Sea, Arctic Ocean, and Norwegian Sea fishers specialize in cod, herring, mackerel, and haddock. The less saline Baltic Sea is important for flounder and eels, in addition to cod and herring. Oysters and sardines provide the principal take in the Bay of Biscay and other Iberian Atlantic waters.

In Europe's new industrial order, the core has diminished in size and the periphery expanded (Figure 11.4). If the stricken manufacturing districts of Britain, northern Spain, and Eastern Europe are excluded, then the new core, represented by high-tech and craft industry concentrations as well as North Sea petroleum, displays a thinner profile than the old one. Even so, the traditional pattern of a manufacturing core and primary industrial periphery remains intact.

Environmental Damage

Not surprisingly, the industrial core/periphery pattern in Europe has a sinister mirror image reflection in damage to water, land, and air. The Industrial Revolution and the prosperity it brought exacted a terrible price in environmental quality. No part of Europe has been exempt from this damage, but the highly industrialized core has suffered most, as suggested earlier, in the discussion of forest death in Chapter 2 (Figure 2.9). The greatest concentration of environmental damage has occurred in the *Black Triangle,* the borderland between eastern Germany, the Czech Republic, and southern Poland. The northwestern part of Čechy (Bohemia) is widely acknowledged to be the most polluted section of Europe (Figure 11.5). Visits to ravaged industrial towns such as Eisleben and Bitterfeld in Germany provide a sobering experience for any sensitive person.

Nor was the damage limited to the natural environment. The graceful humanized landscapes of preindustrial Europe—the fine old towns and aesthetically pleasing rural landscapes—also suffered harm. Industrial activity has altered or obliterated many of the myriad places that endow Europe with its special human character, prompting geographer Douglas Porteous to coin the word *topocide*—the deliberate obliteration of a place—to describe the fate of his native Howdendyke in Yorkshire. The "Faustian bargain" which industrialized Europe made now exacts its price.

Such warnings came very early. After a brief initial period of optimism about industrialization in the period before 1775, the more sensitive Europeans—poets and artists—sensed that something was amiss. They expressed their alarm in the form of paintings and poems, beginning in the last quarter of the eighteenth century. The Scottish poet Robert Burns visited an iron foundry "lest we gang to Hell, it may be nae surprise," and many artists of the period left paintings of the

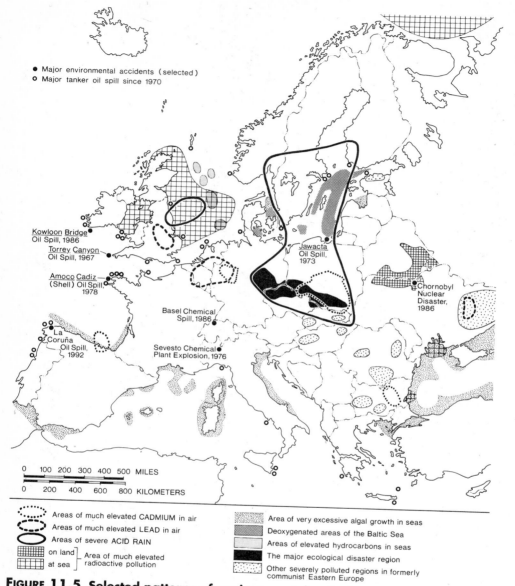

● Major environmental accidents (selected)
○ Major tanker oil spill since 1970

Kowloon Bridge
Oil Spill, 1986

Torrey Canyon
Oil Spill, 1967

Amoco Cadiz
(Shell) Oil Spill
1978

Jawacta
Oil Spill,
1973

Chornobyl
Nuclear
Disaster,
1986

Basel Chemical
Spill, 1986

La
Coruña
Oil Spill,
1992

Sevesto Chemical
Plant Explosion, 1976

0   100 200 300 400 500 MILES
0   200   400   600   800 KILOMETERS

‑‑‑‑ Areas of much elevated CADMIUM in air
‑‑‑‑ Areas of much elevated LEAD in air
◯ Areas of severe ACID RAIN
▦ on land ┐ Area of much elevated
▦ at sea ┘ radioactive pollution

▨ Area of very excessive algal growth in seas
▤ Deoxygenated areas of the Baltic Sea
■ Areas of elevated hydrocarbons in seas
■ The major ecological disaster region
▒ Other severely polluted regions in formerly
  communist Eastern Europe

FIGURE 11.5 Selected patterns of environmental pollution. The core of Europe has been most disastrously affected, but the peripheries have not escaped, due to the discharge of polluted rivers, the practice of dumping toxic wastes in the sea, and oil spills in the transport lanes. (Sources: François Carré, "Aperçu sur la pollution de la mer du Nord," *Hommes et Terres du Nord.* 1992:3, 142; *The Economist Atlas of the New Europe,* New York, USA: Henry Holt, 1992, 203, 210; *Geographica Polonica,* 59, 1962, 51; Dan Ionescu, "Romania: The A to Z of the Most Polluted Areas," *Report on Eastern Europe,* 2:19, 1991, 20–25; Richard Petrow, *In the Wake of the Torrey Canyon,* New York, USA: David McKay, 1968, frontispiece; *Concise Statistical Yearbook of Poland, 1991,* Warszawa, PL: Central Statistical Office, 1992, 25; Hugh Clout *et al., Western Europe: Geographical Perspectives,* Harlow, GB: Longman, 2nd ed., 1989, 182; Thompson, 45.)

industrialized districts that convey a sinister, foreboding landscape. Such warnings continued over the following centuries, and the Welshman Richard Llewellyn, in 1939, penned the poignant novel *How Green Was My Valley*, a classic lament of the economic oppression of his people and the ravaging of their countryside by industrialization. The European land today lies burdened with slag heaps, its soil poisoned by toxic waste, its streams and lakes polluted, its air darkened.

The ongoing environmental problems represent, in most cases, the consequences of deliberate, repeated, and habitual actions bound up in the processes of primary and secondary industry. Western Europeans have made some impressive strides in altering such behavior and in repairing some of the more visible damage, though the task at times seems impossible. Disposal of hazardous toxic wastes in the seas and in landfills continues, though the Netherlands now bans the latter practice.

In other cases, catastrophic industrial accidents, rather than deliberate action, causes environmental damage. Western Europe has suffered repeated oil tanker disasters, and chemical factories have experienced several major disasters, most notably at Seveso in northern Italy and at Basel in Switzerland (Figure 11.5). Without doubt, the greatest of all industrial accidents occurred at the Chornobyl nuclear power plant in Ukraine in 1986 (Chernobyl is the obsolete Russian form of the name). Radioactive pollution spread over much of Europe from Chornobyl, causing noteworthy contamination even as far afield as the reindeer-herding districts of northern Scandinavia. Closer to the site of the disaster, Ukraine has lost 5 million ha (12.4 million acres) of farmland and Belarus 20 percent of its arable land, possibly permanently (Figure 11.5).

The likelihood of future industrial accidents remains great. Lithuania experienced a nuclear "event" at its Chornobyl-style Ignalina plant in 1992, as did St. Petersburg at its Sosnovy Bor plant and the town of Balakovo near the lower Volga River. Some if not most Eastern European nuclear reactors receive inadequate maintenance, due to budgetary crises and bureaucratic inertia.

The human consequences of these environmental problems and disasters are profound. For example, at Seveso, where the chemical factory exploded, high rates of leukemia, lymphoma, and liver cancer rates plague the people exposed to the dioxin cloud; Belarussian children have an elevated incidence of thyroid tumors, a legacy of Chornobyl; Bulgaria's fishing industry has been devastated by dieoffs of mackerel, sturgeons, and anchovies; at Bitterfeld in Germany, air pollution caused diminished lung capacity and impaired immune systems in children; and in Russia's Kola Peninsula, devastated by nuclear waste and nickel smelters, respiratory and genetic diseases proliferate.

The Green Vote

One European reaction to the problem of industrial pollution has been the rise of *Green* politics. Characterized by ecological platforms, skepticism of technology, opposition to the collusion of industry and government, rejection of consumerism, and a desire to change basic lifestyles, the Green movement arose

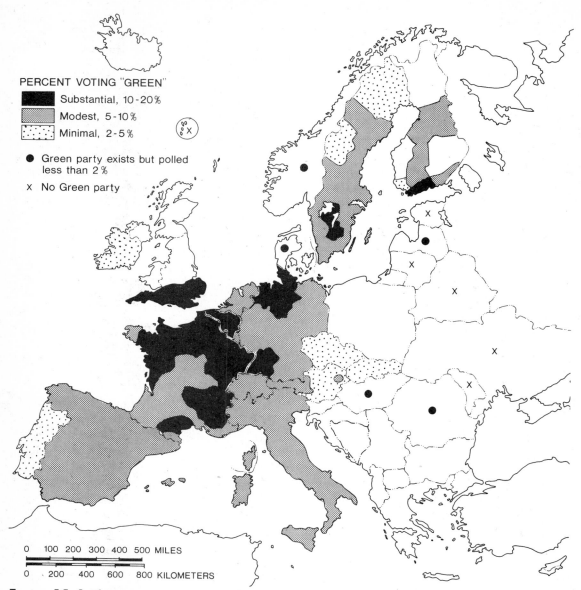

FIGURE 11.6 The "green" vote in selected elections, 1980–present The pattern reveals a core/periphery configuration, with a Green heartland in northern France, Belgium, southern Germany, and England south of the Severn-Wash line. This heartland coincides with prosperous areas experiencing major ecological problems. For Finland, the percentages shown are not votes but instead Greens as a proportion of elected representatives. (Sources: Gertjan Dijkink and Herman van der Wusten, "Green Politics in Europe," *Political Geography*, 11, 1992, 7–11; John Sallnow and Sarah Arlett, "Green Today, Gone Tomorrow?" *Geographical Magazine*, 61:11, 1989, 10–14; Vanlaer, 1984, as cited in Chapter 7; James R. McDonald, Eastern Michigan University, paper read at Association of American Geographers national meeting, 1993; and various national statistical yearbooks.)

mainly in the 1980s, centered in environmentally troubled yet wealthy countries such as Germany. In the German national elections of 1994, the Greens carried 7.3 percent of the popular vote. The combination of pollution and prosperity seems essential to Green success.

The Greens emerged as a major electoral force in the Western European elections of 1989 (Figure 11.6). In spite of their radical positions, they regularly achieve over a tenth of the vote in a sizable part of northwestern Europe, centered in northern France, parts of the Low Country, southwestern Germany, and England. South of the Severn-Wash "divide," which separates Great Britain into a deindustrialized, troubled north and a prosperous south, the Greens take close to 20 percent of the vote. In the severely polluted east, the Greens fare best in northern Čechy and in the former East Germany. In Norway, typical of the less polluted European periphery and dependent upon enterprises such as whaling, the Greens have failed to poll as much as one percent of the vote in any province. In Greece, on the opposite periphery of Europe, they have been similarly unsuccessful.

The industrial geography of Europe, as we have seen, is in flux. New patterns and industries emerge as old ones decline. High-tech and craft industries form only part of the changing economic geography. To obtain a more complete picture, we must now turn to another category altogether—the so-called "service" industries. Chapter 12 is devoted to that growing sector of the economy.

Sources and Suggested Readings

Judith Alfrey and Catherine Clark. *The Landscape of Industry: Patterns of Change in the Ironbridge Gorge.* London, GB: Routledge, 1993.

Boris Braun and Reinhold E. Grotz. "Support for Competitiveness: National and Common Strategies for Manufacturing Industries within the European Community." *Erdkunde.* 47 (1993), 105–117.

David Burtenshaw. *Saar-Lorraine.* London, GB: Oxford University Press, 1976.

R. H. Campbell. "Scottish Shipbuilding: Its Rise and Progress." *Scottish Geographical Magazine.* 80 (1964), 107–113.

Laurent Carroué. "La Bavière: un nouveau centre de gravité pour les industries européennes de haute technologie." *Revue Géographique de l'Est.* 31 (1991), 27–41.

F. W. Carter. "Pollution Problems in Post-War Czechoslovakia." *Transactions of the Institute of British Geographers* 10 (1985), 17–44.

Ronald H. Chilcote. "Spain's Iron and Steel: Renovation of an Old Industry." *Geographical Review.* 53 (1963), 247–262.

C. S. Davies. "Dark Inner Landscapes: The South Wales Coalfield." *Landscape Journal.* 3 (1984), 36–44.

C. S. Davies. "Wales: Industrial Fallibility and Spirit of Place." *Journal of Cultural Geography.* 4:1 (1983), 72–86.

K. C. Edwards. "Historical Geography of the Luxembourg Iron and Steel Industry." *Institute of British Geographers, Transactions and Papers.* 29 (1961), 1–16.

I. M. Evans. "Aspects of the Steel Crisis in Europe, with Particular Reference to Belgium and Luxembourg." *Geographical Journal.* 146 (1980), 396–407.

J. Ferrão and C. Jensen-Butler. *Industrial Development in Portuguese Regions, 1971–1979.* Aarhus, DK: University of Aarhus, Geographical Institute, 1984.

Douglas K. Fleming. "Coastal Steelworks in the Common Market Countries." *Geographical Review.* 57 (1967), 48–72.

Anthony C. Gatrell and Andrew A. Lovett. "The Geography of Hazardous Waste Disposal in England and Wales." *Area.* 18 (1986), 275–283.

Derek Gregory. *Regional Transformation and Industrial Revolution: A Geography of the Yorkshire Woollen Industry.* Minneapolis, USA: University of Minnesota Press, 1982.

Reinhold E. Grotz and D. Wadley. "Economic and Spatial Change in German Manufacturing, 1970–1986. *Tijdschrift voor Economische en Sociale Geografie.* 78 (1987), 162–175.

Peter Hall. *The Industries of London Since 1861.* London, GB: Hutchinson, 1962.

Peter Hall, Michael Breheny, Ronald McQuaid, and Douglas Hart. *Western Sunrise: The Genesis and Growth of Britain's Major High Tech Corridor.* London, GB: Allen & Unwin, 1987.

Richard T. Harrison. "The Labour Market Impact of Industrial Decline and Restructuring: The Example of the Northern Ireland Shipbuilding Industry." *Tijdschrift voor Economische en Sociale Geografie.* 76 (1985), 332–344.

Richard Hartshorne. "Upper Silesian Industrial District." *Geographical Review.* 24 (1934), 423–438.

A. G. Hoare. *The Location of Industry in Britain.* Cambridge, GB: Cambridge University Press, 1983.

Pat Hudson (ed.). *Regions and Industries: A Perspective on the Industrial Revolution in Britain.* Cambridge, GB: Cambridge University Press, 1989.

Guy Jalabert and Maïté Grégoris. "Turin: de la ville-usine à la technopole." *Annales de Géographie.* 96 (1987), 680–704.

Philip N. Jones. "On Defining a Western European Automobile Industry: Problems and Potentials." *Erdkunde.* 47 (1993), 25–39.

Russell L. King. *The Industrial Geography of Italy.* New York, USA: St. Martin's Press, 1985.

John Langton. *Geographical Change and Industrial Revolution: Coalmining in South West Lancashire, 1590–1799.* Cambridge, GB: Cambridge University Press, 1979.

John Langton. "The Industrial Revolution and the Regional Geography of England." *Transactions of the Institute of British Geographers.* 9 (1984), 145–167.

Ian R. Manners. *North Sea Oil and Environmental Planning: The United Kingdom Experience.* Austin, USA: University of Texas Press, 1982.

David R. Marples. "Chernobyl': Five Years Later." *Soviet Geography.* 32 (1991), 291–313.

David R. Marples. "A Correlation Between Radiation and Health Problems in Belarus'?" *Post-Soviet Geography.* 34 (1993), 281–292.

John E. Martin (ed.). *Greater London: An Industrial Geography.* London, GB: Bell, 1966.

John Morris. "Global Restructuring and the Region: Manufacturing Industry in Wales." *Tijdschrift voor Economische en Sociale Geografie.* 78 (1987), 16–29.

T. G. Nefedova, V. Streletsky, and A. Treivish. "La Ruhr, la Haute Silésie et le Donbass dans la trajectoire historique des vieilles régions industrielles européennes du charbon et de l'acier." *Revue Belge de Géographie*. 116 (1992), 41–48.

J. North and D. J. Spooner. "The Geography of the Coal Industry in the U. K. in the 1970s: Changing Directions?" *GeoJournal*. Vol. 2 (1978), pp. 255–272.

Jeffrey P. Osleeb and Craig Zumbrunnen. *The Soviet Iron and Steel Industry*. Totowa, USA: Rowman & Allanheld, 1985.

Heather S. Pardoe and John A. Matthews. "Chernobyl [137]Cs Fallout in Pollen Traps from the Jotunheimen-Jostedalsbreen Area, Southern Norway." *Norsk Geografisk Tidsskrift*. 43 (1989), 231–235.

Chris C. Park. *Chernobyl: The Long Shadow*. London, GB: Routledge, 1989.

Sidney Pollard. *Peaceful Conquest: The Industrialization of Europe, 1760–1970*. Oxford, GB: Oxford University Press, 1981.

Norman J. G. Pounds. "Historical Geography of the Iron and Steel Industry of France." *Annals of the Association of American Geographers*. 47 (1957), 3–14.

Norman J. G. Pounds. *The Ruhr: A Study in Historical and Economic Geography*. London, GB: Faber, 1952.

Norman J. G. Pounds. *The Upper Silesian Industrial Region*. Bloomington, USA: Indiana University Press, 1958.

Claudia Popescu. "Romanian Industry in Transition." *GeoJournal*. 29 (1993), 41–48.

J. Douglas Porteous. *Planned to Death: The Annihilation of a Place called Howdendyke*. Toronto, CDN: University of Toronto Press, 1989.

Allan L. Rodgers. *The Industrial Geography of the Port of Genova*. Chicago, USA: University of Chicago, Department of Geography, Research Paper No. 66, 1960.

Lloyd Rodwin and Hidehiko Sazanami (eds.). *Industrial Change and Regional Economic Transformation: The Experience of Western Europe*. London, GB: HarperCollins Academic, 1991.

David Sadler. "Privatising British Steel: The Politics of Production and Place." *Area*. 22 (1990), 47–55.

David Sadler, Adam Swain, and Ray Hudson. "The Automobile Industry and Eastern Europe." *Area*. 25 (1993), 339–349.

Matthew J. Sagers and Theodore Shabad. *The Chemical Industry in the USSR: An Economic Geography*. Boulder, USA: Westview Press, 1990.

Allen J. Scott. *New Industrial Spaces: Flexible Production and Regional Development in North America and Western Europe*. London, GB: Pion, 1988.

Marc de Smidt and Egbert Wever. *An Industrial Geography of the Netherlands*. London, GB: Routledge, 1990.

Adrian Smith. "Uneven Development and the Restructuring of the Armaments Industry in Slovakia." *Transactions of the Institute of British Geographers*, 19 (1994), 404–424.

David M. Smith. *The North West*. (Industrial Britain Series). New York, USA: Augustus M. Kelley, 1969.

G. P. F. Steed. "The Northern Ireland Linen Complex." *Annals of the Association of American Geographers*. 64 (1974), 397–408.

Jon Thompson. "East Europe's Dark Dawn: The Iron Curtain Rises to Reveal a Land Tarnished by Pollution." *National Geographic*. 179:6 (1991), 36–69.

John N. Tuppen. *France: Studies in Industrial Geography*. Boulder, USA: Praeger, 1980.

David Turnock. "The Pattern of Industrialization in Romania." *Annals of the Association of American Geographers*. 60 (1970), 540–559.

M. Vanier. "Troyes, vieille ville du textile en mutation." *Annales de Géographie*. 98 (1989), 658–675.

J. W. Wabe. "The Regional Impact of De-Industrialization in the European Community." *Regional Studies*. 20 (1986), 27–36.

David Walker. "Industrial Location in Turbulent Times: Austria through Anschluss and Occupation." *Journal of Historical Geography*. 12 (1986), 182–195.

Kenneth Warren. *The British Iron & Steel Industry Since 1840: An Economic Geography*. London, GB: Bell, 1970.

Peter Wells and Michael Rawlinson. *The New European Automobile Industry*. New York, USA: St. Martin's Press, 1994.

Allan M. Williams. *The Western European Economy: A Geography of Post-War Development*. London, GB: Hutchinson, 1987.

Mark Wise. *The Common Fisheries Policy of the European Community*. London, GB: Methuen, 1984.

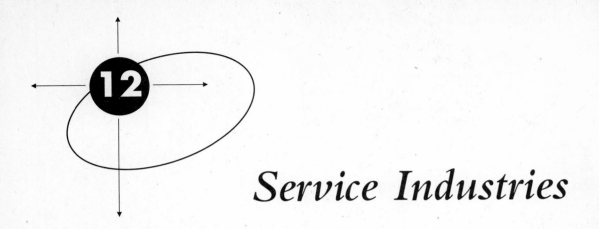

Service Industries

Service industries involve neither the extraction of resources nor manufacturing but instead include a broad range of activities such as government, transportation, banking, retailing, and tourism. Oddly the term **postindustrial** denotes the rise to dominance of service industries in modern Europe, coincident with the decline of primary and secondary industries.

No general agreement exists on how to categorize these diverse enterprises. Some geographers prefer to distinguish *market,* or private, services from *governmental,* or public services. Others suggest that the primary distinction should be between *producer* and *consumer* services. Many label all service industries as **tertiary** economic activities, while others subdivide them into tertiary (transport, trade, energy) and **quaternary** sectors (insurance, banking, research/development, wholesaling, retailing, advertising, legal counseling, health care, education, tourism, and so on). Still others recognize a **quinary** sector of service industries devoted solely to the generation and spread of knowledge and information, based in universities, research, and consulting, and heavily reliant upon computers. We would do best to avoid this classification controversy and simply focus upon some of the more important among the numerous, heterogeneous service industries.

The most outstanding fact concerning service industries in Europe is their disproportionate growth since about 1930. While most service activities have always been present, a marked increase has occurred, especially in recent decades and in the western part of Europe. Well over half of the labor force in many countries and provinces now finds employment in service industries (Figure 12.1). In Austria, for example, jobs in the services sector rose from 30 percent of the work force in 1961 to 55 percent in 1990. Eastern Europe lags behind the western part of the culture area in this respect, but even there the proportion often exceeds 40 percent.

No service activity better epitomizes Europe than **transportation and communication**. European culture has for centuries thrived upon the most complex and complete network of any region of comparable size in the entire world. As suggested in Chapter 1, the dense mesh of transportation facilities provides one

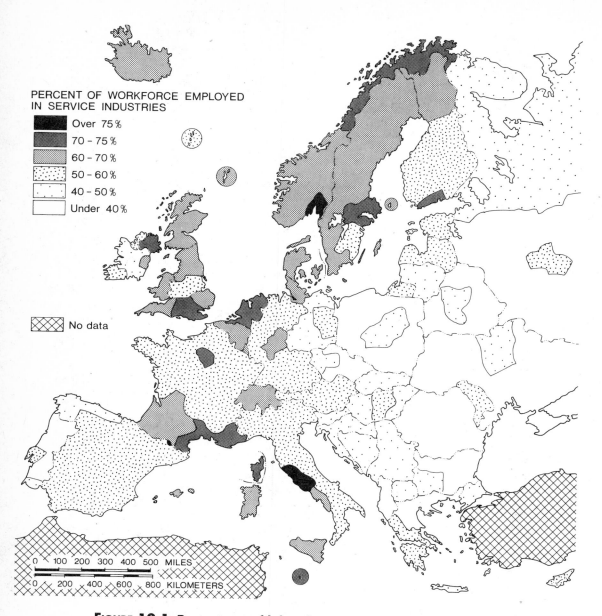

FIGURE 12.1 Percentage of labor force employed in the service industries.
These diverse activities include government, transport, trade, finance, retailing, energy supply, tourism, education, health, and other services. An east/west contrast can be detected within Europe.

defining trait for the European culture area (Figure 12.2). The resultant flow of trade goods and information can only be described as remarkable. Given this predilection, we should not be surprised at the rapid reknitting of transport facilities now occurring in the wake of Communism's fall and removal of the Iron Curtain. Within two months of the reunification of Germany, for example, 150 new crossing points of the defunct Iron Curtain border had opened in that country.

Highways

Europe's roads have provided a crucial component of the service sector at least since the time of the Romans. Desiring to rule more than the Mediterranean shores, the Romans built a truly astounding network of stone-paved roads connecting all parts of their Empire within Europe (Figure 12.3). They constructed some 320,000 km. (200,000 mi.) of highway in the Empire as a whole, and some remain in use today. Construction on the oldest of these Roman roads—the *Appian Way* from Roma southeast to Brundisium (modern Brindisi) on the Adriatic coast—began in 312 B.C. Laid out by surveyors in long, straight stretches where terrain permitted, the Roman highways offered a mobility previously unknown to merchants, the military, and the common folk. Roman engineers bridged even major streams such as the Rhône, and some of these splendid stone spans remain in use today after 2000 years of traffic, flood, and warfare. Among them are the bridges over the Tagus River at Alcántara and the Guadiana at Mérida, both in southwestern Spain. Contrary to the popular saying, not all roads led to Roma (Figure 12.3). The network had few major focal points, and even those have rarely retained their importance in the modern age. In France, for example, the Roman road junctions lay at Durocortorum (modern Reims) and Arelate (Arles) rather than Paris, while the main junction in Spain, Caesarea Augusta (modern Zaragoza) possesses less significance today.

For nearly a millennium following the collapse of the Empire, the surviving Roman highways continued to be the best in Europe, a tribute to the care and precision of their builders. The decline of trade during the Dark Ages curtailed the use of roads, as did political fragmentation. A rebirth of major mercantile activity in medieval times, coupled with the internal security provided by the feudal system, renewed the demand for roads. The new routes hardly rivaled their Roman predecessors. Pavement was a rarity. Numerous streams remained unbridged, and as a consequence, river-ford sites typified many emerging towns. In time, new road patterns emerged. Regions that had undergone political unification, such as France and the United Kingdom, developed highly centralized road patterns by the eighteenth or nineteenth centuries, with the major routes radiating out from the national capital (Figure 12.4). Paris was the all-important hub of French roads, and Dublin served a similar function within Ireland. No transport focal point existed within the network of politically fragmented Germany, reflecting the lack of centralized organization. Some new routes unused in earlier times arose. St. Gotthard Pass through the Alps, ignored by the Romans, emerged as the great north-south route between Italy and the Rhine

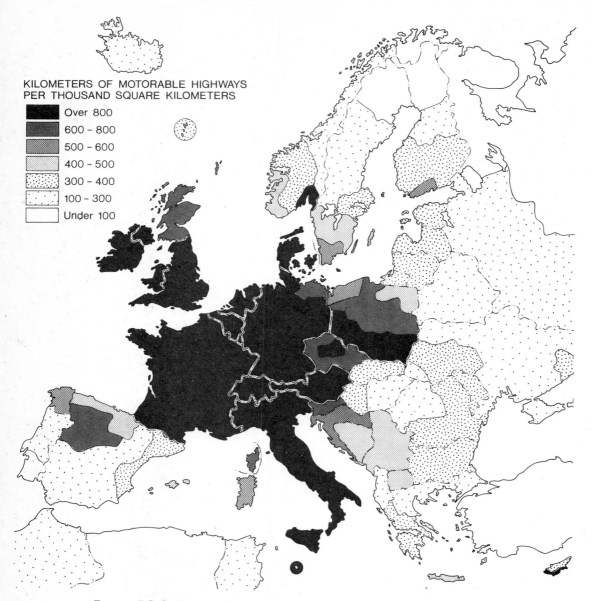

FIGURE 12.2 Motorable highways, kilometers per 1000 sq Km. The European road density exceeds that of any other sizable part of the world. A pronounced core/periphery pattern exists.

Valley in the Middle Ages, supplanting Splügen Pass to the east. The importance of the Gotthard route survives to the present.

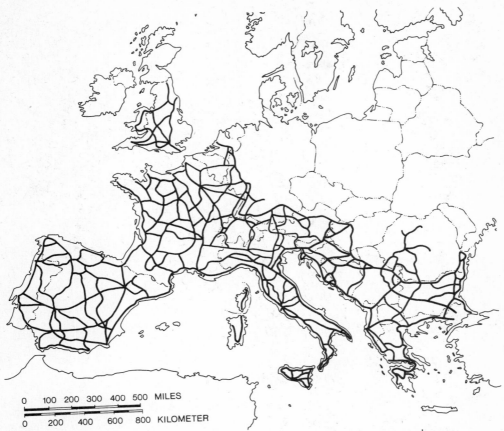

FIGURE 12.3 The Roman roads in Europe. The political borders are modern.
(Source: After *Westermanns Grosser Atlas zur Weltgeschichte*, Braunschweig, D: Georg Westermann, 1956.)

Improvements in the post-Roman roads came very slowly. John McAdam, for whom *macadam* roads are named, built all-weather highways in England in the early 1800s, paved with several thin layers of tightly packed crushed rock set in place by the application of water. The dawn of the modern era of bridge building occurred in 1826 when the British constructed a steel suspension bridge linking the large island of Anglesey to the coast of Wales.

Continued improvement and elaboration of Europe's highway system occurred in the 1900s largely because of the automobile, and a pronounced west/east contrast developed. Western Europe's middle class gained the financial ability to purchase cars only after midcentury. In 1950, a mere 6,100,00 private automobiles existed in non-Communist Europe, about one for every 48 persons, but by 1970 the total had increased tenfold and by 1986 to 112,400,000, so that one Westerner in three owned a car (Figure 12.5). Truck traffic also increased

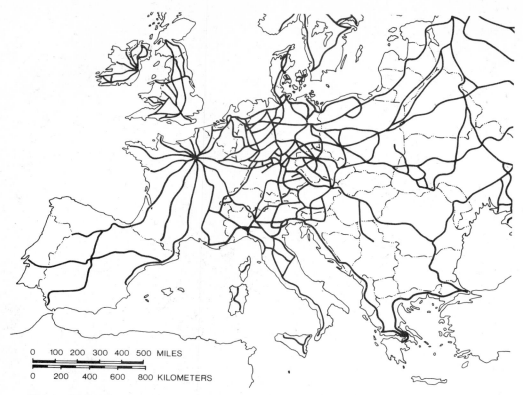

FIGURE 12.4 Main post roads in Europe, 1850. Note the highly centralized pattern in France and the lack of a dominant focal point in central Europe also note the core/periphery pattern of road density. Compare it to Figure 12.6. The political borders are modern. (Source: After George W. Hoffman, ed., *A Geography of Europe*, New York, USA: Ronald Press, 3rd ed., 1969, 107.)

rapidly in Western Europe and today carries 64 percent of all freight, as contrasted to less than half as recently as 1970. Even for movement within cities, Western Europeans now use automobiles more commonly than mass transit.

Eastern Europe remains a region of relatively low automobile ownership, lesser truck usage, and sparser highway network (Figures 12.2, 12.5). Indeed, private car ownership offers one of the sharper, more abrupt contrasts between European east and west. Highway infrastructure even deteriorated in the east since the 1970s, and one of the first major tasks undertaken by the German government after reunification in 1990 involved upgrading roads in its new eastern provinces. Automobile ownership nevertheless increases in eastern Europe, even in the poorest countries such as Albania, where the number of cars rose from 3,000 to 120,000 between 1985 and 1994.

A pronounced core/periphery pattern can also be detected in Europe's roads (Figure 12.2). The densest highway network exists in the center, while peripheries have a sparser pattern. Iceland only recently completed its circuminsular

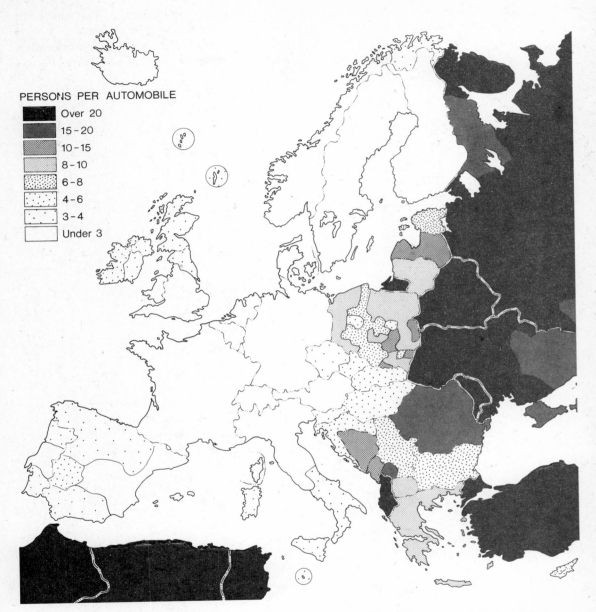

FIGURE 12.5 Persons per automobile. Private car ownership remains largely a Western European trait, serving to differentiate traditional capitalistic countries from the formerly Communist east, as well as from the Third World, non-European countries to the south.

road, and some mainland settlements in Norway remain unconnected to the country's highway system. The core/periphery pattern appears even more strikingly in the network of controlled-access expressways (Figure 12.6). The European Union has invested heavily in expressway connections in the core area.

Efforts to integrate Europe's highway system have progressed for decades, with the aim of more effectively meshing together the various national networks

——— Controlled access divided highway

0   100 200 300 400 500 MILES
0   200   400   600   800 KILOMETERS

FIGURE 12.6 Controlled access, divided highways. Germany built the prototype of such expressways in the 1930s and they remain a trait of the European core.

of roads. The "European highway" designation is one result. In addition to their national number, many routes also have a standard *E* designation. For example, the *E8* highway runs from 'sGravenhage eastward through Hannover, Berlin, Poznan, Warszawa, and Minsk to Moskva. The *E1* extends from Sicilia in the far south to Roma, Genova, Lyon, Paris, LeHavre, and, after a ferry connection, to London. New routes of this type are in the planning stage, such as the *Via Baltica*, an upgraded highway from Tallinn to Riga, Vilnius, and into Poland.

Highway construction and universal adoption of automobiles has brought problems to Western Europe and especially to the densely populated core region. As John Whitelegg noted, high levels of motorization constitute a major source of "disturbance, nuisance, health hazards, land-take, and ecological disruption," not to mention an appalling death rate from accidents and frequent gridlock traffic jams on the freeways. Germany, the epicenter of these problems, has seen picturesque towns such as Idar-Oberstein mutilated by highway construction, watched forests die from automobile exhaust, and suffered nearly 350,000 traffic accidents annually resulting in death or injury in its western provinces alone. Public opinion has begun to turn against additional road building in Germany, and recently construction on the A–49 expressway south of Kassel in Hessen province ended due to opposition. "Hessen grün und rot machen A–49 tot" ("Hessian 'Greens' and 'Reds' kill A–49") noted the graffito of one observer. Switzerland plans to eliminate all transit truck traffic by early in the next decade to reduce noise and pollution.

Railroads

Europeans invented the railroad, just as they did the all-weather highway, and Europe possesses almost one-third of the world's rail mileage. Woven into a splendid network covering nearly all parts of the culture area, Europe's railroad system greatly enhances the mobility characteristic of these peoples. Only an east/west difference in track gauge presents a hindrance.

Railroad network density is greatest in Germanic Central Europe, and a pronounced core/periphery pattern exists (Figure 12.7). Outlying islands such as Iceland, Færoes, Shetlands, Baleares, Malta, Kriti, Åland, and Cyprus have no railroad lines at all, nor do the northernmost provinces of Norway. European railroads are state-owned rather than private, with the result that relatively little duplication of routes developed.

The European railroad system derives from the English Industrial Revolution. In 1767 a British ironworks cast the first rails, initially for use by horse-drawn trams. A crude steam locomotive appeared by 1804 and ten years later a locomotive first pulled a train. By 1825 the British opened regularly operated railroad service connecting the industrial towns of Darlington and Stockton on the River Tees in northeastern England. The British invention, prompted by increased demands for bulk transport, spread rapidly to mainland Europe, reaching France by 1832, Belgium and Germany by 1835, Austria-Hungary by 1838, Italy and the Netherlands by 1839, and Switzerland by 1844. By midcentury a railroad network had developed in England, and significant beginnings had been

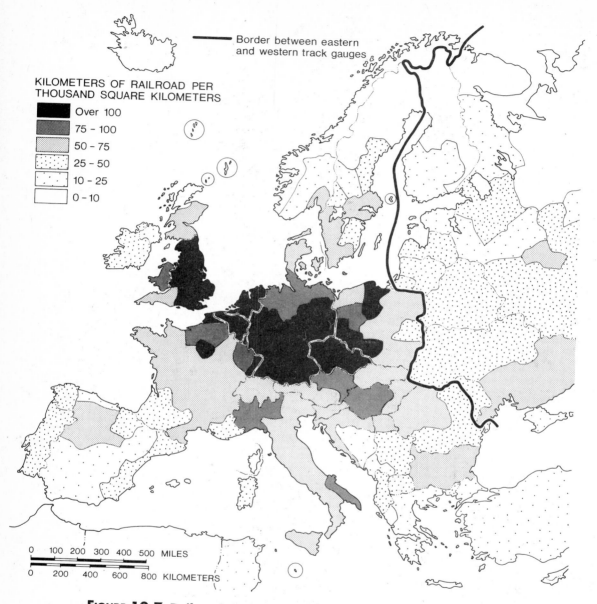

FIGURE 12.7 Railroad density and gauge. A core/periphery contrast is obvious, and the gauge difference adds an east/west component to the pattern. The western gauge is typically 1.64 m (4 ft. 8½ in.) and the eastern 1.74 m (5 ft. 0 in.).

made in the Paris Basin, Belgium, and northern Germany (Figure 12.8). The great era of rail construction ended by 1900 in Europe, by which time nearly all of the present network existed. Albania, the final country to join the railroad age, built its first line in 1947.

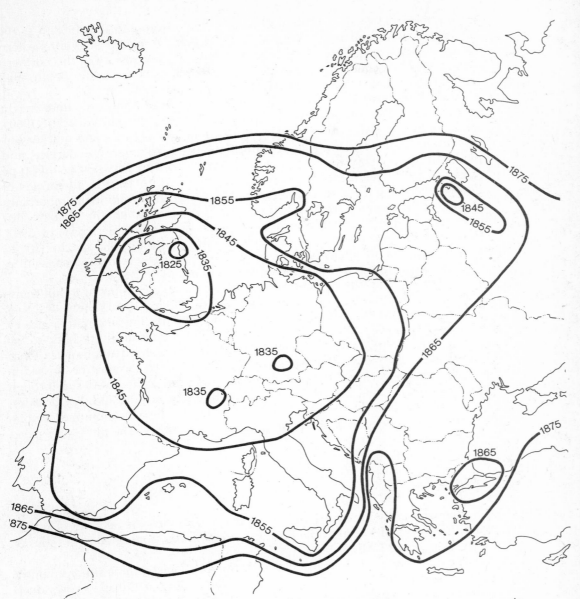

FIGURE 12.8 Diffusion of the railroad in nineteenth-century Europe. A striking core/periphery pattern appears. Political borders shown are modern.

Deindustrialization and the rise of motorized highway transport caused a notable shrinkage of the railroad network in the twentieth century, particularly in Western Europe. As early as the 1920s, over 700 km (435 mi.) of line had been abandoned in Great Britain. In western Germany, the number of passenger rail cars on the *Bundesbahn* (Federal Railroad) declined from 22,600 in 1958 to 18,700 as early as 1967, and the volume of riders decreased in almost every western country. Sweden recently terminated all passenger rail service in the northern two-thirds of its country. Freight movement by rail in Western Europe dropped from 30 percent of all tonnage in 1970 to 18 percent by 1990.

Still, Europeans have by no means given up on rail transport, either freight or passenger. The international Trans-Europ Express, introduced in the 1960s, attracted business travelers by offering luxurious rolling stock and quicker service. Then France led the way in ultra-high-speed passenger rail service, and plans are under way to create a substantial European network of this type (Figure 12.9). If realized, this high-speed system will extend to all corners of Europe, including the east, where railroads retained their traditional importance in spite of deteriorated track quality. Germany plans a 400 km./hr. (250 mi./hr.) train for the Hamburg-Berlin route, across the former East Germany, by 1997. High-speed trains operating in Europe today travel at 160 to 350 km./hr. (100 to 217 mi./hr.) and obviously have no grade crossings. They compete successfully, time- and cost-wise, with many airline connections.

The most compelling evidence of Europe's future commitment to rail transport is provided by the recent completion of the 50 km (31 mi.) Strait of Dover (English Channel) *Eurotunnel*, or "Chunnel," which links England and France by railroad (see Figure 12.10). Trains move through the tunnel at speeds of up to 160 km./hr. (100 mi./hr.), carrying freight, passengers, and ferried automobiles. Once a major hindrance to land transport, the English Channel can now be crossed in only 33 minutes, terminal to terminal. In fact, rail traffic can move faster through the tunnel than along the antiquated connecting lines in England. For decades, the European rail system has steadily converted to electrification and double-tracking, a trend begun in the more prosperous countries. The ultra-high-speed system is totally electric.

Waterways

Complementing the fine road and rail systems is an intricate network of waterways. It consists of Europe's rivers and peripheral seas, connected by a series of canals (see Figure 2.20).

The interconnected oceans and seas flanking Europe on three sides provide a splendid opportunity for transportation. The outline of Europe shows deep indentations on all shorelines, with the result that no part of the culture area lies any great distance from the sea. Small wonder that Europeans have long taken advantage of the pattern of peripheral seas to move their commodities from place to place.

The Mediterranean, the first sea used extensively for transportation, proved admirably suited to early navigators who possessed few advanced marine skills because ships could sail about its waters without ever losing sight of land. High, rocky coasts with promontories made even more visible by the erection of temples and shrines, guided the sailors of ancient Greece, as did the many mountain-

FIGURE 12.9 The European master plan for 21st-century high-speed railroads. Instigated by the European Community, this plan will be difficult to implement, especially in the Balkans and east. Part of the system, particularly in France, is already operational. (Source: European Community planning documents, 1989 update; and European Conference of Ministers of Transport, Paris, 1990.)

ous islands (see Figure 3.2). By "coasting" parallel to the shore or keeping island landfalls in sight, the sailors overcame much of the danger of sea transport. At a remarkably early date, Mediterranean seamen ventured out beyond Gibraltar as

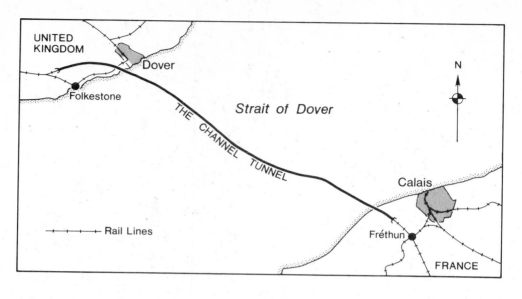

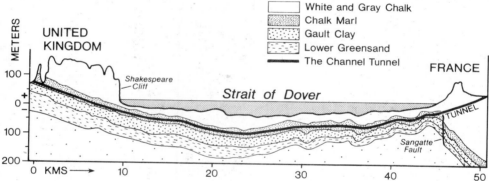

FIGURE 12.10 The Channel Tunnel, providing a railroad link between England and France. Excavation was completed in 1993, linking Britain directly to the ultra-high-speed rail system of the mainland. Also known as the *Eurotunnel*, it follows an undulating layer of chalk marl rock, impermeable to water yet soft enough to drill through with relative ease.

far as Cornwall, attracted by tin mines. Still, at the time depicted in the Homeric epics, about 1200 B.C., the Greeks apparently remained ignorant of even the western part of the Mediterranean. Ulysses' relatively short voyage to western lands such as Malta and Tunisia placed him in unknown waters, where fear and imagination led him to people the shores with one-eyed cannibalistic giants and sorceresses who changed men to swine. In later centuries the Greeks searched out every bay and cove around the Mediterranean and used the sea as the highway of their far-flung commercial empire. The Romans succeeded the Phoenicians and Greeks. They in turn gave way to other great Mediterranean seafaring peoples, including the Byzantine Greeks and Venetians.

The use of the North and Baltic seas for trade came later. By the eighth century a trade in furs, slaves, and amber developed in the Baltic, while merchants in the North Sea handled cloth, wine, and wool. The Middle Ages brought the Hanseatic League, or Hansa, a trading union of many towns, in countries around the shores of the North and Baltic seas. With the Age of Discovery, the Atlantic assumed its present position as the major trade route of Europe.

Complementing the peripheral seas are numerous navigable rivers, improved through dredging, removing rapids, constructing locks, and digging connecting canals. The major use of rivers and canals for transportation began in the Middle Ages, for the classical Mediterranean peoples did not have navigable rivers at their disposal. Only after the commercial focus of Europe shifted north of the Alps did river traffic become important. The Great European Plain is drained by a series of parallel navigable rivers trending southeast to northwest in direction, most of which rise in the hills and mountains south of the plain. Some achieved major use by the 1100s and 1200s, and feudal lords who resided along the banks of such streams as the Rhine collected tolls from ships passing beneath their strongholds. In modern times many rivers have been internationalized, and the countries through which they flow cannot charge unnecessary tolls or restrict traffic.

The navigable rivers of Europe early became bound together by canals. The building of canals antedated railroad construction, beginning in earnest in the late 1700s and reaching a peak in the first half of the nineteenth century. Most canals connected the different rivers on the Great European Plain. The English led the way in canal building as well as railroads, and by 1790 they had established a good network. Some 8000 km (5000 mi.) of canals existed in the United Kingdom by the middle 1800s, and the Industrial Revolution experienced a "canal phase." Inland waterways became the prime carriers of bulky products with a low per-unit value, particularly raw or semiprocessed materials. Canals and rivers provided of the most important linkages for early industrial districts.

By the end of the great era of European canal-building, barges could cross the entire Great European Plain, from France to Russia (see Figure 2.20). The densest concentration of canals anywhere in the world lay in the region from the Seine and English Scarplands eastward to the Odra/Oder. That link remains open today, part of which is Germany's *Mittelland Canal*. Other major water linkages included the *Kiel Canal*, shortening the distance between the Baltic and North seas and the *Canal du Midi* through the Gap of Carcassonne. Russia long ago linked the headwaters of the Volga, Don, and Neva rivers with canals to allow movement through the East European Plain.

After the great age of canals ended, many became derelict, bypassed by railroads and highways. Once-famous waterways such as the Göta Canal of Sweden became largely recreational routes used by vacationers. Canals experienced a decline even more profound than that afflicting the railroads. By 1948, some 6,500 km (4000 mi.) of the British waterway system had been abandoned. Usage continues to decrease; inland waterways carried 12.5 percent of Europe's freight tonnage in 1970 but only 8 percent by 1990.

Even so, several European countries have continued to upgrade their waterways for transport use, most notably Germany and France. Canalization of the Mosel/Moselle River with 14 locks between Thionville in Lorraine and Koblenz, where the Mosel joins the Rhine, greatly enhanced the navigability of the river in the 1960s, ironically just before deindustrialization struck hard at the Saar-Lorraine district. Romania opened the *Danube-Black Sea Canal* in 1984, shortening the route by avoiding the river delta, and in 1992 Germany completed the new *Main-Danube Canal*, linking the Rhine River/North Sea area with the Black Sea by way of Nürnberg. The latter canal, which parallels an outmoded predecessor, can accommodate huge "Eurobarges" carrying as much freight as 78 truck trailers. The Main-Danube Canal created huge controversy. Critics point to the attendant environmental destruction and label it an economic white elephant. "Build it and they will come" seems a dubious policy in the modern age. The canal opened almost precisely at the time when political barriers between Eastern and Western Europe fell, giving its boosters cause for hope.

The elaborate network of seas, rivers, and canals focuses on Europe's numerous port facilities, most of which lie at the transshipment points between inland waterways and the open ocean. A string of major ports lines the shores of the North and Baltic seas, at the mouths of the rivers of the Great European Plain. These include, from west to east, Bordeaux on the Garonne, Le Havre on the Seine, London on the Thames, Antwerpen on the Schelde, Rotterdam-Europoort on the Rhine, Bremerhaven on the Weser, Hamburg on the Elbe, Szczecin on the Odra, Gdańsk on the Wisla, Riga on the Daugava, and St. Petersburg on the Neva (see Figure 2.20). In contrast, most major ports of Southern Europe, including Barcelona, Genova, and Napoli, are generally not riverine but instead lie some distance removed from the silted river deltas. An exception is Marseille, where a major port, Fos, now operates west of the city at the mouth of the Rhône. Lying at the southern access to the core of Europe, Marseille-Fos increased traffic volume enormously since World War II and ranks as Europe's second largest port. Europoort-Botlek, serving Rotterdam and the rest of the Randstad Holland, as well as the European industrial heartland, ranks as the greatest port of Europe, reflecting the huge volume of traffic carried by the Rhine and Maas rivers. Rotterdam began to grow rapidly in the last three decades of the nineteenth century, coincident with the rise of the Ruhr and other industrial areas along the Rhine. By 1938 the Dutch port ranked as the largest in Europe in terms of tonnage handled, and in 1962 it became the number one tonnage port in the world, surpassing New York City.

Pipelines

Rudimentary pipeline transport can be traced back to the aqueducts built widely in Southern Europe to supply water for Roman towns. Some Roman systems remain functional. Most pipelines date from after World War II, when petroleum and natural gas began to displace coal as the primary fuels consumed in the major industrial centers of Europe.

A network of oil and gas pipelines now laces Europe, connecting to peripheral and external sources. Russian oil and gas fields in the hinter reaches of the East European Plain send much of their produce westward by pipeline to Ukraine, Belarus, and Central Europe, with a major depot at Lviv. North Sea oil flows to Great Britain, Denmark, Germany, and the Netherlands in a series of pipelines, some of which cross the floor of the sea.

The Middle East remains the largest supplier of petroleum for Europe. To accommodate this oil, pipelines lead northward from the Mediterranean, beginning at Trieste and Genova in Italy, Marseille in France, and Málaga in Spain. Two of these lines cross the Alps to the German city of Ingolstadt on the Danube River in the province of Bayern, a major refining center. The pipeline from Marseille passes north through the Rhône-Saône Corridor, Belfort Gate, and Upper Rhine Plain, reaching Karlsruhe in southwestern Germany and the Lorraine area of France. Since virtually all pipelines have been built since 1950, their routes reflect international planning. Cooperation within the E.U. led to the selection of southern Germany as an oil-refining center, fed by the pipelines originating in France and Italy. In Europe as a whole, pipelines now carry about 10 percent of all freight by tonnage.

Air Transport

The European transport system has been further supplemented in the twentieth century by air transport. Europe has a dense network of air routes and a large number of airlines, including Lufthansa (Germany), Alitalia (Italy), Air France, Sabena (Belgium), Swissair, KLM (Netherlands), British Airways, Aer Lingus (Republic of Ireland), S. A. S. (Sweden, Denmark, Norway) and others. The largest volume of traffic moves through London's Heathrow Airport, Rhein-Main near Frankfurt, Charles de Gaulle at Paris, Schiphol at Amsterdam, and Leonardo da Vinci near Roma. Congestion at some of these airports, especially London Heathrow, caused additional ones to be built or enlarged. Competition has also arisen. München now seeks to rival Frankfurt with its splendid new facility in the virtual center of post-cold-war Europe.

When travel restrictions between east and west loosened after 1990, airlines proved better able than any other mode of passenger transport to exploit the demand for increased movement within Europe. Years will pass before the railroad and highway infrastructure in the east can be upgraded sufficiently to allow ease of movement, but airline connections are already in place. Even eastern cities formerly difficult to reach by air, such as Riga, now enjoy much enhanced airline linkages.

All of Europe's transport systems are in the midst of revolutionary change, leading to ever-increased mobility and exchange. The term *Euromobile*, used as the title of a recent book, perhaps best describes this evolving situation. Not only will east and west be firmly knitted together, but also the movement of people, information, and commodities within and between all countries will become even more intense. The inherent unity of the European culture area is ever more vividly reflected in the system of transport and communications.

Energy Production

Europeans consume vast amounts of energy in sustaining their high standard of living. In fact, a high per capita consumption of electricity and other forms of energy provides one defining trait to help us bound the European culture area (Figure 12.11). A sizable service industry exists to supply the needed power.

Traditionally, indigenously produced *coal* provided the greater part of Europe's primary energy, but after about 1950, when consumption levels in western Europe began rising beyond all expectations, coal gradually lost its dominance. Petroleum and natural gas eventually surpassed coal in most of Western and Southern Europe, though most oil must be imported, placing Europeans in a vulnerable position. The sharp oil price increase instigated by the Organization of Petroleum Exporting Countries in 1973 sent shock waves through Western Europe, and the Russian turnoff of the subsidized oil flow to its former empire and sphere of domination in Eastern Europe in 1990 had a similarly traumatic impact.

One European reaction to the rapidly growing need for energy and the problem of foreign dependency was increased development of indigenous sources such as hydroelectric and geothermal power (Figure 12.11). The nuclear power industry also grew in response to rising consumption. The United Kingdom put the first nuclear power plant on line in 1956, followed by France two years later and western Germany in 1961. Some countries, most notably France, now depend upon nuclear plants for the greater part of their electricity (Figure 12.11). Certain others, under pressure from "Greens" or in the fear of terrorists, became disenchanted with nuclear energy and curtailed production. Italy phased out its modest industry altogether. By contrast, some newly independent eastern countries, including Lithuania and Slovakia, had to increase their nuclear dependence when cheap Russian oil ceased to flow. Regrettably, some Eastern European power plants remain dangerous, due to obsolete design, inadequate maintenance, or poor management, raising the specter of another Chornobyl-scale disaster (Figure 12.11). Armenia, suffering acute power shortages, reopened an obsolete, earthquake-damaged nuclear reactor, and Bulgaria's power plants remain notoriously dangerous.

These widely differing decisions at the national level produced a vivid geography of primary energy in Europe (Figure 12.11). This complex spatial pattern reflects the European quandary and lack of consensus concerning energy—how to provide an adequate supply safely, dependably, and at an affordable cost, while at the same time avoiding profound ecological damage. Europeans must find a solution to this pressing problem if their prosperity and high living standards are to survive. Always on the eastern horizon lie the irradiated meadows and fields of the Chornobyl hinterland.

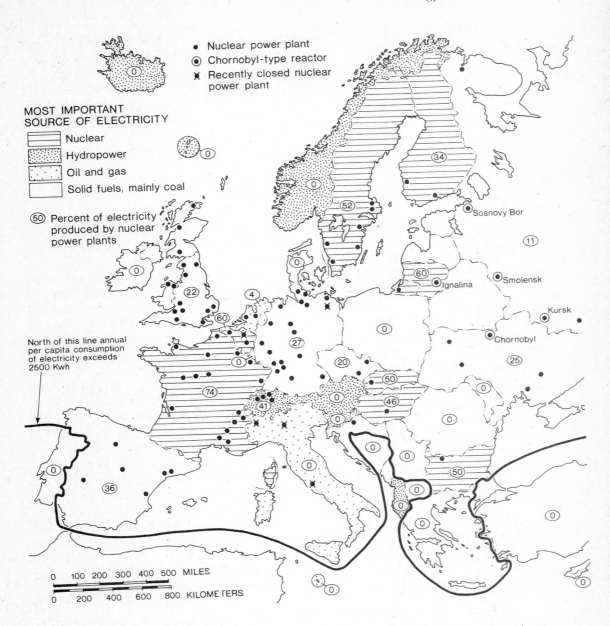

FIGURE 12.11 The geography of electrical energy. The troubled Ignalina plant in Lithuania, still manned by Russian personnel, has recently been "adopted" by Sweden, which has taken steps to render it less dangerous. (Sources: Peter R. Mounfield, *World Nuclear Power*, London, GB: Routledge, 1991, 101, 113–117, 130–133; John Cole and Francis Cole, *The Geography of the European Community*, London, GB: Routledge, 1993, 126; United Nations, *Energy Statistics Yearbook 1992*; World Bank statistics; *European Marketing Data and Statistics 1992*, London, GB: Euromonitor.)

Part of the answer hopefully lies in new methods and technologies of energy conservation, a field in which Europeans rank as world leaders. Still, stupidities proliferate. For example, pigs from the Netherlands go by truck to Italy for slaughter, in order that the prestigious label "Parma ham" can be affixed to the meat, yielding a higher price, while Bavarian potatoes journey to Italy for washing, only to be reshipped to Germany to sell, wasting fossil fuel and clogging Alpine highways in order to benefit from cheap Italian labor.

Producer Services

An entire sector of postindustrial activity consists of higher-order services catering to large business enterprises. These producer services include banking, accounting, advertising, legal services, research/development, insurance, marketing/wholesaling, real estate brokerage, various types of consulting, and the processing and provision of knowledge and information. Such activities, as well as many corporate headquarters, cluster strikingly in the inner core of Western Europe, revealing the dominant economic position of that small part of the culture area and of the "big three" members of the E.U.—Germany, France, and the United Kingdom (Figure 12.12).

London and Paris early became the financial centers of the world. While later surpassed by New York and Tokyo, they remain very powerful, especially within Europe. London still boasts eight of the world's largest 20 insurance firms. Zürich ranks as a world-famous banking center, and Swiss accounts attract deposits from the famous and infamous alike. Frankfurt-am-Main emerged as the banking and monetary center of the E.U.

That service sector devoted to the generation, storing, and processing of diverse types of information forms a mainspring of the service sector in this age of rapid technological change. It includes an institutionalized research and development component and subsidiary consultancy firms. This information sector tends to be clustered in the same European inner core that houses financial services (Figure 12.12). Locationally, the information services remain linked to the major centers of high-tech manufacturing, in particular the western suburbs of London, the southern and southwestern satellite cities of Paris, the Randstad Holland megalopolis, and southwestern Germany (Figures 11.4, 12.12).

As Europe enters the twenty-first century, this striking concentration of producer services represents the most powerful statement of core/periphery contrasts. Even though producer services, in a time of instant communications, need not be concentrated geographically, the fact is that the core of Europe has grown smaller and more powerful in the postindustrial age. Increasingly, the European peripheries find it difficult to keep pace or maintain a status quo. Eastern Europe, in particular, faces well-nigh insurmountable problems in achieving prosperity given the dominant position of the inner core region. Virtually all of the decisions

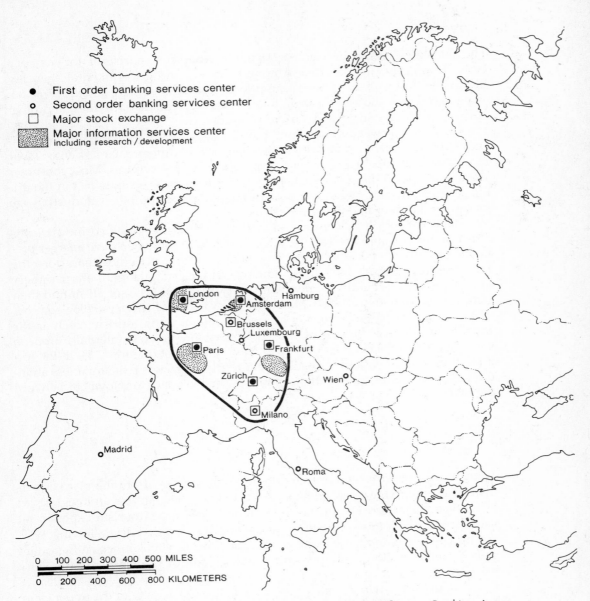

FIGURE 12.12 Major centers of producer service industry. Banking, insurance, research/development, information processing, and other producer services are highly concentrated in an inner core region of Europe.

and innovations that shape and reshape the economy and future of Europe derive from the inner core, from a small, elite group engaged in the producer service industries.

Consumer Services

The remainder, and far greater, part of the service sector consists of, for want of a better term, *consumer* services. Among them we find governmental agencies, health care and welfare systems, educational facilities, retailing outlets, an elaborately developed industry serving tourism and recreational activities, and other enterprises serving social and individual needs.

Most Europeans employed in the service sector work in these consumer-oriented industries. They represent, in the main, a very different, far less elitist labor force than that engaged in providing producer-related services. Most consumer service jobs pay modest wages, usually lower than those recently lost in the primary and manufacturing industries. For many Europeans, the postindustrial age has brought diminished living standards.

The core/periphery contrast so evident in producer-oriented industries is absent in the consumer sector. Peripheral regions, in fact, often have a larger proportion of their total labor force engaged in service activities than does the European core (Figure 12.1). In Scandinavia and Iceland, the northern periphery of Europe, various cradle-to-grave services typical of Nordic socialism find their richest development, causing unusually high levels of service-sector employment. A similar pattern prevails in regions reliant upon tourism, such as the Mediterranean isles. Instead of core/periphery, the greatest internal European contrast in consumer services involves west versus east (Figure 12.1). In the formerly Communist countries, retailing and touristic services remain far less abundant, accounting for most of the contrast in service-sector employment between the two halves of Europe.

Tourism

Tourism—the short-term movement to destinations away from the place of permanent residence for reasons unconnected to livelihood—forms an integral part of the European lifestyle. In the western half of Europe, tourism experienced very rapid growth after 1950 and especially in the two decades following 1965, during which the number of tourists doubled. Tourism constitutes an important growth sector in the economy and provides one of the main reasons why employment in service industries has grown so large.

Prior to World War II, tourism remained an elitist activity of the upper class, but today the majority of western Europeans participates. Each year some 180 million citizens of the E.U. engage in tourism. About 85 percent of all tourists in Europe are Europeans, meaning that overseas visitors now constitute the far lesser part of the industry.

Tourism displays a vivid geography in its sources, destinations, and flows. Most tourists come from the wealthy countries of northern and western Europe, and their vacation destinations most often lie to the south. Over half of all E.U. tourists seek out beaches for their holiday. Spain possesses the greatest concentration of southern seaside resorts, grouped in such coastal districts as the Costa del Sol and Costa del Azahar, as well as the Baleares Isles (Figure 12.13). Between 1959 and 1964, the number of tourists coming to Spain increased from 4 to 14 million and the country's foreign currency earning grew tenfold, marking the beginning of the Iberian beach resort era. Today, a fifth of all cash receipts in Spain derive from tourism, making it the country's largest industry. As is generally the case with tourism, the economic impact in Spain remained highly localized, in a coastal corridor. Even today, the tourist infrastructure remains rather weakly developed in most interior areas, away from the beaches, in spite of the cultural richness of the country.

Many beach resorts also developed in Mediterranean France, in northern Italy, the Dalmacija coast of Croatia, the Black Sea shore of Bulgaria, and Ukrainian Krym. The tourist industry's main shortcoming is extreme vulnerability to economic downturns and political unrest. Empty hotels lined the Adriatic shore of Dalmacija during the recent Balkan war, and refugees took the place of paying guests. Tourist flows to beach resorts tend to be channelized. Two-thirds of the vacationers in Malta, where the tourist boom began in the 1960s, come from the United Kingdom, in part because the islands were once a British colony. Germans prefer the Italian beaches and formerly also patronized Dalmacija very heavily.

The second most common tourist flow is from lowland to highland. Mountain and hill areas attract abundant visitors in both winter and summer, and the Alps, benefitting from central location, dominate the highland tourist industry (see Figure 12.14). Together, Switzerland and Austria receive annually twice as many visitors—27,700,000—as their combined resident population. Here, too, tourists are easily frightened away. Slovenia, gifted with some of the loveliest Alpine scenery, experienced difficulty attracting visitors during the Balkan war, even though it remained aside from the conflict.

At least a quarter of all E.U. tourists seek out rural areas for their vacations. Many farms in favored districts offer guest accommodations. A third of all farmers in Finland's Åland Islands house vacationers, as do about a fourth of those in the Austrian Alps and 16 percent of Scottish islanders and highlanders. In some Norwegian municipalities, the proportion runs as high as 40 percent.

Cultural tourism also ranks high in Europe, directed to places offering museums, well-preserved medieval or Renaissance quarters, theatrical and musical festivals, notable archaeological sites, and the like. Five million tourists visit Venèzia each year, about 56 times the size of the resident population of the city. Stonehenge in England became so overrun by visitors that protective measures became necessary, as also occurred at the Athínai Acropolis. The very names of certain cities—Paris, Wien, Firenze—connote culture and refinement, attracting many tourists. More bucolic in message and appeal, the numerous open-air folk museums of Europe remind visitors of a romanticized, irrevocably lost rural past. Such outdoor museums, centered upon collections of traditional farmsteads relocated from the countryside, appeared first in Scandinavia, the prototype being Skansen in Stockholm, and the concept has spread through most of trans-Alpine Europe, from Kizhi Island in Russian Karelia to the Ulster Folk Museum

FIGURE 12.13 Major tourist destinations in Europe. The most important tourist flow is from north to south, favoring the Mediterranean beaches and Alpine mountain resorts. (Sources: Ferdinand Mayer, ed., *Diercke Weltatlas*, Braunschweig, D: Georg Westermann, 1975, 55, 98–99: George Hoffman, ed., *Europe in the 1990s: a Geographical Analysis*, New York, USA: John Wiley 1989, 184–185; White 1987.)

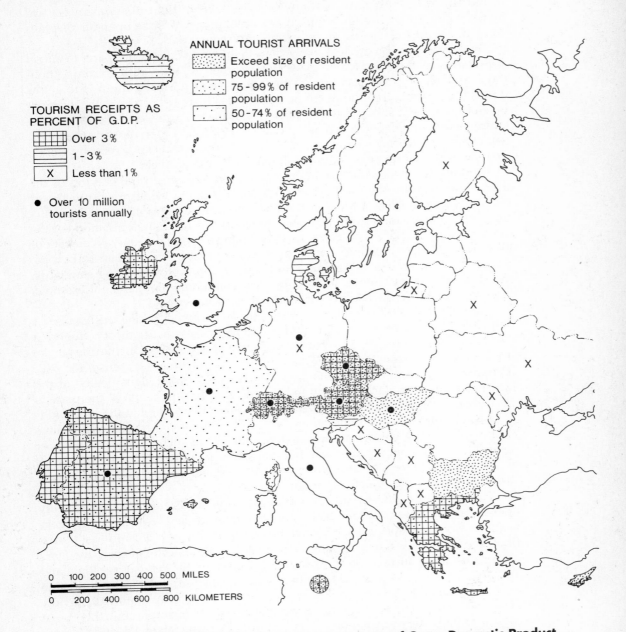

TOURISM RECEIPTS AS
PERCENT OF G.D.P.

	Over 3%
	1 - 3%
X	Less than 1%

● Over 10 million
tourists annually

ANNUAL TOURIST ARRIVALS

	Exceed size of resident population
	75 - 99 % of resident population
	50 - 74 % of resident population

0 100 200 300 400 500 MILES

0 200 400 600 800 KILOMETERS

FIGURE 12.14 Tourism receipts as a percentage of Gross Domestic Product.
Dependance upon tourism varies widely within Europe, with both north/south and
east/west contrasts.

in Northern Ireland and the Schweizerisches Freilichtmuseum in central Switzerland. Following the Skansen example, many of these open-air displays combine the appeals of folk museum and amusement park.

European tourists are less likely than their American counterparts to spend their vacations traveling to one place after another. A "tour" differs from a "holi-day," and Europeans clearly prefer the latter. Their normal pattern is to get as quickly as possible from home to the desired destination—no small achievement given the frequent summer traffic jams on European roads—and then spend the entire holiday there, perhaps making day excursions to other, nearby attractions. Self-contained holiday resorts offering diverse amusements have recently gained in popularity, catering to the European mode of tourist travel.

Linking the penchant for single-destination tourism to the craving of the urban European for the rural countryside led also to the widespread practice of owning vacation homes. Most of these are modest cottages of recent construc-tion, but some are old farmhouses abandoned as the agrarian population left the land and migrated to urban areas. In some Spanish provinces, over 30 percent of all residences were vacation homes by the middle 1980s. Even in Eastern Europe, where tourism remains a less important activity due to lower living standards, the *dacha*, or country cottage, has become very common. In Bulgaria, for example, 32 percent of all city dwellers own a dacha in the countryside.

Another distinctly European type of tourism involves "taking the waters" at one or another of a huge assortment of health resorts, a practice most common in Germany and France. The generous health-care systems of such countries make it possible for citizens to receive treatment, at government expense, for real, imagined, or pretended ailments and afflictions. The road signs posted at the limits of many towns in Germany tell the traveler that the name of the place is *Heilbad* or *Kurort* Such-and-Such, treating one or more problem of the lungs, kid-neys, joints, stomach, or some other part of the anatomy. Amusements receive abundant attention as part of the cure, and the stay at such a place can be most enjoyable. Visitors spend a pleasant holiday, often drawing full wages from work all the while. Needless to say, spas have prospered and proliferated in this subsi-dized system of health-related tourism.

The removal of most political barriers to travel in Eastern Europe recently opened up that huge area to mass tourism from the affluent west. Virtually every formerly Communist country stands to benefit from this new west-to-east tourist flow, and some places and regions, such as Praha, Budapest, Dresden, the Harz Mountains and Thüringer Forest of eastern Germany, St. Petersburg, Riga, and Tallinn have begun to reap the benefits. However, the tourism infrastructure and know-how remains rather primitive in most of the east. Hardy motorists can now drive without restriction through most of Russia, for example, but they must cope with bad roads, substandard hotels staffed by rude personnel, and a scarci-ty of restaurants and service stations. Gasoline is often unavailable at Russian pumps, requiring black market purchases from persons of dubious integrity. Even in eastern Germany, places with major tourist appeal, such as the famous china-manufacturing town of Meissen, lacked hotel facilities as late as 1993. Still,

Western Europeans have a pent-up curiosity about the east, and the tourist flow has begun in earnest.

When mass tourism arrives in full force in the east, residents will find it a mixed blessing, as has earlier proved true in favored destinations in the west. Economic benefits surely come with tourism but so do assorted problems. The experience of the Alps is instructive. As late as 1955, most of that mountain range remained a land of traditional, anachronistic, and in places impoverished dairy farmers living in picturesque log houses. The elitist tourism of the previous century had touched few of these residents and changed little in their way of life. Many young people fled the mountains, seeking a better living in the lowland cities. Then, in a single generation between 1955 and 1975, mass tourism came to the Alps, prompting a pervasive shift from dairying to dependence upon winter and summer visitors. Certain isolated, poverty-stricken places became prosperous, highly desired tourist destinations within a span of two decades. Money injected into the rural Alps by tourism provided a cure for the depressed economy, prompted the construction of an excellent road network, and halted the emigration of the young. As a result, most residents of the Alps benefit from tourism and regard it as a good thing.

Even so, they paid a high price. The local mountain culture underwent disruption. A folk society based upon mutual cooperation, egalitarianism, and respect for tradition gave way to a popular culture in which neighbors competed for tourist income and the old ways were discarded. An ancient adaptive system of land use in ecological balance with the fragile Alpine environment yielded to a new one that required massive and necessarily destructive habitat modification. Ski runs cut through protective belts of communal forests on slopes above the valley floors—the *Bannwälder*—scarred the mountainsides, caused erosion, and removed the natural protection against avalanches. Also, tourism greatly increased the number of people tramping about the Alpine countryside, further damaging the local flora and fauna. Highway construction brought additional massive damage. In short, the people of the Alps lost their ancient traditional culture and the land suffered extensive ecological modification as a result of mass tourism. A proven, sustainable system of land use gave way to an unsustainable and economically vulnerable one. This Alpine pattern has since been repeated in many other tourist districts, such as the Algarve in southern Portugal and the fishing villages of Corsica.

Europe, then, has evolved into a postindustrial status, in which most people find employment in a diverse array of service industries. This development leads the Europeans into uncharted waters, just as the original Industrial Revolution did a quarter-millennium ago. As always, change remains the hallmark of the European way of life. Uncertainties, even pessimism, about the postindustrial future abound among Europeans, including the wealthiest lands, but change is sibling to risk just as innovation is to its sinister twin, destruction. Europeans would have things no other way, unsustainable though they be.

The time has come to sum up the geography of Europe, a daunting task at best. In the concluding chapter, we will seek to join and mingle the findings of the first twelve chapters to establish an overarching regional framework.

Sources and Suggested Readings

G. J. Ashworth and Peter J. Larkham (eds.). *Building a New Heritage: Tourism, Culture and Identity in the New Europe*. London, GB: Routledge, 1994.

Antoine S. Bailly. "Producer Services Research in Europe." *Professional Geographer*, 47 (1995), 70–74.

Mary L. Barker. "Traditional Landscape and Mass Tourism in the Alps." *Geographical Review*. 72 (1982), 395–415.

James Bird. *The Geography of the Port of London*. London, GB: Hutchinson, 1957.

R. ter Brugge. "Nuclear Energy in the Netherlands." *Tijdschift voor Economische en Sociale Geografie*. 75 (1984), 300–304.

Bill Bryson and Gerd Ludwig. "Main-Danube Canal: Linking Europe's Waterways." *National Geographic*. 182:2 (1992), 3–31.

Andrew F. Burghardt. "The Origin of the Road and City Network of Roman Pannonia." *Journal of Historical Geography*. 5 (1979), 1–20.

Jean Cermakian. *The Moselle River and Canal from the Roman Empire to the European Economic Community*. Toronto, CDN: University of Toronto, Department of Geography, Research Publication No. 14, 1975.

Albert S. Chapman. "Trans-Europ Express: Overall Travel Time in Competition for Passengers." *Economic Geography*. 44 (1968), 283–295.

Andrew H. Dawson. "The Service Industries." In *A Geography of European Integration*. London, GB: Belhaven Press, 1993, 122–131.

European Conference of Ministers of Transport. *Prospects for East-West European Transport*. Paris, F: O.E.C.D. Publications, 1991.

Daniel W. Gade. "The French Riviera as Elitist Space." *Journal of Cultural Geography*. 3:1 (1982), 19–28.

Richard Gibb (ed.). *The Channel Tunnel: A Geographical Perspective*. Chichester, GB: John Wiley & Sons, 1994.

Amiram Gonen. "Tourism and Coastal Settlement Processes in the Mediterranean Region." *Ekistics*. 290 (1981), 378–381.

A. E. Green and J. R. Howells. "Information Services and Spatial Development in the UK Economy." *Tijdschrift voor Economische en Sociale Geografie*. 79 (1988), 266–277.

G. N. Gudkova and B. V. Moskvin. "The Development of Motor Roads in the USSR." *Soviet Geography: Review and Translation*. 15 (1974), 573–581.

Derek R. Hall. "Albania's Changing Tourism Environment." *Journal of Cultural Geography*. 12:2 (1992), 35–44.

Derek R. Hall. "Impacts of Economic and Political Transition on the Transport Geography of Central and Eastern Europe." *Journal of Transport Geography*. 1 (1993), 20–35.

Derek R. Hall (ed.). *Transport and Economic Development in the New Central and Eastern Europe.* London, GB: Belhaven Press, 1993.

Magne Helvig. "Transportation, Settlement Structure and Journey to Work in Western Norway." *Norsk Geografisk Tidsskrift.* 44 (1990), 61–75.

J. R. L. Howells. "The Location of Research and Development: Some Observations and Evidence from Britain." *Regional Studies.* 18 (1984), 13–29.

Brian S. Hoyle and David A. Pinder (eds.). *European Port Cities in Transition.* London, GB: Belhaven Press, 1992.

S. Illeris. *Services and Regions in Europe.* Aldershot, GB: Avebury, 1989.

Herbert G. Kariel and Patricia E. Kariel. "Socio-Cultural Impacts of Tourism: An Example from the Austrian Alps." *Geografiska Annaler.* 64B (1982), 1–16.

Baruch A. Kipnis and Eric A. Swyngedouw. "Manufacturing Research and Development in a Peripheral Region: The Case of Limburg, Belgium." *Professional Geographer.* 40 (1988), 149–158.

Douglas G. Lockhart and Susan E. Ashton. "Tourism in Malta." *Scottish Geographical Magazine.* 107 (1991), 22–32.

Arthur Morris and Gordon Dickinson. "Tourism Development in Spain: Growth Versus Conservation on the Costa Brava." *Geography.* 72 (1987), 16–26.

John Naylon. "Tourism—Spain's Most Important Industry." *Geography.* 52 (1967), 23–40.

Peter Nijkamp, Shalom Reichman, and Michael Wegener (eds.). *Euromobile: Transport, Communications and Mobility in Europe, a Cross-National Comparative Overview.* Aldershot, GB: Avebury, 1990.

Michael Pacione. "Italian Motorways." *Geography.* 59 (1974), 35–41.

J. Allan Patmore. "The Contraction of the Network of Railway Passenger Services in England and Wales, 1836–1962." *Institute of British Geographers, Transactions and Papers.* 38 (1966), 105–118.

Roderick Peattie. "The Ruts and Routes of Europe: A Study in Historical Geography." *Journal of Geography.* 53 (1954), 336–341.

Matthew Sagers and Thomas Maraffa. "Soviet Air-Passenger Transportation Network." *Geographical Review.* 80 (1990), 266–278.

Tor Selstad. "The Rise of the Quaternary Sector: The Regional Dimension of Knowledge-Based Services in Norway, 1970–1985." *Norsk Geografisk Tiksskrift.* 44 (1990), 21–37.

Gareth Shaw and Allan M. Williams. "Tourism and Development." In *Western Europe: Challenge and Change,* ed. David Pinder. London, GB: Belhaven Press, 1990, 240–257.

K. F. Shiyanskaya. "The Geography of Soviet Water Transportation by Combined River-Seagoing Vessels." *Soviet Geography.* 26 (1985), 721–727.

G. Škrivanić. "Roman Roads and Settlements in the Balkans." In *An Historical Geography of the Balkans,* ed. Francis W. Carter. London, GB: Academic Press, 1977, 115–145.

Karl Stiglbauer. "Regional Development and the Service Sector in Austria." *Geographia Polonica.* 59 (1992), 7–19.

Sverre Strand. "Roadless Norway." *Scottish Geographical Magazine.* 100 (1984), 49–59.

Sondre Svalastog. "Tourism in Norway's Rural Mountain Districts Twenty-five Years after the Mountain Planning Team's Report." *Norsk Geografisk Tidsskrift.* 42 (1988), 103–120.

David Turnock. "The Danube-Black Sea Canal and its Impact on Southern Romania." *GeoJournal.* 12 (1986), 65–79.

Guido G. Weigend. "The Danube River: An Emerging Regional Bond." *Geoforum.* 5 (1975), 151–161.

James E. Vance, Jr. *Capturing the Horizon: The Historical Geography of Transportation.* New York, USA: Harper & Row, 1986.

Paul E. White. "Italy: Grand Tour to Package Tour." *Geographical Magazine.* 59 (1987), 554–559.

Paul E. White. *The Social Impact of Tourism on Host Communities: A Study of Language Change in Switzerland.* Oxford, GB: Oxford University School of Geography, Research Paper No. 9, 1974.

John Whitelegg. *Transport Policy in the EEC.* London, GB: Routledge, 1989.

Allan M. Williams and Gareth Shaw (eds.). *Tourism and Economic Development: Western European Experiences.* London, GB: Belhaven Press, 1988.

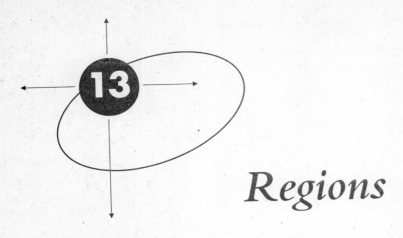

Regions

Europe emerges from our geographical study, paradoxically, as both *one* and *many*. Beneath the overarching unity that prompted our use of the term "European culture area," beneath the façade of a "common European home," we have uncovered major, often ancient cultural fault lines and divides. So far, our overview of this internal division has remained fragmented. We proceeded through eleven topical chapters, each devoted to a different aspect of geography and each presenting Europe as both one and many. Confusingly, perhaps, each chapter revealed a somewhat different internal division of Europe.

Now, in the final chapter, we must try to make sense of all this. We need to draw together all the topical chapters into some sort of comprehensive regional scheme or classification as a way of summarizing what we have learned. The recurrent regional patterns presented in the preceding chapters have been east versus west, north versus south, and core versus periphery. These combine now, in the final chapter, to yield a more complicated sectionalism within Europe.

West Versus East

Repeatedly in our geographical study, contrasts between *Eastern* and *Western* Europe appeared (Figure 13.1). This sectional difference often enjoys fundamental importance, as for example the east/west partition between Greek and Roman Christianity and between the two main divisions of Indo-European languages. Roman, or Western, Christianity eventually provided the path, through Protestantism, to personal freedom, democracy, individualism, capitalism, prosperity, and creativity, while Eastern Orthodoxy, by contrast, fostered enduring paternalism, collectivism, conformity, and ultimately Marxist dictatorship. Some said that Russia, in accepting Communism, turned its back on Europe, but in fact she merely rejected *Western* Europe. The geographer would expect Russia to do so again.

As a result, east versus west continues to describe the most basic internal contrast within Europe. Living standards differ strikingly between the two halves

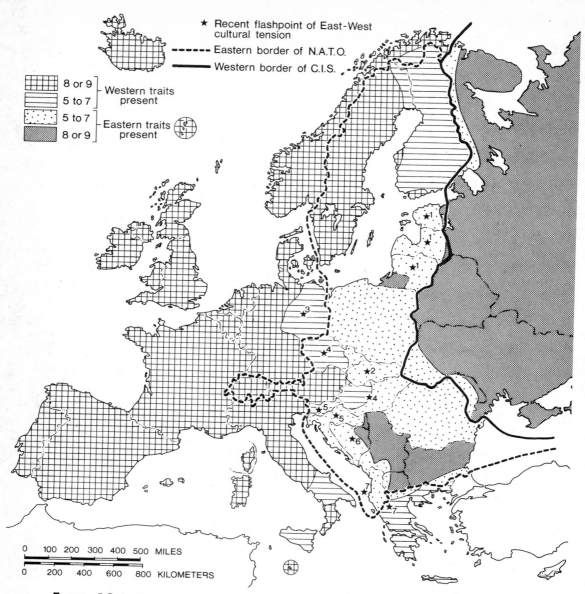

FIGURE 13.1 West versus east in Europe. Nine representative characteristics are included (western trait listed first in each case): Latin/Greek Christianity; Latin/Greek-Cyrillic alphabet; Western/Eastern Indo-European languages; <10/>10 per thousand infant mortality rate; marine/continental climate; <4/>4 persons per automobile; small, compartmentalized terrain units/expansive plains; economy prosperous to struggling/severely-troubled or basketcase economies; and no/yes concerning the presence of totalitarian governments at any time since 1980. Uniate Christians are counted as Latin. Hungary, due to the "neutral" factor of Uralian language, measured equally eastern and western and was divided roughly in half. Flashpoints of tension include: **1** = Baltic republic secessions: **2** = Slovakian secession; **3** = collapse of the German Democratic Republic; **4** = restoration of democracy to the Czech Republic and Hungary; **5** = Croat/Slovene secessions from Yugoslavia; **6** = Bosnian Serb desire to link with Serbia; and **7** = Italian/Greek rejection of Albanian refugees.

of the culture area, whether measured by infant mortality, employment in the service industries, automobile ownership, or more comprehensive indices of prosperity. The two basic types of Christianity also yielded two alphabetic traditions—the Latin versus the Greek-Cyrillic, a legacy highly visible in the landscape and a hindrance to east-west contacts.

Other differences between Eastern and Western Europe add to the image of two separate peoples and lands. The chapter on physical environment revealed a western rimland with mild marine climate, deciduous woodlands, and small, compartmentalized terrain units, contrasted to an eastern heartland with harsh continental climate, coniferous forests, and expansive, unbroken plains. Politically, the West lies fragmented into myriad independent states, while most of the East, even after the collapse of the Soviet Union, forms part of the largest country in the world.

Even seemingly trivial differences contribute to the dichotomy of east versus west. Racially, as we saw, easterners and westerners differ in blood chemistry and cephalic index. The farm villages of the east obey a rigid, planned geometry, while those of the west sprawl chaotically. Peruse the list of books at the end of this chapter. Note that 24 different ones employ the term "Western Europe" or "Eastern Europe" in their titles, a revealing measure of the importance geographers place upon this particular pattern of internal European division.

Not surprisingly, flashpoints of tension and disagreement continue to flare along the east/west divide in Europe. The cold war—the most vivid and profound reflection of east-west conflict—passed into history, but harmony has hardly returned to this great cultural fault zone. Politically, the east/west divide helped prompt Slovaks to secede from Czechoslovakia, Croats and Slovenes to withdraw from Yugoslavia, Krajina Serbs to resist Croat rule, Italians to repulse Albanian refugees, and the Baltic states—after 50 years of subjugation—to leave the Soviet Union. It partially explains both the demise of the German Democratic Republic and the disdain with which many west and east Germans still regard each other.

Expanding by spurts over the decades, the European Union has come to provide the most compelling statement of Western Europe, representing democracy, progress, prosperity, and capitalism. Fortified by the North Atlantic Treaty Organization, a military alliance, the E.U. is a formidable bastion of Western Europe. Politically and economically shattered Eastern Europe, loosely regrouped as the Commonwealth of Independent States, belongs to another world (Figure 13.1). Europe, then, continues to obey an ancient cultural divide, one as old as Europe itself. Truly, as Kipling said, "east is east and west is west," even within Europe.

North Versus South

While less profound today than the east/west divide, the contrast between *Northern* and *Southern* Europe remains substantial (Figure 13.2). This, too, is an ancient cleavage, along which Greco/Roman civilization long ago battled barbarian Germans, Celts, and Slavs. The border of the Roman Empire at its apex, about

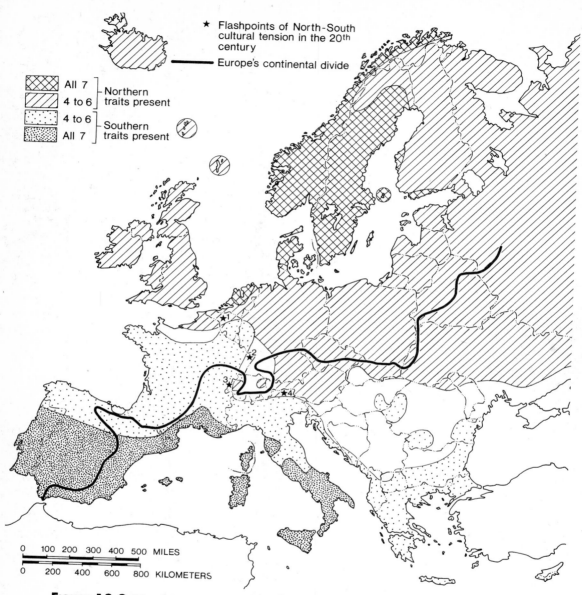

FIGURE 13.2 North versus south in Europe. Seven selected characteristics are included (southern trait listed first in each case): Romance/Germanic languages; Catholicism/Protestantism; part/not part of Roman Empire, A.D. 100; viticulture present/absent; summer drought/year-round precipitation; Mediterranean/Nordic subrace; and stone + earth/wood dominant in folk architectural tradition (half-timbering is counted as wooden). Flashpoints of south/north conflict in the past century include: **1** = French/Dutch tension in Belgium; **2** = French/German dispute over Alsace-Lorraine; **3** = Jura cantonal secession in Switzerland; and **4** = Italian/Austrian dispute in the South Tirol. Unshaded areas do not have as many as 4 northern *or* southern traits. The continental divide separates Mediterranean from Atlantic/Baltic drainage.

110 A.D. still possesses cultural consequence in present-day Europe. It helps explain the south/north contrast of Catholicism versus Protestantism and Romance speech versus Germanic languages.

Chapter 2, on the physical environment revealed the south as a land of mountains, earthquakes, warmth, and summer drought, while the north features plains, hills, and year-round damp. To the south, too, belong viticulture, religious pilgrimage, stone or earthen folk architecture, multi-story unit farmsteads, and the Mediterranean city and subrace, while the northerners drink beer, build in wood, live in rather different types of cities, and more often exhibit secularization and Nordic physical features. North and south look toward different seas, separated by the European continental divide (Figure 13.2).

Cultural conflict along the north/south line, while presently muted, has flared regularly since Classical times. The horrible Thirty Years' War, pitting Catholic against Protestant, ravaged the central section of the divide in the 1600s (look back to Figure 6.5). Perhaps that great and destructive conflict released all the pressure along this cultural fault line, for only minor conflicts, generally of a ethno-linguistic nature, have occurred since (Figure 13.2). The Dutch/French tension in Belgium, the Alsace-Lorraine border dispute between France and Germany, and secession of French-speaking Jura canton from German-speaking Bern in Switzerland, and the restiveness of German-speaking South Tirolers in Italy offer twentieth-century reminders of the north/south split. All of these disputes are either dormant or resolved today, but the north/south cultural division remains viable, if peaceful.

Core Versus Periphery

The contrasts among east, west, south, and north would alone, as the bases for a regional scheme, produce a simple division of Europe into quarters. The resultant spatial classification would be sectorial, with four regions shaped like pieces of a pie.

Europe, however, is not that simply described geographically. Repeatedly in our study, beginning in Chapter 1, another pattern has been revealed: *core* versus *periphery*. Indeed, the very essence of European culture was presented as weakening from core toward peripheries, where Europe meets non-Europe (look back to Figures 1.11 and 1.12).

The European core, to review, is characterized by the densest, most urbanized population, the most industrialized economy, the most productive agriculture (as far back as the medieval advent of the three-field system), the most conservative politics, and the greatest concentration of highways and railroads (look back to Figures 6.2, 7.19, 8.2, 8.13, 10.1, 11.2, 11.4, 12.2, and 12.7). It is the most fertile part of Europe and enjoys the enormous benefits of central location. Examples of the cultural distinctiveness of the core include the Central European city type, the courtyard farmstead, and half-timbered construction (look back to Figures 2.19, 9.14, and 10.22). The core suffers the highest rates of traffic congestion, crowding, and environmental pollution, including acid rain and forest death.

Traditionally, geographers often recognized the core region through their use of the term *Central Europe,* or the German word *Mitteleuropa.* They argued about the boundaries of Central Europe but never questioned its existence. Most acknowledged that the concept of core or Central Europe must somehow be linked to Germany and the other German-speaking lands. The unification of the German Empire in 1871 gave a political expression to Central Europe, as had its medieval predecessor, the Holy Roman Empire (or First *Reich*) (Figure 13.3). The total defeat and disintegration of Germany in 1945 coupled with the East/West cold war that ensued caused the notion of Central Europe to lose favor temporarily, but today we see the core vigorously reascendant. The German task, performed with varying degrees of success, through the centuries, has always been to join together east and west as well as north and south into a viable European core.

Other scholars view the European core in nonpolitical, less German ways. For example, the French geographer Delaisi in 1929 distinguished "Europe A" (core, industrial) from "Europe B" (peripheral, agrarian), and he included all of France, England, and Benelux in the core (Figure 13.3). His classification corresponded well to the designation we made earlier of a "manufacturing core" (look back to Figure 11.2). Overall, this concept of a core area seems preferable (look back to Figure 1.11).

The core/periphery contact zone, too, contains flashpoints of cultural tension. As we noted earlier, many northern Italians, citizens of the European core, seek to secede, separating themselves from southern, peripheral Italy. Catalan, Corsican, Scottish, Breton, Welsh, Slovak, Slovene, and, earlier, Irish separatism can all partly be understood in core/periphery terms.

Eight Regions

Superimposing the core-periphery division upon a Europe already quartered by east-west and north-south partitions produces a more complicated, eightfold regional scheme. Such a classification can be presented as an abstract model that resembles a bull's-eye target placed over a crosshairs sight (Figure 13.4).

The industrial-urban European core thus becomes divided into four regions, including **A:** the Germanic; **B:** north Slavic-Catholic; **C:** the Hungarian-south Slavic-Catholic; and **D:** the Romance Catholic. Likewise, peripheral Europe becomes fourfold, including **E:** the peninsular-insular Mediterranean; **F:** the Balkans; **G:** the Russian-Uralic periphery; and **H:** the Celto-Nordic fringe. Some regions appear larger than the neatly geometric model would predict and others smaller (Figure 13.5). Reality is always complicated. The atrophied character of the eastern half of the European core, including regions B and C, perhaps suggests the lower level of prosperity there.

As a general rule, cores tend to dominate peripheries. Marxist doctrine holds, in fact, that such a relationship is inherent in capitalistic systems. If so, the future

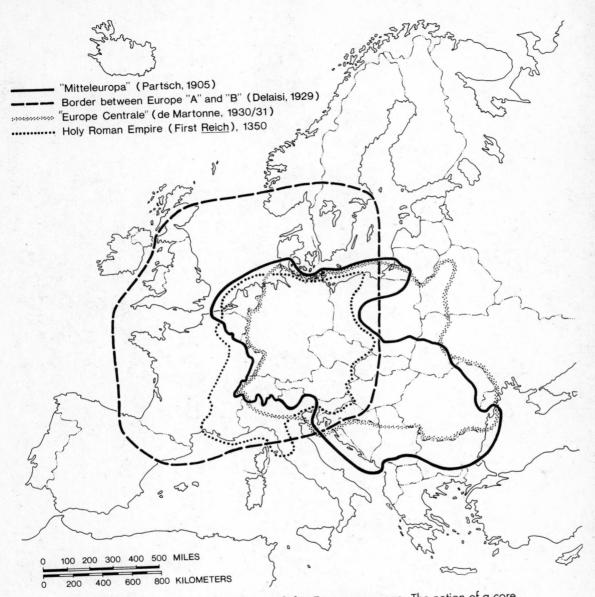

--- "Mitteleuropa" (Partsch, 1905)
- - - Border between Europe "A" and "B" (Delaisi, 1929)
:::::::: "Europe Centrale" (de Martonne, 1930/31)
·········· Holy Roman Empire (First <u>Reich</u>), 1350

| 0 | 100 | 200 | 300 | 400 | 500 MILES |

| 0 | 200 | 400 | 600 | 800 KILOMETERS |

FIGURE 13.3 Some expressions of the European core. The notion of a core, whether expressed by geographers as "Central Europe" (*Mitteleuropa*), as "Europe A" (industrial core), or as the German *Reich*, is quite venerable. See also Figures 1.11 and 1.12. (Sources: Delaisi 1929, 24–25; Partsch 1905 frontispiece; Mutton, 1961, 3.)

of Russia and most of Eastern Europe can hardly be happy, nor can the peninsular-insular Mediterranean or Celto-Nordic fringe aspire to greatness.

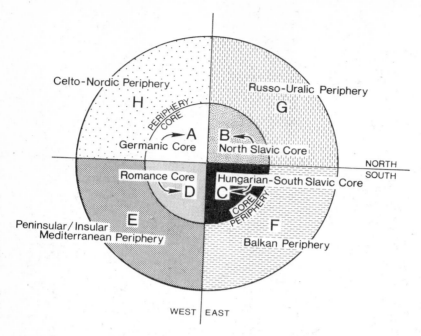

FIGURE 13.4 Europe: a regional model. The bases of the model are north/south, east/west, and core/periphery divisions. Compare the model to Figure 13.5.

Thus we end where we began with the seemingly paradoxical proposition that Europe, geographically, is both many and one. Perhaps to the European mind, trained for two millennia to accept the notion of one God as a Trinity, that proposition makes perfect sense.

General Readings on Regionalism

Jovan Cvijić. "The Zones of Civilization of the Balkan Peninsula." *Geographical Review.* 5 (1918), 470–481.

Darrell Delamaide. *The New Superregions of Europe.* New York, USA: Plume, 1995.

Robert A. Dodgson. *The European Past: Social Evolution and Spatial Order.* London, GB: Macmillan, 1987.

Jean Gottmann. *A Geography of Europe.* New York, USA: Holt, Rinehart and Winston, 4th ed., 1989, chapters 4–21.

George W. Hoffman (ed.). *Europe in the 1990s: A Geographical Analysis.* New York, USA: John Wiley, 6th ed., 1989, chapters 5–11.

James R. McDonald. *The European Scene: A Geographic Perspective.* Englewood Cliffs, USA: Prentice Hall, 1991, chapters 15–23.

Vincent H. Malmström. *Geography of Europe: A Regional Analysis.* Englewood Cliffs, USA: Prentice Hall, 1971.

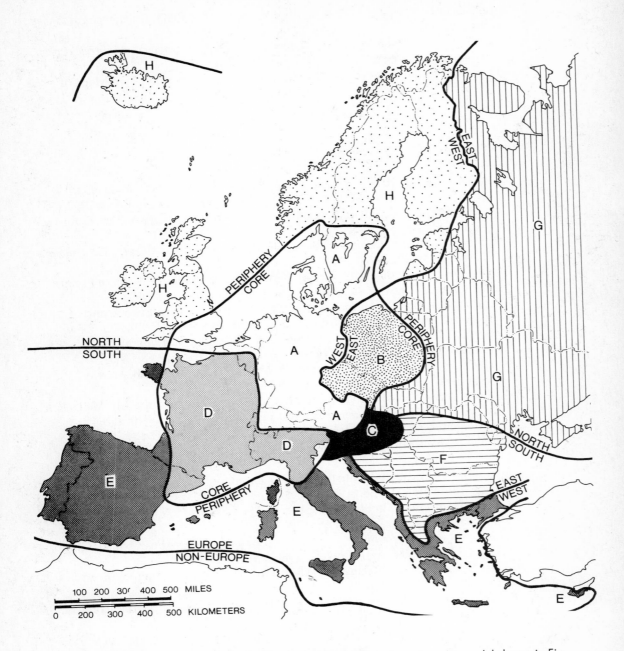

FIGURE 13.5 A regional classification of Europe, based on the model shown in Figure 13.4 and taking into consideration east versus west, north versus south, and core versus periphery. The real world produces great distortions in the neatly geometric model, but all eight of the regional components survive. Why might B and C be so small, as compared to A and D? This map draws upon Figures 1.11, 13.1, 13.2, and 13.3.

Alexander B. Murphy. "The Emerging Europe of the 1990s." *Geographical Review.* 81 (1991), 1–17.

Karl Stiglbauer. "Die Kulturregionen Europas." *Mitteilungen der österreichischen Geographischen Gesellschaft,* 134 (1992), 93–114.

William William-Olsson. "A Prelude to Regional Geography: Two Maps of Europe." *Geografiska Annaler.* 57B (1975), 1–19.

Readings on East Versus West

Andrew F. Burghardt. *Borderland: A Historical and Geographical Study of Burgenland, Austria.* Madison, USA: University of Wisconsin Press, 1962.

David Burtenshaw, M. Bateman, and G. J. Ashworth. *The City in West Europe.* New York, USA: Wiley, 1981.

Werner J. Cahnman. "Frontiers Between East and West in Europe." *Geographical Review.* 39 (1949), 605–624.

Hugh Clout, Mark Blacksell, Russell King, and David Pinder. *Western Europe: Geographical Perspectives.* London, GB: Longman, 3rd ed., 1993.

David A. Coleman. "Contrasting Age Structures of Western Europe and of Eastern Europe." *Population and Development Review.* 19 (1993), 523–555.

Robert E. Dickinson. *The West European City: A Geographical Interpretation.* London, GB: Routledge & Kegan Paul, 1951.

K. H. F. Dyson. *The State Tradition in Western Europe.* Oxford, GB: Martin Robertson, 1980.

E. Estyn Evans. "The Ecology of Peasant Life in Western Europe." In *Man's Role in Changing the Face of the Earth,* ed. William L. Thomas, Jr. Chicago, USA: University of Chicago Press, 1956, 217–239.

A. J. Fielding. "Counterurbanisation in Western Europe." *Progress in Planning.* 17 (1982), 1–52.

Allan Findlay and Paul White (eds.). *West European Population Change.* London, GB: Croom Helm, 1986.

F. E. Ian Hamilton. "The East European and Soviet City." *Geographical Magazine.* 50 (1978), 511–515.

Brian W. Ilbery. *Western Europe: A Systematic Human Geography.* Oxford, GB: Oxford University Press, 2nd ed., 1986.

Philip N. Jones. "On Defining a Western European Automobile Industry." *Erdkunde.* 47 (1993), 25–39.

P. L. Knox. *The Geography of Western Europe: A Socio-Economic Survey.* London, GB: Croom Helm, 1984.

Huey L. Kostanick (ed.). *Population and Migration Trends in Eastern Europe.* Boulder, USA: Westview Press, 1977.

Edward D. Laborde and Alan B. Mountjoy. *Western Europe.* London, GB: University of London Press, 4th ed., 1966.

Roy E. H. Mellor. *Eastern Europe: A Geography of COMECON Countries.* London, GB: Macmillan, 1975.

Francis J. Monkhouse. *A Regional Geography of Western Europe*. London, GB: Longman, 4th ed., 1974.

Hallstein Myklebost. "Regionalism in Western Europe." *Norsk Geografisk Tidsskrift*. 47 (1993), 79–91.

Mary Lee Nolan and Sidney Nolan. *Religious Pilgrimage in Modern Western Europe*. Chapel Hill, USA: University of North Carolina Press, 1989.

John O'Loughlin and Herman van der Wusten (eds.). *The New Political Geography of Eastern Europe*. London, GB: Belhaven Press, 1993.

David Pinder (ed.). *Western Europe: Challenge and Change*. London, GB: Belhaven Press, 1990.

Lloyd Rodwin and Hidehiko Sazanami (eds.). *Industrial Change and Regional Economic Transformation: The Experience of Western Europe*. London, GB: Harper Collins Academic, 1991.

Dean S. Rugg. *Eastern Europe*. London, GB: Longman Scientific & Technical, 1986.

Edward W. Shanahan. *Western and Central Europe: A Regional Geography*. London, GB: Macmillan, 1964.

Clifford T. Smith. *An Historical Geography of Western Europe Before 1800*. London, GB: Longman, 2nd ed., 1978.

David Turnock. *Eastern Europe: An Economic and Political Geography*. London, GB: Routledge, 1988.

David Turnock. *Eastern Europe: An Historical Geography, 1815–1945*. London, GB: Routledge, 1988.

David Turnock. *The Human Geography of Eastern Europe*. London, GB: Routledge, 1989.

Carl C. Wallén. *Climates of Northern and Western Europe*. Amsterdam, NL: Elsevier, 1970.

Paul D. White. *The West European City: A Social Geography*. London, GB: Longman, 1984.

Allan M. Williams. *The Western European Economy: A Geography of Post-War Development*. London, GB: Hutchinson, 1987.

Allan M. Williams and Gareth Shaw (eds.). *Tourism and Economic Development: Western European Experiences*. London, GB: Belhaven Press, 1988.

Readings on North Versus South

Victor Conrad. "The Climate of the Mediterranean Region." *Bulletin of the American Meteorological Society*. 24 (1943), 127–145.

James M. Houston. *The Western Mediterranean World: An Introduction to its Regional Landscapes*. London, GB: Longmans, 1964.

John R. G. Jenkins. *Jura Separatism in Switzerland*. Oxford, GB: Oxford University Press, 1987.

Brian S. John. *Scandinavia: A New Geography*. London, GB: Longman, 1984.

Russell L. King. "Southern Europe: Dependency or Development?" *Geography*. 67 (1982), 221–234.

Lila Leontidou. *The Mediterranean City in Transition.* Cambridge, GB: Cambridge University Press, 1990.

William R. Mead. *An Historical Geography of Scandinavia.* London, GB: Academic Press, 1981.

Marion I. Newbigin. *The Mediterranean Lands: An Introductory Study in Human and Historical Geography.* London, GB: Christophers, 1924.

Ellen Churchill Semple. *The Geography of the Mediterranean Region.* New York, USA: Henry Holt, 1931.

Giuseppe Sergi. *The Mediterranean Race.* London, GB: Walter Scott, 1901.

Avshalom Shmueli. "Countries of the Mediterranean Basin as a Geographic Region." *Ekistics.* 48 (1981), 359–369.

André Siegfried. *The Mediterranean.* Trans. Doris Hemming. London, GB: Jonathan Cape, 1948.

Catherine Delano Smith. *Western Mediterranean World: A Historical Geography of Italy, Spain and Southern France since the Neolithic.* London, GB: Academic Press, 1979.

Axel Sömme (ed.). *A Geography of Norden.* Oslo, N: J. W. Cappelen Förlag, 1960.

Donald S. Walker. *The Mediterranean Lands.* London, GB: Methuen, 3rd ed., 1965.

Allan Williams (ed.). *Southern Europe Transformed.* London, GB: Harper & Row, 1984.

Readings on Core Versus Periphery

Patrick Bailey and Peter Fox (eds.). *Images of Poland: Urban and Rural Studies.* Sheffield, GB: The Geographical Association, 1990.

J. H. Bater and R. A. French (eds.). *Studies in Russian Historical Geography.* 2 vols. London, GB: Academic Press, 1983.

Proinnsias Breathnach. "Uneven Development and Capitalist Peripheralisation: The Case of Ireland." *Antipode.* 20 (1988), 122–141.

Francis W. Carter (ed.). *An Historical Geography of the Balkans.* London, GB: Academic Press, 1977.

Michael Chisholm. *Britain on the Edge of Europe.* London, GB: Routledge, 1995.

Hugh Clout. *Regional Variations in the European Community.* Cambridge, GB: Cambridge University Press, 1986.

Francis Delaisi. *Les deux Europes.* Paris, F: Payot, 1929.

Aubrey Diem. *The New Germany: Land, People, Economy.* Kitchener, Ontario, CDN: Media International, 1991.

Francis H. Eterovich and Christopher Spalatin (eds.). *Croatia: Land, People, Culture.* Toronto, CDN: University of Toronto Press, 1964.

E. Estyn Evans. *The Personality of Ireland.* Cambridge, GB: Cambridge University Press, 1973.

Eric Fischer. "The Passing of Mitteleuropa." In *The Changing World: Studies in Political Geography,* ed. W. Gordon East and A. E. Moodie. London, GB: Harrap, 1956, 60–79.

Pierre George and Jean Tricart. *L'Europe Centrale.* Paris, F: Presses Universitaires de France, 2 vols., 1954.

Stephen R. Graubard (ed.). "Eastern Europe . . . Central Europe . . . Europe." *Daedalus* (special issue). 119 (1990), 1–344.

F. E. Ian Hamilton. *Poland's Western and Northern Territories.* London, GB: Oxford University Press, 1975.

Brian W. Ilbery. "Core-Periphery contrasts in European Social Well-Being." *Geography.* 69 (1984), 289–302.

Russell King. *Italy.* London, GB: Paul Chapman, 1987.

Konrad Kretschmer. *Historische Geographie von Mitteleuropa.* München, D: R. Oldenbourg, 1904.

J. R. Lewis and A. M. Williams. "Regional Uneven Development on the European Periphery: The Case of Portugal, 1950–1978." *Tijdschrift voor Economische en Sociale Geografie.* 72 (1981), 81–98.

Jim Lewis and Alan Townsend (eds.). *The North-South Divide: Regional Change in Britain in the 1980s.* London, GB: Paul Chapman, 1988.

Fritz Machatschek. *Länderkunde von Mitteleuropa.* Breslau, D: F. Hirt, 2 vols., 1931.

Emmanuel de Martonne. *Europe centrale.* Paris, F: Armand Colin, 2 vols., 1930–31.

William R. Mead. *The Scandinavian Northlands.* Oxford, GB: Oxford University Press, 1974.

Alan B. Mountjoy. *The Mezzogiorno.* Oxford, GB: Oxford University Press, 1973.

Alice F. A. Mutton. *Central Europe: A Regional and Human Geography.* London, GB: Longmans, Green, 1961.

John Naylon. *Andalusia.* Oxford, GB: Oxford University Press, 1975.

A. R. Orme. *Ireland.* Chicago, USA: Aldine, 1970.

Hilda Ormsby. "The Definition of Mitteleuropa and its Relation to the Conception of Deutschland in the Writings of Modern German Geographers." *Scottish Geographical Magazine.* 51 (1935), 337–347.

W. H. Parker. *An Historical Geography of Russia.* London, GB: University of London Press, 1968.

Josef F. M. Partsch. *Central Europe.* Trans. Clementina Black. London, GB: H. Frowde, 1905.

Gottfried Pfeifer. "The Quality of Peasant Living in Central Europe." In *Man's Role in Changing the Face of the Earth,* ed. William L. Thomas, Jr. Chicago, USA: University of Chicago Press, 1956, 240–277.

Mario Pinna and Domenico Ruocco (eds). *Italy: A Geographical Survey.* Pisa, I: Pacini, and Napoli, I: Istituto Grafico Italiano, 1980.

Hubertus Preusser. *The Landscapes of Iceland: Types and Regions.* The Hague, NL: W. Junk, 1976.

George Schöpflin and Nancy Wood (eds.). *In Search of Central Europe.* Cambridge, GB: Polity Press, 1989.

Karl H. Schröder and Gabriele Schwarz. *Die ländlichen Siedlungsformen in Mitteleuropa.* Bad Godesberg, D: Bundesforschungsanstalt für Landeskunde und Raumordnung, 1969.

Hans-Dietrich Schultz. "Fantasies of *Mitte: Mittellage* and *Mitteleuropa* in German Geographical Discussion in the 19th and 20th Centuries." *Political Geography Quarterly,* 8 (1989), 315–339.

Dudley Seers, Bernard Schaeffer, and Marja-Liisa Kiljunen (eds.). *Underdeveloped Europe: Studies in Core-Periphery Relations.* Hassock, GB: Harvester Press, 1979.

Dan Stanislawski. *The Individuality of Portugal: A Study in Historical-Political Geography.* Austin, USA: University of Texas Press, 1959.

Dan Stanislawski. *Portugal's Other Kingdom: The Algarve.* Austin, USA: University of Texas Press. 1963.

David Turnock. *Scotland's Highlands and Islands.* London, GB: Oxford University Press, 1974.

G. W. Whittington and I. D. Whyte. *An Historical Geography of Scotland.* London, GB: Academic Press, 1983./

INDEX